Free Jazz and Free Improvisation
An Encyclopedia
Volume I: A–J

Todd S. Jenkins

GREENWOOD PRESS
Westport, Connecticut • London

Library of Congress Cataloging-in-Publication Data

Jenkins, Todd S., 1968–
    Free jazz and free improvisation : an encyclopedia / Todd S. Jenkins.
        p. cm.
    Includes bibliographical references (p.) and index.
    ISBN 0–313–29881–5 (set : alk. paper) — ISBN 0–313–33313–0 (v. 1 : alk. paper) —
    ISBN 0–313–33314–9 (v. 2 : alk. paper)
        1. Free jazz — Dictionaries.   2. Improvisation (Music)   I. Title
    ML102.J3J46   2004
    781.65′136′03—dc22   2004047531

British Library Cataloguing in Publication Data is available.

Library of Congress Catalog Card Number: 2004047531
ISBN: 0–313–29881–5 (set code)
        0–313–33313–0 (v. 1)
        0–313–33314–9 (v. 2)

First published in 2004

Greenwood Press, 88 Post Road West, Westport, CT 06881
An imprint of Greenwood Publishing Group, Inc.
www.greenwood.com

Printed in the United States of America

The paper used in this book complies with the
Permanent Paper Standard issued by the National
Information Standards Organization (Z39.48–1984).

10 9 8 7 6 5 4 3 2 1

*This book is dedicated to
the memory of Joanne Greenough,
my dear jazz friend.*

Contents

List of Entries

Guide to Related Topics

ALPHABETICAL LISTING OF RECORD LABELS

Chronoscope
CIMP (Creative Improvised
   Music Projects)
Circulasione Totale
Contemporary
Cryptogramophone

Delmark
DIW
Durian

Emanem
Eremite
Erstwhile
ESP (or ESP-Disk)

FMP
For 4 Ears

Grob

HatHut
Horo

Ictus
Impetus
Impulse
Incus
Instant Composers Pool
   (ICP)
Intakt

Jazz Composers Orchestra
   Association (JCOA)

Knitting Factory
Konnex

Leo Records

Matchless
Maya Recordings
Meniscus
Moers Music
Music and Arts

Nato
Nessa
Nine Winds
No More

Ogun
Okkadisk (or Okka)
Organ of Corti

Parachute
Po Torch
Potlatch
PSF Records

Random Acoustics
Rastascan
Red Toucan

Saturn
Slam
Songlines
Splasc(h)

Transition

Unit Records

Victo

Wobbly Rail

ALPHABETICAL LISTING OF PERFORMANCE VENUES

Artists House

Bang On A Can Festival
BIMhuis

Empty Bottle

Festival International de
   Musique Actuelle
   Victoriaville
Fire in the Valley Festival
Freedom of the City
   Festival

Guelph Jazz Festival

Knitting Factory

Mopomoso
Music Now Festival

Studio RivBea

Tonic
Total Music Meeting
Town Hall

Uncool Festival of International Contemporary
   Music

Velvet Lounge
Vision Festival

Acknowledgments

Writing about music is like dancing about architecture.

—Frank Zappa

A project this extensive would not have been possible without the assistance of some special people. First, I extend heartfelt thanks to Greenwood editor Eric Levy; series advisor Norbert Carnovale; Simon Barley and Bob Gordon of the American Jazz Symposium; my mother, Jane Taylor; my in-laws, Paul and Carol Bush; my friend, P.A. Whitaker; and my father, Roy Jenkins, who fostered my early love of good jazz and swing.

Thanks to the artists and label heads who put up with my inquiries, including Robert Koester, Bob Rusch, Bruno Johnson, Flavio Bonandrini, Martin Davidson, Marco Eneidi, Vinny Golia, Joe McPhee, and Derek Bailey. (*Please note*: All quotations herein that are not accompanied by a footnote reference are drawn from my telephone or e-mail interviews with the quoted persons.)

Thanks to those in the on-line community whose assistance proved so invaluable, including Darrell Katz, Ray Stadt, Marc Lambert, Jay Soule, Mike Stratton, Remigijus Leipus, and Anthony Fabio. My deepest appreciation to Dave Fields, a veritable repository of avant-garde and philosophical knowledge who loaned me many albums for research, and to Pat Padua, Alan Saul, Kevin Quinn, and Ed Rhodes Jr. for their kind suggestions and fact finding. Profound apologies and thanks to anyone I may have missed.

Thanks to you, the reader, for your interest in this exciting, noncommercial form of music. I hope that these volumes will be informative and of lasting interest. If you see that your favorite performer has been excluded, please forgive the oversight. Compiling this book was a long, hard labor of love, and if the omissions you find are glaring enough, chances are I'm already kicking myself over them.

And last but certainly not least, a world of love and thanks to Christie, Nicholas, and Steven for putting up with many broken dates and lonely weeknights.

Todd S. Jenkins

Introduction

Halfway through the twentieth century, certain developments in American culture began coming to an overdue head. As is usually the case in times of cultural upheaval, the nation's artists reacted in personal yet pertinent ways. One consequent result was the frenetic, cathartic musical form known as "free jazz." The road to freedom was rather long and ugly. As the entertainment market began turning away from jazz toward rock-and-roll, jazz musicians found themselves facing a forbidding challenge: either languish in possible poverty and obscurity, or join the mass exodus into studio work. Jazz had already been wounded by the miserable AFM recording ban in the 1940s, forcing an emphasis on vocalists in place of instrumentalists. Once Elvis got a grip on the charts, scarce hope remained for jazz to endure there. The deaths of a staggering number of jazz legends in the 1950s, from Charlie Parker and Billie Holiday to elders like Fletcher Henderson, Django Reinhardt, and the Dorsey Brothers, hastened the music's decline despite the promising young artists who were on the rise. Jazz clubs nationwide began either closing their doors or changing their booking policies to favor rock acts.

Within jazz's own circles, the scourges of stylistic and racial infighting threatened to dismember it further. Black musicians who had created jazz and kindled most of its important evolutionary steps were still, under archaic segregation laws, not permitted to perform it in large portions of the country. Many of the white performers who had grabbed onto the jazz bandwagon and ridden it to personal success felt little sympathy for their black counterparts and often added fuel to the fire. Traditional, "Dixieland"-style jazz became nearly extinct, save in its motherland of New Orleans and a few other hot spots. (This was true in America, anyway; Britain saw quite a boom of interest in "trad" jazz.) "Cool jazz," created by a multiracial assembly of musicians in the late 1940s as a rejoinder to bebop's complexities, had been all but commandeered by white performers in the subsequent decade. Slightly retailored, it became the reigning jazz style on the West Coast as hordes of Stan Kenton and Woody Herman sidemen dug deeper into its cerebral character.

Back on the East Coast, a cadre of musicians with backgrounds in classical music formulated the "Third Stream," a crossover of classical and cool forms. George Russell and Miles Davis pioneered the "modal jazz" boom, building performances around curious scale patterns instead of the standard chord progressions. Bebop underwent a transformation into the form known as "hard bop," more emotionally ardent with a stronger rhythmic base and sense of the blues. With its house divided against itself time and again into these separatist subforms, jazz began to lose whatever feebly definable identity it had.

The American civil rights movement was beginning to boil over at the end of the 1950s, igniting fires in the hearts of black citizens who rightfully demanded their long-overdue pieces of the pie. The indignities suffered by black Americans were readily apparent in the lopsided music industry, where the true creators of innovative sounds were regularly prevented from reaping the financial fruits of their labors. Fortunately, a number of black musicians realized that their talents put them in a plum position to do something about their lot in life. Political incitement took the form of jazz protest songs and alternative music festivals, which competed with major white-run events. Stages became soapboxes; liner notes, the equivalent of tracts and manifestos. Collectives were formed to create new work opportunities, distribute recordings, and offer arts training to disaffected inner-city youth. Many musicians, perhaps most of them, were more interested in putting food on the table than in participating in active social change. Still, the bulk of America's black musicians gleaned benefits from what seeds were sown by the activists.

A renewed interest in African and Afro-Latin artistic styles altered the face of jazz and other arts, as did the personalization of expression that often accompanies such socially inspired artistic movements. Individual voices tended to be respected on a level equal to the convictions of the masses. This democratization, this balancing out of individual and group positions, was carried over to the ensemble. New performance principles were created that ignored the tired old conventions of Western music. Meter, bar lengths, and harmonic structure were seen as relative and therefore potentially irrelevant. The urban black community's new musical ideas included total abandonment of such restrictions, an exploration of all the sounds that could be drawn out of instruments, the democratic equalizing of ensembles so that the bass player was just as important as the trumpeter, and an emphasis on group improvisation that offered a fresh, spontaneous flow of ideas for the players to weigh and act upon.

The revolution happened little by little, over years. It started, perhaps, with Charles Mingus making room in his works for group improvisation, or perhaps earlier, with Thelonious Monk quirkily avoiding the downbeat from the birth of bebop onward. Whatever the case, the impending revolution in jazz became perceptible when the Cecil Taylor Quartet recorded *Jazz Advance!* for the Transition label in September 1956. The record was fairly well ignored in the marketplace, due more to Taylor's obscurity than poor press. The bad opinions of a few critics, and positive reactions of even fewer, were simply outnumbered by the public's general disinterest in another unfamiliar pianist. For those who heard and knew, however, the record resounded with subversive genius. Taylor's rhythmic notions were advanced well beyond Monk's, and the record overflowed with unconventional harmonies and subtle evasions of traditional musical structure. *Jazz Advance!* did not make major waves until Taylor was well established in the public's mind a few years down the road. In hindsight, it was a frightfully bold step away from the stagnation that threatened to choke the life out of jazz.

Other artists chose to put their artistic positions to use in more directly political ways. Saxophonist Sonny Rollins's liner notes for his 1958 album *Freedom Suite* (Riverside), dedicated to Afro-American equality, were cut by the label hoi-polloi who considered the text inflammatory. The album was pulled from the shelves and eventually reissued under the less menacing title *The Shadow Waltz*, *sans* liner notes. In response to Arkansas Governor Orval Faubus's blasting of national school desegregation, Charles Mingus composed his infamous "Fables of Faubus." The initial 1958 release was instrumental, at Columbia Records' insistence, but two years later, Mingus cut a new version for Candid (*Charles Mingus Presents Charles Mingus*), with incendiary lyrics aimed toward Faubus and his racist comrades: "Tell me someone who's ridiculous / Governor Faubus!" Mingus habitually chose politically provocative titles: "Prayer for Passive Resistance," "Free Cell Block F—, 'Tis Nazi USA" "Oh Lord, Don't Let Them Drop That Atomic Bomb On Me," "Remember Rockefeller at Attica." Gestures like these motivated the jazz community into activism, leading to the creation of fresh new music that still stirs up controversy decades later.

In the 1960s, though its audience was decimated, jazz would become a powerful form of black expression. This consciousness is still a vital part of the music today and has barely faded in the hearts of black musicians who are truly aware of, and concerned with, their unique culture and its advancement. In a 1984 interview (found in the liner notes to Khan Jamal/Pierre Dørge/Johnny Dyani, *Three* [1984, Steeplechase]), vibraphonist Khan Jamal made a statement that would have been right on target two decades before:

> I may play jazz, but first of all I play *Black music*. We have a message. Louis Armstrong had it, and Dizzy Gillespie has it. It may be political, sociological, economical, it may be about good times or bad. It's our way of communicating. You don't have to read heavy books about a country or a people to know what they're about. You listen to the music, you know what they have to tell.

This is the same basic philosophy of racial identity that fostered the Newport Rebel Festival, the October Revolution in Jazz, the Association for the Advancement of Creative Musicians, and the New York loft jazz scene. In all these instances and more, black-produced music was being used to convey the black experience in a singularly artistic manner, a cultural revolution conducted in a manner likely to get people's attention.

Jazz entered the 1960s with an air of tumultuous excitement, a tension-filled state of affairs the likes of which had not been seen since it first emerged from the primordial soup of Storyville. Ten years along, more musical giants would be dead, and rock would have an even greater stranglehold on the American public's listening habits. But in the 1960s, jazz fought back, spreading its name thickly around the globe, broadening and adapting itself to new social circumstances, and nothing would ever be the same.

Controlled Chaos:
The Nature of Free Music

To name something is to wait for it in the place you think it will pass.
—Amiri Baraka

In beginning this discourse on free jazz and free improvisation, we should first address what is perhaps the most difficult notion: defining what constitutes jazz itself. The prospect grates—from its inception, the term "jazz" has always had an elusive definition. To narrow its scope down to music that "swings" or has syncopated rhythms calls, then, for defining what "swing" and syncopation really mean, which then might beg any number of further clarifications. If the emphasis is placed on improvisation, we must discount major works by the likes of Gershwin, Ellington, and Jimmy Giuffre, which are jazz inspired but have completely composed scores. For decades, musical forms that did not easily fit into the more spacious pigeonholes of "classical," "rock," or "country" music have become "jazz" by default. Like the instrumental pop of Kenny G, these endeavors are simply less "non-jazz" than they are jazz. *Caveat emptor*, but so it goes.

Likewise, there is not a pat definition for "free jazz." Granted, synonyms have emerged that reflected certain aspects of the music and its times. "New jazz" or "The New Thing" were fine for their day, but those terms are hardly applicable four decades out, even as the innovations continue. "Out jazz" is preferred by several authors. "Great Black Music" was coined by the Art Ensemble of Chicago to blanket all their efforts, from bebop to blues to free. "Fire Music," from the title of a recording by saxophonist Archie Shepp, had its own vogue. Among today's popular labels are creative improvised music, ecstatic music, modern creative jazz, and action jazz. But all of these are only descriptive names, illustrative yet not sufficient to define the genre in full. The term "avant-garde" is also frequently applied, but free jazz is only a small cog in the machine of modern unconventionalism. Some prefer to restrict the "avant-garde" label to European-inspired art music rather than to modes of black expression, while others are quick to point out that even Louis Armstrong was considered avant-garde in his time. After all, it simply means one is "ahead of the pack."

For the purpose of this book, we shall (prudently) define "free jazz" as a musical form with some degree of syncopation or swing inflection, which also includes some combination of four basic characteristics: nonreliance on traditional musical norms and priorities, emphasis on tone color, open ensemble roles, and collective improvisation. Of course, not all "free" music contains all these characteristics. In fact, the more of these that are common to one work, and the more performers involved, the less "accessible" the music is likely to be. Still, these factors constitute the major building blocks of free jazz and may be applied in myriad ways.

The very name "free jazz" connotes a *freedom from established norms and priorities*; thus, the music, by its nature, departs from traditionally familiar melodic, harmonic, and rhythmic structures. All of these, however, can be used as reference points in free music. As we will discuss later, a principal distinction between "free jazz" and "free improvisation" is simply the degree to which our musical expectations are circumvented.

Much early free jazz, notably that played by alto saxophonist Ornette Coleman, was grounded in the blues as jazz has always been. But the standard blues *structure* (i.e., twelve bars of I-IV-V changes) is not usually a main foundation of free music. That role is given instead to personal expression, one's own interpretations, and instincts as inspired by other musical and environmental elements. Only the basic blues flavor remains, as the form is adapted to the artist's own present goals and circumstances.

It is worth noting here that many old-time blues performances were rhythmically and metrically free. These regularly deviated from the twelve-bar form, now considered the standard of traditional blues, as the freer structure was better suited both to the meter of the lyrics and to the emotions the bluesmen wished to express. It has been said of Robert Nighthawk that he had difficulty performing with other musicians because he was practically incapable of sustaining a 4/4 meter for more than a few measures. His mind was, presumably, more focused upon emotions and lyrics than on a steady pulse. His music certainly did not suffer from the want of meter, although his sidemen might well have. Lightnin' Hopkins and other postwar bluesmen also specialized in extended phrases, which could build a sense of tension or simply give the guitarist a chance to stretch out with a riff or two.

Many free-jazz artists openly experiment with *tone color*, the inherent qualities of the musical sounds they produce. Players customarily stray from standard intonation and timbre to evoke certain moods or clash deliberately with the sounds of other instruments. They may create animal sounds, screams, hums, and whistles through alternate fingerings, embouchures, and vocalizations. Often these tinkerings result in sounds that cannot really be considered "tones" in a classic sense at all. In the Chicago scene in the 1960s, some musicians could do entire gigs or recordings without once producing a traditionally expected sound.

As an example, trumpeter Lester Bowie of the Art Ensemble of Chicago became a virtual one-man band and sound-effects studio through his trumpet. Bowie used vocalizations, half-valve techniques, odd embouchures, and sundry other devices to conjure his intended noises. Like South African expatriate Hugh Masekela, Bowie could even evoke the melodicism of African vocal inflections through his horn. His talents in this regard can be heard on albums by the Art Ensemble of Chicago and his own works, particularly the second solo disc of *All the Magic!* (1983, ECM). Bowie's lifelong body of work is essentially a "how-to" of tone color experimentation. Even without the specialized techniques mentioned, the most basic sound in Bowie's bag— his sharp, vigorous blurting of notes without regard for tempo—is easily recognized. Similarly, a frequent signature of trumpeter Bill Dixon is blowing rapid flurries of notes at a quiet volume, with a characteristic timbre sounding as if he were kissing the mouthpiece. That particular tone color is as much an integral part of Dixon's personal style as fleet blaring was of Bowie's.

Some players choose to alter their instruments to change the sonic characteristics, removing mouthpieces or valves. Cornetist Butch Morris might stuff his mouthpiece into the bell to achieve a certain sound or blow across the bottom of the valves for whistling tones, and trumpeter Dave Douglas removes tubing from his horn for different effects. Reedman John Zorn performed solos with an array of mouthpieces and game calls, sometimes blowing them into a bowl of water. His solo on Big John Patton's "Congo Chant" (*Blue Planet Man*, 1993, Evidence) begins with the sound of Zorn either blowing a mouthpiece into water or using the palm of his hand to stop or change the airflow, bringing out primal ululations. That is followed by a feral saxophone scream, flutters, grunts, and all manner of mayhem that brings open-eared listeners to their feet.

Sometimes the instrument itself is chosen for specific sound qualities. For years, Ornette Coleman played a cheap plastic alto sax because he felt its dry, nasal tone was better suited to his approach than a brass horn. Sticking with such a low-budget horn might seem odd, but Coleman was in good company. Bebop pioneer Charlie Parker also played a Grafton plastic alto for a while, notably at the celebrated Massey Hall concert, and a more influential saxophonist than Bird probably cannot be named. Similarly, Coleman sidekick Don Cherry played a cheap Pakistani pocket cornet that conveyed his signature sound, which he once compared to a dry martini. Electronic modifications can also be utilized to change one's sound, as can be heard in the music of trombonist George Lewis and trumpeters Toshinori Kondo and Greg Kelley.

Some artists have developed their own instruments in order to achieve sounds they heard in their heads but could not reproduce otherwise. Pianist Cooper-Moore fashions diddly-bos (one-stringed drones, used in parts of the American South in prejazz times), hoe-handle harps, and other exotic contraptions as a sideline and plays them in concert. Sun Ra's Arkestra featured many odd fabrications, from mutant bassoons to humongous carved drums, used as much for showiness to complement Ra's spaced-out motifs as for their particular sounds.

Practically every instrument has been subjected to tone color experiments. Eric Dolphy and Roland Kirk revolutionized jazz flute techniques by vocalizing through their horns. The methods they trailblazed remain staples in the flautist's bag of tricks. Kirk's recording of the slow blues "You Did It, You Did It" (*We Free Kings*, Mercury, 1961) is a landmark in jazz flute performance; he sings unison melodies and harmonies over the fingered notes with facility and passion. Dewey Redman broke similar ground for the tenor saxophone by evolving a way to sing while he played, a difficult skill to master, and Albert Mangelsdorff expanded the use of *multiphonics* (playing of chords or intervals through vocal inflections) through similar experiments on the trombone. His talents can be heard to great effect on *Trilogue: Live!* (1977, MPS/ Delta), with two icons of jazz-rock fusion, bass guitarist Jaco Pastorius and drummer Alphonse Mouzon. Manipulating overtones through humming and lip positioning, the trombonist seems to effortlessly blow clusters of five or six notes at once.

Multiphonics are now a standard feature of jazz playing in free or mainstream contexts, but until the 1960s they were mostly unheard of. John Coltrane learned to play multiphonics from an obscure Philadelphian named John Glenn, and Trane's influence eventually made those sounds part and parcel of the jazz *oeuvre*. Pharoah Sanders, Gato Barbieri, and Albert Ayler, each of whom extended Coltrane's legacy in his own way, expanded the production of harmonics through overblowing and alternate fingerings, greatly extending the horn's sound capacity. All these techniques, and more, have added to the character and vocabulary of jazz in general.

Traditionally, the primary melodic roles within jazz ensembles have remained with either horns or chordal instruments (piano and guitar), while the bass, drums, and percussion provided a steady foundation for the others to play and improvise over. In much free music, however, all the instruments are given equal time and uniform chances for expression. *Musical democracy* can operate at its highest in free jazz, where drummers and bassists can carry an equal load with the saxes and trumpets instead of being relegated to the sidelines until their solo niches come up. In some performances, such as "Ghosts" on Albert Ayler's *Love Cry* (1968, Impulse), the horns stick wholly to the written material while the rhythm section improvises freely, a full reversal of the norm.

Free collectives such as the Art Ensemble of Chicago pride themselves on their members' equal opportunities to shine solo. Most of them play various percussion instruments at some points in concert, falling back to let others step to the fore, and bassist Malachi Favors is absolutely essential to that group's philosophy. On a different note, when Ornette Coleman constructed his electric band Prime Time as an extension of his "harmolodic" theories, he intended for each member to perform as both a frontman and sideman at once, playing as melodically as possible without getting in the way of the other performers' own creative impulses. Odd as it appears, the concept tends to work on many levels once the listener gets used to the unexpected density of sound. Air, the trio of reedman Henry Threadgill, bassist Fred Hopkins, and drummer Steve McCall, was another fully democratic ensemble.

Collective improvisation is as old as jazz itself. Players in the earliest New Orleans bands usually engaged in simultaneous improvisations throughout performances, with or without any written arrangements. It was not until Louis Armstrong's rise that a particular horn even moved up front full-time. The key difference is that, in free jazz, group improvisations are not generally based upon set chord patterns or rhythmic structures. There may be available *modes* (scale patterns differing from the traditional Western chordal system), short *melodic references,* or specified *tonal centers* that performers can refer to for inspiration, but their improvisations are not as restrained as in more conventional, chordally based forms of jazz.

Since his emergence in the late 1950s, Ornette Coleman's music has been characterized by short melodic components used as springboards for improvisation. The track "Focus on Sanity" (on his 1959 Atlantic album, *The Shape of Jazz to Come*) barely qualifies as a "composition" in the generally accepted sense. The theme is a quick, choppy four-bar structure that almost sounds like a group improvisation in itself. Following a powerful bass solo by Charlie Haden, the band jumps to another, even shorter, melodic line before Coleman's alto solo bursts out. Except for these brief composed fragments, the musicians are free to play in whatever direction they wish. Granted, this was early enough in Coleman's career that the rhythms and harmonies still hewed close to mainstream jazz, but there is a noticeable difference between "Focus On Sanity" and, say, Art Blakey's hard bop repertoire from the same period. A year later Coleman would again use such short references in his magnum opus *Free Jazz*, but its improvisations and tone sound years removed from the relative safety of "Focus." His evolution thus becomes clear.

Such openness can result in auditory mayhem, even if there is a discernibly logical structure to the piece. The best free performances are often those in which the players do not seem to clash. Even without set boundaries, musicians build structures based upon intuition, anticipation, and logic. The mathematical discipline of chaos theory states that even supposedly random events can have a basis in logical action and reaction. Good free performances reflect this idea of controlled chaos, and players who work together long enough develop an uncanny intuitiveness as to their next moves. One problem that free-jazz specialists face is locating partners who will be compatible and stick around long enough to develop the necessary empathy. The symbiosis between pianist Cecil Taylor and altoist Jimmy Lyons is a prime example. Once located, those partners become invaluable creative resources.

Besides performance styles, the *notation* of written music, the subject of much experimentation in the twentieth century, changed radically in light of the avant-garde. In the handbook for his 1963 performance piece "Treatise," composer Cornelius Cardew (once part of the English improvising collective AMM) surmised that "a composer who hears sounds will try to find a notation for sounds. One who has ideas will find one that expresses his ideas, leaving their interpretation free, in confidence that his ideas have been accurately and concisely notated."[1] That concept is reflected in the abstract notations of experimentalists like John Cage, George Brecht, Morton Feldman, and black free jazzmen Anthony Braxton and William Parker, among many others.

The composers' notational systems may consist simply of verbal descriptions that point the way for the players or geometric and linear diagrams bearing little resemblance to conventional sheet music. Braxton's graphic "song titles" have given DJs fits as they attempted to articulate them on the air (that is, when those records actually made it onto radio). The intimidating cerebrality of these systems has practically guaranteed the limited frequency of their performance. Without the composer present to hold their hands and guide them through each step of the music, most musicians in any field would be unable to follow the written score as it was truly meant to be played. In some cases, however, the point is moot. Multi-instrumentalist Joe McPhee has suggested that his "Watermelon Suite" is specifically intended to be performed by three musicians: a horn player, a bassist, and a drummer. Where anything goes from there is apparently up to the three players themselves. Now that's freedom!

With those clarifications out of the way, you might now wonder why this book distinguishes between "free jazz" and "free improvisation." The general distinctions between music that is considered free jazz and that which is considered free improv, in a more European experimental sense, are that the former uses some type of reference points, be they short composed themes, jazz-based playing techniques, or more general structural suggestions, and some recognizable "swing" inflections or syncopations. Again, this can be an uncomfortable distinction. As guitarist Derek Bailey has put it, "free jazz is a *form* of music, while free improvisation is an *approach* to making music." Bailey prefers the term "non-idiomatic improvisation" for his own music. Fair enough, since it is devilishly difficult to pin him down to a particular idiom like jazz. And that is, in fact, Bailey's intended objective: to improvise without consciously referring to any previously encountered idioms such as jazz, classical, or rock. This is a difficult end to achieve, given the caverns and coils of human memory, but Bailey is one of the form's acknowledged masters.

A sideline form is electroacoustic improvisation (EAI), which includes use of electronic or amplified sound sources. This form, which developed from the experiments of Stockhausen and Cage, was modified by groups like AMM and Musica Elettronica Viva (MEV) in the 1960s utilizing such devices as sine-wave generators, transistor radios, and tabletop electric guitars. EAI performances may range from simple augmentation of acoustic instruments to the exclusive use of electronics in improvisation. Solely due to space limitations, this book will not present much direct discussion of the EAI form, but many of its practitioners are listed in the Encyclopedia.

As you might gather, the distinctions between free jazz and free improv are better heard than described. A comparision of records by two important trombonists, America's Roswell Rudd and Europe's Günter Christmann, might prove adequately revealing. Both are masters of "free" music, but Rudd's playing usually bears recognizable jazz inflections: tone color, flourishes, effects, and such. His jazz-based sensibilities can be heard on, for example, the Jazz Composers Orchestra's eponymous album (1968, JCOA), and his own releases like *Flexible Flyer* (1974, Freedom). Christmann, on the other hand, prefers to produce sounds that are essentially unrecognizable as trombone tones. What Lester Bowie accomplished on the trumpet, Christmann takes to extremes on trombone. His live sextet album *Vario 34-2* (1999, Concepts of Doing) is an exercise in tonal mayhem. The music is completely unstructured and blissfully noisy, with few or no elements that could be conclusively pinned down as coming out of jazz: no swing inflection, no blue notes, no syncopation. Vario's music is no less vital or inspiring, no more or less valid than Rudd's, merely a different breed of improvised animal. Performers from both sides of the free coin will be presented in this volume in (hopefully) equitable measures.

NOTE

1. In Michael Nyman, *Experimental Music: Cage and Beyond* (London: Schirmer Books, 1974), p. 3.

The Path to Freedom

MODERN CLASSICAL ADVANCES

The advances of modern classical music early in the twentieth century had a significant impact on the forms that followed in its wake. These experiments probably affected white free improvisers more than the black musicians who originally conceived free jazz, yet there were exceptions. The music of black artists such as Anthony Braxton and Cecil Taylor was influenced as much by Bela Bartòk's mathematical complexity and Alexander Scriabin's strange chordal and scalar constructions as by Charles Mingus or Eric Dolphy. There are audible traces of these innovations scattered throughout avant-garde jazz, though as time marches on the continuum becomes rather clouded.

Arnold Schoenberg sought an alternative to accepted Western song structures; that is, reliance on a specific key, building of melodies and harmonies around that key, and chords that complement it. He developed two key principles that helped to shape free music: *atonality*, which avoids the strict hierarchy of triad chords fundamental to Western music, and *serialism* or *docecaphony* ("twelve sounds"), which involves arranging the twelve tones of the chromatic scale in nonrepeating series, or "rows," and building a composition out of the different permutations of those patterns. Some of Schoenberg's later disciples (Krenek, Berg, Webern, Boulez, and Babbitt, among others) further mutated the concept into "total serialism" by applying serial principles to rhythmic and dynamic structures as well. Serial ideas later became a perpetual component of *Third Stream* music, the blending of various classical and jazz elements.

Edgard Varèse sought to reach beyond the *tempered* music of the standard chromatic scale to implement the *microtones*, intrinsic to Eastern music, which lie between the notes of that scale. In an off-handed fashion, the opening of Western ears to microtones may have encouraged free jazz's disregard for conventional tonalities and the eventual enthusiasm for "world music." Like the free players, Varèse combined innovation with a desire to provoke the listener to attention and reaction. Among his followers were bop altoist Charlie Parker, who died before he could study with the composer; Harry Partch, who invented peculiar new instruments and scales; and Frank Zappa, who brought the essence of Varèse's experiments with percussion instruments into rock and jazz settings. A number of freemen, including Albert Ayler and Ornette Coleman, recognized that such extension of musical consciousness into microtonal areas rendered the idea of "intonation" pointless. Coleman has claimed that this epiphany arrived "when I realized that you could play sharp or flat in tune,"[1] a remark that still causes some traditionally minded musicians to scratch their heads in wonder.

A prodigy who made millions in the insurance business, Charles Ives experimented with microtones, mixed meters, unusual harmonies, folk music, and *collage* techniques, sewing crazy quilts out of disparate song fragments. His unique works combined folk songs, hymns, marches, and classical echoes, sometimes using unusual percussion instruments as textural devices. Carla Bley and Anthony Braxton are among the jazz musicians profoundly affected by Ives's innovations. Braxton has used similar collage methods since the 1980s, having one musician play a section of one composition while other performers play a different work simultaneously.

Among the other contemporary classical innovations that spread into the new jazz were John Cage's cold naturalism, use of silence, and aleatoric (chance) procedures, such as hand signals or cue cards; Morton Feldman's trials with graphic notation and compositional duration; and Karlheinz Stockhausen's studies of acoustics, artistic psychology, and electronic music. Aleatoric procedures are given a nod in John Zorn's performance games, many of Braxton's works, and Butch Morris's "conductions," in which he leads the ensemble via hand signals. Feldman was influential to many ultraintellectual jazzmen, including Cecil Taylor and reedman Ken Vandermark, who dedicated a series of short pieces to the composer on *Acoustic Machine* (2001, Atavistic) by the Vandermark 5.

PRE-FREE-JAZZ ADVANCES

Inspired by what was happening in contemporary classical circles, jazz composers began to take such bold steps in their own writing. Some experiments fell flat; others had immense effects on the music's nature, changing it for all time. Besides the key element of curiosity, the desire to overcome adversity and discrimination, and to create music that was more acutely personal yet representative of an entire culture, tended to drive these innovations. The racial issues that divided America in the twentieth century came to an artistic head through such investigations.

In 1947, Duke Ellington recorded one of his most unusual compositions, which did not reap much positive attention for perhaps obvious reasons. "The Clothed Woman" was a pointillistic work based upon his "punctuation" piano style of injecting short chordal bursts for emphasis and momentum. The opening and closing sections have no fixed rhythmic structure, and much of the piece hovers about a suspended, nonmodulating bass figure. Ellington had been strongly influenced by classical composers, including key figures of the early-century revolution. Perhaps "The Clothed Woman" was an attempt to introduce those composers' innovations to jazz, and it was prescient of the experiments that Stan Kenton undertook the following decade. However, coming from a black jazz orchestra in the mid-1940s, the piece seems to have been regarded as merely odd or pretentious. In subsequent discussions of Duke Ellington's contributions to American music, "The Clothed Woman" rarely begs a mention. Stravinsky's "Ebony Concerto," written for Woody Herman in the same period, gets far more press. Still, as a small step over the police tape of tradition, Ellington's foray is worth noting.

The bebop movement, born out of 1930s jam sessions and amply realized in the late 1940s, was itself an avant-garde reaction to staleness and racism in jazz. The perception that the "white cats" had bastardized jazz into a pine-fresh commodity by sucking the life, the "blackness," out of it led some black players to experiment with new forms. Celebrated players like altoist Charlie "Yardbird" Parker, trumpeter John Birks "Dizzy" Gillespie, and older hands like tenor sax legend Coleman Hawkins set wild new melodies onto the chords of worn standards. "Indiana," "I Got Rhythm," "Sweet Georgia Brown," and other chestnuts familiar to any jazzman worth his salt were reshaped with complex, manic themes. The expectation was that white players would not be able to keep up technically and that, perhaps, white audiences would get scared off so that jazz would be left to the people who really appreciated it for what it was. And this projection approached reality, at least for a time.

After the Blue Note record label began documenting the music for posterity, bebop became the prevalent face of jazz in most urban areas, and much current jazz is still firmly established on bop principles. However, the relentless emphasis on technique eventually became a sort of sticking point. By the end of the 1950s, the fervent novelty had worn thin, and what was once an impressive swagger became viewed as inconsequential showing off. Bebop gradually mutated into *hard bop*, as players began looking back to their roots once again. Elements of blues and gospel were rewoven back into the bebop form, and the music recaptured some of its soul. Art Blakey, Horace Silver, and Cannonball Adderley were among the jazzmen who hit their stride and established a vogue for hard bop.

Most of the early free players came out of swing, R&B, or bebop backgrounds. One particular bebop giant who was highly influential to freemen was pianist/composer Thelonious Monk. The bearded, behatted Monk was a *sui generis* performer who strictly followed his own lead. Raised on a rich diet of church music and old standards, Monk embraced jazz as a young adult and developed his own ultraeclectic approach to jazz piano. His flat-fingered, scattershot manner is said to have evolved during his days as a barrelhouse pianist on old, worn-out instruments that practically had to be flogged in order to produce any sound. Echoes of Monk resonate in the works of Cecil Taylor, Myra Melford, Misha Mengelberg, and other contemporary pianists who approach the piano percussively.

Monk's experience could serve as a virtual blueprint for the patterns that developed in the free community. He had his own personal sense of rhythm, chordal logic, and melodic structure, which not only made him an instantly recognizable player but reduced the number of compatible sidemen to the barest handful. Monk would habitually cluster notes together in hurried wads of conflicting tones, take long pauses before the next fusillade, or jump up on a whim for one of his peculiar shuffling dances. He was a pioneer in bypassing traditional chord structures, as his recastings of standards like "Just You, Just Me" or "Memories of You" reveal. Monk reshaped musical traditions fearlessly in his own image, using portions of them as scant starting points for wherever his heart and hands led him. He made especially good use of silence as a dramatic device. His compositions often sounded as if Jackson Pollock had flung black spots of ink onto a blank manuscript page. The stilted, uncomfortably edgy "Evidence" is a prime example; unfamiliar listeners almost need to follow along with the sheet music in order to pinpoint the "one."

Monk was once described as "the bebopper who didn't play bebop," and there is ample evidence to support that idea. As a black sheep even among the wolf pack of innovating beboppers, Monk was a standard-bearer for the eventual development of free improvisation as a viable art form. When exposed to the music of Ornette Coleman for the first time, Monk is said to have sneered and quipped, "I was doing that a long time ago." History, to a degree, bears out Monk's claim, but Coleman was among the first players to base entire performances and albums on such techniques.[2]

Later, pianists like Andrew Hill and Herbie Nichols, both undersung legends, drew from Monk's example and moved on to their own innovations. Some free pioneers have devoted much of their careers to interpolating Monk's compositions with free-jazz deliberations, particularly Roswell Rudd and soprano saxophonist Steve Lacy. Similarly, Herbie Nichols's repertoire has been championed by Rudd, Misha Mengelberg, and bassist Ben Allison. In 2000, Anthony Braxton issued two un-expectedly faithful albums of Hill's tunes on the CIMP label. Recommended starting points for exploring the original artists are *Herbie Nichols: The Complete Blue Note Recordings* (1997, Blue Note, three CDs), Hill's classic albums *Black Fire* (1963) and *Point of Departure* (1964, both on Blue Note), and almost anything from the Monk discography.

Though free jazz was eventually regarded as a vehicle of black expression, some of the earliest recorded insights into improvisation, apart from set chordal and rhyth-mic structures, were provided by white players. Perhaps the first of these came in May 1949, when the iconoclastic cool-school pianist Lennie Tristano, a blind white man, recorded two tracks of collective improvisation with his group after the composed pieces for their next album had been taped. These cuts, released years later as "Intu-ition" and "Digression," are considered by some to be the first recorded examples of what came to be called "free jazz." There are no set rhythms or chord patterns, and the tracks convey some of the sterile formality of European classical styles. It has been said throughout jazz's history that white men could not properly convey the authentic feelings behind the music. The argument that Tristano is unable to inject viable jazz passion into these tunes, despite the abandonment of his usually rigid formal struc-tures, seems to hold water.

Another significant session followed five years later (though released before Tristano's works), still ahead of its time and once again the work of white jazzmen. West Coast drummer Shelly Manne, trumpeter Shorty Rogers, and saxophonist Jimmy Giuffre formed an unusual trio in 1954 to record *The Three and the Two* (Contempo-rary) under Manne's name. Giuffre, the composer of Woody Herman's hit "Four Brothers," had exhibited avant-garde inclinations for a few years, but the others had been firmly ensconced in big bands and the California school of cool. Probably at Giuffre's prompting, this trio recorded seven minutes of random thought, which ended up on the album as "Abstract No. 1." Along with "Three on a Row," a composition based on serial techniques, "Abstract No. 1" was dismissed by some critics as a mere throwaway track on an otherwise cool album. But the session pointed the way ahead for Giuffre, who soon became one of the most appreciated and studied musicians in the avant-garde and Third Stream schools. In 1960, he formed a trio, with pianist Paul Bley and bassist Steve Swallow, which reached toward more authentic free improvisation. On their album *Free Fall* (1963, Columbia), the sympathetic presence of his trio-mates keeps Giuffre on a firm jazz path while extending their musical vision.

On the other side of the coin was Los Angeles–born bassist, bandleader, and composer Charles Mingus, a young bebop pioneer and one of the first blacks to regularly push the envelope of accepted structure. By expanding the harmonic and rhythmic potentials of the upright bass, Mingus was instrumental in recasting the bassist's role in jazz ensembles.[3] That sea change eventually helped free up other rhythm players for greater participation in the full jazz experience. Mingus further freed his musicians by choosing in the late 1950s to stop writing his compositions on paper. Instead, he vocally dictated parts to the musicians from his cavernous memory, instilling the basic core of the piece but permitting plenty of elbow room for interpretation. And although he was profoundly inspired by Duke Ellington's works, Mingus developed an individual style that united elements like Duke's orchestral visions, the Holiness Church songs of his youth, and Lennie Tristano's cool musings into a new, stand-alone whole.

In January 1956, Mingus's ensemble recorded "Pithecanthropus Erectus," his ponderous, mythological study of evolution and the presumed hierarchy of social subdivisions that came with it. Mingus was a most serious black activist, fighting civil injustice with his bass and pen, and this recording was one of his greatest achievements in that regard. In the liner notes for the same-titled Atlantic album, Mingus said of the piece:

> it depicts musically my conception of the modern counterpart of the first man to stand erect—how proud he was, considering himself the "first" to ascend from all fours, pounding his chest and preaching his superiority over the animals still in a prone position. Overcome with self-esteem, he goes out to rule the world, if not the universe, but both his own failure to realize the inevitable emancipation of those he sought to enslave, and his greed in attempting to stand on a false security, deny him not only the right of ever being a man, but finally destroy him completely.

"Pithecanthropus Erectus" is an orgy of sneaky crescendos, quick decrescendos, and howling horn spasms. At the piece's climax, the horns clash in free time while blowing incredible multiphonic clusters. It was a revelation, one of the most powerful statements of the modern jazz era. And, as might be expected, it scared the pants off many listeners. For all its impact, some critics, fans, and musicians wrote the album off as a singular distraction, not expecting that an entire musical movement would soon be constructed along similar principles. Even tenorman J. R. Monterose, who shone brightly on the session and was considered a solid foil for Mingus by critics, stated that he did not really understand or enjoy what Mingus was trying to put across at the time.

Mingus's compositions, which usually joined massive, bigger-than-sum orchestrations to periodic passages of collective improvisation, and his commanding presence on bass, made a significant impression upon the course of free jazz. Mingus continued to use such dissonance and freedom throughout his career, notably in ensembles that featured Eric Dolphy on alto sax, flute, and bass clarinet. The live *Mingus at Antibes* (1960, Atlantic) illustrates just how far Dolphy was ahead of the pack. On the extended take of "Wednesday Night Prayer Meeting," trumpeter Ted Curson and tenorman Booker Ervin take impressive but rather conventional solos. Dolphy then sweeps the house clean, creating blissful, atonal lines at whizzing speeds, leaping across wide intervals, and completely disregarding the bar lines in favor of letting his alto speak its mind. Mingus's driving bass and verbal exhortations over drummer Dannie Richmond's splashy rhythms complete the picture, conveying the exciting call-and-response participation of a black church meeting. That energy, that fearless freedom to let it fly, represented a principal point of departure for the free-jazz experience.

Besides his own hybridization of Duke, bebop, and gospel, Mingus explored other musical directions as well. The first movement of his uncompleted "Revelations" was recorded in 1957 for *Music for Brass* (Columbia), a showcase of Third Stream art. "Tonight at Noon" (on *Passions of a Man*, 1957, Atlantic) was an equally complex piece, built upon a bass ostinato and rich with collective improvisations. *The Black Saint and the Sinner Lady* (1963, Impulse) was his magnum opus, an extended suite with incredible (overdubbed) alto sax performances by Charlie Mariano. Mingus was open-minded enough to book Ornette Coleman's quartet for his 1960 protest festival, not to mention working with Archie Shepp, Don Pullen, and Hamiet Bluiett later in life, but once free jazz had become an established form, Mingus had little positive to say about it. His derogatory attitude aside, the inspiration of Mingus's open-ended compositions, his embracing of collective improvisation, and his freeing up of the rhythm section's roles was inarguable. Mingus opened the artistic doors through which free jazz was about to barge.

CECIL TAYLOR STEPS FORWARD

September 1956 marked the recording debut of one of free jazz's principal architects, a conservatory-trained pianist named Cecil Taylor. *Jazz Advance*, issued on the small Transition label, was a quartet session featuring a group of unknowns: drummer Denis Charles, bassist Buell Neidlinger, and a former Dixieland soprano saxophonist, Steve Lacy. The album sounded for the most part like a standard hard bop effort, but Taylor's rhythmic sense was already more abstracted than that of Monk. The unconventional notes and phrases used in their solos and harmonies were a nod toward Taylor's eventual abandonment of traditional musical values altogether. It was a quiet but stern notice that things were going to be changing around the jazz household.

Looking at the album's cover, one would have expected a pretty traditional experience from *Jazz Advance*. Covers of Monk's "Bemsha Swing," Ellington's "Azure," and the standards "Sweet and Lovely" and Cole Porter's "You'd Be So Nice to Come Home to" are present, along with three Taylor originals: "Charge 'Em Blues," "Rick Kick Shaw," and "Song." Lacy only plays on two tracks, and one other is a Taylor solo, so the expectation might be of a pretty straight piano trio session. That, of course, is hardly the case.

The Monk tune begins quietly but catchily, with a Latin rhythm from Charles and a couple of minor figures from Taylor before he starts choppily navigating the melody. When the Latin vibe dies off in favor of a swing pulse, things get more colorful. Taylor begins to revisit sections of the melody, playing through variations of segments and increasingly abstract chordal voicings. A half-hearted blues line mutates into a rapid swing figure, then it's back to the ragged rhythms and variations. Taylor's rhythmic, melodic, and harmonic senses are revealed to be operating on entirely different planes from those of most jazzmen.

Charles, a West Indian native with a broad palette of rhythmic options, does an admirable job of holding things together while Taylor constructs fantasy castles on his foundations. The same with Neidlinger, who is a hazy background image most of the time. Although the blues is clearly present on "Charge 'Em Blues," Taylor's staticky block chords and oddball rhythms continually alter the shades of blue that Lacy adeptly brushes on. The Ellington piece is handled with the most respect, though Taylor still wreaks blissful havoc with the rhythm. The simple title of "Song" belies its vivid complexity; it is almost immediately impossible to pin down the beat between Lacy's adroit turns and the pianist's rollicking randomness. Taylor completely has his way with the Porter tune, exploring every imaginable jazz style, including a few that haven't happened yet.

Taylor's lifelong obsessions with thematic variation and rhythmic fluidity are firmly announced on the disc. Having thrown the gauntlet down so brashly on his first effort, Taylor was sadly ignored and set himself up for years of hardship and misunderstanding that would not reverse course for almost thirty years. But *Jazz Advance* was an important declaration, headaches or no, and from that moment on the winds of change were unleashed upon jazz.

In Chicago, another musical upheaval was occurring at the hands of a bizarre collective called the Arkestra, led by a grand master of ceremonies known as Sun Ra. Ra was a mysterious robed figure who claimed to have come from Saturn, although according to "earthly records" he was born Herman Poole Blount in Birmingham, Alabama, and had once been an arranger for Fletcher Henderson's big band. Ra's theatrical ensemble, clad in wild costumes, played an inventive jazz mixed with free and Latin elements and a wealth of percussion, ethnic, and newly devised instruments. Ra and his devotees were the strangest of the strange, but they apparently made a firm impression on Chicago's young raptors who were looking to cross new musical horizons. Strangely, although the influence of Ra's innovative style on the city's musicians would seem obvious, perhaps unavoidable, few if any of Chicago's premier free players have openly acknowledged him as an inspiration.

On July 12, 1956, the Arkestra recorded the sessions for *Jazz by Sun Ra* (occasionally reissued as *Sun Song*), which was released in 1957 on Transition, giving the Boston label a double play on the free-jazz ballfield. Ra played piano and Hammond organ, and his youthful ensemble included saxophonists John Gilmore and Pat Patrick, trumpeters Art Hoyle and Dave Young, trombonist Julian Priester, and tympanist Jim Herndon. There was already a heavy emphasis on percussion, as several hornmen also played bells, woodblocks, and other miscellanea at intervals. It was the first documentation of Ra's music dealt out to the public, and what a wild revelation it was.

The titles of Ra's compositions alone indicated his innovative perspectives: "Transition" (a nod to their label, no doubt, as well as the impending changes in jazz), "Call for All Demons," "Street Named Hell," "Future," "New Horizons." The utter strangeness of Herndon's tympani erupting out of nowhere for a solo; meters that felt unusual when they really were not; the uncomfortable juxtaposition of Henderson-style arrangements and coolness with minor, jagged harmonies from well beyond bebop: all of these factors and more marked Sun Ra as an earnest innovator who simultaneously embraced jazz tradition and condemned it as insufficient for the midcentury.

About this same time, mainstream jazz audiences in Los Angeles were getting their first startling glimpses of the future when a young Texan alto saxophonist appeared on the scene. His name was Ornette Coleman, and his musical gifts had been fostered in R&B bands around Fort Worth and Dallas. He had been formulating his own notions about jazz and improvisation, working out new tone colors, and extending his solos beyond the tunes' chord progressions. These explorations, not surprisingly, got him fired from his touring gigs. But while stranded in L.A., Coleman met a group of open-minded players and initiated his quiet revolution. Eventually his circle of associates was completed by Oklahoman trumpeter Don Cherry, Midwestern bassist Charlie Haden, and L.A.-native drummer Billy Higgins, a quartet that quickly set about smashing the rules.

Coleman landed his first recording contract in 1958 with Contemporary Records, for which he made two innovative, provocatively titled discs: *Something Else!* (1958, with Cherry, Higgins, bassist Don Payne, and pianist Walter Norris) and *Tomorrow Is the Question!* (1959, with Cherry, bassists Red Mitchell and Percy Heath, and drummer Shelly Manne). Both albums (discussed further under Coleman's Encyclopedia entry), while different from *Jazz Advance* in approach, bore a similarly unsettling blend of tradition and modernity that hinted at, as a later Coleman album title put it, the shape of jazz to come.

While Taylor and Coleman were developing their separate ideas of free improvisation, something equally modernistic was being advanced as a commensurate response to cool jazz. Composer George Russell had originally begun to formulate his Lydian Chromatic Concept of Tonal Organization, the foundation of *modal jazz*, in the mid-1940s. Russell was a supreme jazz innovator; one of the first writers to combine jazz and Latin elements (in "Cubano Be, Cubano Bop" for Dizzy Gillespie's band), he also synthesized bebop and Stravinsky in "A Bird in Igor's Yard," written for clarinetist Buddy DeFranco. In "All about Rosie" (*Modern Jazz Concert*, 1957, Columbia) he updated Charles Ives's aesthetic by layering elements of a Negro children's song into an extravagant Third Stream dessert.

In 1953, Russell published the first edition of his Lydian Concept, the first major work of music theory to be rooted in jazz. It was based on a permutation of a medieval church-music mode, the Lydian, which sharps the fourth note in the scale (i.e., C-D-E-F#-G-A-B-C). The sharped fourth is tonally identical to the flatted fifth that resonated in bebop, but is applied in a completely different manner. The concept ostensibly freed players from the inflexibility of major-minor chordal music, permitting a more vertical development of ideas. The mode could be sustained with no change for as long as the players desired, and its tonal center could be shifted up or down according to the wishes of the composer or performer, opening up new opportunities for improvisational and thematic development. This was important not only to the future development of modal jazz, it also influenced Coleman's *harmolodic theory*, which will be addressed later. Russell later became a principal figure in the Third Stream, as well as combining electronic sounds and jazz in *Electronic Sonata for Souls Loved by Nature* (1960, Flying Dutchman).

Trumpeter Miles Davis, a founding father of the cool school, had abandoned that style quickly and begun to explore modes once Russell's concepts were publicized. Though Davis was not the founder of modal jazz, he arguably made it all the vogue. For his own experiments, Davis assembled an impressive following of disciples, including saxophonists John Coltrane and Julian "Cannonball" Adderley, and pianists Red Garland and Bill Evans. Coltrane, who had worked with both Davis and Monk a few years prior, had gained notoriety for his fleet-fingered skills, while the beauty-attuned Evans was integral to Russell's own modal recordings. The concepts Davis explored gave his sidemen another dash of freedom in which to develop their signature styles.

Davis's first recorded use of modes was the title track of *Milestones* (1958, Columbia). Its harmonically rebellious structure vacillates between two modes (G Dorian and A Aeolian) held down by pianist Red Garland, without any "bridge" or other resolving component. While some stale-hearted critics were confused by the harmonic oddity of "Milestones," it has become a classic over time.

In 1959, Davis's group released what has become the most popular jazz record of all time, the first seriously influential recorded statement of modality in jazz: *Kind of Blue* (Columbia). The music on *Kind of Blue* is moody and impressionistic, refreshingly (or, for some, astonishingly) different from the musings of bebop, by then old hat, and the soullessness of cool jazz. Some tunes sounded like serial compositions, with odd juxtapositions of tones, and tracks like "So What" featured sparse melodies serving as basic idea frameworks. "Flamenco Sketches" hasn't even a melody; it is completely improvised upon five modal options. The music's spacious emotional expressiveness was heightened by its tonal clashes. As had happened at the birth of cool jazz, some celebrated Davis's new creations while others were put off by their modernity. But like it or lump it, modal jazz would become an inexorable force in jazz throughout the next decade, with Davis generally at the helm. From that tide of jazz modality sprang several artists of future renown, especially Coltrane and Evans.

By 1960, Ornette Coleman and his cohorts had polished up their new sound, and in that year they released the document that gave this startling movement its most commonly used label. Issued by Atlantic in an early lapse of inhibition, *Free Jazz: A Collective Improvisation by the Ornette Coleman Double Quartet* was just that: a wild, mostly uncomposed adventure by Coleman's octet that used only a handful of short themes as reference points. The band included Cherry, Eric Dolphy on bass clarinet, young trumpeter Freddie Hubbard, bassists Charlie Haden and Scott LaFaro, and drummers Billy Higgins and Ed Blackwell. The resulting music was astonishing, like nothing ever heard on record before. It seemed to many listeners to have no sound reasoning, no sense of tradition, and no appreciable "musical" content. To others, it pointed the direction in which jazz most logically had to move, turning its back on predictability and heading into uncharted territories. The critics were torn between flaming anti-Coleman rhetoric and delirious praise for this brave step forward. The future had arrived with a bang, though the new jazz still had yet to impress mainstream listeners.

John Coltrane made a new move of his own in 1960 with the release of *My Favorite Things* (Atlantic). The album, a major international hit, marked Coltrane's debut on soprano saxophone,[4] which would become immensely popular by virtue of his influence. For years, Coltrane had shown great potential as a lead voice, but he began to seriously exploit that competence only after his eye-opening experiences with Davis. By 1960, Coltrane's quartet was performing both modal and chordal compositions and using *substitute harmonies*, replacing the standard chords of tunes with alternate chords, which drastically changed the song's spirit while still fitting the melody. His playing had become less restrained and far more explorative. On the title piece, an enduring classic, he soars into the rafters like a songbird searching for an open window. Coltrane had found his passion and translated it into pure musical joy. The transcendent vigor of "My Favorite Things" heralded the spiritual search that would color Coltrane's music for the rest of his days. In fact, the tune stayed in Coltrane's repertoire until his death, each new version a benchmark in his artistic odyssey.

During a recording career that lasted a scant six years, Eric Dolphy inspired a host of third-generation jazz performers who admired his use of vocalizations, sound effects, large intervals, and expansions of the bebop palette. Most of his recordings, as a sideman and leader, are considered essential listening for anyone interested in postbop jazz. Though Dolphy had a nodding interest in the white avant-gardists (he even performed Varése's solo flute piece "Density 21.5"), his experiments usually remained true to jazz's African American roots. He achieved an impressive solidity in his playing, influencing performers like Coltrane and altoist Arthur Blythe while keeping up a consistent degree of soulfulness. He drew inspiration from Parker (especially his rhythmic sense), Monk, and his employers Mingus, Coltrane, and Coleman while becoming inspirational in his own right.

From 1960 to 1964, Dolphy worked extensively with Mingus, and he is featured to fine effect on recordings like *Mingus at Antibes* (1960, Atlantic) and *Mingus!* (1960, Candid). His concurrent time with Coltrane was equally well spent. Dolphy bonded more tightly with Trane than his other employers, and the leader labeled Dolphy one of the most inspiring musicians he had ever met. Their partnership bore delectable fruit on several albums, including *Impressions*; *Africa/Brass*, which Dolphy arranged for an expanded group; *Olé*; and *Live at the Village Vanguard* (all 1961, Impulse).

Dolphy's own albums are excellent almost on the whole, with many textural shifts and bright new ideas to recommend them. (The most essential are discussed under his Encyclopedia entry.) Following a successful tour of Europe with Mingus's quintet, Dolphy remained in Berlin where he set up some dates of his own. *Last Date* (1964, Fontana) documents one of his final concerts, held on June 2, 1964, in the Netherlands. The all-European rhythm section consisted of drummer Han Bennink, pianist Misha Mengelberg, and bassist Jacques Schols. The exposure that Bennink and Mengelberg gained through this gig was pivotal in igniting Europe's subsequent furor for free improvisation. Unfortunately, less than a month later, Dolphy's diabetes flared up and he died of heart failure on June 29. The jazz world had lost one of its most beloved souls, a standard-bearer for the revolution that had just barely begun.

In the wake of Sun Ra's departure for New York in 1960, one of the first Midwest-erners to experiment with free jazz was pianist Muhal Richard Abrams. The next year Abrams assembled his Experimental Band to explore freedom in music. This group, which like the Arkestra used small percussion devices for texture and color, would later evolve into the Association for the Advancement of Creative Musicians, the most important American free-jazz collective.

With the capable assistance of tenor saxophonists Roscoe Mitchell and Fred Anderson, St. Louis trumpeter Lester Bowie, and other young musical leaders, Abrams was about to permanently change the perspective of group performance. One goal of the collective was to facilitate *unity among diversity*, to give each player an equal voice in what was happening musically. Abrams also sought to bring the music to the inner-city public, teaching Chicago's young blacks about their cultural heritage and how they could express their own experiences through the arts. Under Abrams's leader-ship, the AACM became one of urban America's most significant cultural institu-tions. Some of its offspring, principally the Art Ensemble of Chicago and Air, would further reshape the face of jazz in their time.

The mid-1960s also saw the publication of the first academic musicocultural analy-sis of jazz by a black author. One postulated reason that the appreciation of jazz had expanded among white audiences while remaining seemingly static in black commu-nities was a lack of published discourse by black writers who better understood the music's roots. Black authors had too few opportunities to have their works marketed to the general public, and most white American writers, at least on the surface, bore disdain for this "low-brow" art. Some volumes about jazz had been written by white American and European authors from the 1920s onward,[5] and memoirs like Sidney Bechet's *Treat It Gentle* had been issued sporadically. But LeRoi Jones's 1963 book *Blues People* was, as Langston Hughes glowingly pointed out, the first book written (or at least published) by a black writer as a full-tilt overview of jazz. The time was ripe for an intelligently considered black man's perspective on black-created music, and Jones made certain to address the importance of the radical new jazz with energy and ex-citement. Jones later embraced Islam, changed his name to Amiri Baraka, and con-tinued to champion the new musical art as a poet, author, and contributor to *Jazz Review* and *Down Beat*.

CIVIL RIGHTS AND AFRO-AWARENESS

The American civil rights movement was one prime instigator in the propagation of free jazz as a means of black expression (although, despite the implications of cer-tain writers like Frank Kofsky, it was absolutely not a universal incitement). The mid-century revolutions that spread across Africa like wildfire fostered new hopes and ambitions in America's downcast urban blacks, whose own battle for equality was still smoldering. The rhetoric and noble steps of Martin Luther King Jr., Malcolm X, the Nation of Islam, and the Black Panthers all had resounding effects on the American black community.

In 1960, only 17 percent of nonwhite families had an income over $7,000, com-pared with 41 percent of white households. Forty-five percent of the housing available to nonwhites was considered substandard, exactly triple that of whites. The white unemployment rate was 4.9 percent, less than half that of nonwhites.[6] Statistics for both sides would improve dramatically on paper over the next decade, but the racial divide between those numbers remained consistent. The mass migration of blacks to urban America that had begun before World War I had been, for many, perhaps a costlier mistake than remaining in the Deep South. While the increased concentration of blacks within the cities gave the people more opportunities to elect representatives from within their own community, the white power structure severely limited their effectiveness. Desegregation did little to decrease discrimination, and a "backwoods" bigoted mentality could be found around every corner. For most, the urban promise was a vulgar lie. Small wonder that racial politics played a significant role for jazzmen when they ignited their segment of the cultural revolution.

The situation within the music industry was a microcosm of the American minority experience. Many black achievements in the arts, including jazz and the newer rock-and-roll, had ostensibly been commandeered by whites and transformed into something more palatable by white audiences. Oftentimes, the blacks who had helped to create the music were shut out of better-paying gigs and festivals by virtue of their color. Those who were granted grace to perform were often cheated or manipulated for the promoters' gain. Much of the time, black musicians could not stay in the same hotels or eat in the same restaurants as their white bandmates. In *Black Nationalism and the Revolution in Music*, Kofsky likened this circumstance to a territorial colony that uses up its own resources for the benefit of the nation that rules over it. Thus, he maintained, the white men who owned most of the booking agencies, record labels, and production companies reaped the greatest benefits from the labors and talents of black musicians, leaving their cash-cow benefactors in the lurch.

Early in the free-jazz movement, some free and post-bop musicians decided to fight the system, particularly the white-dominated music festivals. Entrepreneur George Wein and his patrons, the Lorillard family, in imitation of classical music festivals, started the Newport Jazz Festival in Rhode Island in 1954. Wein's intentions were good, to be sure. He was attempting to elevate jazz to a more "artistic" status—that is, a status more appealing to the conservative white audiences that patronized such festivals. But in doing so, Wein alienated many nontraditional players, especially those of color, and their urban minority audiences. It may have been that the appearance of Cecil Taylor at the 1957 Newport Festival scared off some much-needed support, or that the weight of white money skewed the promoters' objectives. In any event, Newport became notorious for neglecting the black founding fathers of jazz and exploiting the few black musicians who were allowed to participate.

In a highly visible act of defiance, Charles Mingus and drummer Max Roach staged their Newport Rebel Festival in July 1960 to call attention to the perceived injustices wrought upon black musicians by Wein and his cronies. Among the artists on the roster were Ornette Coleman and his quartet. Against all bets placed by the white promoters, the alternative fest at Cliff Walk Manor Hotel drew a much larger crowd than the main affair, a powerful testament to the Newport cadre's folly and the power of the music they had been neglecting.

Soon the Newport Festival recanted and began hosting a slightly larger number of "out" musicians. The 1965 Newport appearance of John Coltrane and Archie

Shepp, to be further discussed later in this section, proved to be a primary turning point in the music's popularization. White listeners were exposed to a new form of music they had largely been prevented from hearing before, and a good number of them appreciated the power and talent behind it. Blacks, on their own side of the fence, proudly chalked one up for the good fight.

The expeditious growth of Afro-awareness and connected events like the Rebel Festival gradually led to the conceptualization of a music specifically calculated as a means of black expression. Blacks started going "back to the roots" in wardrobe, religion, and music. Traditional African instruments and rhythms became more prominent in performances. Musicians like Randy Weston and Ornette Coleman made pilgrimages to the motherland to seek out their ancestry and the meaning of their lives, sometimes performing with noteworthy groups like Morocco's Master Musicians of Jajouka and Gnawa. Urban American blacks adopted African or Muslim names and bestowed them upon their children. Their specially created free music was aimed to cast away musty "white" notions of what jazz should be, expressing the fury, passion, and pain of their people in urgent times.

Two of the most prominent black activists who arose in the free era were Archie Shepp and Amiri Baraka. Tenorman Shepp was an experienced playwright and poet, and he brought those skills into play in live and recorded performances. Baraka, encountered earlier as Leroi Jones, championed the players who created these new modes of expression, and he took pains to promote and encourage them in liner notes, reviews, articles, and books. He also wrote poetry and plays in explicit street language, which reflected the hard, ugly truths of the urban black experience. His Black Arts Repertory Theater and School was responsible for educating inner-city black youths about their heritage and art.

Besides championing jazz's many forms in print, Baraka has taken part in many live concerts and recording sessions with free jazzmen like Sunny Murray, Air, and Sun Ra. In 1965, he organized a Black Arts Centrum benefit concert that featured Coltrane, Ayler, Shepp, and other top figures of the music; a recording of that event was issued on Impulse as *The New Wave in Jazz* (1965). Baraka recited his poem "Black Dada Nihilismus" on the self-titled disc by the New York Art Quartet (1964, ESP). It is a remarkably proud declaration of the soul-deep bitterness of the black struggle: "Black Dada Nihilismus/ against what life is false/ what breath sucked for deadness/ murder/ the cleansed purpose/ frail/ against God/ if they bring him bleeding, I would not forgive or even call him. . . . Plastique we do not have, only thin heroic blades/ the razor, our flail against them/ why you carry knives, our brutal lumps of heart/ why you stay where they can reach/ why you sit or stand or walk in this place. . . ."[7] Baraka's poetic forms had a sympathetic counterpart in free jazz's instinctive reflexiveness, leading to productive collaborations.

Though New York's music revolution garnered most of the early publicity due to the concentration of jazz press within the city, similar rebellions arose in Detroit, Los Angeles, Chicago, and other urban centers. In *Playing the Changes*, author Craig Hansen Werner hypothesizes that the "Chicago Renaissance," which originated in the 1920s, was an early catalyst that led to the eventual development of the AACM. That artistic uprising within the city's black community led to new exposure and appreciation for black authors and artists, instilling a new sense of pride, identity, and self-respect among the citizens. It fostered an increased desire to become educated, responsible members of society, goals that are echoed in the AACM's mission statement. Along with that cultural flowering came a peaked interest in black heritage, from the plantations back to Africa. The face paint, native costumes, and African instruments of the Art Ensemble of Chicago hint at the importance of roots-awareness during that time.

Despite the Africanization of the jazz mind frame and repertoire, much of the 1960s' musical abstraction seemingly conflicted with traditional African standards of expression. The emphasis on group participation partially reflects a basic principle of African music, the derivation of meaning from interaction. But in free jazz, this is often a function of the musicians' responses to each other, while in African cultures it pertains more to rhythmic directions being inspired by dancers. A Zulu percussion group may conduct an improvisation for twenty minutes or more, with almost imperceptible shifts in texture coming in accordance to the audience's reaction. By its very nature, free jazz is not often danceable, and by that fact alone it is far removed from African concepts of music. In this regard, perhaps the melodically grounded harmolodics of Ornette Coleman comes closest to reflecting African traditions among free styles. Coleman was pleased to learn during a visit to Africa that native musicians in certain cultures had long been performing in the manner he was pursuing. That said, the jazz lofts of the 1970s finally brought the performers closer to their audiences, letting them respond more intimately to the crowd's exhortations. This drawing together brought a corresponding return to this root function of collective performance.

Another occasional conflicting point between free jazz and African music is the dissociation of thought and expression in the New Music. Musicologist John Miller Chernoff wrote:

> In African music, expression is subordinated to a respect for formal relationships, and technique is subordinated to communicative clarity. On this consideration stands the integrity of the music as a social force. . . . The greatest improvised verses and the cleverest lyrics mean nothing unless they work with the chorus to build clarity and not confusion.[8]

In other words, despite sounding random and improvisatory, African music has to be logically structured in a specific cultural context in order to be understood and appreciated by the audience and performers. If this is indeed the case, then the notion construed by some New Thing players—that one could gain some understanding of the black experience in America by listening, for example, to a performance by Pharoah Sanders or Joseph Jarman—would be incomprehensible to an African native, especially a seasoned African musician. The mindset of "I don't get it, but I respect it" is noble but fairly inapplicable to the motherland mentality in this light.

Free musicians, however, counter this by arguing that their music is indeed clear and unconfused from *their* viewpoint, which is the most important. It is closed-minded adherence to European musical standards that prevents listeners from hearing and accepting the logic within free music. Their music does not have "formal relationships" in a Western hierarchical sense. Instead, the performers are equally yoked, each on the same level as a melody player or solo improviser would be in more traditional forms, and therefore better able to create a music with its own internal logic. If the listener does not pick up on that logic, then the blame should not be laid at the performers' feet.

The very notion that there was such a thing as "black" music, and that this music was not accepted by the white public because the artists were generally black, was considered off-base by some musicians who viewed these issues from outside the American perspective. Altoist John Tchicai, half-Congolese and half-Danish, was appalled by the living conditions of jazz musicians when he arrived in New York in 1962. In Europe, these men were treated as "little kings," but in their own land, they lived in near poverty. Tchicai controversially reflected on his position in a 1966 interview:

> Being educated in a European way, I had an easier time adjusting to this environment, more so, perhaps, than a lot of American Negro musicians, because they are in so many ways handicapped by being Negroes and not having the same opportunities as whites. But on the other hand, I think there is also a tendency among a lot of Negro musicians to look only at this—that they are Negroes and that there will always be more opportunities for white musicians. . . . It always takes a little work if you want something, and a lot of Negro musicians are stuck in that position. They can only see that they are being mistreated. . . . Whether you are a black or a white artist, if you are playing the new music that people haven't been exposed to, it's obvious that you will meet a lot of resistance, and you can't fall back and blame it all on the black and white thing. I've heard Negro musicians talk about "black music." The music doesn't have any color. You can't see music, so how can you give it a color?[9]

Nevertheless, the racial division that European artists could not grasp was a sad, glaring truth in America. As a result, many performers ended up leaving the United States, temporarily or permanently, and settling in Europe to play in a more receptive environment. Several founders of the AACM went to Paris for a few years to better formulate their styles. Members of the Black Artists Group of St. Louis also headed for Paris; this movement, combined with loss of state and federal funding for their activities, caused the BAG to fold altogether. Others, like Don Cherry, Eric Dolphy, and even bop tenorman Dexter Gordon, migrated to Scandinavia. One can imagine how disheartened these artists must have been, having to leave their homeland in order to survive, playing black American music for white European fans in order to thrive. This was a sad commentary on American art and culture during the civil rights era.

EUROPEAN DEVELOPMENTS

In Europe in the mid-1960s, a musical movement germinated that came from largely different roots than American free jazz but eventually became an integral part of the new avant-garde. European free improvisation was developing not as an expression of racial identity, since almost all of its practitioners were white, but as an extension of neoclassical art music with exciting elements of black free jazz mixed in. Inspired by the investigations of Taylor, Coleman, Sun Ra, and the AACM, the men sought to further develop the form and transform it into something more relevant to their own cultures. They united the new jazz style with the modern classical experiments of Cage and Schoenberg, systems that were unusual in their own right but less foreign to European ears than what American freemen were creating.

Free jazz was principally introduced into Europe when repressed American musicians crossed the ocean to see if there were more appreciative ears "over there." Indeed, there were, as the successes of Taylor, Albert Ayler, Don Cherry, the Art Ensemble of Chicago, and other artists testified. The acculturation of the civil rights movement into American free jazz expression was somewhat lost on European audiences whose nations had made significantly better strides in race relations. However, they were able to make connections between the structural and technical considerations of free jazz and the unconventional music being produced by Stockhausen, Bernd Alois Zimmerman, and other continental composers. This Euro-avant music, also representing a departure from traditional relationships, meter, and key, seemed to mesh with free jazz for the most part, although arguments persisted over the importance of improvisation in a jazz sense versus the less spontaneous "chance" elements of aleatory music. The more resourceful players managed to use both brands of open play interchangeably.

A predominant feature of the European free scene was the players' keen interest in blending principles of traditional European styles, from martial music to beer-hall choruses to Marxist stage-musical propaganda, into their performances. This was not that far afield from Americans' weaving African, blues, and folk elements into jazz, and it helped the Europeans develop their own characteristic sound from an American-born form. Willem Breuker's Kollektief and the Globe Unity Orchestra were among the larger ensembles to succeed with such cross-pollination of styles; in fact, it became Breuker's principal stock-in-trade. English improvisers like saxophonist Lol Coxhill also used vernacular musics in their performances, while other Britons avoided such components in favor of a more nonidiomatic style that inevitably progressed further away from jazz or any other ascertainable fashion.

In England, a strong core of young players began to ply their trades and develop free music in their own images. One of the earliest was altoist Joe Harriott, a West Indian by birth, who developed his free-form concepts roughly simultaneously with Ornette Coleman, although the two were hardly aware of one another. His albums *Free Form* (1960, Jazzland) and *Abstract* (1962, Columbia) blurred the periphery of compositional form as the players skated through bar lines and evaded chord patterns almost as abruptly as Coleman had been doing.

Guitarist Derek Bailey, keyboardist Steve Beresford, drummer John Stevens, trombonist Paul Rutherford, and saxophonists Trevor Watts, Evan Parker, John Surman, and Lol Coxhill were among the next group of young Britons who embraced free improvisation and created new vocabularies for their instruments. Some of the growing number of South African expatriates in London joined the movement as well, most notably bassists Harry Miller and Johnny Dyani and drummer Louis Moholo, all solid contributors to the scene. Coming from robust backgrounds in African music, these players were able to inject English free jazz with a much-needed dose of the "black sound" that was vital to the American version. As a result of this heady multiethnic mixture, English free music began to sound even more adventurous than that coming from the other side of the Atlantic. Other Britons, like the members of the electroacoustic collective AMM, chose to avoid jazz elements and stick to more academic but interesting techniques with no discernable swing content. Whatever the tactics used, by 1965, when Stevens, Watts, and Rutherford founded the Spontaneous Music Ensemble, the time was ripe for a British improvising revolution.

Elsewhere in Europe, other musicians latched onto the new jazz: in Germany, the exquisitely supple and artistic trombonist Albert Mangelsdorff, trumpeter Manfred Schoof, saxophonist Peter Brötzmann, and pianist Alex von Schlippenbach; in the Netherlands, furious drummer Han Bennink, pianist Misha Mengelberg, bassist Maarten van Regteren Altena, witty saxophonist Willem Breuker; in Denmark, altoist John Tchicai; in Norway, altoist Frode Gjerstad. These experimenters and several of their continental counterparts have frequently joined with English and American free players, making their music a global effort indeed.

Schoof's quintet, Brötzmann's trio, and vibist Gunter Hampel's quintet were the principal architects of the continental free-jazz uprising beginning around 1965. Schoof and Schlippenbach expanded upon the premises of Coleman and Coltrane with distinct conceptions and a marvelous technical command of their instruments, placing them at roughly the level of Bill Dixon and Paul Bley stylistically. *Voices* (1966, CBS) is the cardinal document of the quintet. The robust trio of Brötzmann, bassist Peter Kowald, and Swedish drummer Sven-Åke Johansson took a similar path, with Brötzmann's ferocious horn on the front lines (*For Adolphe Sax*, 1967, FMP). Vibraphonist and bass clarinetist Gunter Hampel, who also worked with Schlippenbach, made a name for himself with early releases like *Heartplants* (1965, MPS). In the Netherlands, Bennink and the Ukrainian-born Mengelberg springboarded from the attention they earned on Eric Dolphy's final recording session. These projects were among the earliest volleys to herald a vital movement's emergence.

Compared with their associates in Britain, Germany, and the Netherlands, Italian jazzmen came into free jazz rather late. Trumpeter Enrico Rava, perhaps the first free pioneer in Italy, began investigating the music around 1962 but did not record his own debut album until a decade later. That said, the Mediterranean Boot can now likely boast more dedicated, consistent free jazzmen than any other European nation. The Italians have quietly created a model of free jazz entirely their own since the 1970s, as rich in earnest melody as it is in humor and abstraction. The Italian Instabile Orchestra boasts among its members most of the key Italian freemen, among them trumpeter Pino Minafra, pianist Giorgio Gaslini, and saxophonist Carlo Actis Dato.

The free musicians of France have historically tended to be among the most insular. They seem to prefer working mostly among their own circles instead of venturing farther into the continent like their German, English, and Dutch counterparts. The few French improvisers who came to wider attention in the late 1960s through the BYG label have rarely been heard from since, at least by Americans. Nevertheless, a decent number of them have worked among the free improv community at large, creating a body of music refreshing in its originality and intriguing in its depth. One of their key inspirations has been American-born soprano saxophonist Steve Lacy, who settled in Paris in 1970 following a three-year residency in Rome and remained there until 2002.

In the Soviet Union, the government's repression of "degenerate music" such as free jazz was every bit as ominous as Hitler's disdain for abstract art. While avant-garde artists worked in frightened obscurity in basements and illegal clubs, only a handful of performers were given official sanction to perform jazz. These loyal artists did their part to keep the doors of cultural *glasnost* open, but it took an emigré named Leo Feigin to bring true Russian jazz to the rest of the world. In 1973, Feigin began releasing smuggled tapes of Soviet musicians who dared to push the envelope of respectability and create music of uncompromising passion. From these bootlegs, Soviet freemen like the G-T-Ch (or Ganelin) Trio built a respectful following of fans who relished their brand of subversive art.

The mixing of European and American influences in creative music had some rather predictable results. The most forward-looking jazz across Europe soon began to spread out into two tangential paths, one more closely linked to the feral freedom of American new jazz, the other a more reserved, simmering style that, in the 1970s, came to be associated with Manfred Eicher's ECM record label in Munich. The so-called "ECM style" includes elements of folk musics from various cultures clustered into neo-jazz contexts. Two particular Norwegian saxophonists are representative examples of these polar opposites within European improvisation: Frode Gjerstad's alto sax playing is energetic in the style of late-period John Coltrane and Albert Ayler, while Jan Garbarek's tenor sound is lamenting, chilly, and often unemotional, undeniably creative but without Gjerstad's overwhelming forcefulness. Small wonder that Garbarek has gained an international following because of his music's accessibility, while Gjerstad remains more of a sideline figure despite an equal measure of talent. Garbarek is perhaps the artist most representative of the "ECM style," having recorded several coolly evocative albums for the label since its inception.

In the long run, the main factor that enabled the continental players to unify these two seemingly disparate musical movements, Eurocentric art music and African American free jazz, was their mutual backlash against hard artistic norms. As John Tchicai summarized it, "the avant-garde has this in common, that we are all young people and that we are all trying to find new ways of being creative and of expressing ourselves. Artistic values change, just as generations change and social attitudes change."[10]

FURTHERING THE REVOLUTION AT HOME

In New York City, trumpeter and composer Bill Dixon was instrumental in bringing free jazz to greater public attention. After leading a powerful quartet with tenorist Archie Shepp, Dixon envisioned a downtown festival celebrating the new music. In October 1964, he booked the Cellar Café for six full nights of concerts that were provocatively billed as "The October Revolution in Jazz." Sun Ra's Arkestra, which had relocated to New York four years before, was featured in the series, as were Tchicai, pianist Paul Bley, and Dixon's sextet. Other lesser-known performers were hired, all of whom would soon become high-profile figures in free jazz: trombonist Roswell Rudd, the remarkable drummer Milford Graves, and bassist David Izenzon from Ornette Coleman's new trio. The Cellar Café was packed to the rafters every night with folks who were enraptured or simply curious about what was going on with modern jazz. The expositional, if not financial, success of the October Revolution gave Dixon and friends some hope that free jazz was indeed a potentially viable art form in America.

Later that same year, this notion of encouragement led Dixon to establish the Jazz Composers Guild, an organization designed to brainstorm the marketing of new jazz to the public. The Guild's mission was to present modern jazz concerts without having to rely on the reluctant nightclubs and promoters in the city. He enlisted Ra, Shepp, Bley, Rudd, Tchicai, Cecil Taylor, composer Carla Bley (then the pianist's wife), Austrian trumpeter Mike Mantler, and pianist Burton Greene to spearhead the operation. However, the Guild folded after about a year due to its members' inability to agree upon a universally acceptable course of action. It was an ironic collapse for a group devoted to an art form that seemed, to mainstream ears, to have no discernable direction of its own.

Mantler married Carla Bley soon after her divorce, and together they restructured the organization into the Jazz Composers Orchestra Association. The JCOA became almost as vital to New York City's free movement as the AACM was to Chicago's. It initially served as a fundraising group for an orchestra that performed and recorded its members' compositions. Bley and Mantler also developed the New Music Distribution Service to supervise the distribution of independent records that had little commercial potential. Several important albums were released under the JCOA's auspices, perhaps the most significant being *The Jazz Composers Orchestra* (1968). That project highlighted the chaotic piano performance of Cecil Taylor, the incendiary tenor saxophone of Pharoah Sanders, and Mantler's film-noirish compositions and arrangements.

Though growing by leaps and bounds within urban circles, the new musicians still languished in relative obscurity outside their own communities. The major music festivals were again paying little attention to what was going on in free jazz, their few attempts having left a bad taste in the mouths of white promoters and audiences. But the music finally came to wider regard on July 2, 1965, when the Newport Jazz Festival in Rhode Island featured two key players from the second and third waves of the new jazz.

John Coltrane, by then a true giant of post-bop jazz, astounded the audience with his intensely emotional expression and unyielding stamina. The performance presaged his impending move into deeper soul searching and freedom. The rhythm section of McCoy Tyner, Jimmy Garrison, and Elvin Jones, Coltrane's most functionally intuitive group, spurred the saxophonist to impressive heights of musical exaltation. Drummer Jones turned in an especially scorching performance during the set, which included a more abstract, furious version of "My Favorite Things" than the famous 1960 studio track.

Earlier that afternoon at Newport, tenorist Archie Shepp had presented an explosive set of original works reflecting the plight of black America: dark, poetic tales of lynchings and drug abuse, tempered with black pride and hope for the future. It was the antithesis of Coltrane's jubilation and a performance like nothing the Newport crowds had ever witnessed before. A few years prior, the Newport Festival had been blasted for being unfairly selective in its bookings, and now the new wave of jazz was striking back with full force. Not long after that performance, Coltrane would enter the last and most controversial portion of his career, as a leading character in the free-jazz invasion, and Shepp would not be far behind.

Following his Newport appearance, Coltrane continued his search for both spiritual and musical truth. He gathered a large ensemble to record *Ascension* (Atlantic), a collective improvisation based loosely on a few modes, a rational extension of his work with Miles Davis. This session officially heralded Coltrane's impending departure from the jazz mainstream. *Ascension* was as powerful a document as Coleman's *Free Jazz*, perhaps even more so, and introduced a number of young players to the world. Tchicai, Shepp, Sanders, altoist Marion Brown, and several others were on hand, and each went on to make their own waves in free jazz. (The album is discussed further under Coltrane's Encyclopedia entry.)

Coltrane soon hired the incendiary Sanders as a permanent member of his band. Pianist McCoy Tyner and drummer Elvin Jones were both unwilling to continue in the free direction Coltrane was pursuing, so his esteemed group, perhaps the most popular jazz band of its time, broke apart. Coltrane moved onward with Sanders and bassist Jimmy Garrison in tow. He hired his second wife, pianist Alice McLeod Coltrane, and drum phenomenon Rashied Ali to fill in the gaps. This new group, more suited to his soul-searching mode, remained with Coltrane up until his death in 1967. His free playing was a disappointment to many prior fans but won over a host of new listeners, and the recorded documents from this era have mellowed with time to earn classic status.

Shepp, Sanders, and Albert Ayler were among the tenor saxophonists who decided to carry on Coltrane's free approach to the horn. Each was a highly volatile player, and each had his own creative ideas that pushed the music to new heights. Ayler became an especially controversial figure by his use of meandering, folklike melodies and loud, maniacal sound production. By the time of his own death in 1970, Ayler had reconfigured the future of jazz along with exploring rock and R&B. Sanders was a ceaseless font of energy, spirituality, and emotion, while the less volatile Shepp continued blending jazz traditions with free elements, poetry, and black activism.

In the wake of Coltrane's death, this second generation continued to advance free jazz as a form of black expression through the 1960s and 1970s. The more outspoken and uncompromising the musicians were, the less work they found in a system dominated by white promoters and label administrators. Many performers founded their own record labels in order to get their music out into the marketplace. More collectives like the AACM developed across the country, along with new urban arts schools and programs. Amiri Baraka and drummer Milford Graves continued to educate inner-city youth about arts and culture. Graves, Sunny Murray, Andrew Cyrille, and other drummers completely recast the role of percussionists along the way, refusing to remain subordinate to a regular pulse for the convenience of others. Graves, in particular, helped change the sound of drumming by adding ethnic percussions to his kit and dumping his bottom drumheads and snare.

While Coltrane was taking jazz to the extremes, his former employer was moving along a different tangent again. In perhaps a bit of regression, Miles Davis's mid-1960s quintet was carving another niche in jazz with a new form of jazz that avoided the confines of chords but did not range beyond modal boundaries. With saxophonist Wayne Shorter and the astoundingly elastic rhythm section of pianist Herbie

Hancock, bassist Ron Carter, and the young drummer Tony Williams, Davis concentrated on moody themes based on blues motives, post-bop processes, and droning ostinato figures. Davis was vocal in his disapproval of the direction in which Coltrane and Coleman were trying to push jazz, and this chordally ambiguous style was about as far into freedom as the temperamental trumpeter was willing to go for now.

The West Coast never had as prominent a free scene as those in New York and Chicago, and what action it did boast was obscured due to the greater congregation of jazz press in the East and Midwest. Nonetheless, a small cluster of free players managed to unite and bring their music to local audiences. Horace Tapscott, an L.A.-based pianist and composer, was the catalyst of much free exploration in California during the late 1960s and the 1970s. As beloved a teacher as he was a performer, Tapscott instilled his musical visions into a select group of sidemen, which included alto saxophonist Arthur Blythe, tenorman Azar Lawrence, and later, multireedman Vinny Golia. He never gained the renown of his counterparts in the eastern United States, but Tapscott did play a vital part in free-jazz's growth and evolution during that critical period.

West Coast collectives of prominence in the 1960s included Quartet and Black Music Infinity, counting among their members Arthur Blythe, drummer/poet/critic Stanley Crouch, flautist James Newton, reedman David Murray, and bassist Mark Dresser (the token white member of Black Music Infinity, as reedman Marty Ehrlich was in Black Artists Group). Each of these men has made his own impact on the music. Crouch, most controversially, gave up on free music in the 1970s and has become one of the form's most vociferous critics. A writer and occasional poet, Crouch usually sides with the Wynton Marsalis school of tradition in the debate over free-jazz's validity.

The New Art Jazz Ensemble, fronted by reedman John Carter and trumpeter Bobby Bradford, was another powerful force in Los Angeles. *Seeking* (1969, Flying Dutchman, reissued 1991, HatArt) is an admirable portrait of their chemistry. In the company of bassist Tom Williamson and drummer Bruz Freeman, a prodigy of subtlety and texture on a par with Steve McCall, the hornmen perform five Colemanesque compositions by Carter and one by Bradford. Carter is a powerhouse on alto and tenor saxes, clarinet, and flute. In later years, he decided to concentrate almost exclusively on the clarinet, which is only heard once here, on the brisk, stair-stepping "Sticks and Stones." He blows rich tenor on "In the Vineyard," taken at a breakneck pace. The tune unmistakably evokes the Coleman quartet of the late 1950s in its perky complexity, aided by Williamson's Haden-like facility on bass. Bradford is the more restrained but no less creative performer, his rounded tone toasting up each tune. "Karen on Monday" is one of the more avant pieces, Carter's buttery alto dancing around Williamson's tappy bass. The two share similar thoughts on "Seeking," a gorgeous flute feature. Bradford's "Song for the Unsung" is a change of pace, with a firm, lurking bass rhythm and question-and-answer horn lines before a hard-bop sensation takes over. It is one bold testament to the West Coast's affinity for freedom.

LOFT JAZZ

As rock music became the vogue, many of the nation's jazz clubs either shut their doors or turned to rock artists as their sole bookings. The absence of club gigs in the late 1960s and the 1970s led many jazz artists in New York to establish new venues within their loft apartments. These lofts were a unique cultural phenomenon that brought the music and its performers closer to those urban denizens who were the main audience base for black free jazz in the inner city. Driven by economic necessity, free players sought to establish a network of locations where they, their students, and patrons could gather to share in courageous expressions. These cooperative studios were assembled in downtown loft apartments for the specific purpose of creating exciting experimental music outside the limitations of commercial studios and stale venues, which were generally out of the players' socioeconomic league. These small locations provided intimate settings in which fans and performers alike could relax, explore, and enjoy the music.

Ornette Coleman's Artists House loft on Prince Street was a popular gathering place, as was Sam Rivers's Studio RivBea, at 24 Bond Street. Studio RivBea (named for *Rivers* and his wife *Beatrice*) operated for many years and was the focal point of many loft concerts, including a seven-night festival in May 1976 that was documented on the excellent *Wildflowers* series, originally released by Douglas Records. Rivers and other loft owners provided an informal, at-home environment for mentoring, the open exchange of ideas, and a comfortable interaction between musicians and audience members. Though the loft musicians were not concretely unified under mission statements like the AACM, there was a strong sense of community and camaraderie among the participants and their loyal fans. By the century's end, most of the lofts had filled their need and gone.

The New York loft scene and Chicago's AACM-related activities soon spawned another group of young improvisers who took up the banner of the free-jazz movement. Trombone virtuoso Ray Anderson, electric guitarist James "Blood" Ulmer, bassist William Parker, and saxophonists Henry Threadgill, Arthur Blythe, Jemeel Moondoc, and David Murray, among others, were responsible for particularly creative advances in the free idiom. Trained at the feet of Coleman, Braxton, L.A. pianist Horace Tapscott, and other mentors, these men and their associates would help to carve the next niche in the style's development, a phase that had roots in both jazz and rock.

MILES BEYOND

Feeling rather like a washed-up jazz relic in his forties, Miles Davis made his own move into rock in 1969, assimilating electric pianos, organ, guitars, and bass into his new group. Miles even electrified his trumpet, blowing through a wah-wah pedal like the one Jimi Hendrix favored for outrageously funky effects. His soloing became a bit freer, with long, loud cascades of notes pouring forth at odd intervals within the songs. The series of live albums taped in 1974–1975 (*Dark Magus, Pangaea, Agharta*, all Columbia/Sony) present his electric band at the peak of its creative freedom, storming every which way over crushing funk beats with little formal chord structure or definable melody. Still, Davis avoided becoming fully immersed in free jazz. Instead, he leaned on these rock, funk, and disco rhythms as buttresses and created a new musical form, known as *jazz-rock* or *fusion*, that was appealing to urban youths but appalling to others who had once appreciated Davis.

Two of Miles's disciples moved straight into freedom upon their discharge from his ranks. In 1970, pianist Chick Corea formed a trio with English bassist Dave Holland and drummer Barry Altschul to record his Blue Note album *The Song of Singing*. Later that year, reedman Anthony Braxton from the AACM was added, and the quartet became known as Circle. For the fleeting two years of its life, this unit created wonderful, richly textured free jazz but issued only a few albums. *Early Circle*, a 1992 Blue Note release, documents some of the quartet's stimulating music. The collection contains two piano-bass duets, two piano-clarinet duets, a percussion work, and other pieces of varied coloration. Braxton's "73° –A Kelvin" is a jagged, Monkish venture featuring the composer on soprano saxophone. This piece sounds completely improvised upon a first, casual listen. However, a distinction can be made by listening to the frequent parallels between the soprano and piano. This will reveal that the first few minutes, at least, of the track have some definite predetermined structure to them. The jostling song structure abruptly freezes to make room for Altschul on surging gongs, then the "melody" returns. This selection indicates Braxton's particular genius at using formal structures while seeming to subvert them.

In 1971, Corea regained an interest in jazz-rock and Latin music. He dissolved Circle and formed the fusion band Return to Forever. His brief wandering from the path of Miles was over, and he was now on a parallel path to popular success as an electric jazz superstar. Now and then, however, he would come back to free music for a time, particularly with a stellar trio including drummer Roy Haynes and Czech bassist Miroslav Vitous. In the meantime, Braxton, Holland, and Altschul each continued down the path of freedom with occasional diversions into more mainstream projects.

In Davis's band, Keith Jarrett had complemented Corea's electric piano lines with liberal doses of sizzling electric organ. Jarrett had left tenorist Charles Lloyd's group in 1969 to join Davis, having played piano, soprano saxophone, and percussion in that unit. During his frequent periods of downtime from Miles's group, Jarrett led his own trio with ex–Ornette Coleman bassist Charlie Haden and ex–Bill Evans drummer Paul Motian. The spontaneity and originality of this unit was startling, eventually leading Jarrett to explore the possibilities of free improvisation.

From 1972, Jarrett gave concerts of completely improvised solo piano music, much of it documented by ECM Records. His approach united classical, jazz, and folk principles into a coherent whole, and despite the totally spontaneous nature of his music, Jarrett became immensely popular to world audiences, jazz fans or not. One of his quirkier habits was a tendency to groan, hum, or sing at high pitch along with his playing, which turned off the less tolerant fans who otherwise dug his music. Jarrett's 1975 album *The Köln Concert* (ECM), recorded live in Cologne, Germany, became an international best-seller, and Jarrett was soon the only jazz artist of the period to gain a global following without caving in to standard forms and motives of established jazz practicum. Jarrett would continue to remain a popular figure in jazz, both as a solo artist and in his groups with tenor saxophonists Dewey Redman and Jan Garbarek.

Since the 1980s, Jarrett has moved further away from free jazz, in favor of interpreting jazz standards with an excellent trio including bassist Gary Peacock and drummer Jack DeJohnette. No doubt this was the wisest move he could have made economically, and it can hardly be considered an artistic compromise given the freshness of the trio's philosophy. As it is, even Jarrett's most pyrotechnic improvisations have rarely approached the visceral power of Coltrane, Coleman, and Taylor.

SPIRITUALITY IN FREE JAZZ

Besides the civil rights movement and the search for deeply personal modes of expression, another driving force behind the explorations of many free-jazz players is spirituality. Many premium documents of the music have openly spiritual foundations: Albert Ayler's *Spiritual Unity*, John Coltrane's *A Love Supreme* and *Om*, and any number of albums by Alice Coltrane or Pharoah Sanders. The search for spiritual truth can be as inspirational as the search for musical truth as an expression of one's real self. These two, in fact, are inextricably linked. If performers had not sought out new ways to convey the truths and doubts they saw deep within their spirits, free jazz might have never been more than a negligible footnote in musical history.

Coltrane and Ayler were unflaggingly open about their spiritual searches, which helped contribute to their lasting impact on our culture. Their searches led fans and fellow musicians to realize the importance of spiritual completeness in life. In *A Love Supreme*, inspired by his overcoming of addiction, Coltrane seemed to be extolling the ideals of Christianity, although in many regards it was closer to Eastern meditative music. Later, due in part to the influence of his second wife, Alice, he looked into Hinduism and other Eastern religions. The controversial *Om* includes not only mantralike meditations but also a reading from the *Bardo Thodol*, the Tibetan Book of the Dead. By the time of Coltrane's death, he still did not seem to have found comfort with one single spiritual path. Still, in all, the example of his searching was powerfully inspirational to a large number of fans. In the San Francisco Bay area is based the Church of St. John Coltrane, a house of worship dedicated to the wise, influential saxophonist.

Alice Coltrane continued her association with Hinduism after John's death, as documented in albums like *Journey in Satchidananda* (1970, Impulse), her most famous and compelling work. While some fans who had shared in Coltrane's spiritual searching embraced her numinous music, others were turned off by the utter weirdness of it all. Alice Coltrane soon took the name Turiya Aparna Satchidananda, founded the Vedantic Center, a popular retreat in California for Eastern studies, and hosted a syndicated TV program of music and spiritual enlightenment.

Ayler was also known for his spiritual explorations, which were even more confused than Coltrane's. In the same missive, he once preached about specific Christian principles, then injected the name of Elijah Muhammad, the leader of the Nation of Islam. *Spirits Rejoice*, *Ghosts*, "Witches and Devils," "Spiritual Unity," "Holy Holy": Ayler's album and song titles dealt with many supernatural and religious subjects. He was preoccupied for most of his career with the concepts of life and death, and each manifestation of these questions and challenges burst forth through his horn. The official verdict of suicide has been disputed by some of Ayler's associates but accepted by others who recognized how haunted the man was by his own mortality and inability to find suitable answers to life's deepest questions.

Due to the revival of African cultural interests, and to a great extent the Nation of Islam's activities, many black musicians converted to the Islamic faith in the 1950s and 1960s as a part of their return to "roots awareness." Many artists assumed new Islamic names to reflect their beliefs; some used these names only occasionally, while others became best known by their Muslim appellations. Reedman William Evans became Yusef Lateef; McCoy Tyner took on the name Sulaiman Saud; Kenny Clarke became Liaquat Ali Salaam; Art Blakey, Abdullah ibn Buhaina. Others kept their given "slave" names but expressed their faith openly through life and music.

Pharoah Sanders is a devout Muslim and, like Coltrane and Ayler, he conveys his spiritual nature through his music. Among his most compelling works, and the least appreciated by "jazz snobs," are the beautifully uplifting "Hum Allah Hum Allah Hum Allah," with vocals by Leon Thomas, and "Let Us Go into the House of the Lord." Although Sanders's faith could doubtless have put him at odds with Coltrane's conflicting dabblings in Hinduism and Christianity, the two tenormen were most complementary partners in their period of shared musical soul-searching.

Charles Gayle is one of the most visceral, impassioned saxophonists on the contemporary New York scene. His bursts of wild creative energy can usually rival those of Pharoah Sanders. But instead of drawing inspiration from Islam, Gayle is a devout Christian whose work is inspired by his views of Jesus Christ and His teachings. Once homeless on the streets of New York, Gayle credits his faith with his gradual increase in public acceptance. Gayle's music, nearly a force of nature in its power, does not reflect conventional Christian gospel music by any stretch of the imagination. His compositions are not likely to be heard in Wednesday night prayer meeting or Sunday service. Improvised performances like "Jesus Christ and Scripture" have the power to clear the hall before the tenorist draws a second breath. His more traditionally structured works, like on *Ancient of Days* (1999, Knitting Factory Works), stick closer to post-bop forms while permitting Gayle to venture far outside. He is clearly inspired by Albert Ayler, though his tunes are more complex than the folksy melodies in which Ayler specialized.

Gayle's tenacity in adhering to the doctrines of his faith, including the biblically ordained viewpoint that homosexuality and abortion are sinful, have cost him more than one job. In his book *Landing on the Wrong Note: Jazz, Dissonance and Critical Practice*, former Guelph Jazz Festival director Ajay Heble outlines the personal and professional reservations that led him to deny Gayle a place in the festival. Such one-sided bigotry, stomping for "tolerance" only when it serves antireligious needs, is typical of the struggle that keeps Gayle balanced between his paychecks and principles. Onstage Gayle wears Emmett Kelly–like makeup in the persona of "Streets the Clown," an itinerant pantomime character. He is often asked by venue managers to stick to playing and not speak, but Gayle will make no promises. He states, "It's part of who I am as a human being. . . . If someone told me, 'Well, you can take the gig but don't do this,' then I'd tell them, 'Well, okay, I probably can't work here. I can't work here, because I don't know if I'm gonna do that or not.' Everything I am trying to say is really a way of saying that something is wrong to me in my heart, and it's killing me."[11]

The various forms of Buddhism (Tibetan, Nichiren Shoshu, Zen) have attracted followers within the jazz community for decades, including pianist Herbie Hancock, saxophonist Wayne Shorter, clarinetist Tony Scott, and reedman Joseph Jarman of the Art Ensemble of Chicago. Jarman became especially steeped in Buddhist philosophy, to the point where he has taken sabbaticals from performing in order to meditate and pursue his odyssey of truth. He took time off from the Art Ensemble in the 1990s for just these spiritual reasons, devoting himself to his Brooklyn dojo, and has since assumed the title "Shaku." His teachings have been helpful to fellow musicians engaged in their own soul-searching, much as he himself originally drew inspiration from Sun Ra's and Muhal Richard Abrams's instructions about clean living. Jarman is regularly asked to give benedictions at shows and festivals, and his faith is as much a part of his present musical conception as Islam is of Pharoah Sanders's.

Reedman John Zorn is one of the motivating forces behind the resurgence of Judaism as an inspiration for artistic expression, particularly in downtown New York. Judaism has long had a tie with avant-garde art, particularly during the twentieth century, and Zorn breathed new life into this association. He and other Downtown performers, including violinist Mark Feldman, reedman Matt Darriau, and trumpeter Frank London, spearheaded a movement known as Radical Jewish Culture. These players have revitalized the Eastern European Jewish musical style known as klezmer, which decades before was blended with traditional jazz elements, and have mixed in the essences of free jazz, European avant-garde, and rock in order to modernize the music and make it relevant once more. Zorn's band Masada, named for the fortress where ancient Jews made a life-and-death stance against encroaching Roman troops, has been at the forefront of the recent Jewish avant-garde revival since the 1990s. His sound-collage compositions for his album *Kristallnacht* (1993, on his own Tzadik label) are alternately tooth-grating and poignant as they recall that despicable event in history.

Other free musicians whose paths have been guided by faith include Wadada Leo Smith, who practiced the Ethopian/Jamaican religion of Rastafarianism before converting to Islam, and the married duo Oluyemi and Ijeoma Thomas of Positive Knowledge, who draw enlightenment from the Baha'i faith. For all the fine free performances produced as a result of such spiritual inspiration, it seems only logical that some artists' spiritual experiences would move them away from such musical freedom. Such was the case with Chick Corea, who became a devoted follower of L. Ron Hubbard's Church of Scientology in the early 1970s while a member of the quartet Circle. Because of the movement's emphasis on appealing to the general populace, Corea was compelled to stop making music of limited commercial interest and move toward a more universally "acceptable" mode of expression. Circle's other members also briefly dabbled in Scientology, but the extreme changes in Corea's personality and artistic aims after he "went clear" caused a rift, particularly between Corea and Anthony Braxton. With Circle behind him and a new attitude of inspiration, Corea established the popular jazz fusion group Return to Forever, producing music that was candy to the ears of mass audiences instead of fodder for free exploration and personal expression. He has come back to free music on occasion, notably with bassist Miroslav Vitous and drummer Roy Haynes (*Trio Music*, 1981, ECM), but Corea's principal focus since the 1970s has been on electronic pop-jazz of varying substance.

POST-COLTRANE, POST-ROCK, POSTMODERN

A certain wag I know recently quipped that Barry Altschul should change his name to "Very Old-School." I was unsure what he was getting at, since "old school" is the literal translation of the drummer's German surname. As it happens, my friend was not even aware of that ironic factoid. His gist was simply that jazz and free drumming had evolved so much since Altschul first recorded with Anthony Braxton that the avant-jazzer's style had actually become old-hat in the twenty-first century. He might have had a point; visionaries like Joey Baron, Jay Rosen, Hamid Drake, Tom Bruno, and Susie Ibarra have stretched the role of rhythm in the jazz ensemble in all directions. But in the "big picture," Altschul's approach remains just as valid as the ubiquitous high-hat rhythm pioneered by Jo Jones with Count Basie in the 1930s or Art Blakey's titanic press rolls. While "jazz" remains increasingly undefinable as the music absorbs more cultural influences, it stays close to its New Orleans roots with equal determination. Still in all, it is jazz's evolutionary characteristic that keeps it perennially popular, to one degree or another, with younger generations. If jazz were still as rudimentary as how Jelly Roll Morton or even Charlie Parker played it, it would be little more than a wistful museum piece entering its second century.

As mentioned earlier, the rise of rock-and-roll to economic supremacy brought many changes to the face of American culture, mostly boding ill for the jazz trade. Rock was a shiny new toy not only to the nation's youth but also to older, "wiser" folks who were hell-bent on staying young, or at least pretending to. As early as 1965, Tom Wolfe remarked that "Intellectuals, generally, no longer take jazz seriously. Monk, Mingus, [Maynard] Ferguson—it has all been left to little executive trainees with their first apartment and a mahogany African mask from the free-port shop in Haiti and a hi-fi."[12] That statement may or may not have been completely truthful, but in some ways it reflected the direction in which jazz was headed. After a couple of decades of dominating airwaves and record shelves, jazz was steadily shoved aside by the pelvis of Elvis, the flashy glitz of Motown, and Phil Spector's "walls of sound." Frank Sinatra even unsubtly labeled rock "the most brutal, ugly, vicious form of expression . . . martial music of every delinquent on the face of the earth . . . phony and false and sung, written, and played for the most part by cretinous goons."[13]

In the 1960s, hundreds of jazz musicians disappeared into the obscurity and general dissatisfaction of studio work as a necessary means of sustenance. Teens who dug Shorty Rogers's wallpaper-music charts for the Monkees' TV show were blissfully unaware of his auspicious contributions to Stan Kenton's band and the cool-jazz crowd at the Lighthouse Café less than a decade before. As for the free players, those who did not pack up for Europe mostly struggled along amidst their own communities, touching small clusters of lives by propagating the heritage of their music and people, and sternly refusing to compromise. For other musicians, it came down to joining them when you just could not beat them. In the face of impending obscurity, Miles Davis all but bypassed the free movement and gained a young audience as the founding father of jazz-rock fusion, an economic (and, in long retrospect, artistic) masterstroke, even if it spelled "sellout" to his die-hard jazz fans.

Despite the persistent interweaving of rock throughout its fiber, jazz had an audible impact on certain facets of rock. Free jazz, in particular, captured the hearts and imaginations of younger icons who were ripe to "fight the establishment" in their own way. Coltrane's late-career modal and free experiments were inspirational to musicians of every walk of life from the mid-1960s onward. Byrds leader Roger McGuinn openly acknowledges the influence of Coltrane on his compositions and performances—namely, the abstract twelve-string guitar intro to "Eight Miles High." Other rock bands—the fledgling Pink Floyd, Iron Butterfly, King Crimson, even Steely Dan—also embraced the music of Coltrane and his partners in adventure to some degree.

The Grateful Dead have been openly recognized by the jazz community for their contributions to American music. The Dead's music was largely redolent of folk and blues forms, but they were also renowned for ponderous, freely improvised excursions on live numbers like "Dark Star." The band admitted the influence of free-jazz icons like Coltrane and Ornette Coleman time and again. The Dead performed some live gigs with Coleman in the 1980s, Dead guitarist Jerry Garcia appeared on Coleman's album *Virgin Beauty* (1988, Portait), and other collaborations were rumored to have been in the works at the time of Garcia's death.

Many jazz fans have difficulty hearing echoes of Coltrane's influence in the Dead's music. This is certainly understandable, as it tended to be more of a structural impression than as any direct adaptation of the saxophonist's style. In a *Rolling Stone* "Raves" column in 1982, Garcia said, "I've been influenced a lot by Coltrane, but I never copped his licks or sat down and listened to records and tried to play his stuff. I've been impressed with that thing of flow, and of making statements that to my ears sound like paragraphs."[14] Since the demise of the Grateful Dead, the jazz community has regularly returned the respect and dedication that Garcia and his friends had for jazz. In 1996, free-minded saxophonist David Murray paid loving homage to the world's greatest cult band on *Dark Star: Music of the Grateful Dead* (1996, Astor Place).

Frank Zappa and the Mothers of Invention blenderized raunchy lyrics, doo-wop inflections, free improv, and the spirit of Edgard Varèse into their recordings and performances. Saxophonist Ian Underwood was responsible for the free vitality on classic albums like *Hot Rats* (1970, Bizarre), and keyboardist Don Preston later recorded with avant-jazzers like trumpeter Michael Mantler. In his own mad way, Zappa was as fiercely political and iconoclastic as Coleman or Archie Shepp had ever been and equally interested in the plight of the common man. Zappa could even boast of a guest spot by Shepp on the album *You Can't Do That on Stage Anymore, Vol. 4* (1991, Rykodisc). Like many of the free pioneers he admired, however, Zappa did not linger permanently on the outer edges. With the more commercial *Overnite Sensation* (1973, DiscReet), Zappa effectively bade farewell to free-jazz influences (but exceptions, of course, did abound).

One of Zappa's offbeat colleagues, Captain Beefheart (né Don Van Vliet), similarly applied free-improv principles to his own bizarre creations, which were usually drenched in hard-rocking blues. *Trout Mask Replica* (1969, Reprise) typifies Beefheart's rock-blues-avant-jazz collage. His frantic stream-of-consciousness poetry spars with the insanely twisted music of guitarist Zoot Horn Rollo, drummer John "Drumbo" French, and other acolytes. Beefheart's music can be extremely difficult listening, more so than the work of Taylor or Braxton for some, but with time and patience, it could be considered almost catchy.

Some forefathers of the punk movement embraced free jazz in developing their personal styles. The MC5, Detroit's leading prepunk group, were strongly influenced by Ayler, Shepp, Coltrane, and Pharoah Sanders. Their live shows often included covers of Sun Ra's "Starship" and Sanders' "Upper Egypt" (both on the collection *Black to Comm*, 1995, Receiver), and the guitar intensity of Wayne Kramer and Fred "Sonic" Smith was an assimilation of their gleanings from the Impulse and ESP catalogs. Lou Reed, the "godfather of punk" and leader of the Velvet Underground, was also a fan of the freemen. John Cale, Reed's VU collaborator, literally came straight out of the avant-garde; he studied with AMM founder Cornelius Cardew and performed with John Cage and LaMonte Young before hooking up with Reed and the Warhol Factory crowd. Their interest in sounds and structures made the Velvet Underground one of the decade's most noisome, yet influential, bands. Reed recalled Archie Shepp's poeticizing of addiction when he sonically recreated the "flash" of a heroin surge in "Heroin" and an amphetamine rush in "White Light/White Heat" (*The Best of the Velvet Underground*, 1989, Verve). Maureen Tucker's austere drumming and Sterling Morrison's acidic guitar, also with precedents in free jazz, built upon VU's primal, urban-tribe mystique. Among those who followed Reed in uniting their free-jazz inspirations and proto-punk rock were Tom Verlaine of Television (*Marquee Moon* (1977, Elektra); *The Blow Up* (1982, ROIR), and Peter Laughner of Pere Ubu and Rocket from the Tombs.

The contemporary post-punk scene has continued to acknowledge the influence of free jazz; namely, saxman Mars Williams, who played with The Waitresses and Psychedelic Furs before joining Hal Russell's NRG Ensemble. Punk icon Henry Rollins, formerly of Black Flag, is a passionate fan of avant-jazz. He recorded the title track for the Charles Mingus tribute *Weird Nightmare* (1992, Columbia) and has performed with Rashied Ali and Charles Gayle (*Everything*, 1996, Thirsty Ear). Rollins was largely responsible for the upturn in Matthew Shipp's career, having released several of the pianist's albums on his 2.13.61 label. The up-yours, antitraditionalist attitude of free jazz is plainly akin to the anarchistic punk aesthetic.

The 1970s were a fairly dismal era for jazz, as the rise of fusion marked a sharp decline of recognizable jazz content in many so-called "jazz" performances. Jazz-rock fusion assumed many forms: the raw edginess of flautist Jeremy Steig and the Satyrs; the horn-driven pop stylings of Chicago, Mike Bloomfield's Electric Flag, and Blood, Sweat and Tears; Chick Corea's multiethnic Return To Forever; John McLaughlin's Eastern-flavored Mahavishnu Orchestra; and the stadium-packing Weather Report, the brainchild of two ex–Miles Davis sidemen, Joe Zawinul and Wayne Shorter. While all had jazz elements, these generally took a back seat to more marketable rock and dance-pop flavors. Hot technical chops were everything, swing a faded memory.

Ornette Coleman moved into the electronic era in his own quintessential way, with an unusual ensemble he called Prime Time. After a little shuffling, the band's core consisted of Coleman's alto sax, two electric guitars, two electric basses, and two drummers. Coleman expanded upon his rudimentary harmolodic theories (a combination of *har*mony, *mo*tion, and me*lody*) to suit the plugged-in group, developing a concept wherein each player could choose the key he wished to play in during the tune. This resulted in a dense, loud fabric of jagged harmonies, bouncing off each other in cyclical fashion as the compositions progressed. Improvisation as it was recognized in jazz, even the free jazz Coleman had pioneered, was pretty much subsumed in the interest of full group interaction.

The electronic trend continued well into the 1980s, as the public embraced the instrumental pop marketed as "contemporary jazz" or "smooth jazz." Within this plugged-in tide, free jazz was nearly forgotten, save the efforts of stalwarts like Arthur Blythe, Henry Threadgill, David Murray, and the loft communities. These artists and their coconspirators produced excellent bodies of work marked by unceasing innovation, yet the economic climate was arid for free artists. Blythe, Murray, Sanders, Shepp, and many others began backing away from free music in favor of structured compositions and jazz standards. Sanders, in particular, began to channel the more accessible style that Coltrane had practiced before embracing freedom. Shepp moved into more mainstream areas, but the corrosiveness of his late-career tenor tone sometimes poorly matched his partners' straighter aims. Shepp's sound was tailor-made for the avant-garde, whether or not he chose to remain on that route. As for Blythe, his secure spot on the Columbia Records roster was rudely sacrificed in favor of a young neo-traditionalist from New Orleans: Wynton Marsalis.

In the 1970s, a fresh wave of free improvisation erupted in Japan, spurred by the volcanic performances of saxophonist Kaoru Abe, guitarist Masayuki Takayanagi, and the psychedelic rock-influenced ensemble Taj Mahal Travellers. Abe died of a heroin overdose in 1978 before he could see the full fruits of his labor borne out in performers like trombonist Masahiko Kono, trumpeter Toshinori Kondo, and bassist Motoharu Yoshizawa. Later, electronic implements played a significant role in Japanese free improvisation, resulting in the dynamic activities of current artists like Otomo Yoshihide and Sachiko M.

As their forebears and inspirations had in previous decades, many freemen retreated to Europe in the 1960s and 1970s, knowing that their music would be welcomed there with open arms, appreciated with open ears. Others ran for the shelter of academia, where steady incomes and the hope of tenure gave them some relief from nagging debts and precarious job prospects. The less fortunate performers huddled closely in the inner cities, where they found a small but loyal following. William and Patricia Parker's Sound Unity Festival, conducted around New York in 1984, helped open new doors and ears to free music, but still the music languished in obscurity. Eventually, jazz adapted itself to its imposing new surroundings, emerging anew and radically changed in many aspects, most apparent in the ongoing fusion of rock, world music, free jazz, and other factors into one scintillating school of performance.

John Zorn is a notorious postmodernist, having embraced Jean-François Lyotard's notion that there are no distinctions between high and low art, capitalized Art and populist entertainment. He often gives the impression of delighting in the discomfort of his audience, in the hope that it might shake them out of complacency and into a new understanding. He is somewhat of an analogue of Andy Warhol, whose subjugation of Marilyn Monroe's glamour into garish, cartoony quadrants correlates with Zorn's friskily subversive "tributes" to Ennio Morricone and Mickey Spillane. Warhol's descent into ugliness with deliberately blurry lithographs of dead accident victims and electric chairs likewise parallels Zorn's liner notes for his albums. These liners are denotative of his shock-value mentality, having included graphic photographs of Chinese criminals being ritually dismembered, Weegee mob-hit snapshots, or Japanese hentai art depicting sexual cruelty and ultraviolent horrors. They illustrate the darkness within men's souls as fluently as the hard poetry of Archie Shepp and Amiri Baraka. Like Warhol's "pop art," in Zorn's hands cultural icons become satirical, less consoling, twisted into disturbing new images that symbolize the follies of our prejudiced principles.

Early in his career, Zorn was as likely to play a tender ballad on his alto sax as he was to stuff a handful of mouthpieces and birdcalls into his yap for an extended solo. The prolific Zorn seems equally comfortable with free interpretation of jazz pieces, spaghetti-Western scores, film noir, rocking surf jams, klezmer, and visceral punk rock. Zorn's willingness to push the envelope until it flies into shreds has alienated him from the main flow of jazz but earned him a devoted, near-cult following. For a time in the 1980s and early 1990s, Downtown New York's avant circle seemed to hover around Zorn's every move. His "game pieces" evolved from early trials like "Pool" and "Archery" to "Cobra," a sophisticated performance system he presented monthly at the Knitting Factory for a few years. *John Zorn's Cobra—Live at the Knitting Factory* (1995, Knitting Factory Works) compiles fourteen live performances of the musical game, played by various ensembles throughout 1994. The sheer variety of noises and ideas batted about in these tracks might make listeners all the more eager to catch a live performance of Cobra in order to understand, if possible, how it all fits together. Zorn sees the boundless potential of the arts as a medium of individual expression and lives out that notion in his compelling, if frightening, music. With such a large array of dissident tactics at his disposal, Zorn fully epitomizes postmodernism in the realm of improvisation.

As jazz musicians have fallen under the pervasive influence of rock, so then have certain free-jazz artists been lauded by the rock community for their inspiring creativity. Guitarists Thurston Moore and Lee Ranaldo of the alternative rock mega-band Sonic Youth honed their chops in avant-garde composer Glenn Branca's incredibly loud guitar orchestras and have performed with the astonishing master drummer William Hooker, Roswell Rudd, and the David S. Ware Quartet. The exotic virtues of Sun Ra's "space music" are frequently extolled by Trey Anastasio, the leader of the band Phish, heirs apparent to the Grateful Dead. The group's love for free jazz manifests itself in their extended improvisations. In 1996, Anastasio gathered an eclectic group of ex-Ra sidemen, jazz, and rock performers to release the ambitious free album *Surrender to the Air* (Elektra). Anastasio hired former Ra sidemen Michael Ray and Marshall Allen, Phish drummer Jon Fishman, and noise guitarist Marc Ribot, among others, for a session of free exploration. While hordes of Phish fans were no doubt disappointed at the results, the more open-minded embraced the freakish sounds of Anastasio and company engaging in good-spirited collective improv.

Guitar virtuosos Henry Kaiser and Fred Frith jump between styles as easily as changing socks, from rock to jazz to world music to noisy hoo-ha. Kaiser has performed with Derek Bailey (witness their incredible duo album *Wireforks*, 1995, Shanachie), Ry Cooder, David Lindley, native Malagasy musicians, and the shifting personnel of the art-rock band Golden Palominos. Frith was a founder of the progressive jazz-rock unit Henry Cow (which was influenced by Sun Ra), duetted with Canadian guitarist René Lussier, and has led his own sessions. Both men have collaborated with Rova and participated in projects with ex–Captain Beefheart drummer John "Drumbo" French and British guitar wizard Richard Thompson, Frith taking bass duties both there and in John Zorn's Naked City. Kaiser and French have also worked together on each other's recordings and in the short-lived Crazy Backwards Alphabet (self-titled, 1992, SST), probably the only band to include both a hard-rocking version of Albert Ayler's "Ghosts" and a Russian rendition of "Surfin' USA" in their sets. These represent but a handful of contemporary artists whose music is best left uncategorized but which has included some aspects of free jazz.

Last Exit, the quartet of guitarist Sonny Sharrock, saxophonist Peter Brötzmann, bass guitarist Bill Laswell, and drummer Ronald Shannon Jackson, created some of the most frighteningly potent electric free improvisation to date. At their best, the band came close to representing the consummate realization of a free-rock fusion. Last Exit's 1986 self-titled debut album (on Enemy) resembles the soundtrack for the arrival of a slavering demon horde, full of crushing intensity that does not give in until the final tone. "Discharge" begins with barrelling triplets from Laswell and Jackson. Forty seconds in, Sharrock bursts forward with razor-edged power chords, Brötzmann following close behind with excoriating fury. Sharrock falls out, granting the saxophonist a brief lead, then the guitar strikes again with even greater intensity. After three minutes of sustained hell, Brötzmann ends the piece all alone with a lengthy gutbucket honk. Such raw, unyielding power is prevalent throughout the album, with enough variations of approach to keep it interesting. Laswell's furious bass on "Catch as Catch Can" and "Crackin" is sick enough to give modern hardcore bands pause. Sharrock is at his typically igneous best on "Pig Freedom," blasting out sheets of sound that overwhelm. Behind it all thunder the harmolodic-inspired drum conjurations of Jackson.

A similarly instrumented group of different vision is Music Revelation Ensemble, led by guitarist James Blood Ulmer. Like Ronald Shannon Jackson, Ulmer was a former sideman of Ornette Coleman who absorbed the altoist's harmolodic concepts into his own musical ideas. MRE was designed specifically as a rhythmic foundation for various jazz horn players to perform with in a horizon-expanding manner. As a result, the group comes across as a median between Prime Time and the archetypal Coleman quartet. Ulmer, electric bassist Amin Ali, and drummer Cornell Rochester have put in time with several of the finest saxophone players in creative music: David Murray (on *Elec. Jazz*, 1980), Arthur Blythe, Sam Rivers, Hamiet Bluiett (all on *In the Name Of . . .* , 1993; Bluiett and Blythe on *Knights of Power*, 1996), John Zorn, and Pharoah Sanders (both on *Crossfire*, 1998, all DIW).

Contemporary urban sounds play an ever-growing part in modern free music. As rap and hip-hop came to the forefront of American music, elements of their styles were absorbed into other segments of the musical culture. Turntable artist Christian Marclay has provided scratches and sound samples to the post-punk scene since the early 1980s, in settings ranging from John Zorn's projects to the Golden Palominos. Other sample artists have entered the scene since Marclay broke ground in the field, including DJ Olive, who has toured America in duet with drummer William Hooker, and DJ Spooky. Matthew Shipp has less successfully melded free-leaning jazz with static hip-hop beats on albums like *Nu Bop* (2001, Thirsty Ear), with the help of engineer Chris Flam. An impending collaboration with rap group Anti-Pop Consortium has reaped better advance press, but traditionalist heads have still shaken.

Two enterprising drum 'n' bass producers, John Coxon and Ashley Wales, have done some admirable work in free-jazz contexts. Operating as the duo Spring Heel Jack, Coxon and Wales have recorded several discs worth of pure electronica, along with two free-jazz collaborations (*Masses*, 2001, with Matthew Shipp, William Parker, Tim Berne, and Roy Campbell; *Amassed*, 2002, with Shipp, Evan Parker, Kenny Wheeler, Paul Rutherford, and Han Bennink, both on Thirsty Ear). Another group that shows significant promise in mixing free jazz with immediate present and future styles is Create(!), a rising Long Beach, California–based unit. On *Moth Nor Rust* (2000) and *Patterns* (2001, both Sounds Are Active), Create(!) combines the influences of Ornette Coleman and Sonny Sharrock with underground hip-hop, world music, avant-classicism, and electronica into a wild new fusion it has dubbed "improvdrumn'jazzworshiphopnoise." Any comparisons to prior art (Lester Bowie, Miles Davis's fusion, Zappa) are vague and somewhat moot in light of the ensemble's originality. Given the all-encompassing character of contemporary music, a property that only increases with time, the startling sound of Create(!) and Spring Heel Jack just might define free jazz's future.

Not all contemporary free jazz is aligned with rock or other currently popular forms, of course. There are large numbers of acoustic free players around New York, Chicago, and other major centers of jazz, and any number of labels issuing recordings of their latest innovations. In the 1990s, a tight circle of players formed around reedman David S. Ware and bassist William Parker, two Cecil Taylor alumni who have continued to alter the face of free jazz with astounding success. Ware's quartet was one of the most critically acclaimed units of the decade, and Parker's prodigious output as a leader and sideman have made him perhaps the most prominent bassist of the new century. Among their high-profile associates are trumpeter Roy Campbell, multi-instrumentalist Daniel Carter, and pianist Matthew Shipp. Altoists Jemeel Moondoc and Noah Howard have risen from their relative obscurity in the 1970s to become promising, well-recorded performers and bandleaders. In the musically fertile San Francisco Bay Area, the husband-wife duo of Oluyemi and Ijeoma Thomas present their warm melange of freedom, world music, and poetry (*Another Day's Journey*, 1995, Music & Arts) under the name of Positive Knowledge. They and adventurous young performers like Rent Romus and Ernesto Diaz-Infante continue to change the face of improvised music by the Bay.

The cadre of performers associated with *Cadence* magazine and its record labels are making particularly large waves today. Bassist Dominic Duval and drummer Jay Rosen are almost a house rhythm section for the CIMP imprint, having worked together and separately on dozens of sessions for the label. Recent issues on CIMP feature guitarists Dom Minasi and Bruce Eisenbeil; bassist Joe Fonda; saxophonists Blaise Siwula, Ken Simon, and Anthony Braxton; drummer Donald Robinson; trumpeter Herb Robertson; and trombonists Steve Swell and Tyrone Hill. Ken Vandermark's prodigious volume of work is represented on a number of labels, including Chicago's fine Okkadisk and Quinnah, and spread out over a dozen or more ensembles. Vinny Golia's Nine Winds label and Jeff Gauthier's newer Cryptogramophone imprint document the exciting developments coming out of the western United States.

The future of less jazzy improvisation in America is also in good hands: witness the work of nmperign, the duo of trumpeter Greg Kelley and soprano saxophonist Bhob Rainey. Reedmen Peter Brötzmann and Evan Parker, and the late bassist Peter Kowald have extended the horizons of European free music through collaborations with players from various other cultures. The European free-improv market sees new albums released on a constant basis, and Europe is by far the largest market for such music, with Japan running a close second. Electroacoustic improv is also on the rise again, driven by experimentalists like Otomo Yoshihide, Gunter Müller, Fennesz, Thomas Lehn, and AMM founding member Keith Rowe.

Notwithstanding the burgeoning popularity of free playing in New York, Chicago, and Europe, the anti-free bias in the mainstream jazz community seems to never quite subside. Some former "young lions," usually those who were inspired almost exclusively by the older traditions of jazz, have been quite vocal in their condemnation of the avant-garde. In a 1995 interview, trumpeter Wynton Marsalis said:

> It's not interesting to me to play like that. If I've rejected it, it's not out of ignorance of it. I don't know any people who like it. It doesn't resonate with anything I've experienced in the world. . . . It was with the type of things that late-period Coltrane did that jazz destroyed its relationship with the public. That avant-garde conception of music that's loud and self-absorbed—nobody's interested in hearing that on a regular basis. I don't care how much publicity it gets. The public is not going to want to hear people play like that.[15]

Despite these comments and his reputation as a showy reactionary who wants jazz to stay right where Duke Ellington left it, Marsalis has voiced an appreciation for some of Ornette Coleman's music, and Coleman is rumored to have considered hiring Marsalis for one of his projects. The trumpeter also played a part in Lester Bowie's Hot Trumpet Repertory Company, seeing in the leader someone who shared his love for the Louis Armstrong archetype. His own brother, saxophonist Branford, has extended some of the free-jazz principles developed by Coleman and Coltrane into his own brand of contemporary jazz. During his tenure as Columbia Jazz's artistic director, Branford contracted the David S. Ware Quartet to the label under the pretense that the group represented the music's future. At the same time, it was Branford who arrogantly criticized Cecil Taylor in Ken Burns's epic documentary "Jazz," practically the only direct insult in nineteen hours of film. Branford's description of Taylor's musical philosophy as "self-absorbed bullshit" suggests condemnation of that which he does not understand.

Though Wynton Marsalis's statement might be reasonably correct in terms of the percentage of the listening population that actively pursues the avant-garde, what he does not take into consideration is that the avant players are not always particularly *interested* in playing to the public's fickle tastes. The music they create is an exaltation of a highly personal nature, a celebration or condemnation of the nature of being at the time it is constructed. Its main function at the public level is not to pander, but to educate and open ears that have been slammed shut by ignorance and narrow-minded listening. Whether the audience chooses to *hear* it is not the artist's concern as much as giving them the *chance* to hear it. Likewise, Branford Marsalis had criticized Taylor's statement that his audience needed to prepare for his concerts as much as he does. Anyone familiar with Taylor's music will recognize this as an assertion of basic fact instead of arrogance. It is easy to become overwhelmed by the pianist's music if one is not ready for the experience, but to imply that Taylor should temper his energy for the sake of the unprepared is silly. The impact of Taylor's music remains identifiable, unique, and timelessly vital, never meant to be preserved under glass.

Today, little by little, note by note, the public is listening, is learning, is embracing the free aesthetic once more. While free jazz might not "resonate" well with the Marsalis brothers' life experiences, plenty of other listeners are finding ways to relate to this exciting musical art. They are discovering sounds beyond the ordinary, following whatever impulses the music summons to life within their hearts and minds, and taking something home when the smoke clears. In the boundless universe of music, freedom is most likely where the future lies.

NOTES

1. John Litweiler, *The Freedom Principle: Jazz after 1958* (New York: William Morrow & Co., 1984), pg. 32.

2. A 2-CD collection entitled *The Blue Note Years: The Avant-Garde* (Blue Note, 1998) suitably celebrates Monk's influence on the early free players by sequentially placing three compositions inspired by the pianist: Eric Dolphy's "Hat and Beard," trombonist Grachan Moncur III's "Monk in Wonderland," and Andrew Hill's "New Monastery." Each piece sustains the sort of sharp, disjointed structures and clashing harmonies that characterized Monk's own works, but are taken to the next level of freedom.

3. Mingus actually followed the lead of Wilbur Ware in freeing up the bassist's role. Ware, who came up during the growth of bebop in the 1950s, combined a percussive approach to the bass with a forceful tone, a keen sense of harmony, and a method of motivic improvisational development, which he honed while working with Thelonious Monk and Sonny Rollins, two other prominent motivic improvisers. Ware also played more freely with Sun Ra and Archie Shepp before his death in 1979.

4. *My Favorite Things* was not, however, Coltrane's first recorded use of the soprano saxophone. That distinction belongs to the album *The Avant-Garde* (Atlantic), with Coltrane playing in the company of Modern Jazz Quartet bassist Percy Heath and three associates of Ornette Coleman: trumpeter Don Cherry, bassist Charlie Haden, and drummer Ed Blackwell. That album was recorded on June 28, 1960, a full six months before Coleman's *Free Jazz* sessions. However, it was not released until 1967, seven years after *My Favorite Things*.

5. Pat Padua, film archivist at the Library of Congress, informed the author of this intriguing fact about the early documentation of jazz history. The earliest books in the library's database under the heading "Jazz—History and Criticism" were written not only by white authors, but Europeans at that. These are Emil Frantisek Burian's *Jazz* (Praha, Czechoslovakia: Ot. Storch-Marien, 1928) and Rudolf Sonner's *Musik und tanz: vom kulttanz zum jazz* (Leipzig, Germany: Quelle & Meyer, 1930). This writer was initially intrigued that European authors' analyses of jazz would predate similar analyses by American authors. However, it is quite evident that early jazz was not a well-respected music in its native land. European musicologists formed a distant, curious interest in jazz well before the American literati themselves deemed it worth writing about.

6. Statistics drawn from Gerald Leinwand, ed., *The Negro in the City* (New York: Washington Square Press, 1968).

7. "Sweet—Black Dada Nihilismus," on New York Art Quartet, *New York Art Quartet* (1964, ESP 1004). The poem "Black Dada Nihilismus" was originally published in Jones, Leroi, *The Dead Lecturer* (New York: Grove Press, 1964).

8. John Miller Chernoff, *African Rhythm and African Sensibility* (Chicago: University of Chicago Press, 1979), p. 211.

9. From Dan Morgenstern's interview, "John Tchicai: A Calm Member of the Avant-Garde," *Down Beat*, February 10, 1966, pp. 49–50.

10. Ibid., p. 50.

11. Interview with Robert Spencer, *Cadence*, April 2001, pp. 12–19.

12. Tom Wolfe, "The First Tycoon of Teen," from *The Kandy Kolored Tangerine Flake Stream-line Baby* (New York: Herald Tribune, 1965).

13. Originally quoted in *Western World* magazine, 1957. From Ross and Kathryn Petras, *The 776 Nastiest Things Ever Said* (New York: Harper Perennials, 1995). Sinatra's ranting about rock bears a striking emotional resemblance to this quote from writer Carl Engel: "Only by a bold stretch of fancy can this delirious caterwauling be brought under the head of music proper—or improper; as noise, its significance at times becomes eloquent to the point of leaving little or nothing to the imagination." In this case, however, Engel was writing about jazz way back in 1922! Carl Engel, "Jazz: A Musical Discussion," *The Atlantic Monthly* 130, no. 2 (August 1922): pp. 182–189.

14. In Anthony Bozza and Shawn Dahl, *Rolling Stone Raves* (New York: Rolling Stone Press, 1999).

15. Interview with Tony Scherman, "The Music of Democracy," *American Heritage* Magazine, October 1995.

Chronology of Events

May 1949	Pianist Lennie Tristano's group records "Intuition" and "Digression," two of the earliest freely improvised jazz tracks.
1955	Albert Ayler meets Charlie Parker in person. Steve Lacy joins the Cecil Taylor Quartet. Jackie McLean leads his first session. Births: Pheeroan Ak Laff, Marty Ehrlich, Wayne Horvitz, Hamid Drake, Joe Morris, Bill Laswell, Gerry Hemingway, David Murray, Joey Baron
Dec. 10, 1955	Cecil Taylor records his debut, *Jazz Advance*, for release on Transition.
1956	Marshall Allen joins Sun Ra's band, while Albert Ayler joins the Army. Charles Mingus records *Pithecanthropus Erectus*, his allegory of the rise and decline of "superior man." Albums: John Coltrane's *Tenor Madness* with Sonny Rollins, Andrew Hill's *So in Love* with Malachi Favors, Roland Kirk's *Triple Threat* Births: Denardo Coleman, Steve Coleman, Ned Rothenberg, Marco Eneidi, Vinny Golia, Nels and Alex Cline
July 12, 1956	The Sun Ra Arkestra records material for *Jazz by Sun Ra* (a.k.a. *Sun Song*).
1957	Coltrane records *Blue Train* and joins the Thelonious Monk Quartet. Sun Ra starts the Saturn label. Ran Blake meets Jeanne Lee. Jimmy Giuffre records "The Train and the River." Steve Lacy debuts with *Soprano Sax*. Births: Myra Melford, Phil Durrant, Bobby Previte, Thomas Chapin, Geri Allen
1958	The Delmark label issues its first album. Cecil Taylor's first concert hall performance held at New York's Cooper Union. Ornette Coleman and bandmates perform under Paul Bley's leadership at

	the Hillcrest Club in Los Angeles. Eric Dolphy joins the Chico Hamilton Quintet. Roscoe Mitchell meets Joseph Jarman. Births: Satoko Fujii, Michael Zerang, Thomas Lehn, Thurston Moore
Feb.–Mar. 1958	Ornette Coleman records *Something Else*, his debut, for Contemporary Records in Los Angeles. The band includes Don Cherry, Don Payne, and Billy Higgins.
June 1958	Cecil Taylor records *Looking Ahead!* for Contemporary.
1959	Alice McLeod (later Coltrane) studies piano with Bud Powell. Joe Harriott cuts *Southern Horizons* in London; Jackie McLean waxes *Jackie's Bag* for Blue Note. Bill Evans forms his trio with Scott LaFaro and Paul Motian. Sunny Murray is hired by Cecil Taylor, and Hal Russell by Joe Daley. Ornette Coleman and Don Cherry attend the Lenox School of Jazz in Massachusetts, then book a run at the Five Spot, which garners praise from figures like John Coltrane and Leonard Bernstein. Births: Tatsu Aoki, Drew Gress, Ellery Eskelin, John Lindberg, Simon Fell, Roger Smith, Otomo Yoshihide
Apr. 1, 1959	John Coltrane records *Giant Steps*, documenting his interpretation of Miles Davis's modal jazz experiments about halfway through Davis's *Kind Of Blue* sessions.
Apr. 22, 1959	Davis, Coltrane, Bill Evans, Cannonball Adderley, Wynton Kelly, Paul Chambers, and Jimmy Cobb finish recording *Kind Of Blue* for Columbia. The modal jazz excursion sells vigorously and becomes one of the most popular recordings of all time.
May 22, 1959	Coleman's quartet records *The Shape of Things to Come* for Atlantic Records.
1960	Steve Lacy works briefly with Thelonious Monk, then forms a Monk repertory group with Roswell Rudd. Albums: Joe Harriott Quintet's *Free Form*, Freddie Hubbard's *Open Sesame*, Max Roach's *We Insist—Freedom Now!*, Eric Dolphy's *Looking Ahead* with Ken McIntyre, *The World of Cecil Taylor* with Archie Shepp Births: Matthew Shipp, Erik Friedlander, Burkhard Stangl, Pat Thomas
July 1960	Three-day "Newport Rebel Festival" held at Cliff Walk Manor Hotel in Newport, Rhode Island, organized by Max Roach and Charles Mingus as an alternative to the main Newport Jazz Festival, to protest a lack of racial and stylistic diversity. Ornette Coleman is among the featured artists. Don Cherry and John Coltrane record *The Avant-Garde*, which Atlantic Records does not release for nearly six years. John Coltrane then records the perennially popular *My Favorite Things*.
Dec. 21, 1960	Recording of the landmark *Free Jazz: A Collective Improvisation by the Ornette Coleman Double Quartet*, issued by Atlantic.

1961   Muhal Richard Abrams gathers his Experimental Band to investigate new horizons in Chicago; in Los Angeles, Horace Tapscott creates the Union of God's Musicians and Artists Ascension. Albert Ayler and John Carter seek work in L.A. Bobby Bradford joins Ornette Coleman's band in New York but returns to California and begins playing with Carter. Charlie Haden leaves Coleman's band; the bass chair is given to Scott LaFaro. Eric Dolphy's association with Coltrane begins with *Africa/Brass*. Bill Dixon and Jimmy Lyons begin performing with Cecil Taylor. Taylor's group tapes three tunes, which are later issued on *Into the Hot* under Gil Evans's name. The move is a marketing ploy by Impulse Records to get Taylor's music out to a larger public.
Births: Lê Quan Ninh, François Houle, Ivo Perelman, Phil Haynes, Steven Bernstein
Deaths: Scott LaFaro, Booker Little

1962   Albert Ayler goes to Sweden and meets Sonny Rollins's band. Chris McGregor assembles the Blue Notes in Johannesburg, South Africa. Alice McLeod tours with Terry Gibbs and meets Coltrane. Ted Curson and Bill Barron go to Europe; Paul Bley, Cecil McBee, Gary Peacock, and Burton Greene arrive in New York. Roswell Rudd and Denis Charles join Bill Dixon's ensemble; Joseph Jarman joins Roscoe Mitchell's. Joe Maneri records a set for Atlantic that goes unreleased for thirty-six years. Charles Mingus's band gives a disastrous performance at Town Hall, marred by incomplete charts and unprepared musicians. Cecil Taylor is working as a dishwasher when *Down Beat* names him the best new pianist of the year. Taylor, Jimmy Lyons, and Sunny Murray later perform at the Montmartre Jazzhus in Copenhagen. Albert Ayler gigs with Taylor at the time but does not record with him. The trio of Ornette Coleman, David Izenzon, and Charles Moffett gives a controversial performance at Town Hall, where a string quartet interprets Coleman's "Dedication to Poets and Writers."
Albums: Jackie McLean's *Let Freedom Ring*, *Free Fall* by the Jimmy Giuffre Trio
Births: Rob Brown, Fred Lonberg-Holm

1963   Founding of the British trio Joseph Holbrooke. LeRoi Jones's *Blues People* is published. Albert Ayler and Rashied Ali move to New York. The John Coltrane Quartet and the Joe Daley Trio give powerful performances at Newport. Alex von Schlippenbach and Gunter Hampel begin working together as a duo. Bernard Stollman founds the ESP label. Paul Motian leaves Bill Evans's trio and joins Paul Bley.
Albums: Ran Blake's *The Newest Sound Around*, *My Name Is Albert Ayler* (recorded live in Copenhagen), Charles Mingus's seminal *The Black Saint and the Sinner Lady*, *The New York Contemporary Five*
Births: Dave Douglas, Gregg Bendian

1964   Eric Dolphy tours Europe with Charles Mingus. Bobby Bradford and John Carter form their New Art Jazz Ensemble. Andrew Cyrille joins Cecil Taylor, replacing Sunny Murray. The Blue Notes tour across Europe and become expatriates. Bill Dixon conducts the four-day "October Revolution in Jazz" series at the Cellar Café in New York. The featured artists include Taylor, Steve Lacy, Paul Bley, Andrew Hill, Jimmy Giuffre, Sheila Jordan, Milford Graves, Roswell Rudd, and John Tchicai. Dixon establishes the Jazz Composers Guild as a self-sufficiency league for creative musicians. Graves records with the New York Art Quartet and Giuseppi Logan, then joins the Ayler group. Sam Rivers performs with Miles Davis and Tony Williams, and begins recording for Blue Note. Gruppo di Improvvisazione Nuovo Consonanza founded in Italy.

Albums: Eric Dolphy's *Out to Lunch*, John Coltrane's *A Love Supreme*, Andrew Hill's *Point of Departure*, Archie Shepp's *Four for Trane*, Wolfgang Dauner's *Dream Talk*, Gunter Hampel's *Heartplants*, *New York Art Quartet*, *New York Eye and Ear Control* soundtrack by Albert Ayler, Don Cherry, and others

Births: Axel Dörner, Cor Fuhler, Tony Malaby, Mats Gustafsson, and Ken Vandermark

June 29, 1964   Dolphy dies in Berlin of complications from diabetes at the age of thirty-six.

1965   After the demise of the Jazz Composers Guild, Mike Mantler and Carla Bley recast the concept as the Jazz Composers Orchestra Association (JCOA). The Association for the Advancement of Creative Musicians (AACM) convenes in Chicago. AMM, Spontaneous Music Ensemble, and the People Band are formed in London. Don Pullen and Milford Graves perform and record as a duo. Peter Brötzmann, Sven-Åke Johansson, and Peter Kowald begin playing together. Don Ayler moves from alto sax to trumpet and joins his brother Albert's band. Charles Tyler also joins the Ayler group. Karl Berger enters Don Cherry's quintet. Ornette Coleman's trio swings a gig at the Village Vanguard after several months without work. Later in the year, they perform and record at the Gyllene Cirkeln (Golden Circle) in Stockholm, Sweden. McCoy Tyner and Elvin Jones leave the Coltrane Quartet. Coltrane brings in his new wife, Alice, Rashied Ali, and Pharoah Sanders as permanent replacements.

Albums: Bobby Hutcherson's *Dialogue*, Archie Shepp's *Fire Music*, Don Cherry's *Complete Communion*, Roland Kirk's *Rip, Rig and Panic*, Sunny Murray's *Sunny's Time Now*, Krzysztof Komeda's *Astigmatic*, self-titled debut albums of Pharoah Sanders, Marion Brown, and Roswell Rudd. Albert Ayler's Town Hall concert is recorded by ESP and later released as *Bells*. The blue vinyl LP causes controversy because one side is left completely blank.

Births: Philip Gelb, Stefano Battaglia, Taku Sugimoto

June 28, 1965   John Coltrane records *Ascension* with an ensemble of rising young jazzmen, including Archie Shepp, Marion Brown, John Tchicai, Pharoah Sanders, and Freddie Hubbard. Four days later, Shepp and Coltrane perform their personal conceptions of free jazz at the Newport Jazz Festival, bringing much controversy.

1966   Alex von Schlippenbach's "Globe Unity" is presented by the Berliner Philharmonic Orchestra. Roscoe Mitchell's Art Ensemble, with Lester Bowie, Philip Wilson, and Malachi Favors, debuts at the Harper Theatre in Chicago. Don Cherry tours the United States. Ronnie Boykins quits the Arkestra. Breakup of Joseph Holbrooke. Anthony Braxton leaves the Army, returns home to Chicago, and joins the AACM. Misha Mengelberg meets Willem Breuker; Peter Brötzmann meets Fred Van Hove and Irène Schweizer. Peter Kowald and Brötzmann tour Europe with Michael Mantler and Carla Bley. Musica Elettronica Viva (MEV) is founded in Rome. The first Spontaneous Music Ensemble session is taped but goes unreleased until 1997 (*Withdrawal* on Emanem).

Albums: Cecil Taylor's *Unit Structures*, Manfred Schoof's *Voices*, AMM's *AMMMusic*, Marion Brown's *Three for Shepp*. Chick Corea debuts with *Tones for Joan's Bones*, as does Dewey Redman with *Look for the Black Star*. The Roscoe Mitchell Sextet records *Sound* for Delmark; it is the first recorded document of music created under the auspices of the AACM. Ornette Coleman records *The Empty Foxhole* for Blue Note with his ten-year-old son Denardo on drums. Steve Lacy records *The Forest and the Zoo* in Buenos Aires, with Italian trumpeter Enrico Rava and two African expatriates, bassist Johnny Dyani and drummer Louis Moholo.

Births: Brad Schoeppach (Shepik)

1967   Chuck Nessa leaves Delmark to form his Nessa label. Dewey Redman joins Ornette Coleman's quartet. Albert Ayler performs at Newport in his only appearance at a major American festival. Henry Grimes disappears from the jazz scene. John Tchicai founds Cadentia Nova Danica, Trevor Watts forms Amalgam. New Phonic Art founded in Köln, Gruppo Romano Free Jazz in Rome. Steve McCall and Barre Phillips go to Europe; Enrico Rava comes to New York. ICP label started.

Albums: *Interstellar Space* by John Coltrane and Rashied Ali, Pharoah Sanders's *Tauhid* (on which Sonny Sharrock turns heads with his maniacal guitar playing), Jackie McLean's *New and Old Gospel* with guest Ornette Coleman, *For Adolphe Sax* by the Brötzmann/Kowald/Johansson trio, Marion Brown's *Porto Novo*,

Gato Barbieri's *In Search of the Mystery*, *New Acoustic Swing Duo* by Willem Breuker and Han Bennink, Clifford Thornton's *Freedom and Unity* with Joe McPhee. The Roscoe Mitchell Art Ensemble records some sessions, later issued on *Old/Quartet* and Lester Bowie's *Numbers 1 & 2*. Muhal Richard Abrams records "The Bird Song" (issued on *Levels and Degrees of Light*) with Anthony Braxton, Leroy Jenkins, and other AACM members. Births: Chris Speed, Jim Black, D. D. Jackson

Apr. 23, 1967 An ailing Coltrane gives one of his final performances at the Olatunji Center for African Culture in New York. Impulse released the performance on CD in 2001.

July 17, 1967 John Coltrane dies of liver failure at the age of forty-one.

1968 Albert Ayler performs only two concerts all year. Inauguration of Berlin's Total Music Meeting. Black Artists Group founded in St. Louis. Marion Brown begins a two-year tour of Europe. Chick Corea and Dave Holland join Miles Davis's electric band. Beaver Harris, Grachan Moncur III, and Dave Burrell put together the 360 Degree Music Experience. Irène Schweizer forms a trio with Peter Kowald and Pierre Favre. Archie Shepp performs at the Donaueschingen Festival.
Albums: Peter Brötzmann Octet's *Machine Gun*, Jazz Composers Orchestra's self-titled disc (with a titanic piano improvisation by Cecil Taylor on "Communications #11") and *Escalator Over the Hill*; Spontaneous Music Ensemble's *Karyōbin*; *Three Compositions of New Jazz* by Anthony Braxton, Leroy Jenkins, and Leo Smith; Don Cherry's world-free-jazz fusion *Eternal Rhythm*
Births: Noël Akchoté, Rent Romus, and Ernesto Diaz-Infante
Deaths: Christopher Gaddy

1969 Pharoah Sanders and Leon Thomas score one of free jazz's extremely rare popular hits with "The Creator Has a Master Plan." Roscoe Mitchell and his Art Ensemble associates move to Europe and meet Don Moye. The group is billed "Art Ensemble of Chicago" at a French concert, and the name is officially adopted by the band. Birth, ECM, and FMP labels open for business. Workshop Freie Musik is started in Berlin. First session in London by the Music Improvisation Company. Taj Mahal Travellers founded in Japan. Charlie Haden gathers his Liberation Music Orchestra, and Gary Peacock takes a three-year sabbatical in Japan. Cecil Taylor performs at the Fondation Maeght in St.-Paul-de-Vence, France, with Sam Rivers, Jimmy Lyons, and Andrew Cyrille. Pan-African Festival in Algiers, featuring Archie Shepp, Dave Burrell, Clifford Thornton, Sunny Murray, Alan Silva, and other improvisers. Festival Actuel held in Amougies, Belgium; produced by French BYG label and *Actuel* magazine, the event leads to a number of free-jazz recording sessions, issued by BYG as the Actuel Series.

Albums: Ornette Coleman's *Crisis*, Anthony Braxton's *For Alto*, Gunter Hampel's *The 8th of July 1969*, Manfred Schoof's *European Echoes*, Kalaparusha Maurice McIntyre's *Humility in the Light of Creator*, Jimmy Lyons's *Other Afternoons*, *Mu, Parts 1 and 2* by Don Cherry and Ed Blackwell, Mal Waldron's *Free At Last*, Horace Tapscott's *The Giant is Awakened*, Sonny Sharrock's *Black Woman*, Tony Oxley's *The Baptised Traveller*, George Russell's *Electronic Sonata for Souls Loved by Nature* with Terje Rypdal and Jan Garbarek

Births: Oren Ambarchi, Jim O'Rourke, Mat Maneri, Assif Tsahar, and Briggan Krauss

Deaths: Krzysztof Komeda

1970   Willem Breuker petitions the Dutch Jazz Foundation to request regular government funding for jazz events. Ornette Coleman backs Yoko Ono on "AOS." Barry Guy founds the London Jazz Composers Orchestra; Chris McGregor forms the Brotherhood of Breath. Incus label established. Steve Lacy goes to Paris and stays for over thirty years. Alex von Schlippenbach forms his trio with Paul Lovens and Evan Parker. June Tyson joins Sun Ra's Arkestra. Bob Moog gives Annette Peacock a prototype synthesizer. The quartet of Anthony Braxton, Leo Smith, Steve McCall, and Leroy Jenkins return to the United States. First recording sessions by the quartet Circle.

Albums: Alice Coltrane's *Journey to Satchidananda*, Jan Garbarek's *Afric Pepperbird*, Joe McPhee's *Nation Time* and *The Trio* by John Surman, Barre Phillips, and Stu Martin. In London, Derek Bailey, Evan Parker, and Han Bennink tape *The Topography of the Lungs*, the master tapes of which are later lost.

Nov. 25, 1970   Albert Ayler's body washes up on the bank of New York's East River. Ayler had been missing since November 5. He was thirty-four years old.

1971   Reflection (later known as Air) is formed by Henry Threadgill, Fred Hopkins, and Steve McCall. The Art Ensemble of Chicago returns to the United States; Bobby Bradford goes to England and performs with the Spontaneous Music Ensemble. The Ganelin (G-T-Ch) Trio and Revolutionary Ensemble are founded. Ornette Coleman signs with Columbia Records. Charlie Haden is arrested in Portugal as a political activist. Keith Jarrett leaves Miles Davis and forms his American quartet.

Albums: Circle's *Paris Concert*, *Septober Energy* by Keith Tippett's Centipede

Births: Vijay Iyer, Dylan van der Schyff, and Rhodri Davies

1972   Rashied Ali inaugurates his Survival label. Karl Berger and Ornette Coleman open their Creative Music Studio. Coleman's *Skies of America* is debuted by the London Symphony Orchestra. Mark Harvey founds the Aardvark Orchestra. Several members of the Black Artists Group head for Europe. The Fringe, New Dalta Akhri, and Human Arts Ensemble are founded. Sun Ra's Arkestra films *Space Is the Place*. Iskra 1903 is founded.

Albums: London Jazz Composers Orchestra's *Ode*; Dave Holland's *Conference of the Birds* with Anthony Braxton, Barry Altschul, and Sam Rivers; and *Duo Exchange* by Rashied Ali and Frank Lowe; *Last Tango in Paris* soundtrack by Gato Barbieri

Births: Bhob Rainey

Deaths: Phil Seamen

1973   Ornette Coleman and music journalist/clarinetist Robert Palmer visit Morocco and record a track entitled "Midnight Sunrise" with the Master Musicians of Joujouka, setting a precedent for future collaborations between jazzmen and traditional Moroccan musicians. Derek Bailey attempts to sell his own recordings instead of dealing with a record label. Don Cherry moves to Sweden. Willem Breuker establishes the Kollektief. Cecil Taylor hires William Parker for the first time.

Albums: Don Cherry's *Relativity Suite*, Bobby Bradford's *Love's Dream*, Han Bennink's *Nerve Beats*, Human Arts Ensemble's *Under the Sun*, Marion Brown's *Geechee Recollections*, Keith Jarrett's *Fort Yawuh*

Births: Greg Kelley

Deaths: Joe Harriott

1974   Trombonist Paul Rutherford conducts a series of solo concerts. Cecil Taylor performs at Carnegie Hall. Amsterdam's BIMhuis is opened. BVHaast, Arista, Emanem, Ogun, Moers Music, and IAI labels founded. John Carter drops the alto sax to concentrate on the clarinet. John Surman, Mike Osborne, and Alan Skidmore form the sax trio S.O.S.

Albums: Muhal Richard Abrams with the Art Ensemble of Chicago on *Fanfare for the Warriors*, Cecil Taylor's *Silent Tongues* (solo in Montreux), Edward Vesala's *Nan Madol*, Roswell Rudd's *Flexible Flyer*, Dewey Redman's *Coincide*, *Dialogue of the Drums* by Rashied Ali, Milford Graves, and Andrew Cyrille

1975   Steve McCall returns to New York from Europe; he resumes his role in Air with Henry Threadgill and Fred Hopkins. Rahsaan Roland Kirk is paralyzed by a stroke. Arista buys the Freedom imprint from Black Lion. HatHut and Black Saint labels established. ESP issues its final recording, Ronnie Boykins's *The Will Come, Is Now*. *Cadence* magazine publishes its first issue. Andrew Cyrille leaves Cecil Taylor, Don Pullen leaves Mingus. Phil Minton begins performing as a solo vocalist, and Evan Parker begins recording solo. Live debut of the World Saxophone Quartet.

Albums: Sam Rivers's *Crystals*, Willem Breuker Kollektief's *The European Scene*, Frank Lowe's *The Flam*, Schlippenbach Quartet's

Hunting the Snake, Keith Jarrett's *The Köln Concert* (ECM's best-selling recording ever)

Deaths: Mongezi Feza

1976   Lou Gare departs from AMM. Derek Bailey develops the Company conception. Old and New Dreams and Codona are formed, both including Don Cherry. Arthur Blythe joins the Gil Evans Orchestra and forms his unusual quintet of alto, guitar, tuba, cello, and drums. G-T-Ch Trio signs to Melodiya, the Soviet record label. Ictus, Po Torch, and Horo labels established. George Lewis replaces Kenny Wheeler in Anthony Braxton's group. Ornette Coleman conveys the first Prime Time lineup for *Dancing In Your Head*.

Albums: Paul Rutherford's *The Gentle Harm of the Bourgeoisie*; Hamiet Bluiett's *Endangered Species*; Milford Graves's *Babi Music*; Anthony Braxton's *Creative Orchestra Music*; David Murray's debut *Flowers for Albert*; Pat Metheny's debut *Bright Size Life*. Legendary *Wildflowers* recording sessions at Sam Rivers's Studio RivBea, the first major documentation of New York City's loft-jazz scene.

Births: Tim Daisy

Deaths: Jimmy Garrison

1977   Derek Bailey organizes the first Company Week festival in London. The Claxon, Nine Winds, and Artists House labels debut, as does the British quartet Alterations. The Revolutionary Ensemble is dissolved. Steve Lacy puts together his esteemed sextet; Arto Lindsay goes "No Wave" with the rock band DNA; the String Trio of New York is born. John Tchicai reemerges after an absence of several years. David S. Ware, John Zorn, Henry Kaiser, David Eyges, and Kenny Werner debut on record. Irène Schweizer joins the Feminist Improvising Group.

Albums: Julius Hemphill's *Blue Boyé*, Malachi Favors's *The Natural and the Spiritual*, Ornette Coleman and Charlie Haden's *Soapsuds, Soapsuds*, Richard Teitelbaum's *Time Zones*, James Blood Ulmer's *Revealing*, Air's *Air Time*

Deaths: Rahsaan Roland Kirk

1978   Ray Anderson and John Lindberg begin performing with Braxton. Giovanni Bonandrini takes over Black Saint and signs David Murray. The Art Ensemble of Chicago signs with ECM for a long run of albums. The Cadence Jazz label and Rova Saxophone Quartet are born. The CCMC is founded in Canada. The Human Arts Ensemble folds up. Ronald Shannon Jackson and Raphé Malik join the Cecil Taylor Unit, and Jimmy Lyons founds his own group with bassoonist Karen Borca.

Albums: Art Ensemble's *Nice Guys*, *Metamusician's Stomp* by Andrew Cyrille's Maono, Leroy Jenkins's *The Legend of Ai Glatson*,

Han Bennink's *Solo*, *Reed 'n Vibes* by Marion Brown and Gunter Hampel, Louis Moholo's *Spirits Rejoice*, James Blood Ulmer's *Tales of Captain Black*, Johnny Dyani's *Witchdoctor's Son*, Evan Parker's *Monoceros*

Deaths: Kaoru Abe

1979 George Adams, Dannie Richmond, Don Pullen, and Cameron Brown form their popular quartet. Tim Berne begin recording. Founding of Impetus label, Hal Russell's NRG Ensemble, and Ronald Shannon Jackson's Decoding Society. Cecil Taylor performs for President Jimmy Carter at the White House and performs duets with Max Roach.

Albums: Henry Threadgill's *X-75*, George Lewis's *Homage to Charles Parker*, Dave Burrell's *Windward Passages*, *First String* by String Trio of New York, G-T-Ch Trio's *Catalogue: Live in East Germany*, Barre Phillips's *Journal Violone II*, Steve Lacy's *N.Y. Capers and Quirks*, Cecil Taylor's *3 Phasis*, Rova's *Daredevils* with Henry Kaiser, Joe McPhee's *Old Eyes and Mysteries*, Amalgam's *Wipe Out*, *Black Paladins* by Joseph Jarman and Don Moye

Deaths: David Izenzon, Charles Mingus

1980 Anthony Braxton's contract with Arista expires. Bill Dixon signs on with Soul Note. The Blue Humans and Borbetomagus begin recording. Joseph Bowie forms Defunkt. Inauguration of the Cecma label, André Jaume's octet, Harry Miller's Isipingo, the Music Revelation Ensemble, and Pierre Dørge's New Jungle Orchestra.

Albums: AMM's *It had been an ordinary enough day in Pueblo, Colorado*, Ran Blake's *Film Noir*, Keiji Haino's *Watashi-Dake?*, Barry Altschul's *Brahma*, *Yankees* by Bailey/Zorn/Lewis, David Murray's *Ming*, Ray Anderson's *Harrisburg Half-Life*, *Full Force* by the Art Ensemble of Chicago, Vinny Golia's *Solo*, Julius Hemphill's *Flat-Out Jump Suite*, Jimmy Lyons's *Jump Up*, Marion Brown's *November Cotton Flower*, John Zorn's *Pool*, Vienna Art Orchestra's *Concerto Piccolo*

Deaths: Ronnie Boykins

1981 Joe McPhee formulates his Po Music concept. James Blood Ulmer signs with Columbia. Founding of Leo Records, Detail, Microscopic Septet, Sonic Youth, Ray Anderson's Slickaphonics, Anthony Davis's Episteme, and the Lounge Lizards. Ron Mann films the documentary *Imagine the Sound*.

Albums: William Parker's debut *Through Acceptance of the Mystery Peace*, Lester Bowie's Brass Fantasy's *The Great Pretender*, Anthony Braxton's *Composition 96*, Keith Tippett's *Mujician*, Leo Cuypers's *Happy Days Are Here Again*, Misha Mengelberg's *Regeneration* with Roswell Rudd, Peter Brötzmann's *Alarm*, James

Newton's *Axum*, John Surman's *The Amazing Adventures of Simon Simon*

1982   Steve McCall leaves Air. Johnny Dyani joins Detail. Mike Osborne stops performing for health reasons. John Butcher quits his physics studies to play free music. Trevor Watts unveils his group Moiré Music and the Arc label. Fred Anderson opens his Chicago nightclub, the Velvet Lounge. Founding of Splasc(h) Records.

Albums: Amiri Baraka's *New Music New Poetry*, Art Ensemble of Chicago's *Urban Bushmen*, Vinny Golia's *Compositions for Large Ensemble*, Anthony Braxton's *Six Compositions: Quartet*, ICP's *Japan Japon*, Louis Moholo's *Tern*, Henry Threadgill Sextett's *When Was That?*, Lester Bowie's *All the Magic!*, Material's *Memory Serves*, Steve Lacy's *Prospectus*, Sirone's *Life Rays*, Anthony Davis's *I've Known Rivers*, Ronald Shannon Jackson's *Mandance*, and the debuts of Ethnic Heritage Ensemble and Pierre Dørge's New Jungle Orchestra

1983   Tim Berne signs with Soul Note. Death of Harry Miller. Simon H. Fell starts his Bruce's Fingers label. Canada's Festival International de Musique Actuelle Victoriaville is founded. The King Übü Örchestrü is born. Gerry Hemingway joins Braxton. John Tilbury joins AMM. Rova tours the Soviet Union and records several performances, later released as *Saxophone Diplomacy*.

Albums: Jimmy Lyons's *Wee Sneezawee*, John Zorn's *Locus Solus*, Alfred Harth's *This Earth!*, Muhal Richard Abrams's *Rejoicing with the Light*, Jimmy Giuffre's *Dragonfly*, Jemeel Moondoc's *Kostanze's Delight*, AMM's *Generative Themes*, Amalgam's *Over the Rainbow*, Wadada Leo Smith's *Rastafari*, Anthony Davis's *Hemispheres*

1984   Founding of The Leaders. Matthew Shipp moves to New York. Konnex label founded. In July, the Sound Unity Festival is held in New York. The gathering was coordinated by William Parker, his wife Patricia Nicholson, and Peter Kowald. Not a big financial success, it ignited a spark that led to the Vision Festival ten years later. Hugh Ragin joins David Murray.

Albums: Sun Ra's *Nuclear War*, Thomas Chapin's *Radius*, Ray Anderson's *Right Down Your Alley*, Roscoe Mitchell and the Sound and Space Ensembles, *Supersession* by Guy/Parker/Rowe/ Prévost, *Album Album* by Jack DeJohnette's Special Edition, John Zorn's *The Big Gundown*, Cecil Taylor's *Winged Serpent (Sliding Quadrants)*

1985   Blue Note bought by Capitol Records. Anthony Braxton assembles his acclaimed quartet with Gerry Hemingway, Mark Dresser, and Marilyn Crispell. Steve McCall leaves Air and is replaced by Pheeroan Ak Laff. Steve Coleman tries out his M-BASE conceptions.

Albums: Jimmy Lyons's *Give It Up*, Butch Morris's *Current Trends in Racism in Modern America*, Art Ensemble of Chicago's *The Third Decade*, Simon H. Fell's *Compilation 1*, *Song X* by Ornette Coleman and Pat Metheny, David Moss's *Dense Band*, John Stevens's *Freebop*, Günter Müller's *Planet Oeuf*, Borbetomagus's *Borbeto Jam*, Don Pullen's *The Sixth Sense*

1986   Breakup of Alterations. Marco Eneidi creates his Botticelli label. G-T-Ch Trio tours the United States. Founding of Debris, Charlie Haden's Quartet West, New Winds, and the trio of Lê Quan Ninh, Daunik Lazro, and Michel Doneda. Last Exit record a live session in Paris. It later becomes their self-titled debut on bassist Bill Laswell's label, Enemy Records. Berlin's Workshop Freie Musik conducts the first Cecil Taylor Festival, at which Taylor records *For Olim*.

Albums: Globe Unity Orchestra's *20th Anniversary*, Bobby Bradford's *In Time Was*, David Murray's *The Hill*, Carlo Actis Dato's *Noblesse Oblige*, Curlew's *Live in Berlin*, Lounge Lizards' *Big Heart: Live in Tokyo*, *Moments Précieux* by Derek Bailey and Anthony Braxton, Parker/Guy/Lytton's *Atlanta*, *Sempre Amore* by Mal Waldron and Steve Lacy, Paul Dunmall's *Soliloquy*

Deaths: Jimmy Lyons, Johnny "Mbizo" Dyani

1987   Inaugural Bang On A Can Festival, and the first October Meeting at the BIMhuis. Breakup of G-T-Ch Trio and Globe Unity. Asian Improv, Rastascan, and Victo labels founded. NOW Orchestra and Splatter Trio debut. Knitting Factory opens in its original location in New York's Lower East Side. Benefit concert for Ed Blackwell held in Atlanta.

Albums: Ornette Coleman's *In All Languages* (with Prime Time and his original quartet), Tim Berne's *Fulton Street Maul*, Charles Brackeen's *Worshippers Come Nigh*, Misha Mengelberg's *Dutch Masters*, Alex Cline's *The Lamp and the Star*, John Butcher's *Conceits*, Sonny Sharrock's *Seize the Rainbow*, Elliott Sharp's *Tessellation Row*, Rova's *Beat Kennel*, Air's *Air Show No. 1*, Matthew Shipp and Rob Brown debut with *Sonic Explorations*, Leon Thomas makes a comeback with *Precious Energy*

1988   Cecil Taylor is honored by an extended music festival held in Berlin. Sponsored by FMP, the festival results in the recording of twelve albums' worth of performances. Grateful Dead guitarist Jerry Garcia records with Ornette Coleman and Prime Time. Steve Adams replaces Andrew Voigt in Rova, and Andrew Cyrille replaces Pheeroan Ak Laff in Air. New York's Town Hall begins its "Not Just Jazz" series; the Knitting Factory inaugurates the "What Is Jazz?" Festival. Gush, Acta label, and Berlin Contemporary Jazz Orchestra founded. Parachute label folds.

Albums: Willem Breuker Kollektief's *Bob's Gallery*, John Zorn's *Spy vs. Spy*, Bill Dixon's *Sons of Sisyphus*, Don Cherry's *Art Deco*, Tony Coe's *Canterbury Song*, *Julius Hemphill Big Band*, Misha Mengelberg's *Impromptus*, David S. Ware Trio's *Passage to Music*

1989   Thomas Chapin gathers his trio with Mario Pavone and Steve Johns. Matthew Shipp and David S. Ware begin their partnership. Ken Vandermark arrives in Chicago. John Zorn puts together Naked City. Julius Hemphill retires from the World Saxophone Quartet.

Albums: Alex von Schlippenbach and Sunny Murray's *Smoke*, Cecil Taylor's *The Eighth* and *In Florescence*, Lindsay Cooper's *Oh Moscow*, Pauline Oliveros's *Deep Listening*, *Other Dimensions in Music*, Horace Tapscott's two-volume *The Dark Tree*, London Jazz Composers Orchestra's *Harmos*, Ivo Perelman's *Ivo*

Deaths: Clifford Thornton, Steve McCall, Donald Rafael Garrett

1990   Flying Luttenbachers, Ground Zero, and Italian Instabile Orchestra are assembled. For 4 Ears and Axiom labels founded. John Betsch replaces Oliver Johnson on drums in the Steve Lacy Sextet. Sun Ra suffers his first stroke. Lou Gare returns only briefly to AMM.

Albums: Thomas Chapin's *Third Force*, Don Cherry's *Multikulti*, Peter Brötzmann's *No Nothing*, Myra Melford's *Jump*, Joe McPhee's *Linear B*, Franz Koglmann's *A White Line*, Schlippenbach Trio's *Elf Bagatellen*, Marion Brown's *Native Land*, Glenn Spearman's *Utterance*, Marc Ribot's *Rootless Cosmopolitans*, Giorgio Gaslini's *Ayler's Wings*, *Overlapping Hands: Eight Segments* by Irène Schweizer and Marilyn Crispell

Deaths: Frank Wright, Chris McGregor, Dudu Pukwana

1991   Lindsay Cooper diagnosed with multiple sclerosis. Tim Berne's Caos Totale, Thomas Borgmann's Orkestra Kith 'N Kin, and Painkiller are formed.

Albums: Charles Gayle's *Touchin' on Trane*, Cecil Taylor's *One Too Many Salty Swift and Not Goodbye*, Steve Lacy's *Live at Sweet Basil*, Sonny Sharrock's *Ask the Ages*, David S. Ware's *Flight of i*, Butch Morris's *Dust to Dust*, Gerry Hemingway's *Down to the Wire*, Julius Hemphill Sextet's *Fat Man and the Hard Blues*, Jazz Group Arkhangelsk's *Portrait*

Deaths: John Carter, Beaver Harris

1992   Joseph Jarman quits the Art Ensemble of Chicago. Chicago's Empty Bottle begins showcasing experimental music.

Albums: Denis Charles's *A Scream for Charles Tyler*; John Butcher's *Thirteen Friendly Numbers* and *Concert Moves*; David S. Ware's *Third Ear Recitation*; Lindsay Cooper's *Sahara Dust*; Pat Metheny's *Zero Tolerance for Silence*; Pharoah Sanders's *Crescent, With Love*; François Houle's *Hacienda*; King Übü Örchestrü's *Binaurality*;

Vienna Art Orchestra's *A Notion in Perpetual Motion*; *This Dance Is for Steve McCall* by Roscoe Mitchell's Note Factory
Deaths; Philip Wilson, Charles Tyler, Hal Russell, Ed Blackwell, George Adams

1993   Guelph Jazz Festival and Polwechsel begin. Red Toucan and Random Acoustics labels founded.
Albums: 4-CD boxed set *The Art Ensemble 1967/68*; Tim Berne's *Diminutive Mysteries (Mostly Hemphill)*; Available Jelly's *Monuments*; Dave Douglas's *Parallel Worlds*; Jon Jang's *Tiananmen!*; Myra Melford's *Alive in the House of Saints*; Joe Maneri's *Dahabenzapple*; Don Cherry's *Dona Nostra*, *The Hal Russell Story*, *Les Diaboliques*; Schlippenbach Trio's *Physics*; *Too Much Sugar for a Dime* by Henry Threadgill and Very Very Circus; John Zorn's *Kristallnacht*
Deaths: Sun Ra

1994   Diverse performances of John Zorn's game piece "Cobra" were recorded all year long, collected and released on *Cobra: Live at the Knitting Factory*. To celebrate his fiftieth birthday, Evan Parker performs and records with both of his esteemed trios: Alex von Schlippenbach/Paul Lovens and Barry Guy/Paul Lytton. Final Company Week gathering. Anthony Braxton receives a MacArthur Foundation grant. Debut of Die Like A Dog and Prima Materia. Okkadisk label founded.
Albums: Berlin Contemporary Jazz Orchestra's *The Morlocks and Other Pieces*, David S. Ware's *Cryptology*, Glenn Spearman's *Free Worlds*, Bley/Parker/Phillips's *Time Will Tell*, *Ixesha* by Tony Oxley's Celebration Orchestra, Peter Brötzmann's *Songlines*, Peter Kowald's *Was Da Ist?*, Biggi Vinkeloe's *Mbat*, Tomasz Stanko's *Matka Joanna of the Angels*, Ken Vandermark's *Solid Action*, Bill Dixon's *Vade Mecum*
Deaths: Sonny Sharrock, John Stevens

1995   Durian and CIMP labels founded; Emanem and Ictus labels return to the market. Glenn Spearman and Marco Eneidi form their Creative Music Orchestra. Debuts of Erik Friedlander's Chimera and Lou Grassi's Po Band.
Albums: William Parker's *In Order to Survive*; *Tone Dialing* by Ornette Coleman and Prime Time; Maarten Altena's *Cities and Streets*; Dave Douglas's *Five*; Vijay Iyer's *Memorophilia*; Fred Anderson's *Birdhouse*; Reggie Workman's *Cerebral Caverns*; Thomas Borgmann's *Orkestra Kith 'N Kin* and *Ruf der Heimat*; Clusone Trio's *I Am An Indian*; Ellery Eskelin's *Jazz Trash*; Otomo Yoshihide's *Live*; *Polwechsel*; Hans Reichel's *Lower Lurum*; Rova's *John Coltrane's Ascension*; *Wireforks* by Derek Bailey and Henry Kaiser
Deaths: Julius Hemphill, Don Pullen, Don Cherry

1996   Vision Festival inaugurated. Geri Allen becomes the first pianist in four decades to perform with Ornette Coleman. Joe McPhee, Dominic Duval, and Jay Rosen form Trio-X. Fire in the Valley Festival begins. Aum Fidelity and Eremite labels founded.

Albums: Bailey/Zorn/Parker's *Harras*; AMM's *Laminal*; Myra Melford's *The Same River, Twice*; Bobby Zankel's *Prayer and Action*; Dave Douglas's *Serpentine*; *Western Front* by Carlos Zingaro and Peggy Lee; Ari Brown's *Ultimate Frontier*; Masada's *Bar Kokhba*; Jemeel Moondoc's *Tri-P-Let*; *Mars Song* by Evan Parker and Sainkho Namtchylak; Sun Ra *Singles* collection on Evidence; John Oswald's notorious *Plunderphonics*

Deaths: Masayuki Takayanagi, Sergei Kuryokhin

1997   Butch Morris leads his "London Skyscraper" conduction, a landmark gathering of improvisers. Gunter Hampel reunites his original Heartplants Quintet. Sainkho Namtchylak spends months in a coma after being assaulted. John Butcher replaces Radu Malfatti in Polwechsel. I.S.O., Resonance Impeders, and MIMEO are founded.

Albums: *Sunrise in the Tone World* by William Parker's Little Huey Creative Music Orchestra, DKV Trio's *Baraka*, David S. Ware's *Wisdom of Uncertainty* (the first with Susie Ibarra in the quartet), *The Sign of Four* by Bailey/Bendian/Metheny/Wertico, *Colors* by Ornette Coleman and Joachim Kühn, Peter Kowald's *Touch the Earth—Break the Shells*, Matthew Shipp's *Flow of X*, Willem Breuker Kollektief's *Pakkepapèn*, *Expatriate Kin* by Fasteau/Few/Howard, Raphé Malik's *The Short Form*, Arthur Blythe's *Synergy* and *Today's Blues*, Miya Masaoka's *Monk's Japanese Folk Song*, Fonda/Stevens's *Parallel Lines*, Chris Burn Ensemble's *Navigations*, Charles "Bobo" Shaw's *Junk Trap*, Aum Fidelity's 2-CD set of recordings from the Vision Festival, *Vision One*

Deaths: Charles Moffett

1998   Peter Brötzmann gathers his Chicago Tentet. David S. Ware moves to Columbia Records, and Art Ensemble of Chicago returns to Atlantic. Olu Dara moves from free jazz trumpeter to blues singer and guitarist. Founding of Grob, Cryptogramophone, Wobbly Rail, and Potlatch labels. Ground Zero breaks up.

Albums: Ware's *Go See the World*, Art Ensemble's *Coming Home Jamaica*, Derek Bailey's *Play Backs*, Bright Moments' *Return of the Lost Tribe*, Die Like A Dog Quartet's *From Valley to Valley*, *Ancestral Homeland* by Roy Campbell's Pyramid Trio, Cecil Taylor's live *Q'ua* and *Q'ua Yuba*, Lisle Ellis's *Children in Peril Suite*, Chicago Underground's *12 Degrees of Freedom* and *Playground*, Satoko Fujii Orchestra's *South Wind*, Milford Graves's *Grand Unification*, Joel Futterman's *Southern Extreme*, Trio X's *Rapture*, *Yo, Miles!* by Wadada Leo Smith and Henry Kaiser, *nmperign*, *Test/Live*, *We Are Not at the Opera* by Sunny Murray and Sabir Mateen, Aaly Trio's *Stumble* with Ken Vandermark, *Downtown Lullaby* by Zorn/Sharp/Previte/Horvitz, New Winds' *Potion*

Deaths: Thomas Chapin, Denis Charles, Motoharu Yoshizawa, Glenn Spearman, Tom Cora

1999   Los Angeles Knitting Factory opens but books almost no jazz art-
              ists, free or otherwise. Funding for Berlin's Workshop Freie Musik
              is discontinued. Uncool Festival begins. Ken Vandermark gets a
              MacArthur Foundation grant. Meniscus, Erstwhile, and between
              the lines labels founded.
              Albums: Steve Lacy's *The Rent*, Italian Instabile Orchestra's *Litania
              Sibilante*, Joseph Jarman's *Pachinko Dream Track 10*, *Momentum
              Space* by Taylor/Redman/Jones, Charles Gayle's *Ancient of Days*,
              Ritual Trio's *Conversations*, *Join Us* by Bluiett/Jackson/Thiam,
              Home Cookin' by Assif Tsahar and Susie Ibarra, Hugh Ragin's *An
              Afternoon in Harlem*, Evan Parker's *Foxes Fox* and *Drawn Inward*,
              Misha Mengelberg's *Two Days in Chicago*, London Improvisers
              Orchestra's *Proceedings*, ICP's *Jubilee Varia*, Anthony Braxton's
              News from the 70s
              Deaths: Fred Hopkins, Leon Thomas, Clifford Jarvis, Jaki Byard,
              Horace Tapscott, Lester Bowie

2000   Cosmosamatics assembled. Music Now Festival begins. Joseph
              Holbrooke reunites to tour Europe and America. Matthew Shipp
              becomes the curator for Thirsty Ear's "Blue Series" of experimental
              jazz albums.
              Albums: Vandermark 5's *Burn the Incline*, Ornette Coleman's *The
              Complete Science Fiction Sessions* (an enhanced reissue), New York
              Art Quartet's *35th Anniversary*, Bill Dixon's *Berlin Abbozzi*, *Mayor
              of Punkville* by William Parker's Little Huey Creative Music Orches-
              tra, Whit Dickey's *Big Top*, *PoZest* by Lou Grassi's Po Band with
              Marshall Allen, Art Ensemble's *Naked*, Derek Bailey's *Incus Taps*
              and *Mirakle*, Mats Gustafsson's *Windows*, *Equal Interest*, Boulder
              Creative Music Ensemble's *Faith*, Not Missing Drums Project's *The
              Gay Avantgarde*, *Inscape – Tableaux* by Barry Guy's New Orchestra,
              Cuong Vu's *Bound*, Michel Portal's *Dockings*, Peter Brötzmann's
              Chicago Tentet's *Stone/Water*, Steve Lacy's *Hooky*, Richard
              Grossman's *Where the Sky Ended*, *After Appleby* by Marilyn Crispell
              with Parker/Guy/Lytton, Ori Kaplan's *Delirium*, *No Greater Love* by
              Joe McPhee's Bluette, David S. Ware's *Surrendered*, Wadada Leo
              Smith's *Golden Quartet*, John Tchicai's *Infinitesimal Flash*
              Deaths: Jeanne Lee

2001   Charly Records issues *Jazzactuel*, a 3-CD collection of tracks from
              BYG's Actuel series. Thurston Moore contributes the liner notes.
              Earth People and Nommonsemble assembled. Freedom of the City
              Festival inaugurated. Reunion of the G-T-Ch Trio. Cecil Taylor
              performs in duo with Elvin Jones, then tours with Tony Oxley and
              Bill Dixon. Charlie Haden wins a Grammy for *Nocturne*, his al-
              bum with Latin jazz pianist Gonzalo Rubalcaba. Alfred Harth
              moves to Korea. Henry Kaiser performs for scientists in Antarc-
              tica. Kenny Werner helps bring free improv to the masses with
              his *Effortless Mastery* instructional video and an Aebersold play-
              along recording.

Albums: *Live in New York* by Archie Shepp and Roswell Rudd, Billy Bang's *Vietnam: The Aftermath*, Peter Brötzmann's *Fuck de Boere*, John Coltrane's *The Olatunji Concert*, Matthew Shipp's *New Orbit*, Carlo Actis Dato's *The Moonwalker*, ICP Orchestra's *Oh My Dog!*, Dave Holland's *Not For Nothin'*, Marco Eneidi's *Cherry Box*, Trio X's *On Tour: Toronto/Rochester*, London Improvisers Orchestra's *The Hearing Continues*, John Butcher's *Points, Snags and Windings*, *Sankt Gerold* by Bley/Parker/Phillips, *Alan Silva and the Sound Visions Orchestra*, *J.D. Parran and Spirit Stage*, poire_z's *Presque_Chic*, *Spirit House* by Jemeel Moondoc's Jus' Grew Orchestra, Misha Mengelberg's *Four in One*, Fred Frith's *Digital Wildlife*, Evan Parker's *2 x 3 = 5*, Henry Threadgill's *Everybody's Mouth a Book* and *Up Popped the Two Lips*, Vandermark 5's *Acoustic Machine*, David S. Ware's solo *Live in the Netherlands*
Deaths: Makanda Ken McIntyre, Billy Higgins

2002   Steve Lacy returns to America, taking a teaching position at New England Conservatory. A social worker in Atlanta finds Henry Grimes living in L.A. and coaxes him back into performing. Byard Lancaster's arrest for performing on a corner in Philadelphia brings the plight of street musicians to public attention.
Albums: Derek Bailey's *Ballads* and *Pieces for Guitar*, *3 Pianos* by Beresford/Weston/ Thomas, Daniel Carter's *Language*, *Splay* by Jim Black's AlasNoAxis, *Seasoning the Greens* by Bill Cole's Untempered Ensemble, Jeff Gauthier's *Mask*, *The Hands of Caravaggio* by MIMEO and John Tilbury, Dave Holland's *What Goes Around*, Andrea Neumann's *Innenklavier*, *Wrapped Islands* by Polwechsel and Fennesz, David Eyges's *Wood* and *Sky*, *Black Water* by Vijay Iyer and Rudresh Mahanthappa, William Parker's *Bob's Pink Cadillac* and *Raining on the Moon*, *Freedom in Fragments* by Rova with Fred Frith, Steve Lacy's *Work*, *The Year of the Elephant* by Wadada Leo Smith's Golden Quartet, Matthew Shipp's *Nu Bop*, *Free Jazz Classics, Volumes 1 and 2* by the Vandermark 5, *Double or Nothing* by Aaly Trio and DKV Trio
Deaths: Peter Kowald, Wilber Morris, Mal Waldron

2003   The city of Berlin announces that it is canceling supporting funds for the Total Music Meeting. Joseph Jarman returns to the Art Ensemble of Chicago. Tim Mulvenna leaves the Vandermark 5; Tim Daisy steps in as drummer. After Michael Dorf leaves the Knitting Factory company, the New York venue ceases most of its jazz bookings.
Albums: Art Ensemble's *Tribute to Lester* and *The Meeting*, Thomas Borgmann's *Cooler Suite*, Vijay Iyer's *Blood Sutra* and *In What Language?*, *Positive Knowledge Live in New York*, Elliott Sharp's *The Velocity of Hue*, Grachan Moncur III 3-CD boxed set from Mosaic Select, Roswell Rudd's *MaliCool*
Deaths: Frank Lowe, Peter Niklas Wilson

A

AACM (Association for the Advancement of Creative Musicians): a loose aggregation of players founded in Chicago, Illinois, in 1965 by pianist Muhal Richard Abrams as a workshop for development of new ideas in jazz and modern black music. The cooperative was the first organization of its kind to develop a distinct vision and mission statement for its members and the community. The AACM artists were notorious for stretching the boundaries of music beyond the groundwork laid by Coltrane and Coleman, developing patterns of controlled chaos, exploring myriad possibilities of collective improvisation, and pushing their instruments to new peaks of range and sound.

In 1961, Abrams, dissatisfied with jazz's ostensible lack of meaningful evolution, founded his Experimental Band, a sadly unrecorded project that explored group interaction in unstructured musical environments. Abrams taught composition and used the Experimental Band as a rehearsal group to test out students' talents and ideas. From the Experimental Band's essence, the AACM was established with a lucid agenda for promoting personal, social, and spiritual growth and education among its members and the community. Among the group's initial contributors were saxophonist/composers Anthony Braxton, Henry Threadgill, and Kalaparusha Maurice McIntyre, trumpeters Leo Smith, Lester Bowie, and Bill Brimfield, drummers Steve McCall and Jack DeJohnette, violinist Leroy Jenkins, pianist Jodie Christian, composer Phil Cohran, and members of the soon-to-be Art Ensemble of Chicago.

The organization has provided social and musical training to inner-city disadvantaged youth for decades now, ensuring the continuation of its legacy among future generations. The AACM's mission statement, intact since its inception, reflects its commitment to supporting and encouraging the community as well as the performers within it. The group's specific goals are to cultivate young musicians and create music of a high artistic level via programs designed to magnify creative music; to conceive an atmosphere conducive to artistic endeavors for the artistically inclined; to provide free training in the arts for disadvantaged urban youth; to encourage new sources of employment for musicians; to set an example of high moral standards for musicians and uplift the image of creative performers; to increase the level of respect between creative musicians and musical tradespersons; to uphold the traditions of cultured musicians as handed down from the past; to stimulate spiritual growth in musicians; and to assist other complementary charitable organizations.

Through the vision of Bob Koester, owner of the Delmark record label and Jazz Record Mart, the AACM artists were able to put their musical creations onto vinyl and market them to the mass jazz audience. In 1966, seeing the rich creative potential within the music, Koester and producer Chuck Nessa documented an ecstatic performance by saxophonist Roscoe Mitchell. *Sound* (1966, Delmark), the first AACM session ever recorded, provided a telling documentation of the city's new music scene. The group plays with more energy and abandon than even Coltrane and Coleman's groups in the same period. On "Ornette," drummer Alvin Fielder provides a fairly steady foundation for the other players to explore at will, while Mitchell's alto tears fistfuls out of the musical fabric with high-velocity runs and squeals. "The Little Suite" sets a pattern that would later typify the Art Ensemble, mixing various musical styles that at first glance would seem mutually exclusive. In the case of this track, harmonica and scratchy noises like a creaky rocking chair convey the initial impression of a slow, hot day on an Appalachian front porch. High, loud note flurries might recall a fly buzzing around one's head. A staccato motif for trumpet, flute, and bass comes forth, terminating in buzzy horn sounds, rattles, a cartoony flourish. An exotic march follows with Bowie leading the parade. Without warning, a period of fierce, free playing erupts, then scale running on recorder and bass. A similar schizophrenia reigns for the remainder of the ten-minute cut. The title piece, broken on CD into two tracks instead of the originally issued composite, is a landmark of improvised music. Once the plaintive theme is completed, hardly a "traditional" sound is to be found coming from the horns. Often it is hard to determine who is playing what, as cat meows, death rattles, wolf howls, and chatters fly about. The album is a textbook example of how to use tone color and embouchure to affect music's emotional content. This is not about melody and harmony; this is about *sound*.

Other significant recordings further outlined the AACM's bold vision: Joseph Jarman's *Song For* (1966); Abrams's *Levels and Degrees of Light* (1966), featuring singer Penelope Taylor and the debut of Anthony Braxton; Braxton's own *Three Compositions of New Jazz* (1968); McIntyre's *Humility in the Light of Creator* (1969). These landmarks illustrate not only the eclecticism of the AACM's members but their emphasis on democracy and group interaction. Though some performers might play more forcefully or dynamically than others, no one is more or less important to the collective concept than anyone else. The Chicago sound was a force unto itself.

The AACM's principles and practices are still alive and well in the new century, thanks to the activities of older performers like Fred Anderson and younger lions like drummer Kahil El'Zabar and tenorman Ed Wilkerson. Anderson, an original AACM member, is one of Chicago's highest profile free jazzmen. El'Zabar leads the Ethnic Heritage Ensemble, which has included Wilkerson, trombonist Joseph Bowie, and saxophonist Ernest Dawkins, who leads his own New Horizons Ensemble. These and other performers continue to carry the AACM's banner as free music continues to grow and develop within the city.

Aaltonen, Juhani (b. Kouvola, Finland, 12 December 1935): reeds player. Aaltonen is one of Europe's veteran jazzmen, having played in bop and dance bands since the late 1950s. He studied flute at Sibelius Academy in the 1960s before coming to Berklee in Boston for a dose of jazz. He fell under the spell of Coltrane there, then returned to a studio job in Finland, excited about the possibilities of free jazz. Aaltonen also explored a fusion of jazz, rock, and folk, which made for a satisfying partnership with Edward Vesala, a like-minded drummer who became his regular employer (*Nan Madol*, 1974, ECM). Aaltonen maintained the fusion angle with Eero Koivistoinen, Wigwam, and Tasavallan Presidentti, played big band jazz with Thad Jones and Mel Lewis, and issued his debut, *Etiquette* (Love), as a leader in 1974. He has also performed with Peter Brötzmann, the New Music Orchestra in Helsinki, the Nordic All-Stars, Arild Andersen, and the UFO Big Band. In the 1980s, the Finnish government gave Aaltonen a fifteen-year grant that enabled him to pursue his musical interests more independently.

Aaly Trio: Scandinavian free trio, consisting of saxophonist Mats Gustafsson, bassist Peter Jansson, and drummer Kjell Nordeson. They have collaborated on several occasions with saxophonist Ken Vandermark and have recorded albums for the Okkadisk (*Stumble*, 1998, with Vandermark), Silkheart, and Wobbly Rail labels. The name is derived from a track by the Art Ensemble of Chicago, "Lebert Aaly," which is itself a near anagram of Albert Ayler's name.

Aardvark Orchestra: large ensemble led by pianist Mark Harvey since 1972. Based in Cambridge, Massachusetts, the group is one of the more successful big bands to work in free territories. Among its members are trumpeter Greg Kelley, reedmen Arni Cheatham and Brad Jones, and tubaist/trombonist Bill Lowe (*The Seeker*, 2000, Leo).

Abdullah, Ahmed (b. New York, NY, 10 May 1947): trumpeter and bandleader. An admirable and free-spirited hornman, Abdullah came to prominence in the New York lofts and worked with Marion Brown, Arthur Blythe, Sun Ra, and Charles Brackeen, among others. He has led the Solomonic Quintet since the late 1980s. His album *Live at Ali's Alley* (1978), recorded at Rashied Ali's loft, was the first album released on the Cadence Jazz label. As of this writing, Abdullah is heading up Diaspora with Cody Moffett, Alex Blake, Masujaa, and Carlos Ward.

Abe, Kaoru (b. 1949, Japan; d. 9 September 1978): alto saxophonist. Abe was a groundbreaker in Japanese improvised music who died before he could see the eventual fruits of his labor. His solo work and collaborations with Masayuki "JoJo" Takayanagi and Toshinori Kondo in the 1970s set the standard for his improvising countrymen who followed. Abe was a power player in the vein of Ayler, whose unfortunate penchant for spreading out to other instruments Abe also inherited; the guitar and harmonica on his later, drug-fueled works were about as appealing as Ayler's bagpipe chanters. He and his wife, writer Suzuki Izumi, are the subjects of the film *Endless Waltz*. Abe's talents are perhaps best represented on CD by the fine *Aida's Call*

(1999, Starlight), *Trio 1970* (1995, PSF), and albums issued under Takayanagi's name. He can also be heard on Derek Bailey's Japanese project *Duo & Trio Improvisations* (rec. 1978; issued 1989, DIW) and Milford Graves's *Meditation Among Us* (rec. 1997; issued 2003, Kitty).

Abrams, Muhal Richard (b. Chicago, IL, 9 September 1930): pianist, bandleader, and composer. Abrams was one of the "second wave" pioneers of free jazz; his early Experimental Band was perhaps the most significant free group after the units of Coleman and Taylor. Abrams is fluent in all the dialects of jazz piano, from stride to bebop to the avant-garde; he has also performed and recorded on soprano and alto clarinets.

Abrams studied piano as a teenager, continuing his education at Chicago Musical College. By age nineteen, he was a professional pianist and arranger, joining drummer Walter Perkins's group MJT+3 in 1957 and performing with tenor saxophonist Eddie Harris. During that time, Abrams also wrote charts for saxman King Fleming and was a first-call backup pianist for musicians visiting Chicago.

Inspired by the free jazz movement in New York City, Abrams formed his own Experimental Band in 1961 and began adding to the free vocabulary. In 1965, that group evolved into the Association for the Advancement of Creative Musicians (AACM; see entry), a collective dedicated both to exploring creative music and educating inner-city youth in the arts. As the president of the AACM, Abrams was a beloved teacher to subsequent giants in free music, including Anthony Braxton and the members of the Art Ensemble of Chicago. He was the ideal mentor for Chicago's improvisers: a socially conscious, consummately professional black musician with a soul-deep well of creativity. His methods, patience, and focus were the key to the future success of innumerable musicians. Abrams has likewise been recognized as a composer with a flair for working free space into seemingly rigid structures.

Abrams's recorded debut was the seminal *Levels and Degrees of Light* (1966), the third AACM release on Delmark. Each of the three tracks features different personnel, among them Anthony Braxton, Kalaparusha Maurice McIntyre, Thurman Barker, Leroy Jenkins, vibraphonist Gordon Emmanuel, singer Penelope Taylor, and poet David Moore. "The Bird Song" is a twenty-three-minute exercise in extremes, with Moore reciting deliberate-metered verses about birds, winter, and "brothers imprisoned in chicken wire," followed by hard silence. "My Thoughts Are My Future—Now and Forever" includes a protracted vocal statement of its title, which recalls Sun Ra's lyrical creations. *Levels and Degrees of Light* is an exhilarating experience, representative of the AACM's wide palette of artistic objectives, and it was a most auspicious debut for Abrams.

Abrams's follow-up was *Young in Heart, Wise in Time* (1969, Delmark). The first track features Abrams's majestic solo piano scaling the spectrum of jazz history from stride (a key influence on his personal style) up to the avant-garde. *Things to Come From Those Now Gone* (1972, Delmark) is closer to the spirit of *Levels and Degrees* in its variety. Opening with a duet for Abrams's piano and Wallace McMillan's flute, the disc cycles through many moods, from Euro-avant to high-pressure freebop.

Sightsong (1975, Black Saint) is a different animal entirely, a duet collection with bassist Malachi Favors. Dedicated to bebop figures like tenorman Johnny Griffin and bassist Wilbur Ware, the tracks are packed with a firm sensation of swing and blues that sets the date apart from the partners' usual offerings. *Lifea Blinec* (1978, Novus) is a strong quintet date with Joseph Jarman and Douglas Ewart on various reeds, Amina Claudine Myers on piano and percussion, and Barker. Most performers have vocal spots as well. *Spiral—Live at Montreux 1978* (Novus) is one of Abrams's best solo efforts, on which he uses a number of sound production techniques. He clusters fistfuls of notes together á la Cecil Taylor, reaches inside the piano to pluck the strings like a giant harp, and delves into lopsided stride and blues.

Abrams's long association with the Italian label Black Saint has resulted in some of his most enduring dates. *Spihumonesty* (1979) is a surprising adventure with Myers, Roscoe Mitchell, George Lewis, bassist Leonard Jones, vocalist Jay Clayton, and Yousef Yancy on the howling theremin. *Mama and Daddy* (1980) features one of Abrams's better large ensembles. Better yet is *Blues Forever* (1981), with an expanded group and several more tunes. Abrams pays homage to Ellington and Sun Ra in appropriate measure, bowing to the big band tradition while moving it ever forward. A larger ensemble yet recorded *Rejoicing with the Light* in 1983. One of Abrams's most abiding efforts, this album crackles with jubilant energy and gospel sensibilities. By turns uplifting and contemplative, Abrams's works show off the respectable talents of each and every band member; no one is a mere supporting player here, even if no solo turn is granted. Abrams's expansion of the big-band concept through democracy is inspirational.

Subsequent recordings by Abrams have had their ups and downs: the satisfying if rather dodgy septet disc *View from Within* (1984); the ever-shifting lineups on *Colors in Thirty-Third* (1986); the inclusion of jazz whistler Joel Brandon on the exciting *Blu Blu Blu* (1990, all on Black Saint). Whatever the setting, Abrams's all-encompassing love of jazz's history is reflected in his dense but likable compositions. *Family Talk* (1993, Black Saint) is a sextet session that sounds like an orchestra, thanks to the master's arranging skills and Jack Walrath's trumpet prowess. *Song for All* (1997, Black Saint) is a more recent triumph.

Acta: label established in 1988 by John Butcher, Phil Durrant, and John Russell. The roster has included free and structured improvisers and other new music performers. The label carried one of the last records of the Spontaneous Music Ensemble, as well as many albums featuring Butcher and Chris Burn.

Adams, George (b. Covington, GA, 29 April 1940; d. New York, NY, 14 November 1992): tenorman and flautist. An incredible improviser, Adams was inspired by the pre-bebop styles of Ben Webster and Paul Gonsalves, and the free playing of John Coltrane and Albert Ayler. He was notable as a sideman with Charles Mingus and Gil Evans, and for his 1980s quartet with two former Mingus mates, pianist Don Pullen and drummer Dannie Richmond. As a college student in Atlanta, Adams was instructed by reedman Wayman Carver, a former sideman of Benny Carter and Chick Webb. He moved to Cleveland, Ohio, to continue his studies, working in various organ trios. After moving to New York in 1968, Adams worked for several years at a time with major players such as drummers Roy Haynes and Art Blakey, Mingus, Evans,

and pianist McCoy Tyner. In 1979, Adams, Richmond, and Pullen formed their acclaimed quartet with bassist Cameron Brown (*Live at the Village Vanguard, Vol. 1* and
Vol. 2, 1983, Soul Note). Adams continued with the quartet and occasional side
projects like Phalanx until his death at age fifty-two.

Adams, Steve (b. Rockville Center, NY, 1952): reeds player. A graduate of the Boston
School of Contemporary Music, Adams is one of the most estimable saxophonists on
the West Coast. He has collaborated with Vinny Golia (*Circular Logic*, 1998, Nine
Winds), Cecil Taylor, Sam Rivers, John Zorn, Dave Holland, Anthony Braxton, Ken
Filiano, and the avant-rock group Birdsongs of the Mesozoic, as well as composing
for the California Shakespeare Festival. Adams has been a member of Composers in
Red Sneakers, Your Neighborhood Saxophone Quartet, and Graham Connah's Sour
Note Seven, but his most visible gig has been with Rova, where he replaced Andrew
Voigt in 1988. He has taught music at North Shore Community College, Governor
Dummer Academy, and the School of Contemporary Music.

Air: free jazz trio, founded in 1971 when Columbia College in Chicago commissioned
reedman Henry Threadgill to arrange the music of Scott Joplin for a theater production. Threadgill enlisted bassist Fred Hopkins and drummer Steve McCall to perform
the music; this trio, which was then called Reflection, broke up the following year.
McCall spent over a year in Europe, returning to New York in 1975. He joined again
with his trio-mates, and the band took on the name Air. The saxophonist has a knack
for making even the most abstruse tunes unforgettable. Hopkins's incredible fluidity
is a stringed counterpart of McCall's effortless drumkit maneuvers, all in equal partnership with the quixotic reedman. Air was one of the most consistently democratic
groups in jazz and, after the Art Ensemble of Chicago, this trio was the next most
significant offshoot of the AACM. Besides alto sax and flute, Threadgill also performed on hubkaphone and hubkawall, large percussion instruments made of discarded
hubcaps. The degenerate doo-dads were as close as Air came to using "little instruments" in the usual AACM fashion, but they fit the bill.
    Recorded in September 1975, *Air Song* (India Navigation) was the trio's debut.
Threadgill traded horns on each of the four tracks, and the amount of vitality and
flooding sound emitted by the three musicians set listeners on their ears. The trio soon
had the opportunity to tour widely, so they made the rounds of America, Europe, and
Japan, signifying that the AACM ideal did not rest solely upon the Art Ensemble's
shoulders. Upon their return to the United States, the members of Air settled in New
York City and became involved in the burgeoning loft-jazz scene.
    The following year brought *Live Air* (1976, Black Saint), a step up in Threadgill's
composing and the trio's interaction. "Portrait of Leo Smith" and "Eulogy for Charles
Clark" acknowledge their friendship and appreciation of fellow AACM members.
Air Raid (1976, India Navigation), recorded in July, adds further textures: musette
(a French double reed) on the title piece and the clanking hubkaphone.
    Air Time was recorded for Nessa in 1977, several years after Roscoe Mitchell's Art
Ensemble debuted on the imprint. The resulting music was less shocking but no less

creative, with Threadgill adding the bass flute to his arsenal. *Live at Montreux 1978* (Arista/Novus) is an excellent document of their live prowess a few years along. The trio members' interactions were nothing less than telepathic throughout this fine session.

On *Air Lore* (1979, Arista/Novus), the group's most popular album, Air moved back to its roots in a way by interpreting two compositions each by Jelly Roll Morton and Scott Joplin. Their transmogrification of ragtime piano music in a pianoless, avant-garde mold was an astonishing wake-up call to the jazz purists who considered the older forms of jazz to be timeless, static museum pieces. The way too short *Air Mail* (Black Saint, 1980) signaled a return to Threadgill's original compositions, and the undersung *80 Below '82* (1982, Antilles) straddled both fences by wedging an anarchistic rendition of Morton's "Chicago Breakdown" in with three originals. The blues content was left fairly well intact on the latter album; perhaps their trip to yesteryear led the trio to reevaluate the importance of prior jazz developments.

The Antilles disc was the swansong for Steve McCall, who returned home to Chicago in late 1982. He was replaced by Pheeroan Ak Laff, an equally capable but significantly different drummer who gave the trio a less subtle grounding. Threadgill and Hopkins felt the personnel shift was meaningful enough to warrant a name change, so the trio became New Air. The next album, *New Air: Live at the Montreux Int'l Jazz Festival* (1983, Black Saint), speaks to the difficult switch Hopkins had to make. Interacting with McCall had become second nature for the bassist, and he had a difficult time settling into a groove alongside Ak Laff's seething animation.

Threadgill himself may have been growing tired of the trio's limitations by the mid-1980s. In between Air albums, he had been involved in sessions with David Murray's octet and his own sextet and septet, garnering critical acclaim for those larger ensembles. *Air Show No. 1* (1987, Black Saint) is noteworthy not only as the final recording of the premier free-jazz trio but as the debut recording of vocalist Cassandra Wilson, now a major star in her own right. Wilson managed to integrate herself ably into Threadgill's difficult but danceable material, writing lyrics for some tracks and improvising wordlessly on "Side Step." Hopkins is clearly over his mental block; his vibrant intro to "Don't Drink . . ." ranks among his best work with the group. Ak Laff is in similarly tight form.

In 1988, Ak Laff departed New Air, and Cecil Taylor veteran Andrew Cyrille took over for a handful of live concerts. Cyrille never recorded with the group, however, and shortly after his arrival, the concept of Air was put on indefinite hold.

Ak Laff, Pheeroan (Paul Maddox; b. Detroit, MI, 27 January 1955): drummer. Early in his career, Ak Laff played with vibraphonist Jay Hoggard, then in Leo Smith's group New Dalta Akhri. He performed off and on for several years with altoist Oliver Lake in both a trio and the reggae-flavored ensemble Jump Up. He further developed his subtly powerful sense of rhythm with pianist Anthony Davis in his quartet and the group Episteme. In 1982, after tenures with pianist Amina Claudine Myers and trumpeter Baikida Carroll, Ak Laff replaced Steve McCall in Air, where he remained until 1985. He has since worked as both a leader (*Global Mantras*, 1998, Modern Masters, with Lake and Carroll) and a capable sideman.

Akchoté, Noël (b. 1968): guitarist, the titular heir to Raymond Boni's free-guitar throne in France. Since the 1990s, Akchoté has become one of the most innovative voices in the electrified avant-garde. He still seems wet behind the ears at times, letting the thrill of technical execution replace tasteful consideration, but his potential and talent are inarguable. A sense of twentieth-century avant-garde techniques seasons Akchoté's recordings, especially *Soundpage(s)* (1993, Deux Z), on which he improvises as inspired by a collection of television soundbites. The leader tries to assimilate his generation's popular culture as Willem Breuker does with older folk motifs, updating Charles Ives for the new millennium. Akchoté displays a love of Ornette Coleman on *Lust Corner* (1998, Winter & Winter), duos with visionary guitarists Eugene Chadbourne and Marc Ribot. Akchoté is a perfect partner, equally balanced, never falling behind or squeezing out his cohorts. Thus far, he has recorded two related solo albums, *Alike Joseph* (2000) and *Simple Joseph* (2001, both Rectangle), with electronic enhancements to produce dialogues with himself.

Ali, Rashied (Robert Patterson Jr.; b. Philadelphia, PA, 1 July 1935): free drummer. Ali gained renown as John Coltrane's rhythmic foil in the tenorman's last few years. He studied at the Granoff School in Philly and worked in R&B and jazz ensembles, including a period with Sonny Rollins. In 1963, Ali moved to New York City and became involved with free jazz, performing with Albert Ayler, Sun Ra, Pharoah Sanders, and others. Elvin Jones, Coltrane's most acclaimed drummer, influenced him, and through his association with Sanders, he managed to replace Jones in Coltrane's band in 1965. Ali helped drive the tenorman's exciting free explorations until his death in 1967, including the fascinating final duo *Interstellar Space* (1967, Impulse).

Ali joined pianist Alice Coltrane for a time, then led his own groups. He became an activist for musicians' rights, helping to organize the 1972 New York Musicians' Festival. Ali established his own record label, Survival, and operated the loft Ali's Alley from 1973 to 1979. The 1973 album *Duo Exchange* (Survival; reissued 2000, Knit Classics) with tenorist Frank Lowe powerfully documents their respective talents. With Milford Graves and Andrew Cyrille, Ali performed in the concert series "Dialogue of the Drums." *Moon Flight* (1975, Survival; reissued 1999, Knit Classics) contains strong quartet and quintet performances. In the 1980s, Ali was less visible in the public eye, though he made some appearances with Phalanx. Over the last decade, he has emerged with the band Prima Materia, playing new interpretations of music by Coltrane and Ayler.

Allen, Geri (b. Pontiac, MI, 12 June 1957): pianist and composer. Allen studied under trumpeter Marcus Belgrave at Cass Technical High School in Detroit, then continued her education at Howard University and the University of Pittsburgh. After some side studies with bebop pianist Kenny Barron, Allen began her career in earnest. Her strong knowledge of jazz history and piano styles has made her an asset in many settings, from her own choice mainstream recordings to edgier fare with Ravi Coltrane, Charlie Haden, Paul Motian, and Steve Coleman's Five Elements. In 1996, Allen became the first pianist in four decades to record with Ornette Coleman, resulting in the pair of *Sound Museum* discs (Harmolodic/Verve). She is married to mainstream jazz trumpeter Wallace Roney.

Allen, Marshall (b. Louisville, KY, 25 May 1924): multireedman, one of Sun Ra's trinity of saxophone giants. Allen worked with pianist Art Simmons in Paris for a period, then toured Europe with bop tenorist James Moody. He relocated to Chicago in 1951, where he met Ra and joined the first incarnation of the Arkestra in 1956. Along with John Gilmore and Pat Patrick, Allen headed up the front line for Ra's outlandish "space music" for over three decades. He performed on alto sax, flute, piccolo, percussion, kora, oboe, bassoon, and other instruments during his tenure with Ra. (See entry for Sun Ra.) Since the bandleader's death, Allen has led the Arkestra and performed as a sideman, notably with guitarist Trey Anastasio's project Surrender to the Air and drummer Lou Grassi's PoBand.

Altena, Maarten (Van Regteren) (b. Amsterdam, Netherlands, 22 January 1943): bassist and composer. Altena honed his craft at the Sweelinck Conservatory from 1961 to 1967, becoming involved with free music during that time. He has since been at the forefront of European free jazz, performing with Steve Lacy, Derek Bailey, Burton Greene, the Instant Composers Pool, and many others. Altena made a particularly stellar contribution to Marion Brown's classic album *Porto Novo* (1967, Arista/Freedom). Since 1975, Altena has led his own ensembles and toured worldwide as a soloist. He founded the Claxon label in 1977, and in 1978 received the Dutch National Jazz Prize. In the 1990s, he led an ensemble devoted to performing interpretations of classical and new music, from John Dowland to Brian Eno. A remarkable composer and arranger, his recordings, like *Rif* (1987) and *Cities & Streets* (1995, both HatHut), show Altena's gift for using particular ensemble configurations to the best advantage.

Alterations: British quartet of keyboardist Steve Beresford, guitarist Peter Cusack, bassist/hornman David Toop, and percussionist Terry Day, founded in 1977. Like the Art Ensemble of Chicago and Day's prior ensemble the People Band, each member performed on various instruments during the course of his shows. Wildly postmodern in blending jazz, rock, avant-garde, and ethnic elements, the band endured until 1986 and is best represented by *Live* (2000, Intuitive), which collects three 1980s concert tracks.

Altschul, Barry (b. New York, NY, 6 January 1943): drummer. His rhythmic and stylistic sensibilities have led to his music being dubbed "freebop." As a youth, Altschul was initially self-taught on drums. He studied with Charli Persip as a teenager, and in 1964, he began his fruitful relationship with pianist Paul Bley. He joined the Jazz Composers Guild in that same year and remained after its metamorphosis into the Jazz Composers Orchestra Association, with which he performed until 1968. In 1970, he joined the influential group Circle with Chick Corea, Anthony Braxton, and Dave

Holland. Two years later, Circle disbanded, but Altschul remained associated with Holland. He played with Braxton and Sam Rivers on Holland's important album *Conference of the Birds* (1972, ECM), then performed with both saxophonists' bands from 1974 onward. Since 1978, he has taught drumming and has occasionally led his own dates, starting with *You Can't Name Your Own Tune* (1977, Muse). *Brahma* (1980, Sackville) is one of Altschul's best, a searing trio with trombonist Ray Anderson and bassist Mark Helias; "Con Alma de Noche" is priceless.

Amalgam: see **Watts, Trevor**.

Ambarchi, Oren (b. Sydney, Australia, 1969): guitarist. Like Keith Rowe, with whom he has duetted, Ambarchi is a noise experimenter who pulls unthinkable sounds from his instrument. He began as a drummer, absorbing free jazz as delivered by John and Alice Coltrane. Attending an Orthodox Jewish school in New York was a dream come true because it put Ambarchi right in the free-jazz cauldron. Fellow Jew John Zorn became an inspiration, as were avant composers like Alvin Lucier, but it was Keiji Haino's guitaristics that convinced Ambarchi to switch instruments.

    After a couple of years, he returned to Australia and formed the noise-punk band Phlegm. Zorn remembered the young man and invited him to perform at the 1993 Radical Jewish Culture Festival. Ambarchi also signed with Zorn's record label, Tzadik, and recorded *The Alter Rebbe's Nigun* (1999) with Phlegm drummer Robbie Avenaim. The guitarist recorded *Insulation* (Touch) that same year, and it became popular in the British electroacoustic realm. He teaches improvisation at the University of Sydney. Ambarchi has recorded with Günter Müller and Voice Crack (2003, Audiosphere), Taku Sugimoto, and turntablist Martin Ng.

America: French-based label that specialized in reissues of American jazz recordings. Besides a long list of quality blues and mainstream jazz albums, America also issued records of various quality by the Art Ensemble of Chicago, Archie Shepp, Anthony Braxton, Jacques Coursil, Albert Ayler, Paul Bley, Clifford Thornton, and Frank Wright.

AMM: free improvisation ensemble. Formed in 1965, roughly the same time as the Spontaneous Music Ensemble, the English group evolved from the free-jazz trio of tenor saxophonist Lou Gare, guitarist Keith Rowe, and drummer Eddie Prévost. Gare and Rowe had been members of pianist Mike Westbrook's progressive band, performing an exotic meld of jazz, cabaret, classical, and stage music. When former Westbrook bassist Lawrence Sheaff joined his friends and Prévost, the kernel of AMM was formed. Their explorations were more related to the academic avant-garde than the music created by the British free-jazz community, relying upon unusual devices like transistor radios and tabletop guitars as sources of sounds and inspirational direction. The meaning of the enigmatic name has been widely speculated upon, with guesses ranging from "Avant-garde Music Machine" to "Ain't Making Money" to the ammeter used to measure electrical power levels.

In 1966, cellist, pianist, and composer Cornelius Cardew joined AMM after the members had participated in a performance of his graphic composition "Treatise." The lineup of Cardew, Rowe, Prévost, Gare, and Sheaff cut its first album, *AMMMusic 1966* (Matchless/RER), in that year. The disc's soundscape included transmissions and feedback from transistor radios and Rowe's howling, scratching electric guitar, along with Cardew's thundering free piano. On "Ailantus Glandulosa," the radios, tuned to talk shows and ethnic programs, are turned on and off at intervals to offer a sort of disembodied commentary on Gare's honking tenor and the ever-seething drums. This is unimaginably difficult music to listen to on the first few tries; not even the strangest sci-fi soundtrack could prepare unsuspecting listeners for the experience. But once the scary novelty of absent melody and massive noise wears off, it becomes easier to get absorbed in the nuances and variations occurring within. Sheaff retired from music shortly thereafter and was replaced by percussionist Christopher Hobbs, but the others remained together until 1972, when Cardew also departed.

The Crypt: 12th June 1968, The Complete Session (1968, Matchless) is a gravelly masterwork consisting of (on CD) three spacious selections, with Gare providing the barest threads of jazz sensibility. The two longest tracks couldn't be more different from each other: one industrially intense, the other more along the lines of kitchen music, with open spaces and restraint to the point of near inaudibility. The third piece dances in the middle ground between quietness and crunch.

Keith Rowe took a brief hiatus from AMM in the mid-1970s, leaving Prévost and Gare to function as a duo dubbed AMM II. *To Hear and Back Again* (1974, Matchless) is the pair's sole record, and the absence of Rowe's skronking guitar leaves Gare to follow his jazz roots with a bit more liberty. In his ability to pull out decidedly non-saxophonic sounds, Gare is reminiscent of the Art Ensemble of Chicago's hornmen. That said, this album is nothing like Roscoe Mitchell's *Sound*, or Coltrane's sparring with Rashied Ali on *Interstellar Space*; the European agenda is written all over it, especially during quieter passages. Gare's violin offers a fresh change of pace. Gare and Prévost also worked with Evan Parker and the London Musicians' Cooperative before the saxophonist left in 1976, after a brief reunion with Rowe.

It had been an ordinary enough day in Pueblo, Colorado (1980, Japo/ECM) is by the Rowe/Prévost duo, billed as AMM III. The spare combination of guitar and drums results in surprisingly dense textures, and the music is perpetually more melodic than the first disc (a relative judgment, of course); credit Rowe's skill in manipulating his instruments for maximum effect. On "Radio Activity," Prévost uses a violin bow on the edges of his cymbals to produce unearthly overtones while Rowe plays two guitars at once, presenting wildly overdriven tones above a low drone from a motorized propeller striking his tabletop guitar. "Spittlefield's Slide" puts Prévost out front for a long, technical solo augmented by Rowe's percussive muted picking. "For A" features further guitar trickery: a metal bar inserted between the strings of the tabletop instrument is jostled up and down to create an unsettling siren-like effect, while Rowe blasts metallic riffs with his second guitar.

After AMM's second duo phase, pianist John Tilbury came in to make the unit a permanent trio. A disciple of Morton Feldman, Tilbury was well attuned to the "contemporary classical" avant-garde, leading AMM further away from a palpable spirit of free jazz. *Generative Themes* (1983, Matchless) features their new arrival on prepared piano, tossing his credentials onto the desk right away.

Subsequent recordings by AMM are increasingly more difficult to describe in print, given their absolutely unique content. *Combine + Laminates + Treatise '84* (1984, Matchless) includes a fine rendition of Cardew's graphic opus "Treatise" along with a longer improvisation. Cellist Rohan de Saram, of the Arditti String Quartet, joined the band for *The Inexhaustible Document* (1987, Matchless), giving the music a more classical character. *IRMA* (1988, Matchless) is the score for a Tom Phillips opera, uniting AMM with Phil Minton and saxophonist Lol Coxhill for one of the best surprises in their discography. Gare returned briefly in 1990 for a concert captured on *The Nameless Uncarved Block* (Matchless), marking another slide toward more "traditional" free jazz for the unit. On *Fine* (2001, Matchless), a strange accompaniment for a dancer, Prévost alters his attack to concentrate on bowing, rubbing, and scratching at his drumkit while Tilbury waxes melodic. The remainder of AMM's recordings is pretty much of a piece, each with refreshing shocks to the system in store.

Laminal (1996, Matchless) is an important addition to the group's catalog: three discs chronicling three live performances at different phases in the group's development. The AACM, Sun Ra, and kitchen music butt heads on the first show, on which Cardew, Hobbs, and Prévost stir up a dazzling array of percussive textures. The other two concerts are by the Tilbury/Rowe/Prévost trio.

Aside from AMM, its members have all been active in other projects; see individual entries for Prévost, Rowe, and Tilbury.

Andersen, Arild (b. Lilleström, Norway, 27 October 1945): bassist. Andersen is a staple of sessions on the ECM label, having served as both sideman and leader since the mid-1970s. Along with several of his countrymen, Andersen studied modal jazz theory with George Russell as a young man. In 1968, he met Don Cherry at the Molde Festival and appeared on Cherry's world-jazz album *Eternal Rhythm* (Saba) that same year. A long string of lucrative gigs followed: longtime partner Jan Garbarek, Sonny Rollins, Stan Getz, Sam Rivers, vocalists Radka Toneff and Karin Krog. In the 1980s, he leaned toward fusion with drummer Alphonse Mouzon's group. His quintet Masqualero, co-led by drummer Jon Christensen, was a major force in Norwegian jazz in the 1980s.

Anderson, Fred (Jr.; b. Monroe, LA, 22 March 1929): tenor saxophonist. Anderson was a founding member, in 1965, of the Creative Jazz Ensemble and of the Association for the Advancement of Creative Musicians (AACM), working as a leader and sideman with other AACM artists. He played a pivotal role on Joseph Jarman's 1966 album *Song For* (Delmark), an early document of the organization's visions. Since then, he has mentored many creative musicians, fulfilling the AACM's musical education agenda. Anderson's playing style conveys a good sense of jazz history, carrying on the disparate influences of Coleman Hawkins, Lester Young, and Ornette Coleman. Douglas Ewart, Hamid Drake, and Billy Brimfield have been especially promising partners. Anderson owns and performs at the Velvet Lounge, a popular venue in

Chicago. Unfortunately, there are comparatively few recordings of Anderson available, especially from the period of 1980 to 1993, when he remained quite active as a live performer. *Birdhouse* (1995, Okkadisk) and *The Milwaukee Tapes, Vol. 1* (rec. 1980, issued 2000, Unheard Music) are among the best of his recent output; Hamid Drake shines on both outings.

Anderson, Ray (b. Chicago, IL, 16 October 1952): trombonist. Anderson is one of the finest trombone players in jazz today, combining a crystal-clear tone with a strong sense of adventure and humor. He was once afflicted with Bell's palsy, a mild facial paralysis, but this did not hinder his abilities as a top-notch musician. He has built upon Albert Mangelsdorff's style of multiphonic playing, producing chords through the trombone by vocalizing.

Anderson grew up with AACM trombonist George Lewis and played in jazz and funk groups while in school. During a short, valuable residency in California, he performed with tenorist Keshavan Maslak and drummers Charles Moffett and Stanley Crouch. In 1972, he moved to New York, performing with Maslak, Lewis, and pianist Anthony Davis. In 1977, he met Barry Altschul in Anthony Braxton's artful quartet and began long associations with both the drummer and reedman. His tenure with Braxton's quartet from 1978 to 1981, and his prior activities in the New York loft scene, gave him deeper insight into the possibilities of creative music.

Anderson has also performed with Roscoe Mitchell, Leo Smith, pianist George Gruntz, and tenorist Bennie Wallace, and has made several colorful albums as a leader beginning with *Harrisburg Half-Life* (1980, Moers). In the 1980s, Anderson led the vital funk-jazz group Slickaphonics, which emphasized his use of electronic enhancements and multiphonics. He built a highly empathic rapport there with bassist Mark Helias, and they have continued their partnership in the trio BassDrumBone with drummer Gerry Hemingway (*Right Down Your Alley*, 1984, Soul Note). Anderson also leads a quartet, the Wishbone Ensemble (quartet plus violin and percussion), his electric Alligatory Band, and the Bonified Big Band.

Aoki, Tatsu (b. Tokyo, Japan, 1959): bassist. Aoki, a resident of Chicago since 1978 and graduate of the city's Art Institute, has assimilated elements of both traditional Japanese music and AACM conceptions into his style. He is a favorite sideman of Fred Anderson (*On the Run*, 2001, Delmark) and pianist Bradley Parker-Sparrow, and leads ensembles like Healing Force and Tri-Color. Aoki has recorded more than a dozen recordings under his own name, including a half-dozen discs of solo bass improvisations. In 1998, Aoki recorded a collection of duets with Malachi Favors (2×4, Southport), demonstrating their individual but compatible approaches. He founded the Chicago Asian-American Jazz Festival in 1996 and is the president of Asian Improv Records.

Arc: label created by British alto saxophonist Trevor Watts in 1982, following the folding up of A Records. Arc's releases have included albums by Watts's groups Amalgam, Moiré Music, and the Drum Orchestra.

Arista: New York–based label, founded in 1974 by Clive Davis. The label featured a wide range of jazz performers, from Anthony Braxton's free-art music to the pop fusion of the Brecker Brothers. The company's two subsidiary labels were particularly important to free jazz. Arista-Freedom did occasional new releases but mostly specialized in reissues of sessions on Freedom, Polydor, Black Lion, and other European labels. Arista/Novus issued new sessions by Henry Threadgill (with and without Air), Muhal Richard Abrams, John Scofield, and others. From 1975 to 1985, the company held the rights to the old Savoy label's catalog, finally selling it off to Muse. Steve Backer was Arista's major producer for most sessions; he carried the Novus imprint with him to RCA after leaving Arista. The label has stopped issuing new material but has continued its reissue program.

Art Ensemble of Chicago: free-jazz ensemble, born out of the AACM. In 1967, Chuck Nessa, an employee of the Delmark record label, which had broken the AACM's music out to the public, established his own label to release new albums by Roscoe Mitchell and Lester Bowie. At the time, Mitchell worked in a quartet with Bowie, Malachi Favors, and drummer Philip Wilson. Beginning in May 1967, they recorded several sessions for Nessa's eponymous label that made listeners stand up and take serious notice of just what was happening in Chicago. *Numbers 1 and 2* (1967) was released under Bowie's name, and *Congliptious* (1968) under Mitchell's. *Old/Quartet* (1975, all Nessa) documented rehearsals by the band during that same period. The collective congealed quickly due to the members' intuitiveness and individual listening capabilities, and they were active in this format for about a year until Wilson left to tour with Paul Butterfield's Blues Band.

A limited-edition boxed set *The Art Ensemble 1967/68* (1993, Nessa) collects previously released tracks and outtakes from all the above sessions. The comprehensive five-disc package provides a convenient look at the evolution of this legendary community of friends and artists. The tracks, which date from May 18, 1967, to March 11, 1968, also document the impact of the several personnel changes that occurred. The set begins with a series of theme statements by the quartet, starting with a slow, mysterious dirge that Bowie soon takes over. It is almost classical in its austere structure, but that ends as the music falls downstairs to land humorously on its tail. Mitchell's "Old" is a rather slow jazz tune with a definite swing rhythm, colored in various places by Bowie's muted burbling. A magnificent solo immediately, permanently establishes the trumpeter's identity as a unique force. Mitchell's subsequent alto solo is just as unusual in a different way, restrained despite his high-range squeals and fragmented idea chains. "Tatas-Matoes," Bowie's tribute to the James Brown band, is represented in rehearsal and studio forms; in both cases, the pivot point is Favors's vibrant, fluid bass work. "Quartet No. 1" is a twenty-two-minute exercise in extremes, which begins at the quietest possible volume. The title is ironic, as the musicians seem to spend as much time playing separately as together. Favors inaugurates the half-hour "Quartet No. 2" with focused bass strumming, revealing himself as a force to be reckoned with on the instrument. Clicks, clacks, and whistles flit around as Favors conjures spirits; these give way to slide whistles, pounded tambourines, and melodic snippets from Bowie. Melodicas, birdcalls, tribal drums, staccato trumpet, and gentle sax mooings ensue. These improvisations reward close listening, the only way to pick up on the true subtleties of the group's intuition. "Number 1" is a long trio improv, which is focused on long tones, the horns egged on by gong splashes and each other. After an animated free-for-all, Bowie, Mitchell, and Favors interact in rigid staccato, then spread out into more drone permutations.

In this period, August 1967, Wilson left the group and was replaced by Joseph Jarman. Though it is highly unorthodox to replace a drummer with a saxophonist, within the democratic context of this group it made a trivial difference: Jarman was as rhythmic as Wilson had been melodic, and traditional ensemble roles had little place here, anyway. Though Thurman Barker was an exceedingly capable drummer, on parts of this boxed set he did not have the same kind of hold-your-own egalitarian mindset that had made Philip Wilson such an asset on earlier sessions. Robert Crowder was even more of a traditionalist, but on Mitchell's jaunty "Carefree," the dance track "Tatas-Matoes," and the occasional martial sections of "Congliptious/Old," his firmness is a definite plus. The latter is a gem in the Art Ensemble canon: fire-engine sirens, roaring bass sax, splashy cymbals, ballad sections, and all the sparse "little instruments" that signified the Ensemble and the AACM at large. Also of interest are the solo features on disc five. Perhaps the one track that best sums up the Art Ensemble aesthetic is Bowie's "Jazz Death?" After he poses the question, "Is jazz, as we know it, dead?" Bowie romps through the full compass of trumpet sounds, from bugle calls to Dixieland, Ziggy Elman swing, and avant-garde blare. He finally kills the question by replying, "That all depends on what you know," and we sense the nudge-nudge, wink-wink in his voice.

Jarman suffered two grievous emotional blows when two of his closest friends passed away within about a year of each other. Pianist Christopher Gaddy died in March 1968 of heart disease, and Charles Clark, one of the most beloved young AACM members, suffered a cerebral hemorrhage in April 1969. Their passings cemented the saxophonist's decision to join the Art Ensemble full-time instead of continuing his own pursuits. In 1969, he and the other members relocated to Paris to exercise their artistic fancies in a more accepting and better paying environment. During their stay in Europe, they recorded an astonishing eleven albums for various labels, cut three film scores, and obtained both a fifth permanent member and a permanent name. In a billboard for a particular concert, the ad artist referred to the group as "The Art Ensemble of Chicago" instead of "The Roscoe Mitchell Art Ensemble." That new appellation stuck, ironically, since they had left Chicago in frustration and would not return home for two years.

As mentioned earlier, one of the immediate defining characteristics of the Art Ensemble was its use of "little instruments" for textural and sound effects. Little instruments became a signature feature of AACM projects, none more so than the Art Ensemble. Gongs, drums, bicycle horns, whistles, African and Asian percussions, banjos, folk instruments, and steel drums found a role of some sort in the group's conception, all cycled through seemingly at random as the situation called for them. The Art Ensemble's first Parisian album, *Reese and the Smooth Ones* (1969, BYG) is one very long performance with an overwhelming emphasis on those small sounds. The music is episodic, shifting in mood and momentum like turned pages in a thriller. Dynamic fluctuations, open spaces, overblowing, and multiphonics are principal attributes. In a similar vein is *People in Sorrow* (1969, Nessa), another long work that changes almost imperceptibly in dynamics over forty minutes until it reaches an unbearable roar.

The Paris Session (1972, Arista) is a two-disc album recorded in June 1969 and originally issued in part on *Tutankhamun* (1969, Black Lion). There is a heavy emphasis on theater, particularly vocalizations and disembodied narrative, on this date. *A Jackson in Your House* has recently been paired with *Message to Our Folks* (both 1969, BYG) on the long-awaited Charly Records reissue. The first session, recorded in Paris in June 1969, was dedicated to the memory of Charles Clark; "Song for Charles" is Mitchell's tender tribute to the bassist, and Favors is nicely featured. Jarman recites his arcane poetry on "Ericka": "Mother once freaked on acid, father of the new frontier, becomes the maiden London, Hiroshima's cry. . . ." *Message to Our Folks* was taped in August 1969 and is similar in nature. On "Old Time Religion," a faux preacher exhorts his three-man congregation to spiritual awakening in a heady call-and-response. Charlie Parker's "Dexterity" is one of the very few bebop classics the Art Ensemble ever attempted, and it fares pretty well at a slightly relaxed tempo. "Rock Out" is a real oddity, a parody of hippie-rock with Jarman on electric guitar, Favors on poofy-toned Fender bass, and the others on various drums. The closing piece, "A Brain for the Seine," is a long, disturbing pageant of shifting moods.

The absence of a consistent drummer did not generally affect the Art Ensemble, since each member played various rhythmic instruments besides their principals. Eventually, however, the chance came to hire another spiritual brother to round out the group's sound. Drummer Famoudou Don Moye, a native of Rochester, New York, met the others in 1970 while playing in Rome with Steve Lacy. After a few rehearsals, the men decided that Moye was the perfect candidate for the fickle rhythm seat. Moye was billed as playing "sun percussion," a convenient blanket term for his simply staggering array of world drums and musical devices. Moye's first AEC project was the soundtrack to the French film *Les Stances á Sophie* (1969, Nessa). Bowie's wife, soul singer Fontella Bass ("Rescue Me"), was featured prominently on the centerpiece, "Théme de Yoyo." Moye adds a vital strength to the ensemble sound while still freeing the other musicians to perform on whichever devices they choose.

The AEC returned to America in 1971, where they planned to perform solely for festivals, workshops, and profitably sized concerts while each member developed a solo career. The strategy was inspired by that of Ornette Coleman a decade before; the Art Ensemble clearly expected to be treated according to its true musical merits instead of the whims of corrupt club owners. It gave its first post-return concert at Mandel Hall in its titular hometown. *Live at Mandel Hall* (1972, Delmark) documents the seventy-four-minute set, divided into four interconnected sections. Don Moye was officially welcomed into the fold by the appreciative crowd, particularly for holding his own in the humorous street-march section. Visuals and stage presence played as big a part in the AEC's live shows as the music; a recording could not adequately capture the full picture. The African face paint and clothing worn by Moye, Jarman, and Favors contrasted strikingly with Bowie's own favored garment, a white lab coat, and Mitchell's straightforward attire. As part of their cultural outreach, the drummer and bassist assumed African-inspired names, becoming Famoudou Don Moye and Malachi Favors Maghostut, respectively.

That welcome-home date was followed by *Bap-Tizum* (1972, Atlantic), the first of two excellent discs the band recorded for the major label. This disc was recorded live at the Ann Arbor, Michigan, Blues and Jazz Festival. The album cover bears the words "Great Black Music," the AEC's official motto (appended later with "Ancient to the Future," indicating that it embraced the fullness of African American musical creativity). The disc is rich with the band's typical DJ-choking titles. The primeval snarls, grunts, and hums of "Immm" remind the audience that this is not their average bebop repertory company. There are no horns present yet, only percussion and voices in French, African dialects, and babble. The horns come out for "Unanka," setting up an increasing drone leading to plaintive tones of fragile beauty. The honking, soaring tenor sax, probably played by Jarman, recalls the spiritual bent of John Coltrane. "Odwalla," the group's prowling theme, closes the session with baritone and bass saxes on the front line. As difficult as the big horns are to swing, Jarman and Mitchell make swift work of the tune. This significant festival appearance proved to America that the Art Ensemble of Chicago meant business.

The Art Ensemble's second and last (for then) Atlantic recording was *Fanfare for the Warriors* (1974), on which Muhal Richard Abrams joined the others on piano. One of their most important works, "Nonaah," is a violently hiccupping Mitchell piece with difficult unison passages. Mitchell has frequently revisited the piece in live AEC shows, often as a solo spotlight for his flute or alto sax. The title track is not really a fanfare, but rather a stentorian announcement of the heroes' arrival, as choppy sax passages soar into mania for all players.

After being dumped by Atlantic, the Art Ensemble traded off with a few more labels: Paula, Prestige, Black Lion, even its own AECO imprint. Finally, it landed a contract with ECM, which resulted in some of its most enduring recordings. *Nice Guys* (1978), its debut on the label, represents a turning point in its vision. The ECM approach to record production was letter-perfect for its subtle dynamic range, able to capture the tiniest breaths through horns or tame the fiercest roars.

Full Force (1980, ECM), which contains a few more glances over the historical shoulder, demonstrates that acknowledging past influences does not mean belly flopping into their restrictions. "Charlie M," Bowie's tribute to Charles Mingus, begins appropriately with the growling Ducal trumpet that inspired the bassist. "Magg Zelma" is one of Favors's conceptions, visited time and again in other settings. At the session's end, "Full Force" returns the ensemble to improv mode with a cavalcade of bassoon, piccolo, and Bowie's quintessentially personal trumpeting.

The two-disc *Urban Bushmen* (1982, ECM) captures the band live in Munich in 1980. The set is not well recorded, almost bootleg quality, but it holds excellent moments by all the performers. The title of *The Third Decade* (1985, ECM) refers to the AACM's entering its third decade of service to the community. Several elements make this recording unique in its discography. "Prayer for Jimbo Kwesi" is unusual for having a synthesizer as principal voice; it is a captivating cyclical piece. "Funky AECO" is odd due to Favors's heavy-handed electric funk vamp. The spirit of James Brown rears its head again. "Walking in the Moonlight," composed by Roscoe Mitchell's father, is delivered as a sort of drunken lovers' stroll. The first half of the title piece is a sharp percussion feature reminiscent of an urban kid's step routine; the second half liquefies into roaring sirens, gong splashes, blasts of traffic noise. If it was intended as a premonition of what the AACM's third decade would bring, it was a dire portent indeed.

After its heyday with ECM, the Art Ensemble continued to find regular work but faced artistic crises. Collaborations with African drummers (*Art Ensemble of Soweto*, 1989, DIW) and Cecil Taylor (*Thelonious Sphere Monk: Dreaming of the Masters, Vol. 2*, 1992, DIW) were not as successful as hoped for. By 1989, a sense of going through the motions prevailed; on *Alternate Express* (DIW) from that year, only the long jam "Kush" reaches the group's previous heights of sonic dynamism. In 1992, Jarman left the group and music altogether for a time to concentrate on his Buddhist dojo in Brooklyn. The void was deeply felt, but the quartet motored on.

Coming Home Jamaica (1998, a return to Atlantic) was recorded in that island nation in the summer of 1995. The junket was financed by the Odwalla Juice Company, whose name was inspired by the AEC's theme song. The rendition of "Odwalla" here is anything but inspired, however. The highest point is Bowie's entertaining "Grape Escape." The bass feature "Malachi" goes on for too long—not even Favors's wizardry can resuscitate it—and the faux island grooves of "Lotta Colada" and "Strawberry Mango" (the latter with Bahnamous Bowie on keyboards) are lackadaisical at best. Still in all, there is some freshness to be found within. A better value is the 2002 reissue on the French label Birdology, which adds three previously unreleased tracks.

Lester Bowie's death from liver cancer in August of 1999 was a miserable loss for the AEC. The group's efforts as a trio have rung hollow, the promise of the concept spent now that their most recognizable voice is gone. *Naked* (2000, DIW), resurrecting material recorded by the full quintet in the 1980s, provides a bittersweet memory of the Art Ensemble's former power. *Zero Sun No Point* (2001, Leo), the last AEC disc to feature Bowie, is a dreadful radio-play collaboration with German multi-instrumentalist Hartmut Geerken. This strange, badly edited production features quotes from Sun Ra, Ezra Pound, and Antonin Artaud. Poorly received by critics, the album could have put more nails into the group's coffin. After Bowie's passing, Jarman returned to make the Art Ensemble a quartet once more, but the death of Malachi Favors in February 2004 may have dealt the final blow. Its last two recordings, both good, were *Tribute to Lester* (2003, ECM), by the Mitchell/Favors/Moye trio, and *The Meeting* (2003, Pi) with the full quartet.

Artists House: the name of Ornette Coleman's loft on Prince Street in New York; also a record label founded in 1977 by John Snyder. Over the course of two years, the label released less than a dozen recordings of both free and mainstream jazz, all high-quality sessions. Among the artists featured were Coleman, guitarists James Blood Ulmer and Jim Hall, and altoist Paul Desmond. The label permitted its artists free reign over all aspects of the albums, from artwork to production, including full rights to the music.

Association for the Advancement of Creative Musicians: see **AACM**.

Atlantic: record company and label, founded in 1947 by Herb Abramson and Ahmet Ertegun. Started initially as a race-music imprint, by the 1950s it had become principally a jazz label. In 1953, Abramson was replaced by producer Jerry Wexler, a significant change that resulted in huge commercial success. Ahmet's brother Nesuhi, who became the company's A&R director in 1955, was responsible for the signing of more adventurous jazz artists like Charles Mingus, Lennie Tristano, Lee Konitz, and the Modern Jazz Quartet. In the late 1950s and early 1960s, Atlantic became a vital force in the free-jazz scene, signing both John Coltrane and Ornette Coleman. Coleman's album *Free Jazz*, the first truly major document of the new music, was recorded for the label. By 1966, Atlantic's jazz interest had waned and a subsidiary label, Vortex, was founded for new jazz releases. In 1967, however, that label was sold to Warner Brothers, and the Ertegun brothers returned the jazz contingent to Atlantic. Since the 1990s, the label has engaged in a vigorous reissue program, including boxed sets of Coltrane, Coleman, Les McCann, Rahsaan Roland Kirk, and other major jazz artists.

Aum Fidelity: label, founded in December 1996 by producer Steven Joerg after his departure from the Homestead label. The imprint's name is derived not only from the mystical Hindu mantra, the sound that spoke the universe into creation, but from the title of Charles Mingus's album *Mingus Ah Um* (itself a pun upon Latin conjugations); the label was called Ah-Um Fidelity on its first singles. Its excellent roster includes the David S. Ware Quartet (*Wisdom of Uncertainty*, 1997), William Parker's Little Huey Creative Music Orchestra (*Mayor of Punkville*, 2000), and Joe Morris (*Soul Search* with Mat Maneri, 2000).

Available Jelly: European collective. The group's members have included reedmen Stuart Curtis, Michael Moore, and Barry Block; trumpeter Jimmy Sernesky; trombonist Gregg Moore; and percussionist Michael Vatcher. Their album *Monuments* (1993, Ramboy) is a good document of their intricate and witty music, which like many of the best European improvising cadres, draws from everything from Ornette Coleman to Dixieland, Irving Berlin, and the Balkan States.

Ayler, Albert (b. Cleveland, OH, 13 July 1936; d. New York, NY, between 5 and 25 November 1970): saxophonist and composer. A living contradiction, Ayler was at once one of the most influential and maligned figures of free music, a direct result of his wide-scoped and increasingly strange experiments. Though nurtured in an environment of conventional jazz and gospel, Ayler wrought some of the most unapproachable and frightening performances in jazz history. These were often tempered by moments of rare beauty, but those calms within the storm were usually overlooked in light of his general intensity.

At age seven, Ayler began studying alto sax with his father Edward, a violinist and tenor saxophonist. Edward, staunchly religious and frustrated by his own lack of artistic success, nevertheless encouraged Albert both musically and spiritually for a vicarious satisfaction. The Ayler home was filled night and day with the sounds of jazz, and on Sundays, father and son played together in church. Albert played alto sax and oboe in school, where he also became well known for his golfing prowess. Even as a child, Albert often strayed from the melody in order to see what lay beyond the fence.

As a teenager, Albert studied with Benny Miller at the Cleveland Academy of Music. He worked in various rhythm-and-blues bands around the city, including touring with Little Walter in 1952–1953, but the road-gig lifestyle did not sit well with him at the time. He enrolled in college and began studying Charlie Parker's recordings in depth to try to assimilate some of the alto giant's style. In 1955, Ayler met Parker in person, an inspirational meeting for a young man whom locals were already calling "Little Bird." Albert became so facile in the bebop style that he often warmed up by playing Parker solos backward.

In 1956, Ayler enlisted in the army and continued his musical education while stationed at Fort Knox and later in France. In the service, he met and played with tenor saxophonist Stanley Turrentine, bassist Lewis Worrell, and drummer Beaver Harris, who had been a Negro League baseball player before enlisting. During this time, Ayler switched to the tenor sax, which he felt was better suited for expressing what he felt inside. He also began trying to formulate a new approach to jazz that would speak to listeners on a deeper spiritual level. He was disillusioned by what he saw as the simplicity of bebop's premise and the alienation it had caused among jazz fans. Ironically, in attempting to find a mode of expression that would be more universally appealing, Ayler would soon become one of the most unintentionally divisive figures in jazz.

Worrell joined Ayler in exploring new forms, though they were condemned by fellow musicians. Roscoe Mitchell, later a founder of the Art Ensemble of Chicago, also played with Ayler and drew much inspiration from his ideas. The spiritually emotive sounds that John Coltrane was forging on his records with Miles Davis at that time helped validate Ayler's search. The simple beauty of "La Marsellaise," the French national anthem, had a strong impact on his musical sense. Though he jokingly called the song "La Mayonnaise," he worked it into many live sets and began constructing other tunes around segments of the anthem.

Following his discharge in 1961, Ayler tried to make a go of it in Los Angeles. But, like Coleman before him, he found nothing but stone walls and headaches. He received encouragement from comedian Redd Foxx, of all people, but the West Coast "cool school" simply shut him out. Ayler had equally poor luck in his hometown of Cleveland. Musicians who had once worked with him happily there could just not relate to his new approach. No one saw merit in his union of Coltrane's post-bop style with R&B and spirituals. Albert was then concentrating on soprano sax and was fortunate to gig with Roland Kirk now and then, but most jazz clubs would not welcome him.

Finally fed up, early in 1962 Ayler headed to Sweden, where at least some solid commercial gigs were forthcoming. He led a bebop combo there and was able to experiment more in public, although he still encountered resistance from some club owners. In October of that year, Ayler made his first recordings with two Swedes, bassist Torbjorn Hultcrantz and drummer Sune Spangberg. The trio laid down "Lover Man" "I'll Remember April," "Tune Up," "Good Bait," Ornette Coleman's "Free," and three takes of "Softly As in a Morning Sunrise," among others. The session is notable for the uncomfortable teaming of the straight-playing Swedes and the adventurous Ayler, who blissfully deconstructed all of the melodies in loose rhythms while the bassist and drummer chugged along in the usual bebop style. The saxophonist was already worlds ahead of two players he had been working with for months.

Ayler met Sonny Rollins, Don Cherry, Billy Higgins, and Henry Grimes when Rollins's band toured Europe in 1962. Rollins's recordings had been a major influence on young Ayler, particularly the way he shaped the sound of each individual note for the greatest impact. Ayler found kindred spirits in the band members, jamming with them several times during the tour. Other jazz legends passed through Ayler's circle and expressed their appreciation for his advances: tenormen Don Byas and Dexter Gordon, and pianist Erroll Garner, hardly the type of musicians one would expect to find value in the avant-garde.

Ayler had the fortune to perform in Copenhagen with Cecil Taylor during one of the pianist's tours and sustained his occasional relationship with Taylor after moving to New York in 1963. Ayler was not available when Taylor's band recorded their famous set at the Café Montmartre, but he made his own waves soon enough. He was already beginning to form his radical approaches to rhythm, phrasing, and note articulation when he recorded for a Danish radio program in January 1963. The session was released as his first album, *My Name Is Albert Ayler* (also called *Free Jazz* in some reissues), on the Debut label. The title was an announcement to the world to sit up, listen, and take notice of a radical new voice.

The band that Ayler scraped up for the session was interesting, if not entirely appropriate: drummer Ronnie Gardner was an expatriate American; pianist Niels Brondsted was staunchly traditional and therefore rather limiting; and bassist Niels-Henning Ørsted Pedersen was only sixteen years old, though he had already gained renown for his inventive maturity. "Bye Bye Blackbird" is the most forbidding track due to Ayler's extremely off-pitch soprano sax. Though the approach might have been intended to recall Coltrane's recent experiments with Indian music, the effect is indescribably painful even for those accustomed to free playing. Charlie Parker's "Billie's Bounce" comes off as almost a deliberate parody of the bop legacy that Ayler was trying to toss, and on other tracks the saxophonist is held back by the stiff traditionalism of the other players. That said, it is clear that Gardner and Pedersen made a gallant effort to follow Ayler's unpredictable lead. Not the case with Brondsted, who is thankfully absent from the free improv "C.T." That track is perhaps the most successful, still not a match made in heaven as the rhythmists attempt to lure Ayler in directions for which he rarely bites.

Even in Europe, gigs were rare for Ayler due to his eclectic approach, so he returned briefly to New York in mid-1963. He renewed his acquaintance with Cecil Taylor and joined his quartet with Sunny Murray and Henry Grimes. The group held down a regular gig at the Take Three club and drew in fans like John Coltrane. Ayler began building a solid reputation among musicians as a viable voice. Like most of his contemporaries, he was not able to market his music to the mass jazz audience, yet he kept struggling for his art without compromise.

A fortuitous jam session one night, at which Ayler soloed unaccompanied for twenty minutes, caught the ear of Bernard Stollman, who had established a record label called ESP. Stollman had become interested in the new directions jazz was taking and hoped to find some new blood to document. On the merits of that jam session at the Baby Grand, Ayler became the first performer contracted to ESP. It took well over a year for the contract to bear fruit, so Ayler was forced to retreat to Cleveland for several months. He attempted to sell a few boxfuls of his first album on street corners, and despite his lack of success, Ayler made a powerful impression on local musicians like Frank Wright.

After a while, Ayler moved back to Harlem, living in his aunt's house and making new friends in the music community. He jammed with Ornette Coleman a few times and wrapped up his association with Taylor on good terms, playing a New Year's Eve set at Lincoln Center. In January 1964, Ayler wed a woman named Arlene Benton, a marriage that produced one daughter and lasted a scant two years.

A month after his wedding, Ayler had a record date with several friends who would drift in and out of his bands for the rest of his life. The session, held at the request of the Danish Debut label, resulted in two albums' worth of material. Ayler, Grimes, Murray, and pianist Call Cobbs recorded a set of spirituals, which were declined by both Debut and ESP. Cobbs, a fellow Clevelander, would remain Ayler's most frequent collaborator. The tracks are less than interesting because Ayler does not improvise, and except for his unusual approach to the melodies, these renditions are fairly stagnant. His soprano sax playing is, however, blissfully improved from "Bye Bye Blackbird." These spirituals were eventually issued on *Swing Low, Sweet Spiritual* (Osmosis) in about 1981.

Of much greater interest is the last part of the session, which marks the first documentation of Ayler's own compositions on record. Cobbs was replaced by trumpeter Norman Howard for "Spirits," "Saints," "Witches and Devils," and "Holy, Holy." The latter two also feature second bassist Earle Henderson, an earlier compadre. All the players are well suited to Ayler's methods, working at the extremes of their instruments to match his seething power. Notes cluster into shapes that are not pitch-specific, creating a new sonic architecture.

These four compositions illustrate the folky simplicity that would mark most of Ayler's works, based on diatonic scales like childhood circle songs and nursery rhymes. This bare thematic austerity is probably essential to Ayler's schema, since the band performs so energetically that melodies that are more complicated would quickly collapse. The listeners' ability to relate to the tunes' ultrabasic structures provides a tenuous handhold and enables a deeper appreciation of the performance. Ayler's astonishing signature vibrato, wider than any since Coleman Hawkins's in the 1930s, was now becoming more prominent. These tracks were issued on Debut as *Spirits* (occasionally reissued as *Witches and Devils* on Arista and other labels) in 1964.

Ayler was briefly a member of the Jazz Composers Guild, staying on just long enough to build a bond with bassist Gary Peacock. The two men formed a trio with Sunny Murray, and in June 1964 they performed a set at the Cellar Café that was later released as *Prophecy* (1978, ESP). The set included "Spirits," "Wizard," "Prophecy," and the first recording of one of Ayler's most enduring themes, "Ghosts." Its rhythm is almost martial; one can readily imagine it as a bugle call wafting hauntingly across a battlefield. "Wizard" is barely even a composition, simply a few bars hunkered together, similar to the springboard themes utilized in Coleman's *Free Jazz* and Don Cherry's *Complete Communion*.

That gig was an encouraging warm-up for the July studio date that would become Ayler's first ESP release and the label's first jazz effort, *Spiritual Unity*. The trio revisited "Spirits," "Wizard," and two takes of "Ghosts." It is clear that Ayler was already confident in his vision and the ability of his bandmates to make history by skirting the stale traditions of jazz. Legend has it that the engineer who recorded the session in mono instead of stereo ran out of the booth when the band started playing. The album was a turning point in the development of free jazz, inspiring countless musicians whose interests had first been perked by Coleman or Taylor. "Ghosts" is handled differently from subsequent recordings, with the melody almost secondhand in favor of harmonic exploration. Unfortunately, a full impression of the drumming cannot be gleaned because Murray was badly miked.

Rumors still circulate about dirty business dealings by Bernard Stollman, perhaps fueled by jealous artists who had been unable to get a record deal themselves. Stollman countered that no one could ever have hoped to turn a profit with such an uncommercial offering. Gossip and zero profits aside, there is no arguing that *Spiritual Unity* is one of the most important documents in free jazz. Ayler had been so eager to document his music that money was barely an issue. He was pleased with the final product, viewing it as confirmation that his ideas were practicable.

Ayler's third recording session within one month was the most unusual of all. Michael Snow, a Canadian filmmaker and musician, asked several performers to record a soundtrack around which he would create a movie. Paul Haines, the renowned modern poet, gathered the performers at his loft for the session. Besides the Ayler trio, the ensemble included Don Cherry, Roswell Rudd, and John Tchicai. Combined with Ayler, Peacock, and Murray, the horns became an unstoppable force of frenzied improvisation. The recording and film both ended up being called *New York Eye and Ear Control* (1964, ESP), and the music is incredibly forbidding.

For a while, Art Quartet drummer Milford Graves was added to Ayler's band, pouring more lava out of its jazz volcano. Graves was every bit the innovator that Murray was, experimenting constantly with textures and flow, and the two of them together apparently made Ayler's group a fearsome listen. This quartet inspired John Coltrane to add a second drummer, Rashied Ali, to his own group for better rhythmic density, and Ayler's first records were the inspiration behind Coltrane's *Ascension*. Ayler's personal spiritual searching was also a profound influence upon Trane's last few years of life, as he came to realize that truly effective music conveys what is in the spirit instead of the mind. Coltrane was instrumental in Ayler's signing with Impulse Records, although that association eventually brought about Ayler's artistic downfall.

In September 1964, Ayler's trio was invited to Copenhagen to play several days at the Café Montmartre. The venue manager had apparently remembered Ayler's contributions to Cecil Taylor's group and thought the time was ripe for the saxophonist's return. Despite Stollman's admonitions against it, the trio packed up for Europe and were joined there by Cherry. Between September 3 and November 9, 1964, the band recorded various live and studio sets in Copenhagen and Hilversum, Holland. The sessions included numerous takes on common Ayler themes. The Copenhagen recordings have been reissued under different titles (*Ghosts*, *Vibrations*, *Mothers and Children*) and labels (Debut, Fontana, Arista/Freedom). The Dutch recordings were originally issued as *The Hilversum Sessions* (1964, Osmosis).

As this European tour progressed, the band quickly gelled into an even more promising unit. Murray and Peacock had fully embraced the barely restrained brand of freedom into which Ayler had indoctrinated them, and Cherry turned out to be a surprisingly apt partner. Though Ayler's style was significantly different from what Cherry had experienced with Ornette Coleman, his tenure with Archie Shepp had sufficiently tempered his ears and mind enough to deal with the flaming Ayler. The leader's hybridization of folk, jazz, and avant styles had nearly reached its ideal blend, and his compositional sense had matured to the point that Ayler was creating more complex melodies and arrangements that did not merely get lost in the wash of sound.

Once the tour was over and Cherry and Peacock were back on their own paths, Ayler hired his brother Don to join the band on trumpet. Don Ayler had earned local acclaim as an alto saxophonist, but he learned how to play the trumpet specifically because his brother wanted to re-create the same vibe that Cherry had brought to the band. In May 1965, the brothers played the Village Gate along with Murray, cellist Joel Freedman, and bassist Lewis Worrell. The critics were torn between joy and revulsion. "Holy Ghost" is one of Ayler's strongest statements, as incendiary as John Coltrane's *Ascension* in the hands of a single performer. Don Ayler's trumpet playing is quirky and clearly untrained, and Freedman occasionally sounds out of place. But they contribute as gallantly as possible, supported by the surge-and-drop rhythmic tide.

Next, the band, with Cleveland altoist Charles Tyler in for Freedman, played New York's Town Hall. The same proving ground that made or broke pioneers like Coleman, Mingus, and Taylor, Town Hall seemed to be a key rite of passage for free jazzmen in the movement's early years. Stollman had engineered this gig as a showcase for ESP artists, and Ayler's set resulted in a major controversy. Stollman issued the resulting album, *Bells*, on one side of a colored vinyl disc; the other side was completely smooth. Retailers and buyers screamed fraud, angered that they didn't get what they paid for. A quirk of Ayler's future group performances, the seemingly total reversal of roles between the horns and rhythm section first emerges clearly on the title track. Traditionally in jazz ensembles, the bass and drums provided a solid foundation to support the explorations of the melody instruments. Ayler turned the tables on this practice. In pieces like "Bells," "Our Prayer," and "Ghosts," one or more horns would concentrate on a tightly grounded melodic line while the rhythm players and others were set free to explore. In this performance of "Bells," at least one horn maintains a sense of melody at all times while the other performers, horn or rhythm, improvise around it.

Spirits Rejoice (1965, ESP) was recorded at a Judson Hall showcase. "Angels" marks Call Cobbs's first use of the harpsichord, an element of questionable merit that Ayler nevertheless held onto in later recordings. Worrell was replaced by the double threat of Grimes and Peacock; Tyler, Murray, and Don Ayler rounded out the sextet. The now-typical factors of Ayler's sets are all present: no one improvises on "Holy Family" except Murray, and unison passages abound in other tunes.

After the Judson Hall session, Peacock retired for a time to study Zen Buddhism, leaving Ayler in the lurch for a suitable bass partner. Ayler appeared on Sunny Murray's album, *Sunny's Time Now* (1966, Jihad), then took about three months off to get his head together. After his hiatus, Ayler experimented with Joel Freedman once more in place of a bassist, along with drummer Charles Moffett, but the trial run was apparently unsuccessful. Tempering that headache was Ayler's exciting appearance with Coltrane at a special tenor-sax conclave at Philharmonic Hall. Coltrane's extended ensemble included his wife, Alice, on piano, the Ayler brothers, Pharoah Sanders, Carlos Ward, Jimmy Garrison, and drummers J. C. Moses and Rashied Ali. Among the other headliners were old-school tenor giant Coleman Hawkins and a pair of "modernists," Sonny Rollins and Yusef Lateef. Coltrane's band blew loud and hard on a forty-minute rendition of "My Favorite Things," which by most accounts was the pinnacle of the evening. Sadly, no official recording of Ayler's only performance with Coltrane has ever been issued.

Things started to pick up for Ayler in 1966. He sat in with pianist Burton Greene's group, performed at Leroi Jones's Black Arts Center regularly, and made the rounds of whatever other free gigs he could dig up around the city. Tired of living in Ayler's shadow, Tyler finally quit the band. He was replaced by Michael Sampson, a classically trained white violinist. This move, of course, brought stones down on Ayler's head from the black community, who viewed it as a sellout. The accusations hurt the tenorist, a loving man with barely a racist bone in his body, but he let them slide off his back.

Ayler began to change the organization of his music. While he continued to solo with even more abandon, his improvs became shorter and subservient to more rigidly composed themes. He sometimes connected themes with intercessory improvisations *a la* Coleman's *Free Jazz*, introduced modes into his works, and pieced fragments of tunes together in Ivesian collages. The roiling chaos of his ESP days was tempered by a new spiritual peacefulness, a realization that his emotions could be more accurately expressed with more structure. The tunes he wrote now had greater complexity, with multiple thematic sections arranged almost in suites. All these elements came together in the new musical forms that Ayler felt obliged to offer up to God in exchange for his earthly talents. Still financially supported by his mother and Coltrane, Ayler had a burning desire to connect with the Spirit and get his life together.

In November 1966, Ayler was invited by Joachim-Ernst Berendt to perform at the Berlin Jazz Festival. He assembled a band with Don, Sampson, drummer Beaver Harris, and bassist William Folwell. Harris had been Archie Shepp's drummer for a while; Folwell was an unknown who became an Ayler stalwart. The Berlin offer turned into a European tour with club stops in Paris, London, and Lörrach, Germany. *Lörrach/Paris 1966* (HatHut) indicates that neither Harris nor Folwell seemed comfortable, and since they only soloed briefly, neither player was used to the best advantage. The high point is a cover of Pharoah Sanders's "Japan," featuring excellent (although poorly miked) playing by Sampson. The disc also documents Ayler's first attempt at singing on disc, a disconcerting moaning that recalled Sanders's vocalist partner Leon Thomas, but more primitive and guttural.

The London shows were disastrous; housing problems put the musicians out of communication with the producers, and the near-total absence of improvisation in the set for BBC Television led to the tapes being destroyed in disgust. Harris and the

Ayler brothers stayed with pianist Chris McGregor, a white South African expatriate, and bonded with jazz writer Valerie Wilmer. The musicians finally headed back
to America after being harassed by the British police once too often.

Upon his return Ayler began recording for Impulse, the label that had granted him
a contract on Coltrane's recommendation. Their first set for the label was recorded
live at the Village Vanguard one week before Christmas 1966 (*Albert Ayler in Greenwich Village*), with Coltrane in attendance. The band included the brothers, Sampson,
Harris, Grimes, and Folwell, with Call Cobbs making a guest shot on piano for
"Angels." The group, including a trombonist named either George Schnell or Steele
(depending upon the source), Freedman sitting in for Sampson, and Alan Silva in
for Grimes, also played the Village Theater in February. Ayler played the alto sax for
the first time in years on "For John Coltrane." He had also been experimenting more
with soprano sax and teaching it to his lover and manager, Mary Maria Parks, though
he didn't record on soprano anymore. The orchestrations and performances during
the Village Theater dates are outstanding, making an impact similar to that of Cecil
Taylor's larger units. The weighty presence of Silva and Freedman on the later date
drastically changed the band's sound, adding vivid washes of unexpected color.

Mary Maria has been disparaged at times in the press for having a perceived nega-
tive influence on Ayler, sort of the Yoko Ono of free jazz. These jibes are grossly unfair, as she played a vital role in continually motivating Ayler when he just wanted
to give up. Her love and attention increased the spiritual focus that had already nour-
ished him for years. Through her encouragement, Ayler created a personal concept
of the "universal man," believing that we are all one in the spirit and must therefore
live in peace, harmony, and love.

June 30, 1967, saw Ayler at Newport, his first and last performance at an American jazz festival. Milford Graves replaced Beaver Harris on drums, performing with
Sampson, Folwell, and the brothers. No recordings exist of the show, but word has it
that Ayler and company went over the top in presenting the most solid show possible. It was a high-water mark in Ayler's career, peaking his expectations that he might
finally succeed.

Ayler's joy, however, was short-lived. On July 17, John Coltrane, his friend and
benefactor, died of liver cancer. His passing was not unexpected, and Coltrane re-
quested that Ayler and Ornette Coleman both perform at his funeral, which was attended by over a thousand mourners. Albert, Don, Milford Graves, and bassist Richard
Davis delivered a heart-wrenching performance of "Truth Is Marching In," an Ayler
composition that had been inspired by Coltrane's own music and spirituality. Ayler
is said to have pulled his horn from his mouth and cried out mournfully at first, a
groan of soul-deep anguish, followed later on by a joyous shout symbolizing the ascension of Coltrane's eternal spirit to the hereafter.

Ayler recorded the first session of *Love Cry* (1968, Impulse) one month after
Coltrane's passing. The title track evokes his mentor's classic extended work *A Love
Supreme*, both in the simple melodicism of Ayler's tenor playing and his muezzin-like
chanting. Don Ayler adds some touching counterpoint on trumpet as Silva and Graves
writhe underneath like serpents. The effect is somewhat like a bagpipe lament (in
fact, Ayler used that oddball Celtic instrument in some of his final recordings). The
interaction between the brothers on yet another version of "Ghosts" is almost mili-

tary, with haunting moans out of Silva's bass and near-Caribbean motifs thrown in. Unlike earlier versions, the horns never venture away from the basic theme into improvisation. These two selections in particular provide a telling glimpse at Ayler's spiritual nature and the lifelong preoccupation with life and death that made him so enigmatic. Several tracks feature Call Cobbs's strange electrified harpsichord, novel but never a comfy fit. Silva and Graves are unbelievable, balancing out the unusual elements with a free but firm grounding. Don Ayler, on the other hand, is relegated almost entirely to a supporting role.

As if Coltrane's death wasn't enough of a cross to bear, Ayler faced new pressure from Impulse. The label made an ill-advised decision to pressure the saxophonist into changing his style. His eclecticism was not producing enough sales, so it encouraged him to move into R&B and rock-influenced music. This, no doubt, was the reason for the faddish electrification of Cobbs's harpsichord. Tracks were kept short for the sake of airplay, and Ayler was discouraged from including too many inaccessible factors. Impulse was also responsible for Graves's departure after these sessions, as the label was afraid of his outspoken stance on musicians' rights.

Ayler, to his artistic detriment, acquiesced on most of the label's points. He retreated into depression and performed only twice in 1968. He staged an unusual opera he had composed, about which little is known, and fired his brother from the band. Though this was possibly due to label pressure, Don Ayler contested the idea and claimed that he quit because he disapproved of Mary Maria's influence on Albert. It's clear that Don had a drinking problem by then, which no doubt made matters worse. Following his departure, Don Ayler headed back to Cleveland to clean up physically and psychologically.

Albert Ayler's mental state was also subject to question. He submitted a long, rambling open letter entitled "To Mr. Jones—I Had a Vision" to *Cricket* magazine, edited by Leroi Jones. Ayler described apocalyptic visions, quoted extensively from the Bible, contradicted himself by stating that Elijah Muhammad from the Nation of Islam was God's true prophet, and claimed that God's home was on the planet Venus and that the other planets were only illusions. Ayler was not a drug user, so hallucinogens can hardly be blamed. If nothing else, the letter illustrates the spiritual confusion that had plagued Ayler for years and which was only compounded by Coltrane's death.

September 1968 marked the beginning of the end for Ayler's artistic integrity. Bob Thiele of Impulse talked Ayler into recording a rock-and-roll album, complete with soul vocals and electric bass. *New Grass* was a new low, an abominable effort that put Folwell on bass guitar and funk drummer Bernard "Pretty" Purdie in the rhythm seat. Ayler, Mary Maria, and Rose Marie McCoy provided vocals on some tacky hippie-rock tunes. Mary Maria actually had written the lyrics to some of the songs. Call Cobbs plays harpsichord, piano, and organ, and Ayler uses ocarina and bagpipe chanter in addition to tenor sax. A horn section, with fine jazzmen like trumpeter Joe Newman and tenorman Seldon Powell, was added to several tunes after the fact.

Ayler staunchly maintained that this was the direction he desired to move in, that his radical movement into rock had nothing to do with Impulse. Ayler may have indeed felt that the end was near and that the best way for him to communicate with the audience he hoped to save was to reshape his music into a form they could better appreciate. When all is said and done, however, Impulse Records is still the most logical culprit in Ayler's downfall.

August 1969 saw a slight return to form, although the rock influences were still prominent. *Music is the Healing Force of the Universe* (1969, Impulse) returned Ayler to his blues roots but modernized the influence with the inclusion of Canned Heat guitarist Henry Vestine and Folwell's electric bass. Mary Maria and Ayler again did the vocals; Bobby Few, bassist Stafford James, and drummer Muhammad Ali (brother of Rashied) rounded out the band. They recorded fifteen tracks ranging from fairly straightforward blues tunes to instrumental jazz works that harkened back to Coltrane. The acoustic rhythm section served Ayler well on those latter selections, while Vestine held his own among the twisted blues tunes. The album is definitely not Ayler's shining moment, but it's better than the grotesque R&B of *New Grass*. It stands as his last Impulse album, as the record company soon dropped him like a hot potato.

The tenorman barely found any work at all for almost a year, when he was finally invited to the Fondation Maeght in St. Paul-de-Vence, France. Cecil Taylor's quartet had made a tremendous showing at the venue the prior year, and despite the unequivocal strangeness of Ayler's music, his sets also pleased the audience. Part of this run was documented on the Shandar label as *Nuits de la Fondation Maeght, Volumes 1 and 2* (1970). Mary Maria sang and played soprano sax, Call Cobbs stuck to the piano, and bassist Steve Tintweiss and drummer Allan Blairman stuck out like sore thumbs. Rarely had Ayler encountered such an unsympathetic rhythm section, but his interaction with Cobbs redeemed the shows. Mary Maria's vocals on "Music Is the Healing Force of the Universe" are perfectly complemented by Ayler's gospel-inflected responses on tenor. The saxophonist was at the all-time peak of his form, utilizing overblowing, swoops, and other effects without falling into self-parody (never mind the fact that he wore a dress during one performance). It is a shame that he did not have a more suitable bassist and drummer with whom to interact, as this album shows the promise that Ayler had left in him. The country whose national anthem had been so influential to his musical conceptions was, ironically, the site of his final public performance.

Ayler and the band returned to America that summer. Many friends said that he seemed excited about the prospects for his music. Given that optimism, some dismiss the suggestion that Ayler was suicidal when his body was found floating in New York's East River on November 25, 1970. Others reject the idea that Ayler had gotten on someone's wrong side financially or morally, pointing instead to some police conspiracy or a racist attack. Mary Maria eventually claimed that Albert left the house on November 5, stating that he had to die. She postulated that he probably jumped from the Liberty Island ferry and drowned. Ayler was buried in his hometown of Cleveland, the mother city to which he had continually returned when hard times got the best of him.

Ayler, Donald (b. Cleveland, OH, 5 October 1942): trumpeter, brother of Albert Ayler. Don Ayler was educated at the Cleveland Institute and performed with Charles Tyler as a young man. In 1965, he switched from alto sax to trumpet and began performing with his brother Albert's band, recording such albums as *In Greenwich Village* (on Impulse). He also worked as a sideman with artists like John Coltrane. For most of the 1970s, following his brother's death and his own return to Cleveland, Ayler was only occasionally active as a musician. In the 1980s, Ayler led a septet and began to perform, tour, and record more frequently as both a sideman and leader.

Ayler Records: Swedish label, administered by Jan Ström. Named for the free saxophonist, Ayler specializes in live performances of the hottest variety. Its artist roster is somewhat similar to Eremite's, as its catalog features William Parker, Noah Howard, Jemeel Moondoc, Hamid Drake, and Sunny Murray, in addition to Peter Brötzmann, John Stevens, Axel Dörner, and others.

B

Babkas: Seattle-based trio consisting of alto saxophonist Briggan Krauss, guitarist Brad Shepik (né Schoeppach), and drummer Aaron Alexander. The band's name, resembling the Yiddish word for "nothing," is simply its members' first initials followed by their last initials. Since 1992, they have recorded three albums for Songlines. Babkas's brand of mostly improvised music is intense, passionate, yet often quiet and introspective.

Bailey, Derek (b. Sheffield, England, 29 January 1930): the principal guitarist in European modern improvised music. Most of Bailey's music lacks recognizable "jazz" characteristics. Indeed, in his philosophy of nonidiomatic improvisation, he has deliberately steered away from such ascertainable elements as swing or groove. He owes more to the innovations of Cage and Anton Webern than to Ayler or Coltrane. In fact, *Pieces for Guitar* (2002, Tzadik), a bracing collection of his earliest solo recordings from 1966 to 1967, confirms his fascination with Webern's serialism at that time. Like Anthony Braxton, Bailey has redefined the very nature of music, and his collaborations with established artists of sounder jazz pedigrees have won him broad acclaim. Bailey is the author of *Improvisation: Its Nature and Practice*, the definitive work on spontaneous creativity, which includes interviews with dozens of his key associates.

In the 1950s, Bailey did hold down jobs as a straight-ahead jazz guitarist of some repute. His early ensemble Joseph Holbrooke, with drummer Tony Oxley and bassist Gavin Bryars, began as a fairly mainstream unit. By the group's demise in 1966, however, it was a totally free ensemble working through completely spontaneous means. (See entry for Joseph Holbrooke.) Upon moving to London in that year, Bailey immediately fell in with some local musicians who were pursuing avant-jazz avenues. Evan Parker and John Stevens, in particular, seemed to click with his personal philosophies, and that harmony led to the Spontaneous Music Ensemble (see entry). Bailey also worked with Oxley's sextet, which pursued more grounded improvisations, and the far-out trio Iskra 1903, with Barry Guy and trombonist Paul Rutherford. Bailey's album *The Topography of the Lungs* (1970, Incus), with Parker and Dutch drummer Han Bennink, is an ultrarare classic, more so that the master tapes have apparently been lost.

In 1968, Parker and Bailey formed the Music Improvisation Company with percussionist Jamie Muir and keyboardist Hugh Davies. The MIC marked a bolder step away from jazz traditions than the SME had made thus far, heading toward the more completely nonidiomatic style of which Bailey was the eventual champion. Dissonant and sounding very much of its period, thanks mostly to Davies' contributions, the group's music can be appreciated on the collection *Music Improvisation Company 1968–1971* (1971, Incus).

Iskra 1903 was named for an agitprop newspaper founded by Vladimir Lenin in that year. Communism was a hot ticket in the 1960s (in fact, many improvisers remain staunchly Communist to this day), and the trio's music was as incendiary as Lenin's rhetoric. Rutherford, Guy, and Bailey recorded a scant fistful of tracks, which have been reissued on the 3-CD set *Chapter One 1970–1972* (2000, Emanem). Bailey is the hub around which the others circle, perhaps inevitably so because his conceptions had already advanced beyond traditional ideas. Guy is relentlessly animated, hammering out chords and bowing furiously, while Rutherford's muted trombone and ungainly piano weave the others' threads into ear-catching tapestries. Following this remarkable period, Bailey's spot in Iskra 1903 was taken over by violinist Philipp Wachsmann, radically changing the ensemble's flavor.

On 1971's *Improvisations for Cello and Guitar* (ECM) Bailey teamed with Dave Holland to produce a dark, resonant masterwork. Holland, best known as an outstanding bassist who easily toes the line between freedom and structure, has little trouble jumping off into utter nondetermination à la Bailey. His plucks and scrapes deliciously complement the guitarist's little twangs, flits, and atonal runs. Fans of Holland's mainstream work, even *Conference of the Birds*, would find shocking enlightenment by tuning into this special session.

As deadly serious as Bailey tends to be taken, he often exhibits a more fun-loving side, never more so than in Bennink's company. The album *Derek Bailey and Han Bennink* (1972, Organ of Corti) shows the unpredictability and wit of this odd pairing. Interesting, parallels arise between the drummer's loud, frantic crash-and-burn assaults and Bailey's scampering guitar movements. The duo practically assassinates the spirit of certain standards that serve as jump-off points. *Han* (1988, Incus) documents the old friends' reunion for a series of concerts in 1986. Bailey is uncharacteristically cogent on this record, chording, strumming, and wailing metallically in the wake of Bennink's percussive fury.

In 1973, Bailey attempted to sell his recordings on his own instead of dealing with record stores and labels. He made a series of 1/4-inch reel-to-reel tapes consisting of a series of "Taps," related to his percussive and textural explorations on the guitar. These tapes were Bailey's adjunct to Braxton's *For Alto*, documenting his deliberately individual vocabulary for the guitar. The materials were compiled on *Incus Taps: Solo Guitar 101–104* (2000, Organ of Corti), a fascinating study of his early innovations. Their assaultive dissonance is well removed from the quieter "kitchen music" approach for which he has generally become known. An interview with Bailey about the essence of his concepts is included. The other side of his coin is revealed on *Aida* (1980, Incus), a short, sweet group of three more introspective solo improvisations. There is still power present, but his plectral musings are more restrained, as he reflects upon the attributes of each note. Context and relationships between notes have become key considerations instead of aggressive norm shattering.

In 1976, drawing from the initial experiments of the Music Improvisation Company, Bailey founded the loose collective known simply as Company, a shifting aggregate of players who explore every avenue of the avant-garde. (See the entry for Company.) Bailey has worked with John Zorn, who shares his affection for destroying the traditions of music, on several occasions outside of Company. Zorn's wild-eyed alto screeches and frantic blowing of mouthpieces and birdcalls make for an oddly suitable partnership with Bailey's haywire-machine guitar. *Yankees* (1980, Celluloid) is an essential document of their partnership, teaming Bailey and Zorn with trombonist George Lewis. The music is spare, bizarre, inspired by the New York Yankees' legacy. It is a very difficult record but worth repeated listens. Of similar spirit is *Harras* (1996, Avant), with William Parker instead of Lewis. The bassist casts his magic in ecstatic bowed flurries and vigorous walking. Zorn's noises are more wisely organized, perhaps given sixteen years of maturation, yet Bailey is 100 percent Bailey.

Bailey duets with Steve Lacy on *Outcome* (1983, Potlatch), a combination that pulls new adventurousness out of the prolific soprano saxophonist. Despite their radically different approaches to improvisation, Lacy seems to find reasonable inspiration in Bailey's snaggle-toothed chompings on electric guitar. There is little of the free unity found in the better releases by SME or AMM, but the two men show loving respect for one another while strolling their not quite parallel paths. Guitarist Henry Kaiser is a more suitable partner. Bailey has been a longtime idol of Kaiser's, and the duo date *Wireforks* (1995, Shanachie) was a dream come true for the younger American. This was Bailey's first duet with a guitarist, and he clicks on many levels with the ambitious Kaiser. An empathy immediately arises, with Kaiser catching every nuance of his elder's magic touch but never fearing to lead the way himself. "Safe and Sane" is a misnomer for the closing track; the avalanche of feedback and noise is dangerous, blissfully exciting. Bailey moved further into avant-rock territory on *Saisoro* (1995, Tzadik), a meeting with the Japanese rock duo The Ruins. This union, set up by Zorn, is chillingly strange even given the weirdness of Bailey's output, but it is like a car wreck: somehow, you can't take your eyes, or ears, off of it. Ugly beauty and unpredictable accessibility reign.

Sometime in the 1990s, Bailey developed a fascination for dance beats, particularly the drum 'n' bass genre. He began to habitually improvise along with tracks on a drum 'n' bass radio station and eventually got the idea to make an album of such exercises. On *Guitar, Drums 'n' Bass* (1996, Avant) the beats are provided by DJ Ninj, who is very poorly mixed on the final product. The experiment is not entirely successful; there are periods of silence, as if Bailey was not sure what to do next, and tense excitement when he does lock in with Ninj's fast grooves. *Play Backs* (1998, Bingo) is a greater triumph, with Bailey improvising over prerecorded tracks by other musicians. John French's stone-solid beats on "JF Drums" offer a firm foundation for Bailey to wring the guitar's neck over, while Ko Thein Htay's Burmese percussion instills exotic essences. John Oswald's multitracked snippets of Bailey himself serve as a further proving ground on "JO Complete." Other tracks feature guitarists Kaiser ("HK D&B"), Jim O'Rourke, and Loren MazzaCane Connors, whose mayhem acts as a forum for Bailey to discuss, of all things, what he likes about the name "George."

Throughout his earlier career, Bailey tried to specifically avoid falling into the patterns established by free godfathers like Cecil Taylor and Ornette Coleman. How ironic, then, that on *Mirakle* (2000, Tzadik) he spars with a pair of Prime Time alumni. Times change, conceptions change, and Bailey changes before our very eyes as bassist Jamaaladeen Tacuma and drummer Calvin Weston drag him into the harmolodic funk swamp. The guitarist is still his own man but has a ton of fun with the rhythmists' mighty grooves. Perhaps this serves as another confirmation of the harmolodic concept's universality as preached by Coleman.

Just when one thought Bailey might have run out of surprises, he turned around and did the unthinkable. *Ballads* (2002, Tzadik) is just what you might think: Bailey's interpretations of classic tunes from the traditional jazz canon—"Body and Soul," "You Go to My Head," "Melancholy Baby"! Still, this could be Bailey's greatest miracle yet. He acknowledges the basic theme of each timeless tune before roughly, lovingly reshaping it according to his own vision. We are talking about the godfather of avant guitar, so we cannot expect him to dwell on the melodies for very long. But what a keen surprise to finally hear Derek Bailey address the standards on his own level.

Bang, Billy (William Vincent Walker; b. Mobile, AL, 20 September 1947): violinist and composer. Bang studied violin during his childhood in New York's Spanish Harlem. His professional name also stems from youth; "Billy Bang" was a popular cartoon character. In school, he played as a drummer alongside his friend, folk musician Arlo Guthrie, before returning to the violin. Besides the jazz violinists Ray Nance and Stuff Smith, Ornette Coleman and John Coltrane influenced him. After returning from service in Vietnam, Bang became enraptured with the black and antiwar activism movements and chose to use his talents to express his views toward racism and injustice. In 1972, Bang began playing professionally and studying with Leroy Jenkins, and from 1977 onward he was active as a touring solo artist. That year he performed a concert series at the experimental venue La Mama and founded the String Trio of New York with guitarist James Emery and bassist John Lindberg. Besides the String Trio and his own ensembles, Bang has worked with Sun Ra's Arkestra, Detail, The Group, Ronald Shannon Jackson's Decoding Society, and Bill Laswell's Material. His playing is craggy, abstracted, and emotional, and he performs with a clear sense of swing and understanding of contemporary classical music. *Live at Carlos 1* (1986, Soul Note) is a fine representation of his performance skills.

On *Vietnam: The Aftermath* (2001, Justin Time), Bang comes to terms with his service in the army during that ugly chapter in history. The group includes Frank Lowe, trumpeter Ted Daniel, flautist Sonny Fortune, pianist John Hicks, bassist Curtis Lundy, drummer Michael Carvin, and percussionist Ron Brown. After a taut, suspenseful buildup, the Oriental theme of "Yo! Ho Chi Minh Is in the House" emerges, leading into a percussive, angular solo by the leader. Similar Asian motifs grace other tracks. The album ends with "Saigon Phunk," its disco beat recalling the sort of urban celebration that might have marked a soldier's homecoming in that era.

Bang On A Can Festival: New York festival, inaugurated on Mother's Day in 1987 by composers Michael Gordon, Julia Wolfe, and David Lang. It began as a one-day event on the Lower East Side, with performances of works by Milton Babbitt, Steve Reich, and nineteen other American composers, and has grown into a phenomenon involving educational and multimedia events. Their "house band" is The Bang On A Can All-Stars, including clarinetist Evan Ziporyn (also involved in the Radical Jewish Culture movement), bassist Robert Black, cellists Mark Stewart and Wendy Sutter, pianist Lisa Moore, and drummer David Cossin. Their recordings include *Industry* (1995), *Cheating, Lying, Stealing* (1996, both Sony Classical), and *Renegade Heaven* (2000, Cantaloupe Music).

Baraka, Amiri (Imamu; [Everett] LeRoi Jones; b. Newark, NJ, 7 October 1934): poet and author. Jones was schooled in piano, drums, and trumpet as a youth and has had a lifelong love for jazz. In the 1960s, he became world-famous for his jazz-inspired poetry and writings for such publications as *Jazz Review* and *Down Beat*. In 1963, his book *Blues People* was the first important book about jazz written by a black man. The book, also a significant document of the role of African American music in the nation's culture, garnered him much critical acclaim.

Not long after the publication of *Blues People*, Jones divorced his first wife (a white woman named Hettie), converted to Islam, and took the name Amiri Baraka. Besides occasionally recording with groups like the New York Art Quartet, he continued his efforts as a black cultural activist, establishing the short-lived Black Arts Repertory Theater-School in 1964. After it was closed down a year later, Baraka relocated the school to Newark, New Jersey, and renamed it The Spirit House. Since then, he has continued to be active as a poet, critic, administrator of the Jihad record label, and author of over twenty plays. His second wife, Amina, is also a promising poet. *New Music New Poetry* (1982, India Navigation) is one of his better recordings, in the company of David Murray and Steve McCall.

Barbieri, Leandro "Gato" (b. Rosario, Argentina, 28 November 1934): tenor saxophonist and composer. A clarinetist in his youth, Barbieri learned to play the alto sax in Buenos Aires when he moved there as a teenager. Influenced by Charlie Parker and John Coltrane, Barbieri added a vital bebop flare to composer/pianist Lalo Schifrin's orchestra. He switched to tenor sax and led his own quartet for a time, then relocated to Rome, Italy, in 1962. The next year he joined Don Cherry in Paris (*Gato Barbieri and Don Cherry*, 1965, Inner City) and recorded some of the trumpeter's impressive free-jazz suites. Like many freemen, his debut album was on the ESP label (*In Search of the Mystery*, 1967). *Fenix* (1971, Flying Dutchman) exemplifies his incredible fusion of free jazz and Latin rhythms.

Though he held onto his colossal buzz-saw delivery, Barbieri eventually began to turn away from free jazz in favor of Latin music. He did stay in touch with the free scene for a time, performing with the Jazz Composers Orchestra and Cherry's band. He recorded a fascinating duo collaboration with South African pianist Dollar Brand (*Confluence*, 1968, Arista) and worked with Charlie Haden's Liberation Music Orchestra. His tenure with Haden's group, which performed a good amount of Latin-flavored music, increased Barbieri's desire to return to his roots. Since the 1970s, he has performed mostly in Latin and pop-jazz contexts. In 1972, he composed and performed on the soundtrack for *Last Tango in Paris*, and he became an international star later in the decade with glossily produced albums like *Caliente!* (1976, A&M). His subsequent output has been spotty and definitely populist in character.

Barefield, A. Spencer (b. Detroit, MI, 27 May 1953): guitarist. Barefield is rather unusual in the free-jazz business in that, like James Emery, he concentrates on the acoustic guitar. Rather than being overwhelmed by the potentially high volume of free improvisation, however, Barefield excels at establishing a serious presence in whatever setting he finds himself. A member of the Creative Arts Collective, Barefield has performed with Andrew Cyrille, Richard Davis, Oliver Lake, and most significantly, Roscoe Mitchell since the mid-1970s. He has also recorded a few well-crafted albums of his own (*Live at Nickelsdorf Konfrontationen*, 1984, Sound Aspects).

Barker, Thurman (b. Chicago, IL, 8 January 1948): drummer and percussionist. Barker joined the AACM in Chicago while attending Roosevelt University. He was in on several important early recordings by Muhal Richard Abrams, Joseph Jarman, and the Roscoe Mitchell Art Ensemble, among others. From 1968 to 1980, he found steady work in Chicago pit orchestras while working with Abrams, Anthony Braxton, Sam Rivers, and Maurice McIntyre. Since then he has recorded more widely as a sideman, maintaining his associations with Rivers and Jarman and playing with Amina Claudine Myers, Cecil Taylor, and Pheeroan Ak Laff. *Time Factor* (2001, Uptee Productions) features Barker's impressive quartet with guitarist James Emery, electric bassist Jerome Harris, and pianist/organist Rob Schwimmer.

Baron, Joey (b. Richmond, VA, 26 June 1955): drummer and bandleader. Baron is a sharp observer who taught himself to play drums as a youth. Though he is perhaps best known as a Downtown improviser from John Zorn's circle, Baron's resumé includes jobs with Dizzy Gillespie, Stan Getz, Al Jarreau, Tony Bennett, the Lounge Lizards, the L.A. Philharmonic, and a long stint with guitarist Bill Frisell. He performed with Zorn in both Naked City and Masada and has had a fruitful association with performance artist Laurie Anderson since the late 1980s. He has led his own group, Barondown (heard on *Crackshot*, 1998, Avant), and was in a trio with Marc Ribot and John Medeski.

Barron, Bill (William Jr.; b. Philadelphia, PA, 27 March 1927): tenor and soprano saxophonist, composer, teacher, and bandleader. Barron is the brother of pianist Kenny Barron, and like his sibling, he initially came up in the middle of the bebop movement. Gigs with Jimmy Heath and Red Garland preceded his move to New York, where he briefly fell under the spell of Cecil Taylor. Barron dabbled in free jazz with Taylor and trumpeter Ted Curson but kept a good foot in bebop with Philly Joe Jones's band. He has taught at City College of New York, Wesleyan University, and the Children's Museum of Brooklyn's Jazz Workshop. *Compilation* (2001, Cadence Jazz) documents some of his solid mid-'80s performances at Wesleyan, with Bill Lowe on trombone and tuba, vibist Jay Hoggard, pianist Fred Simmons, bassist Wes Brown, and drummer Ed Blackwell.

Battaglia, Stefano (b. Milan, Italy, 1965): pianist, composer, and bandleader. He took up the piano at age seven and graduated from the Conservatory of Milan in 1984. An outstanding technician, Battaglia is one of Italy's finest jazzmen and is just as respected in classical circles. He performs regularly with Tony Oxley, fellow pianist Enrico Pieranunzi, and the large ensemble Theatrum. Battaglia has recorded two albums of compositions by Bill Evans, one of his principal influences, along with many other discs for the Splasc(h) label (the solo *Life of a Petal*, 1993).

Bauer, Conrad (b. Halle, Germany, 4 July 1943): trombonist and bandleader, the brother of Johannes Bauer. He studied at the Dresden Conservatory and got into out-jazz early with Ernst-Ludwig Petrowsky's band. Exis, formed in 1971, was the first of several free-jazz projects Bauer instigated himself. Since then he has worked with a number of German ensembles, including his present group, Zentralquartett. He has been a favored partner of Derek Bailey, George Lewis, Han Bennink, Peter Kowald, and other freemen. Like many of his associates, Bauer transcends the limitations of his horn to achieve an otherworldly level of performance. He has recorded two albums with his fellow trombonist Nils Wogram for CIMP (*Serious Fun*, 1999, and *Serious Fun + One*, 1999, adding Dominic Duval).

Bauer, Johannes (b. Halle, Germany, 1954): trombonist, brother of Conrad Bauer. From the 1970s, he conducted new music workshops and worked semisteadily as a sideman with East German improvisers. His early recordings on the national Amiga label are now deleted, presumably never to return. He established working relationships with Fred Van Hove (including duo outings), Manfred Schulze, and Jon Rose before joining the growing scene of large improvising ensembles: Globe Unity, the Cecil Taylor European Orchestra, Barry Guy's Now Orchestra, and Tony Oxley's big group, among others. Johannes has often worked with his brother Conny as well, in duo and in the quartet Doppelmoppel. One of his few recordings available as a leader is *Organo Pleno* (1993, FMP). Other recent projects include the Wild Mans Band, Peter Brötzmann's Tentet, and Luc Houtkamp's group.

Bead: London-based record label, founded in the mid-1970s. The catalog includes releases by Evan Parker, Peter Cusack, Marcio Mattos, Philipp Wachsmann, Günter Christmann, Quintet Moderne, and Chris Burn/John Butcher.

Beckett, Harry (Harold Winston; b. St. Michael's Parish, Barbados, 30 May 1935): trumpeter and flügelhornist. Beckett moved from Barbados to Britain in 1954 to work as a professional trumpeter. From 1961 to 1977, he played in a group led by composer Graham Collier, honing his unique, lyrical tone. He also performed with Mike Westbrook, Chris MacGregor's multiracial band Brotherhood of Breath, the London

Jazz Composers Orchestra, and the bands of Tony Oxley, John Surman, and Elton Dean. He was part of Dudu Pukwana's world-jazz group Zila and has been a frequent member of Stan Tracey's Octet since the 1970s. One of his best albums as a leader is *Bremen Concert* (1987, West Wind).

Bendian, Gregg (b. Englewood, NJ, 13 July 1963): percussionist, composer, and bandleader. Like Nels and Alex Cline, with whom he has worked for a couple of decades, Bendian is just as attuned to rock music as he is to jazz. Webern and Varèse also hold a fascination for this versatile percussionist. After attending Rutgers and studying with Steve McCall and Andrew Cyrille, he began immersing himself in the Downtown New York scene. The proximity of Leo Smith, John Zorn, George Lewis, and Bill Frisell inspired Bendian to look further into the possibilities of free improv. Participation in Derek Bailey's Company project was followed by a couple of years with the Cecil Taylor Unit (*In Florescence*, 1989, A&M), one of Bendian's principal goals from his college days. Since then, Bendian has worked with Bailey on several occasions, including *The Sign of Four* (1997, Knitting Factory Works) with guitarist Pat Metheny and drummer Paul Wertico. Other gigs have included playing with William Parker, Evan Parker, and Peter Brötzmann. Bendian leads the electric quartet Interzone, Trio Pianissimo, the Open Aspects Ensemble, and the Mahavishnu Project, the latter a tribute to fusion pioneer John McLaughlin's Mahavishnu Orchestra.

Bennink, Han (b. Zaandam, Netherlands, 17 April 1942): drummer and percussionist. Bennink's musical interests are as wide-ranging as any musician's could conceivably be. He embraces obscure Irving Berlin showtunes and free improvisation with equal relish, and his sense of humor has become the stuff of legend. He can move from head-spinning loudness to feathery subtlety in the blink of an eye and do it all with the music's best interest in mind. His technical prowess is equaled by his innate ability to follow every tiny thread of information that might come from other players in a particular performance. Backstage, he is known to rummage through closets and corners to find objects he might be able to make noise or theater with: PVC pipes, old wooden or cardboard boxes, and discarded stage props. He also performs on clarinet, soprano sax, trombone, and whatever else might be handy.

As a teenager, Bennink learned to play the drums from his father, a professional orchestral percussionist. His brother Peter is a well-respected saxophonist and bagpiper; the two have recorded together on several releases by Instant Composers Pool. Early on, the brothers made the acquaintance of several other Dutch musicians, including Mengelberg. When the influx of American jazzmen to Europe began to take off in the early 1960s, Han was already proficient enough to back those who visited Amsterdam. His performances with the Instant Composers Pool led to meetings with Brötzmann, Alexander von Schlippenbach, Derek Bailey, and other key European improvisers. While his continental compadres worked hard to set their music apart from American jazz styles, Bennink distinguished himself by showing respect for established traditions at the same time as he teasingly subverted them.

The albums issued under Bennink's name tend, as one might imagine, to showcase his unparalleled gifts as an improviser above those of his bandmates. On *Solo*

(1978, FMP), he becomes a virtual one-man band, moving past and through the jazz continuum from Dixieland to the avant-garde. Along the way, he tries out the banjo, trombone, harmonica, clarinet, and viola for short passages, evoking the Art Ensemble of Chicago's continuous instrumental flux. His titanic command of the drum kit is his stock-in-trade, however, and *Solo* will not disappoint fans of the good old skins. The vocalizations he uses in ensemble settings to exhort the players on to new heights serve a more cathartic role in his solo shows, like the pressure valve on a water heater relieving a load of pent-up tensions. *Nerve Beats: 1973* (issued 2000, Atavistic Unheard Music) gives an earlier glimpse at Bennink's solo aesthetic. Typical of his bizarre sense of humor, he wails on clarinet over a mechanical drum-machine beat on the title track. Here, too, Bennink uses trombone, piano, and even didgeridoo as his deficient attention span spins him around the room.

In 1980, Bennink recorded *Jazz Bunker* (Golden Years of New Jazz) with American bizarre-guitar artist Dr. Eugene Chadbourne and trumpeter Toshinori Kondo. Twenty-one years later, guitarist and drummer butted heads once again on *21 Years Later (Train Kept A-Rollin')* (2001, Leo). This show is entirely Chadbourne's, with Bennink in a more conventional drummer's role, an unusual spot for him indeed.

Bennink and Dave Douglas duetted on *Serpentine* (1996, Songlines) five years before Misha Mengelberg's *Four in One* session. This bracing set no doubt prepared them to interact together so flawlessly on the larger group date. A sizzling undercurrent of electricity courses through most selections. A rendition of Ray Noble's "Cherokee" sates Bennink's fascination with American Indian themes (though it is hardly tribal in and of itself). Douglas's deep interest in Eastern musics is manifested in the Hindustani-sounding "Alap," introspective and magnificent. Among Bennink's other worthwhile duets are *Post Improvisation 1: When We're Smilin'* (1999, Incus) with Derek Bailey; the earth-shaking *Dissonant Characters* (1999, HatArt) with Ellery Eskelin; *The Laughing Owl* (2001, Atavistic) with Dutch punk guitarist Terrie Ex; and *The Grass Is Greener* (2002, PSI) with Evan Parker.

Beresford, Steve (b. Wellington, Shropshire, England, 1950): British multi-instrumentalist, versed in piano, organ, trumpet, euphonium, voice, electronics and other instruments. Beresford studied piano from the age of seven and orchestral music in high school. He studied music at York University while playing the organ in a soul cover band. After graduation, he remained in York for a time, performing and promoting free music. Beresford moved to London in 1974, eventually becoming one of the most in-demand studio and concert musicians in the city. He is a popular composer and arranger, receiving many commissions for concert pieces and film, television, and commercial scores. From 1977 to 1986, he was part of Alterations with guitarist Peter Cusack, flautist David Toop, and drummer Terry Day. He was both one of the earliest and latest members of the ever-shifting "ensemble" Company. Beresford has instructed at the Oslo Art Academy, Southampton Institute, and the University of Westminster. On *3 Pianos* (2001, Emanem), Beresford performs in duo and trio configurations with fellow pianists Veryan Weston and Pat Thomas, his cohorts in the London Improvisers Orchestra.

Berger, Karl (Karlhanns; b. Heidelberg, Germany, 30 March 1935): pianist and vibra-phonist. He was educated in classical piano as a child, and after the war, he accom-panied jam sessions with visiting American jazzers including trumpeter Don Ellis and pianist Cedar Walton. In the 1960s, he began playing vibes and listening to free jazz. He studied philosophy and musicology, then joined Don Cherry's quintet in Paris in 1965. Berger can be prominently heard on Cherry's *Symphony for Improvisers* (1966, Blue Note) and *Eternal Rhythm* (1968, Saba). When Cherry wrapped up his U.S. tour in 1966, Berger remained in America to teach and lead his own groups. In 1972, he and Ornette Coleman established the Creative Music Studio in Woodstock, New York, providing an outlet for students' personal musical ideas instead of forcing es-tablished styles upon them. Besides his activities as the director of the Studio, which shut its doors in the mid-1980s but continues as a traveling workshop, Berger has been a guest conductor for international events, toured with his own bands, and performed at percussion festivals. One entertaining recent effort is *No Man Is an Island* (1996, Knitting Factory Works), built upon the poetry of John Donne. Since 1971 Berger has collaborated with vocalist/poet Ingrid Sertso, his partner in the Creative Music Studio.

Bergman, Borah (b. Brooklyn, NY, 13 December 1926): pianist and composer. Of the piano innovators to emerge in the free era, Bergman is certainly possessed of one of the most consistently interesting techniques. He has developed an approach he calls "ambiideation," which refers to the evolvement of two entirely separate streams of ideas in the left and right hands. This double-brained way of thinking lets him cre-ate extraordinary harmonies, Janus-faced melodies, and counterpoints at will, lend-ing him an instantly identifiable sound on an instrument whose limitations can enforce anonymity. His left-hand playing is among the most astoundingly fluid in modern music.

Inspired by bebop greats Bud Powell and Thelonious Monk, Bergman's technique is only barely similar to Cecil Taylor's. He did not take up the piano until the mid-1950s, at which time he dumped the clarinet. His first few albums were solo works (*Upside Down Visions*, 1985, Soul Note, is especially strong), after which he cut some excellent duo sessions with Thomas Chapin, Evan Parker, Roscoe Mitchell, Rashied Ali, and Andrew Cyrille. Since then he has spread himself a little further, exploring trio collaborations (Peter Brötzmann/Thomas Borgmann, Mitchell/Tom Buckner, and Brötzmann/Cyrille) and working with Ivo Perelman.

Berlin Contemporary Jazz Orchestra (BCJO): experimental large ensemble, founded in 1988 by pianist Alexander von Schlippenbach. The BCJO was created to perform and record new works by contemporary jazz composers in Europe (and America, given the inclusion of Carla Bley's works in their repertoire). One year after the demise of the Globe Unity Orchestra, the BCJO played its first concert at radio station RIAS in Berlin, still a strong advocate of the band and its music. The membership was ini-tially drawn from the city limits, but performers from Holland, America, and Japan were quickly assimilated. The BCJO has recorded sporadically thus far but remains active as of this writing.

The Morlocks and Other Pieces (1994, FMP) introduces Japanese pianist/conductor Aki Takase into the BCJO. The album consists of six Schlippenbach compositions, including the magnificent title piece with its plucked-piano ostinato. *Live in Japan, '96* (1998, DIW) melds several other Japanese performers into the BCJO's body. Schlippenbach shares piano duties with Takase, who arranged the opening Eric Dolphy medley of "The Prophet," "Serene," and "Hat and Beard." Takase lovingly reinvents some of Dolphy's most memorable works, and the piano duo alone is worth the price.

Berne, Tim (b. Syracuse, NY, 16 October 1954): saxophonist, composer, and band-leader; one of the most versatile performers in the New York scene today. Berne took up the alto sax in college with the intention of getting involved in R&B. However, once he heard Julius Hemphill, his direction was clear. Berne moved from Oregon to New York to study with Hemphill and ended up managing the elder statesman's career for a time.

In 1979, Berne began recording his own music with a number of prominent or up-and-coming freemen, including John Carter, the Cline brothers, Vinny Golia, and Paul Motian. In 1983, he was contracted to Soul Note; four years and six albums later he moved on to Columbia, becoming one of several free-minded jazzmen who stayed with the label a very short time before being neglected and dumped. Two of his finest recordings, *Fulton Street Maul* (1987) and *Sanctified Dreams* (1988), resulted from the Columbia contract, then Berne moved on to a more fruitful relationship with the German label JMT, where his trio Miniature, with Hank Roberts and Joey Baron, made some appreciable noise.

In 1991, Berne gathered the ensemble Caos Totale, which included Roberts, Mark Dresser, guitarist Marc Ducret, trombonist Steve Swell, and Bobby Previte. He recorded *Diminutive Mysteries (Mostly Hemphill)* (1993, JMT) in tribute to his ailing mentor, then convened the quartet Bloodcount with saxophonist Chris Speed, bassist Michael Formanek, and drummer Jim Black. Bloodcount recorded three live albums with Marc Ducret before JMT folded and the recordings disappeared from print. Berne formed his own label, Screwgun, and began aggressively documenting Bloodcount and other projects. He has led two trios: Paraphrase, with bassist Drew Gress and drummer Tom Rainey, and Big Satan with Rainey and Ducret. Other collaborations include the bands Quicksand, Composure, and Science Friction, duets with Formanek and Roberts, and a guest spot with the Italian jazz ensemble Enten Eller. As might be gathered, Berne is eager to explore any avenues of creative expression, and the results are usually well worth the time. He is one of the stars of the Blue Series currently being issued by Thirsty Ear.

Bernstein, Steven (b. Washington, DC, 8 October 1961): trumpeter. Bernstein is one of the very few exponents of the slide trumpet, actually a soprano trombone. He came up in Downtown New York's ranks as the music director for the Lounge Lizards, followed by a brief tenure with Spanish Fly (with tubaist Marcus Rojas and slide guitarist David Tronzo) and the Kamikaze Ground Crew. Bernstein led and arranged for The Kansas City Band, which had performed in Robert Altman's film *Kansas City* and played on the Verve All Stars Tour. He also arranged the score of *Get Shorty*, for which he received an Oscar nomination. In the late 1990s, Bernstein began leading Sex Mob, now one of the most critically acclaimed units in contemporary jazz. Aside from his own projects, the flexible Bernstein has performed with Carla Bley, Peter Apfelbaum's Hieroglyphics Ensemble, Don Byron, Michael Blake, Tricky, They Might Be Giants, Mel Tormé, and DJ Logic. His humorous, brilliantly executed *Diaspora Soul* (1999, Tzadik) is part of the label's Radical Jewish Culture series.

BIMhuis: Amsterdam performance venue. The facility opened in 1974 as the brainchild of BIM, the Dutch Union of Improvising Musicians, and the Dutch Jazz Foundation. Both Dutch masters, like Willem Breuker and Han Bennink, and key American improvisers such as Sun Ra, Charles Mingus, and Dexter Gordon have graced the BIMhuis stage. Over two hundred concerts per year are staged at the venue, and a record label was inaugurated in 1996. An annual festival, the October Meeting began in 1987 and continues to feature the world's finest improvisers.

Birth: record label founded by Gunter Hampel in 1969. Its releases have almost exclusively been sessions under its founder's name, featuring his blend of free jazz ideas with ethnic musics and other styles.

Bishop, Jeb (b. Raleigh, NC): bassist, guitarist, and trombonist. One of Chicago's most prominent slidemen, Bishop is a first-call technician on trombone, indelibly associated with Ken Vandermark's various projects. After studying at Northwestern in the early 1980s, Bishop played bass with punk and indie-rock bands around Raleigh. He became interested in free jazz during a stay in Belgium, and in 1992, he became the Flying Luttenbachers' bassist. In 1995, he joined Vandermark's quintet, the Vandermark 5, on trombone and occasional guitar. That association opened new doors for Bishop in rock and jazz settings, from Stereolab to John Butcher. In 1998, he began working with Peter Brötzmann's Chicago Tentet. Bishop has recorded with his own trios and duetted with Joe McPhee, Wadada Leo Smith, and others ('98 *Duets*, 1998, Wobbly Rail).

Black Artists Group (BAG): artists' collective, formed in St. Louis, Missouri, in 1968 by drummer Charles "Bobo" Shaw and poet/percussionist Ajule Rutlin. The BAG was modeled after the AACM's example and was intended to provide both an outlet for creative artists around St. Louis and a sense of black cultural awareness within themselves and the community. Besides including musicians, the BAG also included a wealth of poets, actors, sculptors, and painters. Among the initial members were baritone saxophonist Hamiet Bluiett, altoists Oliver Lake and Julius Hemphill, trombonist Joseph Bowie (brother of trumpeter Lester Bowie), and trumpeters Baikida Carroll and Floyd LeFlore.

The BAG conducted concerts and mixed-media events around the city, and its individual members recorded several albums during the Group's too-brief existence. Only one recording, the scarce *Black Artists Group in Paris* (1969, BAG), was issued under the collective's name. A handful of significant subgroups was associated with the collective, including the St. Louis Creative Ensemble, Children of the Sun, and Human Arts Ensemble. The BAG's headquarters contained classrooms, performance and rehearsal spaces, and dormitories.

After several of its key members moved to France around 1972, the BAG stopped receiving grants from the National Endowment for the Arts and the Missouri Arts Council, due in part to suspicions that the BAG's members had radical political ties. A few of the younger members attempted to carry on the project but were eventually forced to disband due to mismanagement. Some remained active in the St. Louis area, while others emigrated to Chicago or New York, where the loft jazz scene was burgeoning. Hemphill, Lake, and Bluiett joined with David Murray in the World Saxophone Quartet, while Joseph Bowie eventually formed the funk-jazz-rock unit Defunkt. Both of those units continue to operate today with altered lineups.

Black, Jim (b. Daly City, CA, 1967): drummer and percussionist. Black is one of the hardest working drummers in New York City, holding down membership in the avant-ethnic band Pachora, a trio with Ellery Eskelin and Andrea Parkins, Tim Berne's Bloodcount, Chris Speed's Yeah No, and Dave Douglas's Tiny Bell Trio. He has been a valued sideman with Satoko Fujii, Laurie Anderson, flautist Robert Dick, Charlie Haden, Carla Bley, and pianist Uri Caine, with whom he has interpreted the music of Mahler and Bach. Black presently leads the rock-influenced AlasNoAxis (*Splay*, 2002, Winter & Winter) featuring Chris Speed, bassist Skuli Sverrisson, and guitarist Hilmar Jensson.

Black Lion: record label, founded in London by Alan Bates in 1968. The label has generally shown two faces, one as a reissuer of classic and obscure dates from the 1940s onward, the other dealing in new releases by American and British artists. Aside from some gems by Sun Ra and Cecil Taylor, little of free-jazz interest came out of the label's coffers. However, its subsidiary label, Freedom, was devoted almost exclusively to fringe jazz. Freedom was sold to Arista in 1975 along with the rights to many Black Lion albums.

Black Saint: Italian record company and label, founded in Milan in 1975 by Giacomo Pellicciotti. Giovanni Bonandrini brought the label into international prominence when he took over the company in 1978. Devoted almost exclusively to free jazz, the label has carried major releases by Roscoe Mitchell, Anthony Braxton, the World Saxophone Quartet, David Murray, and many other American and European musicians. It is the sister label of Soul Note, and it is generally difficult to discern a difference between the two imprints' objectives. The label's name was apparently drawn from Charles Mingus's landmark Impulse album, *The Black Saint and the Sinner Lady*.

Blackwell, Ed (Edward Joseph; b. New Orleans, LA, 10 October 1929; d. Hartford, CT, 8 October 1992): free drummer, an important member of Ornette Coleman's circle. Blackwell was influenced as a youth by the jazz of New Orleans, particularly by drummers like his mentor, Paul Barbarin. The unique flavor of this upbeat martial music remained in Blackwell's playing throughout his life, even in the most openly free settings. He played in R&B and jazz bands for a while, including the groups of Plas Johnson and Ellis Marsalis, then moved to Los Angeles in 1951, where he met Coleman. Between 1953 and 1960, Blackwell lived in Texas, went back to New Orleans, then moved to New York, where he replaced Billy Higgins in Coleman's quartet. Blackwell soon became honored for his fluid but grounded drumming, nicely complementing Coleman's abstract musical conceptions.

In the 1960s, Blackwell worked with groups led by Don Cherry, Booker Little, Eric Dolphy, Mal Waldron, and Archie Shepp, always building upon his status as a premier free drummer. In 1975, he was artist-in-residence at Connecticut's Wesleyan University, and in 1976 he joined his previous Coleman cohorts in the quartet Old and New Dreams. He continued his association with Cherry through the 1970s and 1980s until he was sidelined by severe kidney problems that finally led to his death. Blackwell recorded three albums for Enja, including *What It Is?* (1992).

Blake, Ran (b. Springfield, MA, 20 April 1935): pianist and composer. Blake is a principal figure in the American Third Stream, applying a classical technique to originals and standards like few other pianists of his generation. A graduate of Bard College in New York, Blake also studied at Columbia and the Lenox School of Jazz in the 1950s.

Blake met vocalist Jeanne Lee in 1957, and the pair worked and toured for several years. He debuted on record with *The Newest Sound Around* (1963, RCA, with Lee and bassist George Duvivier), then signed with ESP in 1965 (*Plays Solo Piano*). In 1957, he joined the faculty of the New England Conservatory of Music, where he has remained to this day as the chairman of the School of Contemporary Improvisation. The NEA, the Guggenheim and MacArthur Foundations, and the Massachusetts Artists Foundation have honored Blake for his contributions to music and arts education.

From 1975 through 1992, Blake averaged one album per year, with an astonishing five recordings in 1977 (including *Take One* and *Take Two*, both on Golden Crest, and *Portrait of Doktor Mabuse*, Owl). As these album titles imply, Blake has always been fascinated by film and its soundtracks, particularly the *film noir* era. His records *Film Noir* (1980, Novus) and *Suffield Gothic* (1983, Soul Note) exemplify his approach to such material, balancing silence with sudden chords or rampant lines. A duo album with Enrico Rava, *Duo en Noir* (2000, between the lines), furthered his explorations. His other collaborators include Mary Lou Williams, Anthony Braxton, Jaki Byard, Mal Waldron, Gunther Schuller, Oscar Peterson, Patty Waters, and Clifford Jordan. Blake has occasionally paid tribute to artists like Monk (*The Short Life of Barbara Monk*, 1986; *Epistrophy*, 1991), Sarah Vaughan (*Unmarked Van*, 1995, all Soul Note), and Horace Silver (*Horace Is Blue: A Silver Noir*, 2002, HatOlogy).

Blank, Roger (b. New York, NY, 19 December 1938): free drummer. Blank came from a musical family and was a house drummer in New York until meeting Sun Ra in 1964. He became a resident of Ra's communal loft and performed with John Coltrane,

Ornette Coleman, Leroy Jenkins, Charles Tolliver, Archie Shepp, and fellow drummer Dennis Charles. He led the Melodic Art-tet for a time and cowrote a percussion manual with Ed Blackwell. Little has been heard from Blank since the loft scene dissolved.

Bley, Carla (Karen Borg; b. Oakland, CA, 11 May 1938): composer, bandleader, pianist, and organist. Bley came up in the music of the church and learned the piano by herself with some guidance from her father. At age seventeen, she tired of life on the West Coast and moved to New York City. She worked as a cigarette girl at Birdland with occasional gigs as a pianist. She was married for a few years to pianist Paul Bley, who encouraged her to become a composer; he has since recorded dozens of her works, as have George Russell, Jimmy Giuffre, and Gary Burton. The works of Kurt Weill, Gil Evans, and Charles Ives have inspired her compositions and arrangements. They run the stylistic gamut from exotic extended suites ("A Genuine Tong Funeral," recorded by Burton) to pieces rooted in Americana ("King Korn," "Spangled Banner Minor"). Many, like "Ictus," are themes of amorphous form with no distinct bar lines to separate the phrases.

After her divorce from Bley, she married Austrian trumpeter Michael Mantler, and in 1964 they formed an orchestra associated with the Jazz Composers Guild. In 1965, after the Guild folded, the spouses fabricated the Jazz Composers Orchestra Association to continue the Guild's mission of encouraging creative musicians. The JCOA project brought Bley much attention, particularly when the group recorded *Escalator over the Hill* (1971), a most unusual jazz opera by Bley and writer Paul Haines. Besides the JCOA, Bley worked during this period with Charlie Haden's Liberation Music Orchestra and Gary Burton. She and Mantler also established the New Music Distribution Service, an outlet for independent labels that record music with limited commercial potential.

Since the 1970s, Bley has led a critically acclaimed orchestra and occasional smaller ensembles, including the octet 4x4, gradually turning her back on free-jazz conceptions. Unfortunately, given the economic difficulties of traveling here with a large group, Bley's big band rarely tours America, although it has long been popular outside of the United States. Bley has done many smaller projects with bassist Steve Swallow. She and Mantler divorced in 1991; their daughter, Karen, frequently plays organ and harmonica in Bley's ensembles and has recorded her own unusual jazz-pop albums.

Bley, Paul (b. Montreal, Canada, 10 November 1932): pianist. Bley was trained in both violin and piano as a child. He moved to New York in the early 1950s, working with altoist Jackie McLean's quintet for a time. In 1956, he moved to Los Angeles, leading a quintet that included Ornette Coleman and Don Cherry. This group gave some of the earliest live free-jazz performances in 1958 (see Coleman's entry). Bley went to New York, where he led a trio including bassist Steve Swallow and drummer Pete La Roca. He also performed as a sideman with Don Ellis, Charles Mingus, and others. In 1964, he was part of the "October Revolution in Jazz," recorded *Barrage* (ESP) with Marshall Allen and Milford Graves, and was a founding member of the Jazz Composers Guild.

In the late 1960s, Bley briefly investigated electronic music. He and his second wife, pianist Annette Peacock, performed duets on the new Moog synthesizer (*The Bley/Peacock Synthesizer Show*, 1971, Polydor). In about 1972, he returned to acoustic piano and has continued to be active as a solo and duo artist, often with vibist Gary Burton. His solo album *Open, to Love* (1972), with compositions by ex-wives Peacock and Carla Bley, remains one of the most popular items in the ECM catalog. In 1974, he and painter Carol Goss established the IAI (Improvising Artists, Inc.) label. Bley has instructed at New England Conservatory for several years. He has recorded two arresting trio discs with Evan Parker and Barre Phillips, *Time Will Tell* (1994) and *Sankt Gerold* (2001, both ECM), and has kept up a fruitful relationship with the Steeplechase label. The tense *Chaos* (1998, Soul Note), with bassist Furio di Castri and Tony Oxley, is also excellent. Bley's autobiography, *Stopping Time: Paul Bley and the Transformation of Jazz*, was published in 2000.

Blue Humans, The: shifting ensemble led by guitarist Rudolph Grey, formerly part of New York's post-punk art wave. The group's personnel and style have varied significantly since it was founded in 1980. The inceptive Blue Humans lineup was a trio featuring Grey, Beaver Harris, and Arthur Doyle (*Live N.Y. 1980*, 1995, Audible Hiss). Subsequent members have included Borbetomagus saxophonist Jim Sauter and experimental guitarist Alan Licht.

Blue Note: record company and label, one of the most important imprints in jazz history. Founded by Alfred Lion in New York in 1939, Blue Note presented early sessions by Sidney Bechet, Willie "The Lion" Smith, Ike Quebec, and Earl Hines, among others. Thanks to the vision of Quebec, the label's A&R director until his death in 1963, the label was one of the first to document the rising bebop scene. From 1953, when engineer Rudy Van Gelder joined the label, the quality of their releases garnered Blue Note tremendous international acclaim. The soul-jazz and hard-bop catalog from the 1950s and 1960s is the stuff of legend, including timeless material by Jimmy Smith, Art Blakey, Lee Morgan, Horace Silver, Hank Mobley, and a further host of giants. The label's association with free jazz was always tenuous at best, but some vital documents by Cecil Taylor, Sam Rivers, Andrew Hill, Bobby Hutcherson, Ornette Coleman, Don Cherry, and Jackie McLean were brought out in the 1960s. Starting around 1971, a nearly fatal interest in jazz-rock and commercial music cost Blue Note its exalted stature within the jazz market. After its sale to United Artists in the mid-1970s, Blue Note's significance was at an end. Not until 1985, when the label was acquired by the Capitol group, did a conscientious effort happen to reclaim the throne. Since then, a commendable number of quality new recordings and fine reissues have hit the market. Unfortunately, a number of classic free-jazz records have only been reissued under their limited edition Connoisseur Series, making them fairly scarce on CD today.

Blue Notes, The: South African jazz unit led by pianist Chris McGregor. The group was founded in 1962 with the core lineup of McGregor, tenorman Nick Moyake, altoist Dudu Pukwana, trumpeter Mongezi Feza, bassist Johnny Dyani, and drummer

Louis Moholo. After winning a prestigious national award, the band members moved *en masse* to Europe to escape the oppression of apartheid. Pianist Dollar Brand (now Abdullah Ibrahim) helped them adjust to life outside of South Africa, but the transition was difficult. The ensemble performed to great acclaim at the Antibes Festival, then made the rounds of the continent. After settling briefly in Copenhagen, some of the members broke off from the group. Dyani continued working in Denmark, McGregor, Pukwana, Feza, and Moholo went off to London, and Moyake returned home. McGregor and friends met expatriate bassist Harry Miller and formed a large ensemble, the Brotherhood of Breath, which gained renown around the globe for their remarkable performances (see entry for McGregor). Feza's death in 1975 was a terrible blow to his fellow expatriates, and heartfelt tributes poured out from the European jazz community (*Blue Notes for Mongezi*, 1975, Ogun).

Bluiett, Hamiet (b. Lovejoy, IL, 16 September 1940): baritone saxophonist and clarinetist. He was taught music by his aunt and studied clarinet in school, then flute and baritone at Northern Illinois University. After serving in the Navy, Bluiett relocated to St. Louis and became involved in the Black Artists Group (see entry) with Julius Hemphill, Joseph Bowie, and Oliver Lake. He decided to make the baritone sax his principal instrument, a rarity in jazz and especially the avant-garde. In 1969, Bluiett moved to New York, where he performed with Sam Rivers, Don Pullen, and Charles Mingus, as well as his own groups. In 1974, he reunited with Lake and Hemphill for a single session with Anthony Braxton. The three joined David Murray for a concert in New Orleans, and that group became the World Saxophone Quartet (see entry). The WSQ and his own bands (*Endangered Species*, 1976, India Navigation; *Live in Berlin with the Clarinet Family*, 1984, Black Saint; *Bluiett Baritone Saxophone Group Live at the Knitting Factory*, 1997, Knitting Factory Works) have remained high on his list of priorities ever since, although he has continued to perform as an occasional sideman. His trio with pianist D.D. Jackson and percussionist Mor Thiam (*Join Us*, 1999, Justin Time) has brought recent accolades. Bluiett produces recordings for the Mapleshade label, which also issues his own works (*Bluiett's BBQ Band*, 1995). Around 2000, he dropped the use of his first name.

Blythe, Arthur ("Black Arthur"; b. Los Angeles, CA, 7 May 1940): altoist and bandleader. Blythe grew up in San Diego and studied the alto sax in school with Kirtland Bradford, a Jimmie Lunceford alumnus. He returned to L.A. in 1960 and began working with his mentor, Horace Tapscott. The two founded the Union of God's Musicians and Artists Ascension in 1961 and continued their working relationship until 1974. His fervent fascination with black history earned Blythe the nickname "Black Arthur." Dissatisfied with California's jazz scene outside of the Tapscott circle, Blythe relocated to New York, where he performed with Chico Hamilton, Lester Bowie, Charles Tyler, and Jack DeJohnette and participated in the loft culture. He served a valuable apprenticeship with Gil Evans's orchestra from 1976 to 1980, performing brilliantly alongside fellow altoist David Sanborn on the title track *Priestess* (1977, Antilles).

In the 1980s, Blythe led two of his own ensembles, In The Tradition (with Steve McCall and Fred Hopkins from Air, and pianists Stanley Cowell and John Hicks) and a remarkably popular quintet with cello, guitar, tuba, and drums. At that time, Blythe was signed to Columbia Records (*Light Blue: A Tribute to Thelonious Monk*, 1985) and became one of the highest profiled players on the avant-garde edge, although the label later dropped him in favor of promoting Wynton Marsalis. Thankfully, some of his Columbia dates have now been reissued on CD by Koch Jazz. From 1984, Blythe performed with the Leaders, sharing the front line with Lester Bowie and Chico Freeman. He has partnered many times with electric cellist David Eyges (*Synergy*, 1997, In & Out, with drummer Bruce Ditmas) and served temporarily as a member of the World Saxophone Quartet. A renowned interpreter of standards, Blythe is a master of harmony and emotional expression who has developed a distinctive personal voice.

Boni, Raymond (b. Toulon, France, 15 March 1947): guitarist, composer, and bandleader. Boni's unique take on his instrument stems from his equal interests in Gypsy six-string legend Django Reinhardt and the free piano of Cecil Taylor. The Gypsy factor is amplified by Boni's studies with Gypsies in his neighborhood, while the free-improv impressions did not arrive until later. Boni is trained on piano as well, and his knowledge of keyboards translates into his guitar approach in fluid chords and wide-intervalled single-note phrases.

As a teenager, Boni studied in London, but he gave up the conservatory grind in favor of actual gigging. He returned to France, settled in Paris, and became immersed in the city's nascent free improv scene. In 1973, with his fellow guitarist Gérard Marais, he formed a duo that explored new avenues in free jazz. The pairing has remained semi-active for all the years following, though they have rarely recorded. *La Belle Vie* (2001, Hopi) presents a 1981 concert by the duo. In 1976, Boni formed a democratically oriented trio with André Jaume and Gérard Siracusa, and began working with saxophonist Claude Bernard. In 1978, through Jaume, he made the acquaintance of Joe McPhee and became a regular performance partner. (See McPhee's entry.)

In 1981, Boni relocated to Marseilles, where he began composing for dancers as Bernard had inspired him. His relationship with choreographer Geneviéve Sorin has proved fortuitous. In 1985, Boni toured the Americas with McPhee, bringing his unorthodox, fascinating sound to a new audience. Boni has mentored younger freemen, like bassist Claude Tchamitchian, and has performed with his son, bassist Bastien Boni, and Sorin. Recordings under his own name have been few and far between (1981's *L'Homme Etoile*, HatHut) but are all rewarding. Boni's duo with drummer Eric Echampard is the aptly titled *Two Angels for Cecil* (1999, Emouvance), a tribute to the spirit of Cecil Taylor. Both men appear in Tchamitchian's Grand Lousadzak Ensemble on *Bassma Suite* (1999, Émouvance). *Voices and Dreams* (2001, Emouvance) is a long-awaited, varicolored duet with McPhee.

Borbetomagus: free-noise trio founded in New York in 1979. The core of the group is saxophonists Jim Sauter and Don Dietrich, and electric guitarist Donald Miller. Their music is characterized by extreme levels of intensity and volume, with overtones and clashes created by the overwhelming loudness. Sauter and Dietrich draw every possible sound from their horns, even locking the bells together so that one can vocalize while the other blows through both saxophones. Among their collaborators have been guitarist Thurston Moore, electronics manipulator Brian Doherty, and the avant-garde duo Voice Crack. Their own label, Agaric, has issued sporadic records, including their 1980 self-titled debut.

Borca, Karen: bassoonist. Her instrument's unusual tone and unwieldiness have made Borca perhaps the only full-time bassoonist of significance in free jazz. While Marshall Allen, Ken McIntyre, and a few other reedmen played the bassoon on certain occasions, only Borca has built a serious profile as a specialist on the instrument. Her most regular gig was at the side of her husband, alto saxophonist Jimmy Lyons, either in the Cecil Taylor Unit or Lyons's own bands. She is, as might be assumed, classically trained, but her heart is clearly with jazz. Since Lyons's passing in 1984, Borca has worked with a number of America's finest, including Joe Morris, Alan Silva, Marco Eneidi, and Joel Futterman. Her incredible technical facility on the cumbersome horn has made Borca an appealing addition to many recording sessions, particularly Lyons's *Wee Sneezawee* (1983) and *Give It Up* (1985, both Black Saint). She has led her own units and contributed vocals to some sessions. Borca is also a member of Earth People (see entry).

Borgmann, Thomas (b. Münster, Germany, 1955): saxophonist. One of his earliest jobs in avant-garde music was with the Berlin Art Ensemble in the early 1980s. He worked with Sirone in New York in 1987 and with various European ensembles. In 1991, Borgmann assembled his Orkestra Kith 'N Kin, with an astonishing lineup featuring John Tchicai, Hans Reichel, Lol Coxhill, and Pat Thomas (*Orkestra Kith 'N Kin*, 1995, Cadence Jazz). Two years later came Ruf der Heimat, which included Ernst-Ludwig Petrowsky (*Ruf der Heimat*, 1995) and Peter Brötzmann (*Machine Kaput*, 1996, both Konnex). Borgmann has taken part in two excellent trios: Blue Zoo, with Brötzmann and Borah Bergman (*Ride into the Blue*, 1996, Konnex), and one with Wilber Morris and Denis Charles, who was replaced after his death by Reggie Nicholson. The "BMC Trio" can be heard on *The Last Concert*, 2000, Silkheart; "BMN Trio" on *You See What We Sayin'?*, 1998, CIMP. Borgmann and Brötzmann meet the New York rhythm team of William Parker and Rashid Bakr on *Cooler Suite* (2003, Grob). The saxophonist has worked with Alex von Schlippenbach, Evan Parker, André Jaume, Kip Hanrahan, Vladimir Chekasin, the Bauer brothers, Thurston Moore, and Phil Minton. He has appeared at a large number of festivals and himself administered the Stakkato Festival in Berlin from 1984 to 1996.

Botticelli: label administered by alto saxophonist Marco Eneidi. Originally founded in 1986, the label's inaugural issue was *Vermont 1986* with Eneidi, William Parker, and Denis Charles. After that LP was released, Eneidi put the label on hold for a few years to concentrate on other priorities. He revived Botticelli in 1991 and has sporadically issued recordings under his own leadership, ranging from sizzling quartets and quintets to the twenty-plus-member American Jungle Orchestra.

Boulder Creative Music Ensemble: group based in Boulder, Colorado, and led by reedman Fred Hess. Among the other members have been saxophonists Mark Harris and Glenn Nitta, trumpeter Ron Miles, bassist Kent McLagen, and drummer Tim Sullivan. *Faith* (2000, Cadence Jazz) captures their brand of deft improvisational interplay.

Bowie, Joseph (b. St. Louis, MO, 1953): trombonist. The younger brother of Art Ensemble trumpeter Lester Bowie, Joseph was inspired by the AACM and became a founding member of the Black Artists Group. In the 1970s, Bowie recorded and performed with Oliver Lake, the Human Arts Ensemble, and the St. Louis Creative Ensemble. Around 1980, he formed the group Defunkt, playing a synthesis of free jazz, punk rock, and funk. He also served for a spell as the musical director for soul/R&B singer Fontella Bass ("Rescue Me"), his former sister-in-law.

Bowie, Lester (b. Frederick, MD, 11 October 1941; d. Brooklyn, NY, 8 November 1999): trumpeter, founding member of the AACM and the Art Ensemble of Chicago (see separate entries). A fascinating player with a deep appreciation for his instrument's history, his adeptness with growls and sound effects recalled Cootie Williams and Bubber Miley's performances of Duke Ellington's "jungle music." Bowie also bore a love for the full history of black music, from prejazz styles to the blues, doo-wop, and rap, all of which found some appreciative expression in his recordings and performances. His late-period recordings with his ensemble Brass Fantasy reflect this all-encompassing affection for black creativity.

Bowie came from a musical family and played trumpet from age five. He worked as a session musician for several years, moving from St. Louis to Texas to attend college. He played with James Clay and David "Fathead" Newman, along with various blues artists, and married soul/R&B singer Fontella Bass. After moving to Chicago in 1965, Bowie joined the AACM and later became a founding member of the Art Ensemble of Chicago. *Numbers 1 and 2* (1967, Nessa), issued under Bowie's name, marked the first recording the AEC's members made together. He toured and recorded with the group for three decades and lived with them in France for a few years. More recently, Bowie has led From the Root to the Source, which explored the history of black music in America; the Hot Trumpet Repertory Company; the New York Organ Ensemble; and the extremely popular Brass Fantasy. All these groups frequently presented a retrospective of black American music from ragtime to hip-hop. Bowie was a member of The Leaders and worked as a sideman for David Murray, Archie Shepp, and Amina Claudine Myers. Of the discs issued under his name, *The Great Pretender* (with Brass Fantasy, 1981, ECM), *Rope-A-Dope* (1975, Muse), and *All the Magic!* (1982, ECM, 2 discs) rank among the best.

Boxholder: label based in Woodstock, Vermont. Their presently small but growing catalog includes live and studio recordings featuring William Parker, Joe McPhee, Bill Cole, Ken Vandermark, Raphé Malik, and others.

Boykins, Ronnie (b. Chicago, IL, 1935; d. Brooklyn, NY, 20 April 1980): bassist, most notably for Sun Ra and the Arkestra. He came out of Chicago's legendary DuSable High School music program under Captain Walter Dyett, backing blues and jazz artists like Muddy Waters and Johnny Griffin as a youth. He joined Sun Ra in 1958 and stayed with the Arkestra until 1966 through many tours and recordings. He also led the Free Jazz Society and played with the Melodic Art-tet and the New York Contemporary Five. Boykins was a valuable sideman for a variety of artists: Rahsaan Roland Kirk, Archie Shepp, Sarah Vaughan, Steve Lacy, Mary Lou Williams, and Elmo Hope. His melodic inventiveness was perhaps second only to Charles Mingus's in Boykins's heyday, which added a special character to the Arkestra's rhythm section. In 1975, he led *The Will Come, Is Now*, the final recording issued on ESP.

Brackeen, Charles (b. White's Chapel, OK, 13 March 1940): bop and free reedman. Brackeen studied saxophone, violin, and piano as a youth. He moved to California in 1956 to work with trumpeter Art Farmer and vibist Dave Pike. He also associated and played with Ornette Coleman's sidemen on both coasts: Charlie Haden, Don Cherry, and Billy Higgins in L.A., and Cherry, Ed Blackwell, and David Izenzon in New York. In New York, he performed with the Melodic Art-tet, Frank Lowe, and his then-wife, pianist Joanne Brackeen. *Worshippers Come Nigh* (1987, Silkheart) is a favored item in his sparse discography.

Bradford, Bobby (Robert Lee; b. Cleveland, MS, 19 July 1934): trumpeter, cornetist, and composer. Bradford spent his youth in Texas; he took up the cornet at age fifteen and attended high school with David Newman, Cedar Walton, and James Clay. He moved to Los Angeles in 1953 and performed with Ornette Coleman, Eric Dolphy, and Gerald Wilson, among others. After serving in the military, he rejoined Coleman in New York in 1961, then returned to Los Angeles. There he played with John Carter in the New Art Jazz Ensemble, which became one of the more prominent free outfits in California. Bradford spent time in Europe in 1971, recording with the Spontaneous Music Ensemble during his stay. He returned to Coleman's New York band briefly, then settled into teaching college in California. However, he frequently returned to Europe to work again with SME associates like Trevor Watts and John Stevens (both appear, along with bassist Kent Carter, on *Love's Dream*, rec. 1973; reissued on CD 2003, Emanem). Besides leading his own Mo'tet, he has performed frequently with Carter, David Murray, John Stevens's Freebop band, and Charlie Haden's Liberation Music Orchestra. *In Time Was* (1986, Circulasione Totale) and *One Night Stand* (1997, Soul Note) are among his best recordings.

Braxton, Anthony (b. Chicago, IL, 4 June 1945): reeds player, composer, and bandleader. Braxton has always been somewhat of an anomaly, even among his early comrades in the AACM. He shares with Cecil Taylor a substantial academic background in Western music, but while the elder Taylor largely cast those dictums aside as irrelevant to black creative musicians, Braxton embraced and expanded upon them. A profound intellectual who made a living playing chess in the 1960s when his music was not paying the bills, Braxton, perhaps chiefly among African American free musicians, utilizes European avant-garde concepts in his music as much as African-based motifs, if not more so. As a result, his body of work has become one of the most scrutinized in new music, alternately praised for its intellectual complexity and condemned for the same.

Braxton specializes in complex works of unconventional notation, inspired more by the avant principles of Cage, Ives, Stockhausen, and Iannis Xenakis than by American free jazz. He would argue, however, that there are plenty of African-rooted elements in his music as well. He views the continuum of musical history and development as based on ritual and spiritual factors, "vibrations" that resonate throughout the course of humanity and therefore cannot be pinned down to what is stringently European, African, or otherwise. This concept of vibration saturates Braxton's worldview, from music to relationship dynamics to metaphysics. His musical conceptions are based upon a theoretical structure he calls "conceptional transference," derived from complicated mathematical principles. His "Tri-Axium" concepts have focused on permutations of the number three; the "Trillium" operas, of twelve.

Despite his square-peg approach to the music, and his resultant lambasting by confused critics and listeners, Braxton has had plenty of support from the rest of the free-jazz community, European improvisers, and academic circles. He has worked with jazz legends Max Roach and Dave Brubeck, performed in duos with electronic musician Richard Teitelbaum and pianist Marilyn Crispell, and played with key English improvisers like Derek Bailey and Kenny Wheeler. Braxton has also frequently collaborated with large ensembles, such as the London Jazz Composers Orchestra and his own Creative Music Orchestra. His imagination knows no bounds, as evidenced by some of his most ambitious projects. Composition 9 was written in 1969 for four amplified shovels and required a pile of coal, costumes, and choreography. In 1971, he conceived Composition 19 for four groups of twenty-five tuba players each, complete with twenty pages of schematic notation and instructions. His "Trillium" operatic conception consists of thirty-six interchangeable dialogues, grouped to form twelve operas of three acts each. He has conceived pieces to be played by a hundred orchestras at a time and scores for multiple orchestras located in different cities, linked by satellite communications. The ultimate extension of this madly ambitious concept would involve orchestras on far-off planets and in other galaxies! His scarce efforts as a sideman have sometimes lacked the rhythmic energy and fire of his own works, but at his best, Braxton is a performer of truly commanding presence.

Braxton uses his own abstract formulaic notations (said, in a manner that recalls Sun Ra, to be inspired by mystical references from ancient Egypt and other cultures) for the titles of his compositions. In the 1980s, he began retroactively using opus numbers as well, to the relief of catalogers and DJs. (These opus numbers will be used in referring to specific compositions throughout this section, whether or not they were used on the records discussed.) His music is not generally categorized as "Third Stream," though it may fit into that mold as easily as "free jazz." He has developed, among other tools, a list of one hundred "language types," which indicate forms the performers should use for their musical expressions. A broken horizontal line might connote staccato playing; tight waveforms, trills; home-plate-shaped symbols, multiphonics. Graham Lock's *Forces in Motion* offers intermittent insights into these arcane codes, but for the most part they might remain impenetrable to the average listener. His students and sidemen concur that the only way to truly understand Braxton's music is to work through it with the man himself.

An introverted child, Braxton spent much time in his South Side home listening to jazz, early rock-and-roll, and classical records. He took up the clarinet as a high-school freshman and fell under the spell of Charlie Parker, Eric Dolphy, and Paul Desmond. He continued his education at both the Chicago School of Music and Roosevelt University, studying composition, harmony, and philosophy, then entered the army for two years. He considered a career as a philosophy teacher but abandoned that idea in favor of music, where he could philosophize uniquely.

In 1966, after leaving the service, Braxton returned home and joined the AACM, for which he performed and taught harmonic theory. He had previously met Joseph Jarman, Roscoe Mitchell, and other members in college. The AACM was a significant springboard for Braxton's career, although he was not active in the organization for very long. Muhal Richard Abrams, the group's founder, emphasized newness of song and rhythmic structure and experimentation with sonic texture, along with the importance of arts and education to the community. All of these notions held an appeal for Braxton, and he absorbed them thoroughly during his three years of AACM membership. He soon developed his own distinctive vocabularies for the instruments he played, particularly the alto saxophone, drawing from the legacies of Parker and Dolphy but not content to remain at their lofty levels.

Braxton made his recorded debut with Abrams's band on the seminal album *Levels and Degrees of Light* (1966), the third AACM release on the Delmark label (discussed under Abrams's entry). His performances on two of the three tracks were cheerful, bright, with an attractive tone. He interacted splendidly with violinist Leroy Jenkins, who became his performing partner of choice in a subsequent trio with trumpeter Leo Smith.

The Braxton trio was a strange beast. The novelty of two horns and a stringed instrument, not counting the small percussion devices they employed, was revolutionary but perfectly in line with the AACM's visions. In 1968, the group recorded the astonishing *Three Compositions of New Jazz* (Delmark). The record shocked many listeners' sensibilities with its outlandish formulaic titles and naturistic soundscapes, which sounded like little else on record. The two Braxton compositions (Leo Smith's fine "The Bell" is also included) point the players in certain directions, which are determined both by Braxton's set rules and by the musicians' own perceptions. The twenty-minute track "(840M)—REALIZE—44M—44M" (this is a linear approximation of the title diagram; the opus number is 6e) begins with a three-part vocal chant. Textures build as the performers alternate between whistling and chanting, then bells and percussion emerge hesitantly. These are followed by alto sax, harmonica, xylophone, and so forth. The performers cycle continuously between instruments and voices, rhythmic snippets, stabbing horns. There are definite snatches of melody and comeliness interspersed, though at times they are almost too subtle to notice. Closing one's eyes while listening can help conjure sundry images: swarming bees, winding of clocks, children at play, elephants on parade. This is by definition music made for the imagination, spawned from Braxton's search for total openness of the musical spectrum. Upon repeated listenings, the charm of Braxton's early vision becomes palpable.

The artistic triumph of *Three Compositions* was followed by Braxton's equally shattering *For Alto* (1968, Delmark), an epic two-record set of solo alto saxophone meanderings that showcased Braxton's specially developed vocabulary for the horn. With this project, Braxton began to more acutely explore his personal principles of musical construction and improvisation, a blend of both the AACM's teachings and those of European art music. The eight pieces are dedicated to various friends and influences, including Cage, Taylor, and Leroy Jenkins. The descriptions given for the pieces ("medium fast pulse relationships," "ballad language") are somewhat helpful in translating the composer's ideas as realized on disc, although at times their meaning is blurred. What is clear is the radical change that Braxton brought to prevailing notions about the alto sax, Dolphy's strides notwithstanding. No longer left on the pedestal where Charlie Parker had placed it, nor relegated to a supporting role behind the tenor sax in big bands, it became once more a viable tool for seriously creative music.

In 1969, the trio, now dubbed the Creative Construction Company, moved to the presumably greener pastures of Paris along with Roscoe Mitchell's Art Ensemble. In June, not long after its arrival, the group recorded *Silence* (1969, Freedom/Black Lion). Jenkins's appropriately named "Off the Top of My Head" took up the first side of the LP, Smith's title track, the second. Shortly afterward, the trio encountered drummer Steve McCall, another AACM veteran. McCall was a virtuoso on a par with Sunny Murray and Ed Blackwell, able to temper his assertiveness with an acute sensitivity to volume, color, and form. McCall joined the group, which spent a productive year in Europe before returning to Chicago. A classic session that came out of Braxton's spell in Paris was *The 8th of July 1969* (1969, Birth), led by Gunter Hampel. (See Hampel's entry.)

Braxton and friends were involved in several more projects during their year in Europe, including sessions for the BYG label, which was tied into the Actuel music festival. Braxton and Jenkins appeared on trumpeter Jacques Coursil's *Black Suite* (1969, BYG Actuel). In August, several of the same players worked in bassist Alan Silva's Celestrial Communications Orchestra on *From the Luna Surface* (1969, BYG). Braxton and Jenkins also appeared on the fine matchup *Archie Shepp and Philly Joe Jones* (1969, America). All these sessions indicate the limitless opportunities that Europe afforded, and the ripe possibilities when musicians from increasingly disparate cultures get together to sculpt new artistic forms. As for the Creative Construction Company, the group dropped that handle and recorded two sessions issued under Braxton's name by BYG. *B-X°/ N-O-1-47^A* (1969) and *This Time . . .* (1970) presented a return to the AACM aesthetics as the men cycled through instruments like cigarettes.

In the springtime, hopeful that their employment prospects might have improved back home, the four men returned to the United States. On May 19, 1970, the band recorded two albums of material at the Peace Church in Washington, D.C. The results were issued on the Muse label as *Creative Construction Company* (1970) and *CCC, Volume 2* (1971). Ornette Coleman supervised the session, on which Muhal Richard Abrams on piano, clarinet, and cello, and Richard Davis on bass joined the band.

As promising as that quartet appeared, it did not last long. Smith soon left to form a partnership with altoist Marion Brown. The following year, Jenkins assembled the

Revolutionary Ensemble and McCall formed Reflection (later called Air). Braxton performed briefly with Musica Elettronica Viva, forming a lasting bond with synthesist Richard Teitelbaum. Braxton appeared with Jeanne Lee on Marion Brown's *Afternoon of a Georgia Faun* (1970, ECM), one of the earliest releases from that fledgling German label. Brown's group also included drummer Andrew Cyrille and pianist Chick Corea, who would play a vital role in the next, all-too-brief phase of Braxton's career, the quartet Circle (see entry for Circle).

Since the 1960s, Braxton has added many instruments to his previous duo of alto sax and clarinet. His love of tonal extremes has led him to use both the tiny sopranino sax and gigantic contrabass sax, of which he owns one of only a half-dozen or so in the world. He has also developed a novel but interesting usage of the contrabass clarinet. Surprisingly, Braxton has rarely performed or recorded on the tenor saxophone, the most popular reed in jazz since Coleman Hawkins's day. The textural variations enabled by his array of instruments enabled Braxton to expand upon the AACM's notion of sounds beyond the expected. His collaboration with Joseph Jarman on *Together Alone* (1971, Delmark) delineates the similarities and differences in their applications of the AACM's conceptions.

In early 1971, during the tribulations of Circle, Braxton managed to swing a couple of side jobs in Paris. He appeared again with Silva's Celestrial [sic] Communications Orchestra on the hour-plus *My Country* (1971, Leo), which also featured excellent work by Steve Lacy. *The Complete Braxton, 1971* (Freedom) presents two days of sessions at Polydor Studios in London. Corea and Braxton duet on two compositions; three others feature Dave Holland, Barry Altschul, and trumpeter Kenny Wheeler. Odd one out is Composition 4, Braxton's piece for five tubas, on which he conducts the London Tuba Ensemble.

Saxophone Improvisations—Series F (1972, America) was another solo triumph. The opener, Composition 8i, is dedicated to chess master Bobby Fischer in a nod to one of Braxton's other pastimes. Here he presents three of the piece's five short sections, continuing the pulse-relationship explorations of *For Alto*. Choppy tones and grating blats are supplemented by high, quiet squeals and humanoid wails, a subtler lyricism, then honks and buzzsaw rips in the third phase. The other three selections are alternately light-hearted, poetic, and fluttery (with occasional abrupt strangling-duck noises).

Braxton returned to France in March 1972 for a performance of his Composition 25, dedicated to Ornette Coleman. This is another of the most unusual pieces in Braxton's canon, as it calls in certain places for 112 bells and 100 balloons, rubbed to elicit squeaks and groans. Braxton claims he opted for balloons because they were cheaper than electronic components that could approximate the sounds in his head. The twelve parts of the composition can be arranged in any order, and each performer selects his own tempo for his parts. The performance was released in three-LP sets by Ring and Moers Music as *Creative Music Orchestra 1972*.

On May 22, 1972, Braxton made a promising appearance at New York's Town Hall, just as many of his predecessors in free jazz had done. The album *Town Hall (Trio & Quintet) 1972* (issued 1992, Pausa) presents two colors of Braxton's music. A trio with Holland and drummer Philip Wilson, another AACM stalwart, features long, intense improvisations culminating in a surprisingly swinging rendition of the tired standard

"All the Things You Are," a real triumph for the reedman. The second half teams Braxton, Holland, and Altschul with tenorman John Stubblefield and Jeanne Lee, whose vocal acrobatics practically steal the show.

November 30, 1972, saw Braxton take part in one of the most treasured sessions in free jazz. *Conference of the Birds* (1972, ECM) was recorded under David Holland's name and included six of the bassist's compositions. Barry Altschul and saxophonist Sam Rivers rounded out the powerful quartet. Named for a poem by a Sufi mystic poet and the inspirational bird-sounds outside Holland's window, *Conference* resourcefully blends improvisation with fascinatingly constructed compositions to result in a sum greater than its considerable parts. Rivers, a veteran of sessions from Dizzy to Miles to Cecil and renowned for his own prophetic albums, cooperates well with Braxton in this two-reed setting.

In 1974, Braxton toured Europe, making a convincing appearance at the Moers Festival in Germany. He met Derek Bailey there, and the pair recorded *First Duo Concert* (1974, Emanem). The two long sets offer a chance to compare and contrast the American and European approaches to free improv. Braxton, rotating through many reeds, is definitely jazz grounded despite his overwhelming imaginativeness. Bailey, on acoustic and electric guitars with resonant sympathetic strings, exemplifies the extreme atonality of the European school. Somehow or another, thanks to open ears that enable them to work well with so many different musicians, the men manage to find a solid middle ground on which to converse. The partnership was renewed at the 1986 Victoriaville Festival, the source of *Moment Précieux* (1986, Victo). Its two movements of "The Victoria and Albertville Suite" are less successful. Though the men had gained twelve years of experience since their initial duo, they seemed to have a difficult time connecting at the Canadian gig.

New York, Fall 1974 (Arista) marked Braxton's debut with a major American label and his first usage of several ensemble configurations on one album. This disc became one of his most popular releases, thanks to Arista's strong distribution as much as its stellar content. The first three tracks feature Braxton with Holland, Wheeler, and drummer Jerome Cooper. Composition 38a is a duet for Braxton's clarinet and Richard Teitelbaum's synthesizer, hinting at the possibilities of Braxton's collaborations with Musica Elettronica Viva. Next comes Composition 37 with the sax quartet of Braxton (on sopranino), Julius Hemphill (alto), Oliver Lake (tenor), and Hamiet Bluiett (baritone). Braxton's cohorts were prominent in the avant-garde circles of St. Louis at the time but had been heard little outside of the city. (Two years later, they joined the California-born tenorman David Murray and formed the World Saxophone Quartet.) This track hints at things to come, as layers of rhythm and melodic ideas wash over each other with blissful reediness. The closing track, 23a, adds Leroy Jenkins to the first quartet. The contrabass clarinet drags the piece into bitter solemnity, a pit from which Jenkins's valiant violin fails to pull the listener free.

Next up on Arista was *Five Pieces 1975*, which continued the quartet adventures with Altschul reclaiming the drum chair from Jerome Cooper. It begins uncharacteristically with an alto/bass duet on "You Stepped Out of a Dream," another old warhorse. Holland's mighty pulse drives Braxton's seasoned bop articulation without coaxing him too far into freedom. This is yet another track that emphasizes Braxton's appreciation of jazz traditions; he bears a clear love for the tune and closes it with a wonderful high-note figure that lifts the standard far above the maudlin. In a later group improvisation, Braxton switches horns frequently: alto to sopranino sax, clarinet, flute (with Wheeler echoing his flutters), contrabass clarinet (his dry flappings sound almost synthesized). Some critics have dismissed this sort of track as a mere show-off platform, but the reality of Braxton's astonishing technical facility on different horns reduces such charges to jealous grumblings. This is one of Braxton's true masterpieces.

In early 1976, trombonist George Lewis, a phenomenal young technician from the AACM, replaced Wheeler. Wheeler stuck around long enough for the large group recordings issued as *Creative Orchestra Music 1976* (Arista), the first full realization of Braxton's conceptions for larger ensembles. This landmark date features AACM veterans (Abrams, Smith, Roscoe Mitchell, drummer Philip Wilson), older Braxton cohorts (Teitelbaum and pianist Frederick Rzewski from MEV, Karl Berger), and some surprises (trumpeters Cecil Bridgewater and Jon Faddis, and reedman Seldon Powell). Large ensemble freedom has not been universally successful; Sam Rivers's impregnable *Crystals* (1975, Impulse) was a promising idea that was far too overbearing for most listeners in its time. With this session, Braxton showed how it could be done, that striking a fine balance between structure and freedom is essential to convey one's musical message.

Recorded in November 1976, *The Montreux/Berlin Concerts* (1977, Arista) documents the personnel switch with three tracks from Wheeler's final days and three following Lewis's accession. (The CD reissue omits the long, aimless performance by Braxton and Lewis with the Berlin New Music Group.) An especially fruitful year, 1976 also saw Braxton recording fine duets with Lewis (*Elements of Surprise*, Moers Music, and *Donaueschingen [Duo]*, HatArt) and Abrams (*Duets [1976]*, Arista). The duo with Lewis at the Donaueschingen Festival in Germany features two long Kelvin explorations and a short, rewarding venture into Charlie Parker's knuckle-busting "Donna Lee." The disc with Abrams revisits some of Braxton's earliest concepts and includes covers of Eric Dolphy's "Miss Ann," Scott Joplin's "Maple Leaf Rag," and a fey ballad dedicated to Braxton's wife, Nickie.

A more recent worthwhile release is *News from the 70s* (1999, New Tone), a collection of six tracks from 1971 to 1976. Compiled by discographer Francesco Martinelli, *News* is filled with surprises and strong moments. Of chief interest is a nearly sixteen-minute version of Holland's "Four Winds," taped in Graz, Austria, in October 1976. Lewis fills the second horn chair that Sam Rivers held on *Conference of the Birds*, and the resultant textural change is awesome. These tracks were selected from tapes found by Martinelli and Braxton at they scrounged through the saxophonist's basement, and each piece is a bright gem. There are a few misconstruances regarding Braxton's horns; despite some misleading liner-note photos, he does not play contrabass sax here, and he plays alto on Composition -2 instead of sopranino, clarinet, and piccolo as labeled. Those quibbles aside, this is a spectacular release.

Starting in 1977, Braxton explored new ensembles, investigating the sonic and textural possibilities of various instrumentations. His trio efforts that year were less than productive, but in 1978, he had better success with a larger unit. *Creative Orchestra (Köln) 1978* (issued 1995, HatArt) was recorded live in Cologne, Germany, with a twenty-one-piece band of his selection. Lewis, Smith, and Wheeler figured prominently, as did trombone whiz Ray Anderson, pianist Marilyn Crispell, bassist John Lindberg, and reedmen Vinny Golia and Marty Ehrlich. The compositions were more avant-leaning than his previous large-band effort. Also recorded in that year was his two-hour Composition 82 (*For Four Orchestras*, Arista), performed by four Oberlin College student ensembles. The concept is quadraphonic, with the listener in the middle of the four units, the best vantage point to appreciate its unisons and dissonances.

The monolithic scale and relative aridity of Composition 82 would characterize many of Braxton's future compositions, yet he returned to jazz forms just as frequently as he abandoned them. *Birth and Rebirth* (1978, Black Saint), his famed duo set with pioneering bop drummer Max Roach, demonstrates his unflagging appreciation of and affinity for Afrocentric rhythms. In fact, Braxton leans closer to Africa on this album than just about any other in his massive discography, egged on by the phenomenal talents of Roach.

Next, Braxton formed a new quartet with Ray Anderson, John Lindberg, and drummer Thurman Barker. Anderson's clearer tone, more fluid approach to the horn, and gift for multiphonics made him a notably different but entirely suitable replacement for Lewis. *Seven Compositions (1978)* (1979, Moers) is a majestic document of this underappreciated quartet.

Subsequent endeavors for string quartet and duo pianos were followed by *Composition 96* (1981, Leo), one of the major turning points in Braxton's career. He considers it one of his most significant achievements, and it has become one of the most frequent sources of material for his collage performances. Originally conceived for a large orchestra and four slide projectors, which presented photographs taken by his wife, Nickie, the work was described by Braxton as "a ceremonial concert context for positive transformation and historical re-solidification." There is certainly enough to quote from: 240 pages of notation! The 1981 recording featured clarinetist Bill Smith (a former sideman of Dave Brubeck who also dabbles in contemporary classical music), trombonist Julian Priester, and thirty-five collegiate musicians. Snippets of the piece have since been used in innumerable albums and performances with differently sized ensembles.

After Braxton's contract with Arista abruptly ended in 1980, he milled about for several years, working for whichever independent labels were interested. His sole effort for Antilles, *Six Compositions: Quartet* (1982), features bassist Mark Helias, pianist Anthony Davis, and drummer Ed Blackwell. One of Braxton's most broadly appealing pieces, 40b, starts the disc. Dedicated to hard bop altoist Lou Donaldson, this is described in the liner notes as "a post bebop thematic structure that affirms the composite continuum of trans-African creativity and world culture." The initial theme is a tense, exciting post-bop line over a bass ostinato, recalling the archetypal Blue Note sound. It moves abruptly into a herky-jerky atonal line, reminiscent of Eric Dolphy's "Gazzelloni," that magically melds into the theme. This work illustrates Braxton's estimable knowledge of jazz traditions, an awareness that many critics have refused to acknowledge. This album, one of Braxton's most accessible, offers easier insights into his concepts than subsequent releases. It is a shame that he did not hold onto this particular quartet lineup or label for long.

In 1983, Lewis reassumed the trombone chair in the quartet, and Blackwell was replaced by young Gerry Hemingway. *Four Compositions (Quartet) 1983* (Polydor) documents this lineup on less successful material than Braxton had previously realized on record. At the year's end, Braxton separated from the quartet to record the solo *Composition 113* (1983, Sound Aspects), giving the soprano sax much the same vocabulary-expansion treatment that *For Alto* had done for the larger horn. This is another creation intended more for live concert than recording, as it calls for specific staging and a large photograph (of what is not clear). Likewise, the performer's movements are central to the full conceptualization. As bracing as his ensemble performances can be, a Braxton solo is a special joy to behold. His facility on the long horn is phenomenal as he coaxes sounds human, animal, and otherworldly from its shallow depths.

In 1985, Braxton assembled what was considered to be his finest quartet ever, with pianist Marilyn Crispell, bassist Mark Dresser, and Hemingway on drums. Their British tour was documented in witty detail by Graham Lock in *Forces in Motion*, revealing the alternation of accolades and grief that the band suffered while trying to support its unusual art. With this quartet, Braxton began separating performances into "sound territories," collaging whole or partial compositions together in the course of a set, with solo passages often bridging the gaps. Braxton frequently hacked off portions of Composition 96 to act as bridges or supportive sections. Braxton had originally labeled this kind of environmental interaction as "universe forms" but recanted the term later. The basic idea is that his body of music is like a universe unto itself, with the individual pieces capable of being blended together in any combination during a performance. This notion has stricken critics as egocentrism, but in practice, the logical unity of Braxton's compositional approach enables such cross-breeding of works. This modular concept can only be truly understood by hearing it in action, at which time the oneness of his ideas comes clear. Of course, there is a risk in one musician concentrating so hard on his particular segment that he fails to interact well (if at all) with the others, a performance process that composers such as John Cage and Otomo Yoshihide have encouraged at times. Fortunately, Braxton has worked out his modular concepts thoroughly enough that such risk is minimized in his ensembles. It also helps that he has the luxury of hand-selecting his collaborators.

London (Quartet) 1985 (Leo), recorded early on in the British tour, is a magnificent archive of the band's methods. The set runs the gamut from hard bop to circus music to Kelvin repetition structures. The CD consists of two discs containing one track each, these single tracks delineating the two sets performed by the quartet that night at the Bloomsbury Theatre. Since the compositions flow seamlessly into one another, it might have seemed logical to lump them into mega-tracks, but it makes it difficult to pick out the various pieces if desired. One must simply listen for likely transition points in the flux. The London set is an invigorating, enlightening experience that is mandatory listening for anyone remotely interested in Braxton's music.

Braxton's efforts at restructuring the umbrella of modern music eventually earned him the accolades and honors he deserved. He served for several years as a music professor at Mills College in Oakland, California, and is presently a tenured professor at Wesleyan University in Connecticut. In 1994, Braxton was awarded the

MacArthur Fellowship "genius" grant for his outstanding contributions to music. With those funds, he incorporated the nonprofit Tri-Centric Foundation as an outlet for his works. His own books, *Tri-Axium Writings* and *Composition Notes A-E*, document his musical principles, which remain as bafflingly complicated and personal as ever. In the mid-1990s, he began working with what he calls "Ghost Trance" music, repetitive but compelling cycles of melody often extended over long periods. One of the most effective recordings of this phase of Braxton's music is *Ninetet (Yoshi's) 1997, Volume 1* (2002, Leo, 2 CDs), featuring interpretations of his Compositions 207 and 208 by Braxton, reedmen J. D. Parran, Brandon Evans, James Fei, Jackson Moore, and Andre Vida, guitarist Kevin O'Neal, bassist Joe Fonda, and drummer Kevin Norton.

All of this ultra-intellectual complexity places Braxton at the remotest edge of the AACM's cadre. He is certainly one of its most "academic" alumni, with perhaps the fewest discernible hints of jazz in his compositions. Like Butch Morris and many of the European free improvisers, the more concepts Braxton has assimilated from the "classical" avant-garde, the farther his music has moved from what might be comfortably called "jazz." However, Braxton still occasionally surprises the jazz establishment by recording albums of standards, delivered in his notably facile, bebop-inflected style. In the mid-1990s, he performed quartet dates as a pianist, and in 2000 he recorded a pair of excellent, well-grounded albums featuring compositions by Andrew Hill (*Nine Compositions (Hill) 2000* and *Ten Compositions (Quartet) 2000*, both on CIMP) with O'Neal, Norton, and bassist Andy Eulau. Then, just when one thought Braxton might be going soft, he came out with his most audacious project yet: *Four Compositions (Duets) 2000* (CIMP), a collaboration with a young stand-up comedian named Alex Horwitz.

Breuker, Willem (b. Amsterdam, Netherlands, 4 November 1944): saxophonist, composer, and bandleader, one of the most prolific figures in European jazz. An activist who has fought for government arts funding in the Netherlands, Breuker possesses a bottomless love for music in all its guises. Theater, cabaret, comedy, and classical influences have seasoned his various projects over the decades, none more than his big band, the Kollektief. He also has a bit of Braxtonian adventure in his soul, as evidenced by his compositions for three barrel organs and nineteen mandolins.

As a young boy, Breuker began studying voice and clarinet. He was particularly influenced by altoist Piet Noordijk, whom he regularly heard on the radio. He gained an early interest in jazz and improvisation and dabbled in most every form of contemporary music as his studies advanced. Breuker took up the bass clarinet but was soon fired from the band he worked in. He was also denied admission into the Amsterdam Conservatory, but that setback did not keep him from performing professionally while he studied to become a teacher.

Breuker began composing his own works before his twentieth birthday and gained the attention of local musicians by winning numerous prizes at local festivals. His sense of humor got the better of him when he fell into a disagreement with a local composer and deliberately performed horrible renditions of the man's music at a festival. This incident got the attention of pianist Misha Mengelberg, who hired the young reedman for his quintet. There, if only briefly, Breuker had the chance to play along-side his early inspiration, Noordijk, and two future icons of free improv, Han Bennink and Maarten van Regteren Altena. Aside from drummer Pierre Courbois, few Dutch-men had become involved in free jazz up until that time, the mid-1960s.

Bennink and Breuker sometimes performed as the New Acoustic Swing Duo, play-ing a thunderous, witty brand of improvised music. They recorded their first album on their own label, ICP (Instant Composers Pool). The ICP stemmed from their idea of having a rotating cast of players perform together in spontaneous improvisations, altering the lineup according to whim or availability to change the sound. Mengelberg became the third ICP member but fell into arguments with Breuker over direction and leadership. The former friends fell out, with Mengelberg remaining in charge of the ICP, and they did not perform together for over twenty years. (See Instant Com-posers Pool entry.)

Breuker recorded his first album, *Contemporary Jazz for Holland/Litany for the 14th of June, 1966* (ICP) in the autumn of that year, earning national recognition for the politically charged "Litany." Illustrating the rift between the ICP's founders, half of the album features Mengelberg's quintet *sans* Breuker. Subsequently, he recorded with Gunter Hampel (*Assemblage/New Music from Europe*, 1967, ESP; *The 8th of July 1969*, with Anthony Braxton), the Globe Unity Orchestra, and Peter Brötzmann (*Machine Gun*). Breuker also landed sporadic jobs in film, radio, and theater, which kept him afloat while he formulated outside concepts like *The Message* (1971, ICP), a three-act opera written for a mime troupe.

Breuker and some friends approached the Dutch Jazz Foundation in 1970 to re-quest full-time funding for jazz ensembles. Flummoxed by the idea, a number of board members resigned and left the Foundation in the hands of a few who supported Breuker's request. The Dutch Ministry of Culture accepted the group's proposal within a year, and subsidies began to flow a few years later. Breuker won the Dutch National Jazz Prize in 1970 for his efforts in "legitimizing" the music. With steady funding from the national government and the Amsterdam Arts Council, the musicians funded the building of the BIMHuis, which remains one of Europe's most unique venues for cre-ative music. Next came the BVHaast label, created by Breuker and pianist Leo Cuypers for the general purpose of documenting the saxophonist's projects. *Live in Shaffy* (1974) was the label's first release, a free duo featuring its founders. (The 1978 . . . *Superstars*, on BVHaast, is an even better portrait of the pair.)

In 1973, The Willem Breuker Kollektief, a semi-big-band with ten members or more, was formed around a core of friends that Breuker had built up over the prior decade. The WBK's music was a compound of several jazz styles with European pop, propaganda, and theater music. Their live concerts were almost immediately charac-terized by a wild theatricality, with, for instance, the whole sax section falling onto their backs and kicking frantically while playing difficult passages. In spirit, WBK's shows are part Firesign Theatre, part Art Ensemble of Chicago.

The European Scene (1975, MPS) was the WBK's debut on record, and it came as a sincere shock to the systems of jazz enthusiasts and Breuker's free-jazz fans alike. The eleven-piece band included Breuker on various reeds, Cuypers, altoist Bob Driessen, tenorman Maarten Van Norden, trumpeter Boy Raaymakers, flautist Ronald Snijders, trombonists Bernard Hunnekink and Willem Van Manen, French hornist Jan Wolff, bassist Arjen Gorter, and drummer Rob Verdurmen. There are many free moments, and "Riette" is about as far out as the Kollektief goes, with Breuker's horn offering a hilarious burlesque of sound. In November 1975, this same lineup recorded *Live in Berlin* (FMP). From the "Introduction and Oratorium" to the closing spiritual "Our Time Will Come," the Kollektief cheerfully deconstructs any preconceived notions about the sanctity of treasured musical forms. Gorter, Cuypers, and Raaymakers in particular turn in rousing performances on both discs.

The Kollektief was remarkably prolific in its first decade, churning out albums every few months at times. *On Tour* (1977, BVHaast) was taped in Rouens, France. The sequential "Husse" tracks are texturally interesting, but the high points are the daffy country spoof "Potsdamer Stomp" and the totally overboard "Antelope Cobbler." Better sound quality and a bit more tradition can be found on *Summer Music* (1978, Marge). *WBK '79* (1980, BVHaast) contains excellent covers of Weill and Grieg. The two-record set *In Holland* (1980, BVHaast) is one of the Kollektief's finest releases, but unavailable on CD.

Rhapsody in Blue (1982, BVHaast) unites the most ostentatious music of two cultures: America and Italy. The title piece is handled with reasonable loving faith by Breuker and pianist Henk de Jonge, who also has a lovely, grounded solo feature in Gershwin's "Three Preludes." Covers abound on *Driebergen-Zeist* (1983) as the Kollektief attacks Weill's "Benares" and "Pirate Jenny" (with insane new lyrics), Ellington's old chestnut "Creole Love Call," and Prokofiev's "Dance of the Knights."

Klap op de Vuurpijl (1985, BVHaast) saw the Kollektief moving from bracing originality into more of a going through the motions. There are some excellent moments scattered about. But on the longest tune, "Casablanca Suite," the humor starts to sound stale, contrived, and the occasional mood swings are all things we've heard before. *Sendai Sjors & Sendai Sjimmie* (1987, Jazz + NOW), a duet album with Bennink, illustrates how far the reedman had moved away from freedom. Bennink is, as usual, all over the kit and full of inventiveness. Breuker's head, however, doesn't seem to be on the game, even on his energetic bass-clarinet solo "Tlam."

Having neither a heart for free improv nor much interest in pursuing his trademark style collages, Breuker seemed at a crossroads by the mid-1980s. It was ironic, then, that the Kollektief's next album was the one that broke them out to American audiences. *Bob's Gallery* (1988, BVHaast) was the first release on the label to receive good American distribution, and while U.S. audiences were roundly impressed with the WBK's flash and musicianship, it was by no means the group's best. Thanks to Gorter and Raaymakers, and a few inspired offerings from the leader, the disc was strong enough to earn the Kollektief new fans. *Gershwin* (1988, BVHaast), on which the American maestro's tunes were rendered more faithfully than on Breuker's previous homage, continued the market expansion. *To Remain* (1989) and *Heibel* (1990), the latter packaged in a cheese box, have a handful of gems between them. Still in all, it seemed the Kollektief's best days were behind them. More theater works and oddities followed, with a permeating sense of half-heartedness.

Not until *Pakkepapèn* (1997, BVHaast) did the Kollektief truly recapture their stride. Tenorman Alex Coke and trumpeter Andy Altenfelder, among the newer WBK members, distinguish themselves admirably. Raaymakers, Gorter, and Hunnekink are still along for the ride, adding stability to the ship on arduous workouts like

"Pakkepapèn 1" and "Hawa-Hawa." *Psalm 122* (1998, BVHaast) is one of Breuker's most ambitious undertakings, a relating of the Jews' trek to establish the city of Jerusalem as performed by the WBK, a forty-member choir, a string octet, and a barrel organist. Difficult on first listens, the record becomes endearing after repeated spins. Moses would likely not have approved, but Breuker's fans will be delighted.

Other triumphs have ensued in the new millennium. *Parade* (2000, BVHaast) includes a full three-track rendition of the cartoony title work by Erik Satie, as well as two suites: Breuker's shaky "Zaanse Pegels" and Henk de Jonge's masterful "Expectations." *Hunger!* (2000, BVHaast) features strong performances by singer Loes Luca and some high-spirited butcherings of Rossini and "Yes, We Have No Bananas." *Thirst!* (2001, BVHaast) is similar in spirit. WBK's best-of collection is *Celebrating 25 Years on the Road* (2000, BVHaast), and it runs the full gamut of Kollektief tunes from "Rascals" to the old Vincent Youmans warhorse "I Want to Be Happy." *The Pirate* (2000, BVHaast), on the other hand, is an equally essential compendium of outtakes and rarities.

Bright Moments: free-jazz supergroup of sorts, featuring saxophonists Joseph Jarman and Kalaparusha Maurice McIntyre, pianist Adegoke Steve Colson, bassist Malachi Favors, and percussionist Kahil El'Zabar. *Return of the Lost Tribe* (1998, Delmark) is their sole document thus far, a brilliant collective effort.

Brimfield, William (b. Chicago, IL, 8 April 1938): AACM trumpeter. Brimfield also studied violin and piano, and was a pupil of Fred Anderson. He met up with Muhal Richard Abrams during a stint in the army, joining Joseph Jarman's group with Anderson upon his discharge. He featured prominently on Jarman's early Delmark album *Song For*, and has performed in other AACM ensembles such as Abrams's orchestra.

Brötzmann, Peter (b. Remscheid, Germany, 6 March 1941): reedman. Originally self-taught, Brötzmann qualified for admission into the Art Academy of Wuppertal as a teenager by exhibiting an acute level of musicianship. After graduation, he became involved with the German wing of Fluxus, George Maciunas's avant-art movement, as well as performing with local Dixieland bands. In the mid-1960s, he fell in with Swedish drummer Sven-Åke Johansson and bassist Peter Kowald, both involved in Wuppertal's embryonic free scene. Their trio became one of the principal forces in German free music, opening the doors of opportunity for new players. As Harriott and Coleman had been unknowing contemporaries, so Brötzmann moved in the same directions as Ayler without them being aware of each other. Brötzmann got in on the ground floor of the Globe Unity Orchestra in 1966, the same year he accompanied JCOA founders Carla Bley and Michael Mantler on a successful European tour. Besides his skills on the tenor and soprano saxes, Brötzmann is the principal free pundit of the tarogato, a single-reed Hungarian horn, which seems a hybrid of clarinet and soprano sax.

In 1967, the Brötzmann/Kowald/Johansson trio recorded its first album, *For Adolphe Sax*. The disc was issued on FMP (Free Music Production), the label founded by the three men to document and distribute European free performances. The title tune is a circus of paint-peeling agitation, with Brötzmann pushing Herr Sax's invention to limits of which he never could have conceived and would hardly have approved. Long unavailable, it has finally been reissued on CD through Atavistic Records' Unheard Music program.

The follow-up, *Machine Gun* (1968, FMP), is usually ranked among the greatest free albums, European or otherwise. The expanded band consists of Brötzmann on baritone sax, Evan Parker on tenor, Willem Breuker on tenor sax and bass clarinet, Fred Van Hove on piano, Kowald and Buschi Niebergall on bass, and both Han Bennink and Johansson on drums. Structurally the group is similar to the Coleman Double Quartet on *Free Jazz*, with a piano and an extra saxophone in place of the two trumpets. The first few seconds of the title track are earthshaking, as a mammoth barrage of sound is brought down on the listeners' heads in unrelenting droves. The three saxophonists blare out huge, dissonant, staccato chords while rattles of percussion bounce around in the background like shrapnel and falling bricks. A moment of blissful relief comes with Parker's solo turn, but he soon turns up the heat, and the ensemble obliterates him with loud screams. On the sidelines, Van Hove ironically pounds out chords that are often beautiful but eventually break down into speedy runs and hammers. After some comparative downtime, the band stretches and roars to open the way for Breuker's furious solo. Brötzmann leads the parade out over a drunken big-band riff that dissolves into chaos. *Free Jazz* certainly has nothing on *Machine Gun* for sheer power.

In the aftermath of *Machine Gun*, Brötzmann became a chieftain of European free jazz, recording a dazzling number of sessions for FMP. Many of his best early works have long been unavailable due to the label's habitually flaky reissue practices, but *Nipples* (1970) is available again, and *Balls* (1969) and other classics will soon return to the market thanks to Atavistic's Unheard Music imprint.

The title track of *Nipples* is performed by the sextet of Brötzmann, Bennink, Niebergall, Van Hove, and a pair of then up-and-coming British improvisers: Evan Parker and Derek Bailey. The white-hot severity of the music is kindred to Coltrane's *Ascension*, but the energy level is the only certain comparison. The horns lay out multiple patterns of notes, which are then repeated and altered at will. Like a pack of wolves fighting for dominance, those with the most forceful presence tend to wrest command.

Fuck de Boere (Dedicated to Johnny Dyani) (2001, Atavistic) presents two lengthy live tracks recorded at the Frankfurt Jazz Festival. A version of "Machine Gun" from 1968 is smoother and less charismatic than the studio original, but that's a relative statement if ever there was one. It sounds as if the band members were more familiar with the tunes ins and outs by festival time, with the deeper comprehension reducing the urgency somewhat. This is still a phenomenal performance nonetheless. The title of "Fuck de Boere," taped in 1970, stems from the late bassist Johnny Dyani's disdain for the white government in South Africa. The track conveys the frustrated anger of Dyani and his people, resulting in a searing condemnation of racist imperialism through music and Mingusian spectacle.

In 1971, Brötzmann, Van Hove, and Bennink gave a series of concerts in Berlin at the same time that some top American jazzmen—among them Miles Davis and Ornette Coleman—were in town. As *Live in Berlin '71* (1991, FMP, 2 CDs) shows, these gigs amounted to a vigorous, if light-hearted, "up yours" to the visitors who spun their brand of improv for the German crowds. Albert Mangelsdorff is also present, blatting multiphonics all around Van Hove's sarcastic nods to musical convention.

In 1975, the trio (without Mangelsdorff) recorded the more restrained *Tschus* (FMP), notable in part for the surprising shortness of its tracks. This is a jazzier outing than most anything else this team recorded together, though it does not lack for crunchy moments. Bennink vocalizes just as insanely as he assaults everything in reach of his drumsticks; Brötzmann ranges from leonine roars to lambish softness; Van Hove holds the whole shebang together with his inimitable flexibility.

Brötzmann's first solo album came in 1976. *Solo* (FMP) exhibits some of the influences that the reedman did not always wear on his sleeve in group efforts, along with his sporadically displayed sense of humor. That wit is best evidenced on the lumbering "Humpty Dumpty" (no relation to the Ornette Coleman tune) for bass saxophone and the twisted march "Eine Kleine Marschmusik." Solo performances are, by nature, revealing ventures that lay bare the player's strengths and weaknesses with no other sounds to hide behind. At this point, Brötzmann still seems an artist in development, in search of his own identity. By the time of *Nothing to Say: A Suite of Breathless Motion Dedicated to Oscar Wilde* (1996, FMP), his more recent solo outing, Brötzmann had become a well-established and completely confident player. His ideas on the Wilde homage are more concise, pared down to the bare essentials for conveying the message of each track. The switching of instruments carries a stronger sense of textural purpose, not that Brötzmann was ever vulnerable to mere showmanship. Comparing the two recordings, perhaps with the rarer *No Nothing* (1990, FMP) between them, paints a clear portrait of his maturation.

Over the course of his career, Brötzmann has recorded with several different trios. It is an excellent format for him, providing the ideal balance of openness and support. For 1979's *3 Points and a Mountain . . . Plus* (FMP) Brötzmann teamed up with Bennink and Misha Mengelberg on a most memorable session. Mengelberg's presence seems to encourage the others to hold back on the dynamics and have fun with the soundflow. Excellent moments of inspiration abound, and the title track is the most precious offering.

Brötzmann performed with drummer Günter Sommer and British bassist Barre Phillips in the early 1980s at some festivals, and in 1988, the trio reunited for *Réservé* (FMP). This trio is a completely different animal from the ones with Bennink, Van Hove, and Mengelberg, thanks to the limitless drive of Phillips, who joins the fray partway through the second half-hour track and assumes the role of referee. The brilliance of the trio's interaction makes one wish that the bassist had been present on the title track to temper the heat level.

In 1991, in the spirit of musical ecumenicism, Brötzmann got the chance to perform at Berlin's Total Music Meeting with two icons of American free jazz: AACM bassist Fred Hopkins and ex-Coltrane drummer Rashied Ali. The persistent compatibility between the Americans' jazz-based approach and the more open European style was readily confirmed. The fabulous *Songlines* (1994, FMP) is the result of that union. Brötzmann seems to hold himself back from his usual bombast. Whether that is due to his own uncertainty in the setting or an egotistical belief that the others could not keep up is moot; the music is the thing. The empathy between Hopkins and Ali is immediate, and it does not take long for Brötzmann to connect to their wavelength. This is an important distinction between these two cultures, musically and politically. American free jazz has so often been about group democracy, while European improvisers have been more inclined toward shows of individual strength, leading to battles royal. On both sides, of course, exceptions abound. At any rate, the democratization of roles on *Songlines* results in an exciting set that does not completely drain the listener of energy.

Brötzmann's recent trio features two younger Scandinavians: Danish electric bassist Peter Friis Nielsen and Swedish drummer Peeter Uuskyla. They have recorded two albums together, *Live at Nefertiti* (1999, Ayler) and *Noise of Wings* (1999, Slask). The electrified sound of Nielsen's bass is rousingly different and matches nicely with Uuskyla's dynamic drum technique.

Brötzmann occasionally distinguishes himself in duo sessions as well, and two in particular come highly recommended. *Wie Das Leben So Spielt* (1989, FMP) marks his meeting with Swiss altoist Werner Lüdi, who was shamefully obscure outside of European circles until his death in 2000. Lüdi's alto tone is somewhat reminiscent of Trevor Watts's, very melodic and appealing even when he pushes the envelope. The contrast with Brötzmann's raw delivery is particularly helpful on a session that has no rhythmic support. In complete contrast is *Last Home* (1990, Pathological), a frighteningly intense pairing of father and son. Avant-rock guitarist Caspar Brötzmann is known to a small but loyal audience in America as the frontman of the crunching band Massaker. Those fans are likely open-minded enough to be aware of his old man, but they still might blanch at the prospect of a duo for electric guitar and equally loud reeds. This set makes it glaringly obvious where Caspar got his unorthodox musical pedigree, as the two act out the ultimate in domestic violence.

Besides countless European recordings and appearances, Brötzmann has regularly worked with players in the United States. His most famous American association was Last Exit, a jazz-thrash quartet with guitarist Sonny Sharrock, electric bassist Bill Laswell, and former Coleman/Taylor drummer Ronald Shannon Jackson. (See the entry for Last Exit.) A crushingly powerful unit, Last Exit was not well represented on records and folded upon Sharrock's death.

Brötzmann's Chicago Tentet is an acclaimed multiethnic unit with such young stars as saxophonists Mats Gustafsson and Ken Vandermark, trumpeter Toshinori Kondo, trombonist Jeb Bishop, cellist Fred Lonberg-Holm, bassists Kent Kessler and William Parker, and drummers Michael Zerang and Hamid Drake. The level of playing on the three-disc *Chicago Octet/Tentet* (1998) and *Stone/Water* (2000, both on Okkadisk) is a cross between Globe Unity and *Machine Gun*: potent, inventive compositions welded to astoundingly passionate improvisations.

Recorded in 1998, *Chicago Octet/Tentet* features Brötzmann, Gustafsson, and trumpeter/saxophonist Joe McPhee in partnership with some of the Windy City's finest post-AACM freemen: Drake, Lonberg-Holm, Kessler, Zerang, Bishop, Vandermark, and reedman Mars Williams. From the opening notes of "Burning Spirit (for Kazuka Shiraishi)," this ensemble delves into the open-composed neighborhood of Cecil Taylor's large-band works. The first tune features a marvelous section wherein various players snatch portions of Brötzmann's tenor solo and make their own variations on them while he continues to unravel his skein of ideas. *Stone/Water* is a single composition of just over half an hour's length. It would have been nice to fill up the album with more material, but then again the sheer force of what is here is enough to sate most appetites. Kondo and William Parker, whose rapport with Kessler results in marvelous low-end magic, replace Mars Williams and McPhee here. Kondo, a less traditional trumpeter than McPhee, augments his horn with electronic processing for shearing tone effects when he's not dipping into a 1970s fusion mode. The drummer and the fluid Vandermark contribute much to the final outcome.

Brötzmann has been acclaimed for his work with the Die Like A Dog Quartet, including Kondo, Parker, and drummer Hamid Drake. (See the quartet's separate entry.) Brötzmann sometimes works with Drake outside Die Like A Dog, including the unusual duo set *The Dried Rat-Dog* (1998, Okkadisk). Drake and Bennink are among the consummate drummers in free music, each drawing from a well-deep knowledge of jazz and world-music traditions in addition to their open improvisational skills. It is only logical that Drake would prove as satisfactory a partner for Brötzmann as the Dutch genius had been. Drake is a more serious performer than Bennink, engaging in intensified colorations rather than wild-eyed humor on tracks like the tarogato feature "It's an Angel on the Door." On this and other projects, Brötzmann continues to prove that he is eternally full of surprises.

Brown, Ari (b. Chicago, IL, 1 February 1944): saxophonist, pianist, composer, and bandleader. Brown graduated from Wilson College in the mid-1960s along with several other early members of the AACM. At the time, however, he was a pianist for local soul groups. Eventually he took up the tenor sax and explored jazz, with a brief digression due to a mouth injury. Brown became quite a flexible player, performing bop with Sonny Stitt and McCoy Tyner alongside free gigs with Lester Bowie, Anthony Braxton, and Archie Shepp. Since 1989, Brown has been a member of Kahil El'Zabar's Ritual Trio and has recorded a few good dates under his own name (*Ultimate Frontier*, 1996, Delmark).

Brown, Marion (Jr.; b. Atlanta, GA, 8 September 1935): alto saxophonist who came to prominence following John Coltrane's *Ascension* album. A favorite partner of Archie Shepp, Leo Smith, and Gunter Hampel, Brown remains the best altoist that too few people have heard of.

Brown formally studied alto sax in high school, college, and the army, where he fostered an appreciation for the early innovations of Coltrane and Coleman. Upon relocating to New York City in 1965, he quickly made an impression among the cadre of freemen there, particularly Coltrane and Shepp. Brown had not yet developed a firm sensibility of his own, but his potential was clear. He also associated with Coleman, although no recordings resulted from their time together.

His invitation to take part in Coltrane's landmark *Ascension* and Shepp's *Fire Music* brought offers to lead his own record dates, beginning with *Marion Brown Quartet* (1965, ESP). The comparative discomfort in his sound on the Coltrane disc had dissipated by the time he recorded this debut with trumpeter Alan Shorter, tenorman Bennie Maupin, dual bassists Ronnie Boykins and Reggie Johnson, and Rashied Ali. On the three tracks, Brown and the other horns rip through and around the changes like knives on tissue paper, driven by the thunderous rhythm team. *Why Not?* (1966, ESP) places Brown in solid company with Ali, bassist Norris Jones (before he took on the moniker Sirone), and pianist Stanley Cowell. The compositions are better thought out—"Fortunato" became one of Shepp's favorite tunes—and the quartet's power is mighty.

The connection with Boykins opened the door for Brown to work with Sun Ra, which helped to shape his harmonic and rhythmic senses. Shepp's encouragement in the same period led Brown to record *Three for Shepp* (1966, Impulse), a tip of the hat to the honoree's own *Four for Trane*. Shepp's tune "Spooks" is the highlight, with humorously virtuosic performances by Brown and Stanley Cowell. "Delicado" is a typical Brown barnburner, which features Grachan Moncur III's searing trombone. Brown honks, slithers, and growls expertly, remarkably different from Coleman and Jimmy Lyons. He is definitely his own man. The liner notes by Frank Kofsky are a manifesto for "Black Power" that save little room for discussion of Brown's merits, typical of the disrespect Brown has endured. Recorded less than two years after he debuted in New York, *Three for Shepp* was Brown's last major album in America.

From 1968 to 1970, Brown toured around Europe, working with Anthony Braxton and Steve McCall. He met multi-instrumentalist Gunter Hampel, who became one of his most regular partners along with trumpeter Leo Smith. Brown recorded most of *Porto Novo* (1968, Black Lion) with two Dutch powerhouses, bassist Maarten van Regteren Altena and drummer Han Bennink; two additional tracks on the 1994 CD reissue are duets with Smith. An almost unbearable excitement builds in the trio pieces, thanks to Bennink's deranged thundering. The duo with Smith was dubbed the Creative Improvisation Ensemble, an unwieldy name for such a pair of sensitive musicians, but apropos at any length. Brown and Smith alternate between horns and percussion for added effectiveness. Though their duo efforts are texturally interesting, the cooperative brilliance of the Dutch trio makes the disc.

Following his adventures in Europe, Brown made a single album for ECM. *Afternoon of a Georgia Faun* (1970) is similar in spirit to *Porto Novo* in that one track is horn-rich and the other has little more than percussion and voices. The "faun" notion is apt, given the pastoral air of the session; with a little stretch of the imagination, one might picture a hoofed Brown cavorting through the forest primeval. Bennie Maupin and Anthony Braxton both contribute on several reeds, Chick Corea and Gayle Palmore play piano and percussion, and Jeanne Lee's vocals and synthesizers are precious objects. Andrew Cyrille and drummer Bill Malone lurk amid the jungle of exotic sounds on "Djinji's Corner," an eighteen-minute percussion festival.

Back in America, a nostalgic Brown meditated on his Southern roots on a series of projects and the writings of poet Jean Toomer. *Geechee Recollections* (1973, Impulse) sets percussionist Bill Hasson's reading of Toomer's "Karintha" to a tense theme. "Buttermilk Bottom" and the three-part "Tokalokaloka" suite draw on hard blues and folk elements. Smith and Steve McCall offer up delicious contributions. On *Sweet Earth Flying* (1974, Impulse), Toomer's spirit is omnipresent if her words are not; Hasson's recitation on Part Three of the suite is done in his own unintelligible language. Pianists Paul Bley and Muhal Richard Abrams are surprisingly compatible, a testimony to their flexibility. The electric keyboards date the sound somewhat, but Abrams in particular is excellent. In the midst of it all is Brown on alto and soprano, summoning the ghosts of the Black Diaspora in his inimitable style. The third installment of the Toomer-inspired trilogy, *November Cotton Flower* (Baystate) was not recorded until 1980, but it was perhaps one of Brown's best efforts. Pianist Hilton Ruiz is the altoist's foil this time, and his keyboard prowess adds polish to the well-worn "La Placita" and "Fortunato."

In 1977, Brown returned to Europe on tour, recording *La Placita: Live in Willisau* (Timeless) with the prime quartet of guitarist Brandon Ross, bassist Jack Gregg, and drummer Steve McCraven. Brown gives "Fortunato" its finest reading yet for an appreciative Swiss crowd, and offbeat takes on the dusty "Soft Winds" and Sonny Rollins's "Sonnymoon For Two" update the notion of what makes jazz jazz. The occasional metallic edge of Ross's ensuing playing with Henry Threadgill and the Downtown New York crowd is not yet dominant; his lines are tempered with thoughtful melodicism with periodic rises in intensity.

Brown and Gunter Hampel worked together frequently from the mid-1970s. *Reed 'n Vibes* (1978, IAI) is one of their most enduring sessions, impeccably produced by Paul Bley. The two players listen on a microscopic level usually found only within the longest partnerships, resulting in timeless creations. The uncomfortably titled *Gemini & Play Live Sun Ra Compositions* (1983, Birth) is live and ripe with humor.

Illness forced Brown into a layoff of a few years, during which time he managed to record with Steve Lacy and Mal Waldron. Brown returned to form with the exceptional *Native Land* (1990, ITM), recorded with a German group centered on fellow altoist Udo Hagen Zempel. While Brown may not have the full vitality and endurance of his Impulse period, the underlying passions of his heart are clear. In 1992, Brown recorded three sessions: *Echoes of Blue* (2000, Challenge), with the German ensemble Jazz Cussion, and *Offering* (1992, Venus) and *Mirante do Vale—Offering II* (1992, Venus) with his quintet featuring guitarist Jay Messer and pianist Tom McClung.

Since the mid-1980s, Brown's vivaciousness has been dampened due to nagging health problems, including surgery for aneurysms and a foot amputation, a deplorable situation for a tremendous talent who has never really received his due. It is fortunate that Brown's best recordings remain in print for old fans to love and new ones to discover when the time comes.

Brown, Rob (b. 27 February 1962): alto saxophonist and flautist. Brown is a rather underappreciated figure in current free jazz, despite his outstanding work with Matthew Shipp (both debuted on record with *Sonic Explorations*, 1988, Cadence Jazz), Joe Morris, Whit Dickey, and William Parker's Little Huey Creative Music Orchestra since the late 1980s. He has displayed his impressive flexibility on a scant few albums as a leader (*Scratching the Surface*, 1997, CIMP; *Jumping Off the Page*, 2000, No More) but tends to achieve his highest peaks under his peers' leadership.

Bruce's Fingers: British record label founded by Simon H. Fell in 1983. The catalog includes free jazz, improvised music, and contemporary composition. Most releases feature bassist Fell in one ensemble format or another.

Bruno, Tom: drummer. Bruno labored for several years in practical obscurity, drumming in the New York subways under the arts program Music Under New York, beginning in 1975. He joined the New York Artists' Collective and got a few club gigs, along with the occasional recording session (*White Boy Blues*, rec. 1981, issued 2000, Eremite). His technique is easily equal to most other free drummers of the era. Bruno finally broke out to wider appreciation with the formation of his superb quartet Test (see entry) in the early 1990s.

Buckner, Thomas (b. 1941): vocalist and producer. Buckner is one of America's premier "new music" vocalists, regularly collaborating with fringe composers like Robert Ashley, Pauline Oliveros, Morton Subotnick, and Alvin Lucier, as well as free jazz artists Roscoe Mitchell, Henry Threadgill, Joseph Jarman, and Leroy Jenkins. He has recorded solo CDs for the Lovely Music label and has frequently partnered with new music pianist Joseph Kubera and his wife, classical Indian dancer Kamala Cesar Buckner.

Buckner began to develop his singular avant-garde style in the 1960s in Berkeley, California. He founded the 1750 Arch record label and concert production company, and first worked with Mitchell at that time. The piece "Words," from *Roscoe Mitchell and the Sound and Space Ensembles* (1984, Black Saint) is an intriguing crossover between black free jazz and white Third Stream music. Mitchell and Gerald Oshita perform on alto and baritone saxes, respectively, while Buckner sings freely from a selected list of thirty-two uncommon words. Their interaction offers an interesting study of the breakdown of both musical phrases and word structures. The resulting patchwork recalls Dada poems like Kurt Schwitters' "Ursonate," with actual words in place of nonsense syllables. This typifies Buckner's unique gift for uniting contemporary classical vocal concepts with black free jazz. He has debuted several works by Mitchell, including the orchestral "Fallen Heroes" and *Pilgrimage* (1995, Lovely Music) with Mitchell's New Chamber Ensemble.

Burn, Chris (b. Epping, U.K. 1955): pianist and composer. Once immersed in the musics of Stockhausen, Cage, and Henry Cowell, Burn has also worked in various jazz, free improv, and dance situations. He has worked with John Butcher for over two decades, in quartets and duos (*Fonetiks*, 1984, Bead). Burn's eight-piece Ensemble has achieved high marks for creativity and has been supplemented by harpist Rhodri Davies, trumpeter Axel Dörner, and other improvisers at times. He has participated in Company projects, received numerous awards for recordings and media work, and is a member of the London Improvisers Orchestra. *Navigations* (1997, Acta) presents a solid overview of the Chris Burn Ensemble.

Burrell, Dave (Herman Davis; b. Middletown, OH, 10 September 1940): pianist. An alumnus of Berklee College of Music, the University of Hawaii, and the Boston Conservatory, Burrell played with Tony Williams and Sam Rivers around Boston. He moved to New York in 1965, performing with Grachan Moncur III and Marion Brown. Burrell was a founding member of the Untraditional Jazz Improvisational Team, with

Byard Lancaster (1965), and the 360 Degree Music Experience (1968), with Beaver Harris and Moncur. In 1969, he gave a stellar performance at the vital Pan-African Festival in Algiers, then toured and recorded with Archie Shepp, Alan Silva, Pharoah Sanders, Sunny Murray, and others. In his playing and composing, Burrell blends jazz, opera, and ethnic musics. Among his finest recordings are *High Won-High Two* (1968, Arista) and the live *Windward Passages* (1979, HatHut).

Butcher, John (b. 1954): British saxophonist, largely self-taught. Butcher set out on the path of a physicist early in life, yet in 1982, he left his PhD on indefinite hold in order to pursue his career in avant-garde music. It is the good fortune of his fans that Butcher bid bugger-all to the lab life and followed his heart into this strange and unknown territory. His use of multiphonics and overtones is shocking, advanced well beyond the levels achieved by American free jazzmen in the late 1960s. Since the mid-1990s, he has released a steady number of albums under his own name and with other projects, each pushing the jazz envelope further. Stockhausen was an early and lasting influence laid upon Butcher by his longtime friend and partner, pianist Chris Burn. Stints in the London Improvisers Orchestra and SME have further polished his reputation.

Thirteen Friendly Numbers (1992, on his own Acta label) was Butcher's first solo release following several group efforts. Its impact was roughly akin to that of Braxton's *For Alto*, Bailey's *Incus Taps*, Paul Rutherford's *The Gentle Harm of the Bourgeoisie*, all recordings that burst the bubble of contemporary thinking about their chosen instruments. Like Braxton, Butcher prefers to work on one section of the vocabulary at a time: sustained squeals on this track, flutters on that, chords elsewhere. These numbers are hardly friendly in the conventional sense; Butcher's sax technique is too foreign, too demanding of his audience, upon first listen; appreciation comes with time.

Though inspired by Evan Parker's innovations, Butcher uses an extended array of sounds in a more subtle fashion, setting him apart from the rampaging honkers who have dominated free improv so far. *Fixations (14): Solo Saxophone Improvisations 1997–2000* (2001, Emanem) displays the lasting power of his nearly scientific concepts.

Anomalies in the Customs of the Day: Music on Seven Occasions (1998, Meniscus) is a collection of duets between Butcher and various creative musicians from Europe and America recorded from 1996 to 1998. The Americans seem to be his most sympathetic partners: Gino Robair and Michael Zerang both provide outstanding percussive guidance, and cellist Fred Lonberg-Holm brings a rich charm to his one track with Butcher. Trombonist Jeb Bishop and violinist Terri Kapsalis are less successful, but Veryan Weston finds a positive stride on three tracks.

Since the mid-1980s, Butcher has maintained a fertile partnership with violinist and electronics manipulator Phil Durrant. At times, as on *Secret Measures* (1999, Wobbly Rail), Durrant has kept the violin packed and stuck to manipulating Butcher's saxophone sounds. Manipulating, indeed; Durrant practically exploits the reedman's ideas, throwing them back in his face, completely changing their tone and context or carrying on animated conversations in hushed tones. *Requests & Antisongs* (2000, Wobbly Rail) is cut from the same cloth, and both discs are simply amazing. On *Intentions* (2001, Nuscope), Butcher and Durrant (on violin this time) meet with Canadian cellist Peggy Lee. Their use of silence and dynamics is powerful, and Lee predicts Durrant's thought-streams time and time again. Lee's husband, drummer Dylan van der Schyff, is Butcher's foil of choice on *Points, Snags, and Windings* (2001, Meniscus). Their enthralling intuition is on the level of Parker/Lytton or Taylor/Murray, a psychic patterning of call, response, and anticipation.

Butcher found another appropriately sensitive partner in pianist Georg Graewe (or Gräwe). Their meeting is captured on 1999's *Light's View* (Nuscope), and the saxophonist apparently finds much appeal in the neoclassical approach of the pianist. Graewe demonstrates his objective facility well, striking out or embracing the sax phrases as he deems fit. Graewe is the more melodic of the two, but Butcher's personal sense of structure sees him through.

On *12 Milagritos* (2000, Spool), Butcher takes on two younger Americans, percussionist Gino Robair and bassist Matthew Sperry. Robair is metrically conscious but also as flexible as they come. Sperry is a true surprise, a phenomenally facile technician whose swoops, chords, and bowing drive the session onward. Here Butcher achieves heights of energy he has only hinted at in other situations. *The Contest of Pleasures* (2001, Potlatch) is an all-horn gathering with clarinetist Xavier Charles and trumpeter Axel Dörner, and *Vortices and Angels* (2001, Emanem) is an entertaining collection of duo tracks, two with Derek Bailey and three with Rhodri Davies.

BVHaast: Dutch record label, founded in 1974 by Willem Breuker and Leo Cuypers. The label has documented a vast range of musical styles, from Breuker's Kollektief ensemble to harmonium music, modern gamelan, and Burton Greene's klezmer projects.

Byard, Jaki (John Byard Jr.; b. Worcester, MA, 15 June 1922; d. Queens, NY, 11 February 1999): pianist, saxophonist, composer, and bandleader. Byard's piano technique covered the spectrum of jazz, from Jelly Roll Morton up through Cecil Taylor, yet he managed to maintain a personalized style that united elements of all the jazz waves. He came to prominence in Earl Bostic's R&B/jazz band in the 1950s, then got into more progressive jazz with Herb Pomeroy and Maynard Ferguson. Charles Mingus tipped Byard off to exciting new sounds when he joined the bassist's band in 1962. A vital, if short-lived, friendship with Eric Dolphy led Byard further toward the edges of free jazz, though he was still very interested in playing boppishly with Zoot Sims, Al Cohn, and vocalist Chris Connor. Roland Kirk and Third Stream pianist Ran Blake were other interesting collaborators of the well-rounded Byard. His first album as a leader, *Blues for Smoke* (1960, Candid), was followed by a lucrative contract with Prestige Records that lasted through the decade. Of those albums, *Out Front!* (1961) and *Sunshine of My Soul* (1967) are especially strong; the latter is by a red-hot trio with David Izenzon and Elvin Jones. Byard also recorded for Muse and Soul Note while teaching, variously, at the New England Conservatory, Harvard University, and Jackie McLean's respected program at Hartt School of Music.

C

Cadence: magazine and record company founded by Robert Rusch. Frustrated with the lack of published coverage of truly creative music, Rusch founded *Cadence* magazine in 1975 to give a voice to avant-garde artists who were working hard to advance the state of contemporary music. One of the magazine's most reliable supporters has been saxophonist and Coltrane transcriber Andrew White, who purchased full-page ads for several years to keep *Cadence* afloat and still contributes funds today. Rusch has come up with many innovative promotions to set *Cadence* apart from the crowd, including hawking high-quality socks, T-shirts, and even cloth diapers!

In 1978, the Cadence Jazz record label was inaugurated with the release of trumpeter Ahmed Abdullah's *Live at Ali's Alley*. In keeping with its "Jewel Box Begone" policy against annoying industry-standard packaging, Cadence Jazz issues its CDs in scratch-free vinyl envelopes. A second imprint, CIMP (Creative Improvised Music Projects), began issuing audiophile-quality recordings in 1995, starting with *The Redwood Sessions* by Evan Parker, Barry Guy, and Paul Lytton with guest Joe McPhee. CIMP's specialty is gathering groups of performers who might have never worked together to experiment in the studio. In the true spirit of a family business, Rusch's son, Mark, usually records CIMP's sessions, while daughter Kara designs all of the album covers. Several talented improvisers, including the reliable duo of bassist Dominic Duval and drummer Jay Rosen, have fostered lasting relationships with Rusch and his labels. Cadence also oversees North Country Distribution, which distributes creative recordings from hundreds of worldwide record labels.

Though *Cadence* magazine presently covers all forms of jazz and creative music to some degree, free jazz and improv remain its principal focus. Its format has remained relatively steady over a quarter century. Each issue features two or three interviews with creative musicians, along with a great number of reissue and new-release reviews. The center section of each issue contains a list of thousands of recordings available for purchase through North Country. The sale of these recordings has contributed to the magazine's continued success on the market. At present, *Cadence* and *Signal To*

Noise are among the very few internationally distributed magazines that specialize in free music and the avant-garde.

Cadentia Nova Danica: Danish jazz ensemble, founded by John Tchicai in 1967 upon returning to his homeland from America. The band began as a nonet but grew to include nearly thirty members, among whom were trumpeter Hugh Steinmetz, bassists Finn Von Eyben and Steffen Andersen, saxophonists Karsten Vogel and Max Brüel, and violinist/reedman Kim Menzer. *Afrodisiaca* (1969, MPS) is their triumph. The band was hired by Danish Radio that year and lasted until Tchicai's departure in 1971.

Campbell, Roy, Jr. (b. Los Angeles, CA, 29 September 1952): trumpeter. Campbell's family moved to the Bronx when he was an infant; his father was a trumpeter who played with Ornette Coleman on occasion. In his youth, Campbell studied piano, flute, and violin but did not take up the trumpet until he was seventeen. As a teenager, he frequented local clubs and hobnobbed with Lee Morgan, Kenny Dorham, Woody Shaw, and other hard-boppers. At Manhattan Community College, he took arranging classes with Yusef Lateef and formed his first group, Jazz Spectrum, while playing R&B, Latin, and reggae on the side. Hearing Albert Ayler and Pharoah Sanders records turned him on to the possibilities of free jazz, so he investigated Studio RivBea and worked with Carlos Garnett (*Cosmos Nucleus*, 1976, Muse), Jemeel Moondoc, and Ken McIntyre. Since the 1980s, he has performed with David Murray, William Parker, Peter Brötzmann (subbing for Toshinori Kondo in Die Like A Dog), and held other high-profile positions. Campbell is a member of the Little Huey Creative Music Orchestra (led by Parker) and Other Dimensions in Music, and leads his Pyramid Trio with Parker and drummer Zen Matsuura (*Ancestral Homeland*, 1998, No More).

Carl, Rüdiger: multi-instrumentalist. Carl performs on tenor sax, clarinet, accordion, and percussion and is one of Europe's most active improvisers. He debuted in 1972 with *King Alcohol* (FMP) and has continued to release discs on the label every few years. His musical partners have included Joëlle Léandre, Irène Schweizer, Carlos Zingaro, Paul Lovens, and Philipp Wachsmann. Carl has been a member of the Canvas Trio, COWWS, and Globe Unity.

Carroll, Baikida (E.J.; b. St. Louis, MO, 15 January 1947): trumpeter. Carroll was educated at Southern Illinois University and the Armed Forces School of Music, where he directed a band; he also studied music in Germany. Upon his return to St. Louis, he joined the Black Artists Group and directed a free-jazz big band. He was among the BAG leaders who relocated to Europe in 1973. He has led his own bands (*Marionettes on a High Wire*, 2001, Omni Tone) and played with R&B and jazz musicians from all walks, including Julius Hemphill, Oliver Nelson, Muhal Richard Abrams, Oliver Lake, and David Murray. Carroll has also composed jazz pieces and film soundtracks.

Carter, Daniel (b. Wilkinsburg, PA, 1945): multi-instrumentalist. One of the most compelling studies in David G. Such's 1993 book *Avant-Garde Jazz Musicians: Performing 'Out There,'* Carter has become one of the principal players in free jazz's revitalization. Besides Joe McPhee, he is one of the few musicians proficient on both trumpet and reeds. Carter began his career as a doo-wop singer in his teens. The clarinet was his first instrument, followed by saxophone in high school. His extensive musical education included studies at the U.S. Armed Forces School of Music, Hunter and Goddard Colleges, SUNY at Stony Brook, and the New School for Social Research under Jimmy Giuffre and Robert Lillienfeld.

In the 1970s, Carter performed with William Parker, Dewey Johnson, Billy Bang, bassist Earl Freeman, and other freemen in the Music Ensemble, born out of the loft scene. Parker has remained a principal partner, along with Matthew Shipp. Carter is also a member of Test, Other Dimensions in Music, Post Prandials, Tenor Rising/ Drums Expanding, and Out Da Concrete. His formidable talents have brightened records and concerts by Sam Rivers, Sun Ra, Cecil Taylor, Bob Moses, Gunter Hampel, Mat Maneri, Zusaan Kali Fasteau, Spring Heel Jack, the One World Ensemble, Yo La Tengo, the Saturnalia String Trio, and DJ Logic. Carter's first recording under his own name was 2002's *Language* (Origin), with bassist Reuben Radding and drummer Gregg Keplinger.

Carter, John (b. Fort Worth, TX, 24 September 1929; d. Inglewood, CA, 13 March 1991): altoist, clarinetist, and composer. Carter performed in Fort Worth with Ornette Coleman and Charles Moffett as a teenager, then studied music at Lincoln University in Missouri and the University of Colorado. He taught music in Fort Worth's schools from 1949 to 1961, when he moved to Los Angeles. Carter continued working as a teacher and formed a friendship with trumpeter Bobby Bradford. In 1964, the two men founded the New Art Jazz Ensemble. *Seeking* (1969, Flying Dutchman; reissued 1991, HatArt) is an admirable portrait of the leaders' chemistry. With bassist Tom Williamson and drummer Bruz Freeman, a master of subtlety and texture on a par with Steve McCall, the hornmen perform five Colemanesque compositions by Carter and one by Bradford. Carter was a true powerhouse on alto and tenor saxes, clarinet, and flute. In later years, he decided to concentrate almost exclusively on the clarinet, which is only heard once on this early album.

In 1974, Carter abandoned the alto saxophone, concentrating exclusively on the clarinet from then on. From 1976 to 1978, he was part of the Little Big Horn jazz workshop with Bradford, Arthur Blythe, and James Newton, with whom he formed the Wind College in 1983. Through those educational projects, Carter made a lasting impression on many Californian improvisers. His interesting Clarinet Summit of the period was a quartet of three sopranos and a bass.

Carter toured and recorded frequently up until his death. He is most appreciated today for a series of five recordings under the conceptual umbrella "Roots and Folklore: Episodes in the Development of American Folk Music." The albums in the series include *Dauwhe* (1982, on Black Saint), *Castles of Ghana* (1985), the scarce *Dance of the Love Ghosts* (1986), *Fields* (1988), and *Shadows on a Wall* (1989, all on Gramavision). Each suite reflects upon a different aspect of the African American experience, from freedom in the homeland to slavery and back to a more dubious freedom in America.

Carter, Kent (b. Hanover, NH, 12 June 1939): bassist. Carter came from a background in country and western music. He studied jazz at Berklee in the early 1960s and worked as a house musician backing artists like Sonny Stitt, Phil Woods, and Lucky Thompson. He joined and recorded with the Jazz Composers Orchestra in 1964, touring Europe the following year with Paul Bley and performing with Steve Lacy. Carter was a member of Amalgam and Detail, and played with Alan Silva and Mal Waldron. He is also proficient on piano and all members of the violin family. One of his best discs as a leader is *The Juillaguet Collection* (1996, Emanem), a duet with violinist Albrecht Maurer.

Cavallanti, Daniele (b. Milan, Italy, 6 June 1952): reedman. Cavallanti is one of the best saxophonists in the current Italian cadre, a vital part of the Italian Instabile Orchestra, the Jazz Chromatic Ensemble, Guido Mazzon's Gruppo Contemporaneo, and the octet Nexus. Cavallanti has recorded only sporadically under his own name, starting with *Times for Peace* (1994, Splasc(h)). He is a standout contributor to Tiziano Tononi's very entertaining *Awake Nu: A Tribute to Don Cherry* (1996, Splasc(h)).

CCMC (Canadian Creative Music Collective): Toronto, Canada–based improvising ensemble, active since 1978. Its members have included altoist John Oswald, pianist Michael Snow, vocalist Paul Dutton (those three perform on the live disc *aCCoMpliCes*, 1998, Victo), keyboardist John Kamevaar, bassist Al Mattes, and drummer Jack Vorvis. Snow is also an accomplished avant-garde filmmaker; the (in)famous soundtrack to *New York Eye and Ear Control* was recorded by Albert Ayler, Don Cherry, and other free jazzmen in 1964 (ESP).

Cecma: Italian record label, established in 1980 by photographer Cecco Maino. Its first release was David Murray's *Solo Live* (1980); later Cecma artists included Hugh Ragin, Roscoe Mitchell, Anthony Braxton, and John Lindberg.

CELP: label founded by André Jaume in 1987. The catalog features sessions by Barre Phillips, Raymond Boni, Joe McPhee, Jimmy Giuffre, and other artists, often with Jaume on hand.

Centazzo, Andrea: percussionist. An excellent orchestral musician and doctor of musicology, Centazzo is perhaps best renowned for his contributions to the avant-garde since the late 1970s. He has collaborated with John Carter, John Zorn, Don Cherry, Evan Parker, Henry Kaiser, Lol Coxhill, Steve Lacy (*Clangs*, 2000, RDC), and in trio with Lacy and Kent Carter. One of his specialties is multimedia presentations, which unite video projections and his original music. *Situations* (2000, Robi Droli/Newtone) is a worthwhile release featuring Lol Coxhill, Franz Koglmann, and Giancarlo Schiaffini. Centazzo and his wife, Carla Lugli, founded the Ictus label in 1976.

Chadbourne, Eugene (b. Mount Vernon, NY, 4 January 1954): guitarist and vocalist. Chadbourne grew up in Boulder, Colorado, and, like most of his peers, was influenced by the Beatles and Jimi Hendrix. However, he initially moved backward on the musical timeline and became interested in acoustic Delta blues. Jazzwise, he preferred the rising tide of free jazz to most other forms. These widely separate influences, paired with his morbidly wacky sense of humor, helped to define Chadbourne's later musical direction.

Chadbourne studied journalism, then fled to Canada as a conscientious objector during the Vietnam War. In 1976, after President Carter declared amnesty for C.O.s, Chadbourne moved to New York and became involved in the avant-jazz scene there. After starting up the Parachute label, the guitarist met John Zorn and began a long period of collaboration. He also formed his warped band Shockabilly, performing covers of rock and blues hits as well as his own politically satirical tunes and improvisations. Since that time, Chadbourne has worked with California rockers Camper Van Beethoven, Han Bennink, Carla Bley, fellow guitarists Nöel Akchoté and Marc Ribot, and others.

Chancey, Vincent (b. 1950): French horn player. Chancey began playing at the Chicago Conservatory at the age of eleven after studying the cornet in school. His interest in jazz began four years later, when he heard guitarist Wes Montgomery, but he did not play jazz himself until he was twenty-three years old. Chancey obtained his degree in music from Southern Illinois University, then moved to New York to seek out jazz hornist Julius Watkins for lessons. After performing with Monty Waters's big band, Chancey met vocalist/pianist Alison Mills and joined her quartet with David Murray and Abdul Wadud. That led to an invitation to work with Don Cherry, then further jobs with Murray, Muhal Richard Abrams, Carla Bley, Sun Ra, George Russell, Lester Bowie's Brass Fantasy, and Wilber Morris. Chancey worked with Bley from 1978 to 1984; her wise insights into ensemble performance shaped his understanding and flexibility, as did the Abrams and Sun Ra associations. Chancey has led his own trio, Third Order, and has recorded with other ensembles (*Welcome, Mr. Chancey*, 1993, In & Out; *Vincent Chancey and Next Mode*, 1996, DIW).

Chapin, Thomas (b. Manchester, CT, 9 March 1957; d. Providence, RI, 13 February 1998): alto saxophonist, flautist, and bandleader. Chapin, like Glenn Spearman, was a tragic figure of the free-jazz resurgence who died too early. His bebop-derived tone and facility, indebted to Jackie McLean, and endless idea flows are well represented by a decent discography.

Chapin's love for jazz began with the boisterous recordings of Earl Bostic and Roland Kirk. He studied with Kenny Barron and Paul Jeffrey at Rutgers, then moved into McLean's well-respected program at Hartt College of Music. After graduation, Chapin stuck close to mainstream jazz for a time, spending five years as musical director of Lionel Hampton's band and then working with Chico Hamilton. After leaving Hamilton's group, Chapin began to work with saxophonist Ned Rothenberg in more avant-garde settings. During his short stint with Machine Gun, he fused hard-edged metal with free jazz with respectable results.

Chapin's first recording as a leader, *Radius* (1984, Muworks), was an indicator of things to come, bristling with power and thoughts of freedom. Two years later, Chapin became a regular fixture at the newly opened Knitting Factory in downtown New York. In 1989, Chapin assembled a trio with bassist Mario Pavone and drummer Steve Johns, who was later replaced by Michael Sarin. The trio's albums and live shows were among the most staggering to emerge from the Downtown scene, rife with titanic bursts of energy and post-bop technicality (*Third Force*, 1990, Enemy). Chapin explored other ensemble arrangements, often adding guests to the trio, but that threesome remained his best canvas. Never averse to mainstream jazz, Chapin recorded a couple of bop-oriented discs for Arabesque and a session with bassist Ray Drummond, but free jazz was his principal stock-in-trade until his death from leukemia at the age of forty.

Charles, Denis (b. St. Croix, Virgin Islands, 4 December 1933; d. New York, NY, 24 May 1998): drummer. Charles began as a bongo player at age seven and taught himself to play the trap set in his twenties by listening to albums by Art Blakey and Roy Haynes. After moving to New York in 1945, he played in various Caribbean bands around town. In 1954, he became Cecil Taylor's first regular drummer, and the group recorded *Jazz Advance* in 1956. With Taylor and Archie Shepp, Charles performed for Jack Gelber's stage play "The Connection," which featured tenorist Dexter Gordon as an actor. Job opportunities followed with Gil Evans, Jimmy Giuffre, Don Cherry, and his former Taylor bandmate, Steve Lacy. In the late 1960s, however, Charles hit a dry spell and work became quite scarce for him. He was "rediscovered" a few years later and became a regular fixture in New York free music again. Tours and records followed with David Murray, Wilber Morris, Frank Lowe, Billy Bang (including most of his best 1980s albums), Charles Tyler, and others.

Traditional Caribbean music was always close to Charles's heart. An island-flavored set with Sonny Rollins on tenor wasn't very successful, but Charles triumphed with his own album, *Queen Mary* (1989, Silkheart), inspired by themes from his homeland. That session was one of only three to be issued under Charles's own name during his lifetime; the others, also fine, were *Captain of the Deep* (1991, Eremite) and the tribute *A Scream for Charles Tyler* (1992, Adda). Charles died of pneumonia at age sixty-four, just a few weeks after recording *The Last Concert* (2001, Silkheart) with Thomas Borgmann and Wilber Morris. Charles is the subject of Véronique Doumbé's documentary film, *Denis A. Charles: An Interrupted Conversation*.

Chekasin, Vladimir Nikolayevitch (b. Sverdlovsk, Russia, 24 February 1947): reed and keyboard player. Chekasin studied violin as a child, later taking up alto sax and clarinet. He led his own band from 1967 to 1971, during which time he attended the Mussorgsky State Conservatory. In 1971, he moved to Vilnius, Lithuania, where he formed the acclaimed Ganelin Trio (also known as the G-T-Ch Trio; see separate entry) with Vyacheslav Ganelin and Vladimir Tarasov. Besides the trio, he has toured and recorded with his own groups and taught music at the Lithuanian State Conservatory. Chekasin adopted the practice from Rahsaan Roland Kirk of playing two horns simultaneously, which added to the theatricality of G-T-Ch's live experience. He has only rarely recorded under his own name (*Nostalgia*, 1984, Leo).

Cherry, Don (Donald Eugene; b. Oklahoma City, OK, 1936; d. Malaga, Spain, 19 October 1995): trumpeter, composer, and bandleader who, with Ornette Coleman, helped pioneer free jazz. Cherry was one of the most unique figures in jazz's history. The cover of the *Jazzactuel* compilation (2001, Charly) is a prime example: a photo of Cherry wearing goofy dark goggles and a plastic propeller beanie, blowing on a bamboo flute. He was given to outlandish costumes made of vivid African cloths, wearing his hair in a bizarre dreadlock mutation, and roller-skating through the streets of New York City. His love of life and the people around him were inspirational to all who encountered him, as was his matchlessly peculiar music.

Cherry's approach to both standard and pocket cornets was out of New Orleans by way of Miles Davis, sophisticated yet ever balanced on the edge of freedom. Cherry hardly bore titanic chops, but his artistic fearlessness made up for an early lack of technical facility or logically sequenced ideas. He was in love with music itself, not just the rules and regulations that had been erected to comfortably contain it. In that regard, as well as by his impeccable listening skills, Cherry was an ideal partner to most everyone who was lucky enough to work with him.

Cherry was of mixed African American and Choctaw blood. In the 1940s, the family moved to Los Angeles where Don's musician father worked in hot-spot nightclubs that brought in the great big bands. Cherry's interest in jazz started early and was so intense that he went across town to Jefferson High School to study in Samuel Brown's music program; among his bandmates were trumpeter Art Farmer and pianist Horace Tapscott. Cherry started a band with tenor saxophonist James Clay called the Jazz Messiahs, a prophetic title.

The Cherry family lived next door to Jayne Cortez, the future wife of Ornette Coleman. She was seriously interested in ethnic musics as well as jazz, and her enthusiasm infected young Don as well. Not long afterward, he met Coleman and joined the altoist in exploring new dimensions of musical expression. Their mutual ability to give the impression of the human voice through their horns was a special unifying part of their relationship. Once the famous quartet began to take off, Cherry was clearly an equal partner on a creative level, although Coleman got most of the credit. It was not until the band moved to New York that Cherry's personal genius was seriously recognized. That belated praise led to lucrative opportunities apart from the Coleman unit: work with Coltrane, Sonny Rollins, Albert Ayler, Steve Lacy, and Archie Shepp. After seven albums, Cherry left Coleman's band on friendly terms in a quest to make his own impact. (See Coleman's entry.)

The New York Contemporary Five, Cherry's group with Shepp and altoist John Tchicai, barely lasted two years but made a profound mark on jazz in that time. From there Cherry pursued a career as a leader. The year 1965–1966 saw three important dates for Blue Note: *Complete Communion*, *Symphony for Improvisers*, and *Where Is Brooklyn?* The first two dates were structured similarly to Coleman's *Free Jazz*, with several small composed themes serving as inspirational points wrapped up in endless improvisations. The band on *Communion*, recorded on Christmas Eve 1965, included Leandro "Gato" Barbieri, Henry Grimes, and Ed Blackwell, all of whom would remain prominent in free jazz for the next several years. Barbieri's power is especially daunting. Those four players were joined on the *Symphony* date by Karl Berger, French bassist J. F. Jenny-Clark, and Pharoah Sanders on tenor sax and piccolo. That session featured eight small themes as improvisation platforms, and the combined might of Barbieri and Sanders is almost too much to bear. Cherry's third Blue Note date resulted in *Where Is Brooklyn?*, a classic almost equal to the others. A quartet with Sanders, Grimes, and Blackwell, this unit dispensed with the thematic-string motif to navigate five originals. These sessions helped establish Cherry as a force to be reckoned with on his own merits, as opposed to a sideman for Coleman. All three albums were available in a limited-edition boxed set, *The Complete Blue Note Recordings of Don Cherry* (Mosaic).

In 1968, while Coleman was on hiatus conjuring new visions, Cherry assembled a multicultural group for a special appearance at the Berlin Jazz Festival. The leader had been exploring Asian and African music for a while, thanks in part to the inspiration of Jayne Cortez, and he chose to experiment with Balinese gamelan instruments in Berlin. The band included trombonists Albert Mangelsdorff and Eje Thelin, Swedish reedman Bernt Rosengren, Karl Berger, Joachim Kühn, Arild Andersen, French drummer Jacques Thollot, and Sonny Sharrock. Most of these performers would go on to greater acclaim after this fine date, which marked Andersen's first recording. The concert was issued on LP as *Eternal Rhythm* (1968, Saba), and it remains one of the most unusually pleasurable records in free jazz. All the Europeans share in the camaraderie, making this one of the earliest sessions to dissolve the cultural no-man's-land in jazz.

Cherry worked with Rosengren off and on for several years, gigging around European clubs and exploring further fusions of world styles and jazz. *Brotherhood Suite* (1997, Flash) collects a number of their live tracks from the late 1960s. This is some remarkable free-bop, summarized in the title suite on which Cherry gets into some taut minimalistic piano before diving into hot trumpet interaction with Rosengren's tenor sax. Turkish trumpeter Maffy Falay, one of Cherry's finest collaborators and inspirations, joins in on "A.B.F."

In August of 1969, Cherry and Blackwell recorded a series of duets that were originally issued on two separate BYG albums. They are united on *Mu, First Part and Second Part* (1995, Affinity). Blackwell's adaptation of traditional jazz and African rhythms into his own quintessential style were ideal for Cherry's adventures in fusing world musics with jazz. The trumpeter gives equal time to piano, flutes, and vocals on this utterly unique collection. "Teo-Teo-Can" typifies the eclecticism of the package: Blackwell jingles a long string of bells as Cherry continually chants something like "cootie-cootie-cootie" with charming rhythmic effects; he then switches to playing folky flute as Blackwell uses a shaker. It's essential to understanding the full range of the trumpeter's vision.

Another outstanding Cherry/Blackwell duo date is *El Corazón* (1982, ECM), presenting more of their fine collaborative magic with some rather cool production, courtesy of the German label. Thelonious Monk's "Bemsha Swing," which Cherry had recorded with Coltrane on *The Avant-Garde* almost twenty years before, is wedged into a very interesting medley on the first track. Some of the compositions are reminiscent of Coleman, others of Cherry's period cultural explorations. "Voice of the Silence" shows how Cherry's command of the horn had improved since the Coleman days.

Live Ankara (1969, Sonet) again finds Cherry in the company of Maffy Falay, who arranged a half-dozen traditional themes for his guest. Cherry was only the second American jazzman to visit Turkey since Dizzy Gillespie made a stop there in 1956, yet the musicians he found to accompany him there were as attuned to jazz sensibilities as any of the Europeans of the time: percussionist Okey Temiz, tenorman Irfan Sümer, and bassist Selçuk Sun. The set list includes Pharoah Sanders's "The Creator Has a Master Plan," two short Coleman compositions, and six Cherry originals. The rich exoticism of tunes and instrumentation makes for a gorgeous listen, and the leader is enchanting on trumpet, piano, flute, and the double-reed *zurna*. Temiz is the real discovery, classically trained on a profusion of percussion instruments, including copper hand drums. He continued to work with Cherry for some time, including in a trio with bassist Johnny Dyani. *Live Ankara* is paired with 1973's *Eternal Now* (Sonet, an update of the *Eternal Rhythm* concept) on the Verve collection *The Sonet Recordings*.

Cherry made a sidestep to Dartmouth College in 1970 for a brief shot at teaching, also studying classical Carnatic vocal techniques from India. In 1973, Cherry worked with the Jazz Composers Orchestra, with which he recorded the timeless *Relativity Suite* (JCOA). His vocal training and fondness for the *doussn'gouni*, a folk guitar from Mali, bear sweet fruit on "Mali Doussn'gouni," which features a terrifying tenor sax improv by Frank Lowe. Among the foreign sounds to be heard are his wife Moki's *tamboura*, an Indian drone lute; Selene Fung's *ching*, a Chinese zither; a number of violinists including Leroy Jenkins; and Jack Jeffers's pounding tuba.

From 1973 to 1977, Cherry lived in Sweden, where he raised his family, including two now-famous stepkids, Neneh and Eagle Eye Cherry. From there he regularly traveled between America and the Middle East and, of course, worked with notable Scandinavian jazzmen. *Brown Rice* (1975, A&M) dates from this period but was recorded in New York with Charlie Haden, Billy Higgins, Frank Lowe, Ricky Cherry on electric piano, and others. It is more of a period piece than most anything in Cherry's discography, owing to the funky rhythms of "Degi-Degi" and the title track. Haden plays his bass through a wah-wah pedal, as he had with Ornette Coleman on "Rock the Clock," with equally disturbing results. Another completely new direction came with *Hear and Now* (1976, Atlantic), produced by Narada Michael Walden. This rock-soaked session features drummers Tony Williams and Lenny White, Walden on tympani, vocalists Cheryl Alexander and Patty Scialfa (yes, Springsteen's backup singer), Niel Jason and Marcus Miller on bass, tenorman Michael Brecker, and Collin Walcott on sitar.

From 1976 to 1984, Cherry was a member of Codona, a nonpareil world-jazz trio with Walcott and Brazilian percussionist Nana Vasconcelos. Walcott was also a member of Oregon, an eclectic quartet that blended folk music, jazz, and ethnic elements in a similar manner as Codona, while Vasconcelos was a first-call percussionist in New York's circles. Cherry did a little of everything: cornet, pocket trumpet, wooden flutes, doussn'gouni, kalimba, percussion, even singing. There was not much in the way of free jazz to be found on the group's albums (*Codona* [1976], *Codona 2* [1978], and *Codona 3* [1982, all ECM]) but much to love for fans of truly exotic fare. The band's name derived from the first two letters of each member's surname. Walcott's death in a bus crash in November 1984 closed this chapter of Cherry's life on a sad note.

Also in 1976 came the birth of Old and New Dreams, a quartet of Ornette Coleman alumni: Cherry, Dewey Redman, Charlie Haden, and Ed Blackwell. Partially a Coleman repertory ensemble (and a wonderful job they did of giving a new polish to the altoist's classic compositions), the group also played original works. This was during the period when Coleman was first experimenting with Prime Time; fans who were turned off by his new electrified direction found solace in the acoustic Dreams. (See entry for Old and New Dreams.)

After a few years of relative obscurity, Cherry exploded back onto the scene with *Art Deco* (1988, A&M), a wondrous update of his sound and musical thoughts. It's like old home week, as the band is James Clay on tenor, Charlie Haden, and Billy Higgins. Monk's "Bemsha Swing," "Body and Soul," and three Coleman pieces are on tap, and "Maffy" is a tribute to Cherry's late Turkish friend, Maffy Falay. Clay is phenomenal on all he surveys. His prior fading into the unspectacular Texas jazz scene apparently did little to hamper his chops and musical growth.

Spiritually *Multikulti* (1990, A&M) was an extension of the prior set, but with an entirely different lineup. Blackwell again sounds unhindered by his nagging health problems, conversing gloriously with Vasconcelos. Peter Apfelbaum, a clever young tenor saxophonist with world-music aspirations of his own, is outstanding on most of the tracks. His own band, the Hieroglyphics Ensemble, backs Cherry on two brightly brocaded pieces, and the trumpeter sounds like he is in paradise. African percussion abounds on most selections. Karl Berger, Carlos Ward, and tubaist Bob Stewart add important coloration to this wondrous session, which is only detracted from by Cherry's tentative poetry reading.

In 1993, Cherry returned to Europe to record *Dona Nostra* (ECM) with a collection of the continent's finest out-jazzers. Okay Temiz is a welcome sight on drums, pianist Bobo Stenson is in excellent form, and saxophonist Lennart Aberg, bassist Anders Jormin, and drummer Anders Kjellberg fill the studio with their stark Nordic pride. The antiseptic ECM sound suits the Norsemen but adds a discomfiting resonance to Cherry and Temiz.

As health problems began to hold him back, Cherry's playing and ability to show up for gigs took serious hits. In his last couple of years, he performed less frequently and ended up relocating to Malaga, Spain. Cherry died there on October 19, 1995, forever remembered as one of jazz's most beloved and colorful personalities.

Chicago Underground: Less a set ensemble than a concept, the Chicago Underground has ranged from a duo to a quintet. Cornetist/keyboardist Rob Mazurek and percussionist Chad Taylor are the core members, adding bassists Noel Kupersmith and Chris Lopes, guitarist Jeff Parker, and trombonist Sara P. Smith at intervals. Parker and Smith are members of the funk-jazz band Isotope 217, with which Mazurek has collaborated. As the Chicago Underground Duo, Mazurek and Taylor have recorded three albums beginning with *12 Degrees of Freedom* (1998, Thrill Jockey). As a trio with Kupersmith, they have done two Delmark sessions, *Possible Cube* (1999) and *Flamethrower* (2000). Parker was added for *Chicago Underground Quartet* (2001, Thrill Jockey). The Chicago Underground Orchestra, actually a quintet of Mazurek, Taylor, Parker, Smith, and Lopes, issued *Playground* (Delmark) in 1998.

Christi, Ellen (b. Chicago, IL): vocalist. Christi studied opera with Met singer Galli Campi, jazz vocals with Jeanne Lee, and piano with Jaki Byard, all of which contributed to her uncanny harmonic sense. She has since become one of America's most significant avant-jazz vocalists, working with Reggie Workman, William Parker, Butch Morris, Rashied Ali, Andrew Cyrille, Ed Blackwell, Ray Anderson, clarinetist Tony Scott, and many other major figures. Christi has also ventured to Switzerland, Italy, Africa, and other locales seeking new musical experiences. She is a founder of the New York City Artists' Collective, the European quartet Alienstalk, and the Network Records label. *Live at Irving Plaza* (1998, Soul Note) is with the group Menage, including vocalist Lisa Sokolov, William Parker, Tom Bruno, and pianist Rahn Burton.

Christmann, Günter (b. Srem, Poland, April 1942): trombonist, bassist, cellist, and bandleader. Inspired as a youth by Dixieland jazz and driven to overcome the effects of polio, Christmann studied the banjo and trombone. In the 1960s, he embraced free jazz upon hearing Coltrane and Coleman. Soon he was playing free with Rüdiger Carl, Paul Lovens, Peter Kowald, and his own band in fresh extrapolations of the American free-jazz style. Percussionist Detlef Schonenberg was another regular partner; the two performed in duet on Christmann's debut, *We Play* (1973, FMP). His liquid approach to the trombone, a mutation of Kid Ory's New Orleans "tailgate" style, was influential to a host of younger players like George Lewis.

In 1973, Christmann joined and composed for the Globe Unity Orchestra, where he worked with premier European improvisers. Since 1975, he has occasionally performed as a solo artist. In 1978, he formed a duo with cellist Tristan Honsinger, and the next year Christmann developed the pseudo-ensemble Vario, with a shifting personnel of musicians, actors, and mimes. He has also played in duo with bassist Torsten Müller and electronic musician Harald Boje. His multimedia piece "Déjà vu" featured his solo trombone and cello against film clips and light shows. Poor health has restricted Christmann's live performances for the past several years, but he remains active as a composer.

Chronoscope: label founded by Trevor Manwaring and Peter Finchal. It was initially intended to reissue albums by the Spontaneous Music Ensemble and other European free projects.

CIMP (Creative Improvised Music Projects): see **Cadence**.

Circle: short-lived quartet with pianist Chick Corea, reedman Anthony Braxton, bassist Dave Holland, and drummer Barry Altschul. Corea shared electric piano duties with Keith Jarrett in Miles Davis's new fusion band until 1970, when he left to (briefly) pursue acoustic music. Corea began working in a free format with ex-Davis bassist Holland and Altschul, formerly of the Jazz Composers Orchestra Association. After meeting Corea in altoist Marion Brown's group, Braxton became the fourth member of the new unit, which took on the name Circle.

The quartet was highly influential among young avant-leaning musicians who appreciated the musicians' astounding interplay. Of particular note was the prominent role of Corea in a form of music where pianists had not always been successful. Corea clearly took control of Circle's excursions, building his own style rooted in bop and Spanish music instead of functioning as a mere clone of Cecil Taylor.

The ensemble's handful of albums has cycled in and out of print. *Early Circle* (1992, Blue Note; portions originally issued on *Circling In*, 1976, Blue Note) presents ten tracks recorded in New York City in October 1970. The selections on *Early Circle* demonstrate the taut group concept that the members had formulated, particularly on Holland's "Starp." The pair of spacious "Chimes" trios draws inspiration from miniature tubular-chime introductions, with Braxton's soprano and Holland's cello and guitar engaging in open dialogues with Corea's celeste and piano.

Circulus (1970, Blue Note) is the most difficult to find of Circle's recordings. These performances are not as interesting as those on *Early Circle* or *Paris Concert* (1971, ECM), the group's most celebrated release. That final live album contains the quartet's most surprising performances. Reinventions of Wayne Shorter's "Nefertiti" (from his Miles Davis tenure) and "There Is No Greater Love" demonstrate the applicability of Circle's theories to familiar material. Also included is a fascinating duet by Braxton and Corea. The joyous interaction between the men when they were both on the ball makes the ensemble's demise all the more rueful. Corea decided to abandon free music in favor of populist jazz-rock (hastened, it has been said, by his frequent disagreements with Braxton), bringing one of the most potentially satisfying partnerships in free music to a permanent end.

Circulasione Totale: label established by Frode Gjerstad. The catalog includes albums by Gjerstad, drummer John Stevens, and the Circulasione Totale Orchestra (CTO). The CTO is a group of Norwegian players, founded by Gjerstad as a workshop to foster the growth and appreciation of improvised music. To increase its appeal to young performers and listeners alike, the group includes electric instrumentation and rock-styled rhythms. CTO has been vital in spreading the free-jazz movement across Norway. Their commissioned performance at the 1989 Molde Festival combined free improv with rapping and turntable scratching.

Clark, Charles (b. Chicago, IL, 11 March 1945; d. Chicago, 15 April 1969): bass player with the early AACM. Clark studied with the ingenious Wilbur Ware as a youth and turned professional in 1963. Though his career lasted barely six years, Clark secured a reputation as a powerful and intuitive bassist through his association with Muhal Richard Abrams and the AACM. He appeared on Joseph Jarman's seminal *Song For* and *As If It Were the Seasons*, and was an essential member of Jarman's band. Clark died of a cerebral hemorrhage following a rehearsal with the Chicago Civic Orchestra, which established a scholarship in his name.

Cleaver, Gerald (b. Detroit, MI): drummer. Cleaver has been a fixture of Detroit's adventurous jazz milieu since the early 1990s but did not come into national prominence until he began his association with Matthew Shipp. He studied drums with Victor Lewis, courtesy of an NEA fellowship, obtained his degree in music from the University of Michigan, and began working as an educator while playing with keyboardist Craig Taborn. He often commutes between Detroit and New York City, where he has participated in Roscoe Mitchell's Note Factory and trio, quartets led by Joe Morris, Mat Maneri, and Shipp, and his own sextet, Veil of Names (*Adjust*, 2001, Fresh Sound). Other employers have included Henry Threadgill, Charles Gayle, Eddie Harris, and Reggie Workman.

Cline, Alex (b. Los Angeles, CA, 4 January 1956): percussionist. Alex Cline is the twin brother of guitarist Nels Cline. The brothers have collaborated on various projects since their teenage years, including the acclaimed Quartet Music with violinist Jeff Gauthier and the late bassist Eric Von Essen. Later high-profile gigs included work with Julius Hemphill, Tim Berne, and Vinny Golia. An aficionado of ethnic percussions, Alex Cline has led his own ensembles off and on since 1981, when he recorded *Not Alone* (Nine Winds). His 1987 disc *The Lamp and the Star* (ECM) is a favorite of percussion fans. Cline also performs in Gauthier's quartet, drummer Gregg Bendian's Interzone, Bobby Bradford's Mo'tet, and in duo with reedman Jamil Shabaka. He has recorded three albums for Cryptogramophone, most recently *The Constant Flame* (2001).

Cline, Nels (b. Los Angeles, CA, 4 January 1956): guitarist. Nels Cline is the twin brother of percussionist Alex Cline, with whom he has worked in many settings. The brothers took up their instruments at age twelve. By the late 1970s, they were immersed in the Southern California improv scene that had coalesced around reedman Vinny Golia. Their friendship with bassist Eric Von Essen resulted in the formation of Quartet Music, with violinist Jeff Gauthier as the fourth member.

Cline has spent almost as much time in rock settings as in jazz contexts, having played rock with Bloc, the Geraldine Fibbers, and noise-improv guitarist Thurston Moore of Sonic Youth. Among his jazz credentials are time with Charlie Haden's Liberation Music Orchestra of the West Coast, altoist Julius Hemphill, and a duo with Gregg Bendian, in which they interpret the duo music of John Coltrane and Rashied Ali (*Interstellar Space Revisited*, 1999, Atavistic). He and Alex are also members of Bendian's band Interzone.

In the 1990s, Cline and his trio hosted "New Music Mondays" at the Alligator Lounge in Santa Monica, the only real showcase of avant-jazz in Southern California at the time. His sextet, Destroy All Nels Cline, includes four electric guitarists, while the ironically named Nels Cline Singers are the all-instrumental trio of Cline, bassist Devin Hoff, and drummer Scott Amendola (*Instrumentals*, 2002, Cryptogramophone).

Clusone Trio: one of the most revered and entertaining groups of the 1990s, consisting of drummer Han Bennink, American-born reedman Michael Moore, and cellist Ernst Reijseger. Born out of a supposed one-shot appearance at the Clusone Festival in Italy, the group's shows and recordings ran the full gamut of musical influences and ideas, from old Broadway pop to all-out free improv. Like the best free-jazz ensembles, the Clusone Trio was distinguished by the intricate interactions and musicianship of its members. Reijseger's cello conveys images of guttural native drones and meandering rivers, interspersed with walking bass lines, wild sixteenth-note rolls, and light pizzicatos. Moore gets especially decent mileage out of his bass clarinet, a wonderful complement to the cello. Bennink is Bennink in all his glory: swinging hotly with brushes, falling off a cliff with glorious crashes and clangs, and using odd found objects to make new noises. The intercourse among the three men is astounding, though they (deliberately) never quite seem to land on the same page, engaging more in two-against-one tradeoffs.

   I Am An Indian (1995, Gramavision) is an exciting collection of Native American–themed live tunes. From the opener, Moore's "Wigwam," the trio members throw themselves headlong into clichéd Indianisms as Bennink chugs out primal rhythms and ululates like a brave on the warpath. Other delights are Irving Berlin's "I'm An Indian, Too" (two takes, bisected by Herbie Nichols's "The Gig") and "The Song Is Ended," Dewey Redman's rollicking "Qow," and Bud Powell's "Celia." *Love Henry* (1997, Gramavision) is equally good, if less thematically unified. It includes Berlin's "When I Lost You" and "White Christmas," Kurt Weill's "Bilbao Song," and the title song. This is some of the most consistently enjoyable free-tinged music on record, and it is a shame that Clusone Trio did not persist into the new millennium.

Coe, Tony (Anthony George Coe; b. Canterbury, England, 29 November 1934): reeds player and composer. Millions of moviegoers who are familiar with the skulking tenor sax on the *Pink Panther* theme would be incredulous that the same player had performed extreme free music with the likes of Derek Bailey. This is testimony to Tony Coe's extreme versatility as a jazzman.

   Coe studied clarinet in school and taught himself the tenor sax in high school, aping the style of Ellington tenorman Paul Gonsalves. After serving in the Royal Army bands, he was hired by trumpeter Humphrey Lyttelton in 1957 and remained in that group for five years. Coe led his own bands (*Some Other Spring*, 1964, Hep) and was courted for Count Basie's reeds section, which fell through due to visa troubles. He joined the John Dankworth Orchestra instead, furthering his profile as a mainstream player there and in the Kenny Clarke–Francy Boland and Mike Gibbs big bands.

   In the mid-1970s, Coe worked with Derek Bailey in Company and crossed other boundaries briefly with the United Jazz & Rock Ensemble. With freemen like Tony Oxley, Coe recorded *Nutty (on) Willisau* (1983, HatHut), and in the 1990s, he began an association with the Nato label (producing, among others, the Basque homage *Le Voix d'Itxassou*, 1990). *Canterbury Song* (1988, Hot House) gives an especially good impression of his clarinet work. He recorded with Franz Koglmann's Monoblue Quartet and issued *British-American Blue* (2000) on Koglmann's label, between the lines. In addition, he has been a member of the Lonely Bears, Caravan, and the Melody Four. Denmark awarded Coe the coveted Jazzpar Prize in 1995, resulting in the album *Jazzpar '95* (Storyville).

Cole, Bill: multi-instrumentalist, composer, and bandleader. He studied music at the University of Pittsburgh, holds a PhD in ethnomusicology from Wesleyan, and is retired from Dartmouth's music department. Cole performs on an astonishing throng of percussion and wind instruments with his Untempered Ensemble. His arsenal includes the didgeridoo, the Indian nagaswaram (also a favorite of altoman Charlie Mariano), the Chinese double-reed shenai and multipiped shona, and African agogo bells, among other exotica. *Live in Greenfield, Massachusetts, Nov. 20, 1999* (Boxholder) features William Parker, altoist Sam Furnace, Cooper-Moore, tubaist Joe Daley, percussionist Atticus Cole, and drummer Warren Smith. The performances are inspired by black historical figures from Sojourner Truth to Amadou Diallo, a black man killed by New York police in February 1999. Cole has also recorded for a number of newer free-music labels, has performed with Ornette Coleman, Julius Hemphill, Sam Rivers, Jayne Cortez, and James Blood Ulmer, and has written biographies of John Coltrane and Miles Davis. He is a founder of the arts organization Shadrack, Inc.

Coleman, Denardo (Ornette Denardo; b. 1956): drummer, the son of Ornette Coleman and Jayne Cortez. At the age of ten, Denardo was enlisted as the drummer for his father's Blue Note album *The Empty Foxhole*. Ornette sought a more naive and simple rhythmic foundation for his music at the time and found the perfect foil in his young son. Denardo recorded two more sessions with his father (*Ornette at 12* and *Crisis*), and occasionally toured with him while finishing his education. In 1975, Denardo became a founding member of Prime Time. He has remained with the group since and in the 1980s became their producer. He serves as his father's business manager, heads the family's recording studio in Harlem, and performs in the Firespitters in support of his mother's poetry readings.

Coleman, Ornette (Randolph Denard Ornette; b. March 19, 1930, Fort Worth, TX): Alto saxophonist, composer, and bandleader. Since his emergence in the 1950s, Coleman has risen from the shadows of iconoclasm to become a respected elder statesman of jazz. Coleman is one of the most controversial figures to ever grace the music, due to his persistence in shattering the accepted bounds of musical practice time and again. These practices, however, have ensured him audiences across diverse segments of society, garnering fans who appreciate both adventurous jazz and rock-tinged electric music.

Coleman has not been as widely influential among American jazzers as many of his contemporaries, but he did leave lasting marks upon some of the most important players of the past four decades. Simple rhythmic structures, association with specific motives and tonal centers, an emphasis on a vocal-like tone quality, and a lack of prearranged harmonies characterize his improvisations on alto sax. His manipulations of tone color made a powerful impression on John Coltrane when the tenorman studied with him. However, unlike Coltrane's "sheets of sound," Coleman relies not on high speed and complexity (although he is certainly capable of such) as much as deliberate melodic conceptions taken at different paces. He has long been more interested in substance than flash. His earliest recordings were controversial not for their fury, unlike many who followed him, but for their direct pursuit of a new musical vocabulary. His folklike melodic sensibilities were a powerful inspiration to Albert Ayler. Coleman's use of motives as reference points and his abstinence from set harmonies were principal factors in developing his unique harmolodic musical theory later in his career.

Coleman was born into an impoverished but loving family. His mother, widowed when Ornette was seven, bought her son a cheap alto saxophone when he first showed some interest in music. His cousin, James Jordan, an accomplished saxophonist himself, was an early inspiration. Ornette taught himself to play and read music but was incorrect in many of his assumptions about notation and fingering; he assumed, for instance, that the concert scale began with A instead of C. In high school, he was instructed in the "proper" methods of playing and reading music, but he was still intrigued by the purportedly "wrong" ways he had taught himself and explored them further, anyway. This was one of Coleman's earliest impulses toward exploring new routes of musical creation. He also began to compare the structure of music with those of his other academic interests, mathematics, physics, and chemistry.

Coleman started his own band at age fifteen, playing in R&B clubs around Fort Worth. He had but a single lesson, with saxman Walter "Foots" Thomas, who mostly told him to watch himself in the mirror so he wouldn't make odd faces while he played. In high school, he became friends with several musicians that would play a part in his later career, among them bassist Charles Moffett and tenorist Dewey Redman. After a time, Coleman switched to tenor sax because there were more job opportunities available, though he kept the alto handy.

At age nineteen, tired of Fort Worth's racial and economic obstacles, Coleman headed out on the road with a touring band. His interest in bebop and what lay beyond was not shared by the bandleaders who employed him, and he was fired more than once. Before being chased out of Natchez, Mississippi, by the police for his scruffy hair and dark skin, Coleman recorded for a local label, but the tapes are lost to the ages. In Baton Rouge, a vicious assault left him with broken teeth and a crushed tenor. Coleman eventually found himself terminated by Pee Wee Crayton and abandoned in Los Angeles after his concepts became too advanced for his employer's tastes.

Ornette decided to remain in L.A., where he worked as a houseboy for a white family. It was then that he began formulating his concepts with a group of like-minded young players, including trumpeters Bobby Bradford and Don Cherry, bassist Don Payne, and drummers Billy Higgins and Ed Blackwell. Gigs were few and far between for the struggling altoist, and luminaries like Dexter Gordon chased him off the stand regularly. He returned to Fort Worth in 1952 and set up a "conventional" jazz band but became bored and returned to L.A. He held day jobs as an elevator operator and stock boy for Bullock's while trying to ply his musical trade. He met and married Jayne Cortez during this time, and in 1956 they had a son, Ornette Denardo.

In 1958, bassist Red Mitchell heard one of Coleman's tunes and suggested he take it to Lester Koenig, who ran the Contemporary label. Both hoped that Koenig might hawk the composition to a contracted player. Surprising to all, it was Coleman who ended up with the contract. When Koenig asked him to play the composition on piano, Coleman declined because he couldn't play the piano, so he performed it on alto. Koenig was sold and set up the recording sessions for what became the album *Something Else!* Given the predominance of cool jazz and big bands on the West Coast,

Koenig's gamble was a sizeable one. He initially faced much criticism for parting from the status quo, but his instincts about the potential of Coleman's ideas were prophetic.

Though *Something Else!* was not a monetary success, it broke much new ground in jazz improvisation. Some of the songs were plainly blues-based ("Jayne" and "The Blessing"), melodically mutated and with unusual bar lengths (thirteen, seventeen, even twenty-five bars to a chorus). Already Coleman chose to explore beyond the expected chordal structures, as particularly evident on "Invisible," and investigate pitches outside the stock for better emotional effect. His voice on the horn had a more human quality than those of his contemporaries, which reflected his interest in speaking to the listeners' hearts on a personal level. For all its innovation, this album seems positively tame compared with what Coleman had in store a few years down the road. "When Will the Blues Leave?" and "The Blessing" are among Coleman's most-covered compositions because of their relative simplicity compared with his later body of work.

At this point, we can note another aspect of Coleman's developing musical vision. The well-meaning folks at Contemporary chose to include Walter Norris, a more than capable pianist, in this first session. Norris contributed as well as he could but sounded out-of-sorts in the setting despite a valiant effort. The piano's grounded pitch made it sound foreign in a setting where the horn players bent their pitches in every direction. Following this session and his subsequent tenure with pianist Paul Bley, Coleman avoided using keyboard instruments and guitars for decades because he felt that chordal instruments restricted the atmosphere of truly free improvisation.

By now, Ornette's rapport with Don Cherry had already become almost extrasensory. The young trumpeter from Oklahoma proved to be a perfect foil. Not only could he hold his own at blowing Coleman's tortuous melodies, but his quieter, more contemplative playing was often the antithesis (and thus complementary) to the leader's hybrid vigor. Higgins was also an aptly supportive partner. A consummate listener, the drummer developed the keen ability to maintain time and pulse while venturing out in all directions. Higgins, like Ed Blackwell after him, took the time to become intensely familiar with the mechanics of drumming, often using the overtones from different areas of the drum heads to color the music. All these factors helped make this first album something special, even if the market overlooked it. Don Payne peformed well on bass but soon left the band. He was replaced by a young Midwesterner, Charlie Haden, whose extraordinarily vibrant tone opened up the harmonic possibilities for the group. Coming from a family of musicians based in folk and country, Haden seemed an unlikely candidate to change the face of the bass, but his importance as a boldly original voice was quickly evident.

After the session for *Something Else!*, Coleman and his cohorts worked for Bley, who was most amenable to the type of musical innovations Coleman espoused. This group landed a six-week gig at the Hillcrest Club, one of L.A.'s more open-minded establishments, and they received positive attention from musicians who frequented the club. At least for a time, people were interested in what Coleman was involved in. His plastic alto sax had an edgier, more plaintive timbre than a standard metal horn, and his use of alternate fingerings and embouchures created a new palette of sounds that caught other musicians' ears. The rather pinched tone of Cherry's pocket trumpet, actually a miniature cornet, added its own unusual flavor.

The Hillcrest stint is documented on *Live at the Hillcrest Club—1958* (1976, Inner City). "The Blessing" is revisited with some success, perhaps thanks to Bley being more open-minded than Norris. Two older pieces are also documented, giving Coleman a chance to prove that he could hold his own on mainstream material. Charlie Parker's bebop classic "Klactoveesedstene" is nearly twelve minutes long, and Coleman flaunts his chops admirably through the complex theme and changes, still choosing to stray as he sees fit. The second cover, "I Remember Harlem," is by Roy Eldridge, a beloved trumpeter from a prior generation of jazzmen. The band delivers it in an explorative manner of which Eldridge probably would not have approved, then leaves the old school behind in favor of Coleman's shocking originals. The altoist's "Free" is the final tune on the disc. This piece illustrates his adeptness at reshaping the bebop and blues vocabularies to suit his own desires. The session sounds similar to much of Coleman's output in the late 1950s, not only because of the material but because Bley's piano is miked so badly that this may as well have been a recording by the pianoless quartet! Coleman's anchoring in bebop is as clear as his intention to move beyond that form's entrenched principles.

Early in 1959, Coleman made his second album for Contemporary. Haden and Higgins were not available, so the bass duties were divided between Red Mitchell and Modern Jazz Quartet bassman Percy Heath, and Koenig called in local drummer Shelly Manne, a white player associated with the Kenton/Herman clan of cool jazzmen. In 1954, Manne had cut freely improvised and serial tracks with Shorty Rogers and Jimmy Giuffre, but that was small potatoes compared with what he experienced with Coleman. As Manne later recalled, "When I worked on his session, I didn't feel I was playing a song as much as that I was really playing *with* a person. And somehow I became more of a person in my own playing. He made me freer." (Hentoff, *The Jazz Life*, pp. 242–43.) Manne did not look much further into free jazz exploration, but he was arguably a looser player from then onward.

Tomorrow Is the Question! continued the pattern of in-your-face annunciatory album titles that Coleman proffered. The music did look ahead to the future, although this record is more restrained than its predecessor. The rhythm section clings tightly to the more rigid arrangements, at least early on, conceivably preventing Coleman and Cherry from exploring as far as they would have liked. Blues elements are still present, for example, "Rejoicing," along with scattered simple, folky statements that might have influenced Albert Ayler.

With the moral support of valuable friends, Coleman managed to land a contract with brothers Ahmet and Nesuhi Ertegun at Atlantic Records. Like Koenig, the Erteguns took a commercial gamble in marketing Coleman's new concepts to jazz fans. Cecil Taylor had taken similarly courageous steps to change the sound of jazz, but as of 1959, he had barely made a dent in popular opinion. Whether Coleman could go further was anybody's guess, but Atlantic pressed on.

Between 1959 and 1961, Coleman and friends recorded a sizable number of tracks at the Atlantic studios, some of which were not released until 1970 on *The Art of the Improvisers*. The first full Coleman album issued on Atlantic was May 1959's *The Shape of Jazz to Come*. On the cover is the leader in a black sweater, white shirt and tie, demure but confident, his white plastic alto sax standing out in stark contrast to his clothing and the simple red background. It reflects Coleman's disposition as a person, assured of where he is headed musically but remarkably unassuming and likeable in conversation. That confidence manifests itself well in the album, which begins with a Middle Eastern drone from Haden on "Lonely Woman." This is one of Coleman's most popular works, consistently called a "dirge" by certain critics who failed to perceive the lust for life within its raw emotion. It is also one of his most personal statements; Coleman pours out a staggering volume of heart and soul in melody and solo. Cherry is once again complementary with his own grieving tone. The peculiar "Focus on Sanity" is also present. *The Shape of Jazz to Come* was Coleman's most visionary statement yet, and the fullest confidence of Atlantic Records seemed to be behind it.

Deeply impressed by Coleman's albums and live shows, Percy Heath arranged for Coleman and Cherry to attend a three-week summer session at the Lenox School of Jazz in Massachusetts, established by MJQ pianist John Lewis and composer Gunther Schuller. At Lenox, they received valuable instruction in the music's history, including hefty doses of the Third Stream theories developed by the school's founders. The experience at Lenox made some unusual impressions on the altoist, inspiring a lasting interest in composing for string ensembles.

Next was the astonishing *Change of the Century*, recorded in October 1959 by the quartet. A wider spectrum of styles was represented, starting with the mutant blues "Ramblin'." The tune is a world of fun, its structure marked by throbbing drones by Haden and cheerful exuberance from both hornmen. The horn interaction is invaluable as the two exchange tiny phrases at the end of each chorus and into Coleman's improv. That solo is itself worth the price of admission, Coleman poking good-natured fun at the gutbucket, bar-walking sax style that preceded him. "Free," the tune that ended the Hillcrest Club album with Bley, is reviewed and developed further. "Bird Food" and the title track are fast-paced bop workouts, the first a tribute to Charlie Parker's spirit, if not his technique. As Coleman stated in the liner notes, "the idolization of Bird, people wanting to play just like him and not make their own soulsearch, has finally come to be an impediment to progress in jazz." That statement, while truthful, was an unwelcome wake-up call to established jazzers who had built their reputations on emulating bebop giants like Parker. The many "cool" saxophonists who had worshipped at Lester Young's altar for years took similar umbrage at Coleman's jibe.

In November of 1959, Coleman and Cherry assembled a band for a date at the Five Spot. Fans and players alike derided Coleman during the engagement, insisting that he could neither play nor write music. Unlike his later protegé John Coltrane, the altoist had no credentials to rest upon other than his brief R&B career and a few oddball albums. For him to emerge like a thundercloud in the midst of the mythical New York City jazz scene seemed the ultimate in chutzpah, which did not rest well with much of the downtown music community. Nevertheless, Coleman and the band also reaped a fair amount of praise, with some lauding the visionary young altoist as the next Charlie Parker. No endorsement, however, was more surprising than that of composer/conductor Leonard Bernstein, who frequently attended the quartet's Five Spot shows, as did Coltrane and singer Dorothy Kilgallen.

Coleman and friends continued their call for originality on *This Is Our Music* (1960, Atlantic), on which Higgins was replaced by New Orleans–born drummer Ed

Blackwell. Blackwell had a definite martial feeling to his drumming at times, but coming up in the Big Easy gave him a looseness of attack that assisted the free flow of ideas. He interacts especially well with Haden on "Blues Connotation" and "Humpty Dumpty," as well as the rare cover of "Embraceable You," a chestnut that Charlie Parker himself radically redesigned in the late 1940s. By this inclusion, Coleman formally declared his intent to cancel out Parker's lingering dominance as the voice of the jazz alto. More chutzpah? Perhaps, but it was nothing compared with what lay just around the corner.

That year, Coleman's quartet made a significant showing at the Monterey Jazz Festival and played an even bigger role in Newport, Rhode Island. Coleman and Cherry took part in the Newport Rebel Festival, organized by Charles Mingus and Max Roach, at the Cliff House Manor down the street from the main festival. Their protest of the questionable racist practices at George Wein's Newport Jazz Festival succeeded in getting the promoters' attention and drew a crowd of interested citizens who heard, for the first time, what could be the real future of jazz.

In December 1960, Coleman assembled a double quartet consisting of himself, Cherry, Eric Dolphy on bass clarinet, trumpeter Freddie Hubbard, bassists Haden and Scott LaFaro, and both Blackwell and Higgins on drums. The result was the album *Free Jazz: A Collective Improvisation* (Atlantic), a seminal document of the movement to which the recording lent its name. *Free Jazz* was a thirty-seven-minute free improvisation with merely a set tonal center and brief written statements to introduce and inspire the soloists in turn. Once the improvisations begin, there are no set melodies, rhythms, or chordal progressions; the soloists are free to move in whichever directions their hearts may lead them. Despite its lack of expressive and dynamic variety, the recording was a revelation in the jazz industry. It was simply like nothing ever heard in the music before.

The first sounds heard in "Free Jazz" are rapid nonunison lines from all involved, stopped abruptly by long tones that clash in pitch and immediately change the music's aura. Dolphy begins a wildly groaning, hooting solo in the upper register of the bass clarinet, replied to on occasion by Cherry or other horns in the left channel. The basses have their own say, separate but equal. LaFaro's amazing, fleet-fingered style stands in the forefront, even as others improvise fervently above him. The drummers take similar paths, miraculously maintaining a good pulse despite the maelstrom and their own unrelation. Just when one expects Hubbard or Coleman to start an extended solo turn, they cut off bluntly and someone else starts taunting Dolphy. After he finally winds down, the long tones return and are followed by more quick nonunison phrases before Hubbard takes his shot. The session proceeds in similar fashion until everyone is exhaustedly satisfied. The CD reissue also contains the seventeen-minute first attempt, originally issued in 1971 on the Atlantic collection *Twins*. "First Take" is muddier and less satisfying than the final issue, but as a warm-up, it has some good moments, particularly from Dolphy.

On the whole, "Free Jazz" is exasperating, mind whirling, and addictive after several attentive listens. It's unfortunate that many critics and musicians didn't bother to give it more than one spin before they assailed Coleman unmercifully for his gall. People had been saying for four years that Ornette Coleman was a madman, and this album was allegedly the pudding that contained the proof. Atlantic Records took a beating in the press as well, though the Ertegun brothers stuck by their prize innovator for several more months.

In January 1961, shortly after the *Free Jazz* sessions, Haden left the fold and LaFaro took over bass duties. His playing was extraordinarily limber, his melodicism a step up from Charles Mingus's own innovations. LaFaro and Blackwell immediately bonded, achieving a taut hand-in-glove interaction that was noteworthy considering the music's complexity. LaFaro's dalliance with Coleman, however, only produced one more album before the bassist was snatched up by pianist Bill Evans. *Ornette!*, the next Atlantic disc, carried on some of the *Free Jazz* principles with a quartet lineup. The disc bears four tracks, with arcane titles allegedly inspired by Sigmund Freud's writings. The improvisations are galvanizing, the tunes distinctive and appealing. The recording stands as one of Coleman's finest achievements. It is a particular shame that LaFaro did not work longer with Coleman, Evans, or anyone else; he died in a car accident on July 6, 1961.

In March 1961, Coleman had replaced LaFaro with young Jimmy Garrison, who himself only stuck around for a short time before joining John Coltrane's quartet, where he made further jazz history. Garrison is featured on *Ornette on Tenor* (1961, Atlantic), the only date on which Coleman concentrated entirely on the larger sax. His tone on tenor is a bit rough, his movements tentative at times. All things considered, the session is an artistic success. The edginess of Coleman's timbre, particularly in the lower register, is prescient of the sound that Archie Shepp would popularize a few years later. That tone and its resultant gutbucket effect on Coleman's vibrato suit the retro, boppish air of some tunes.

Coleman did not tarry much longer in the position that *Free Jazz* had placed him. Cherry soon left and was replaced by Bobby Bradford, another Texan. Shortly thereafter, Coleman canned the quartet concept altogether and put together a trio with bass virtuoso David Izenzon and drummer Charles Moffett, his old chum from Fort Worth. The absence of other horns in this trio format gave Coleman more elbow room to expand his own expressiveness, but the hole left by Cherry's departure was palpable until the leader restructured his concepts to fill the void.

Coleman was pleased with the trio and felt that the music they were creating deserved better exposure than the nightclub circuit. In December 1962, he rented New York's Town Hall for a special concert where the trio debuted. Three main pieces were featured: "Doughnut," the dirge "Sadness," and a twenty-four-minute take on "The Ark." As if Coleman's trio concepts weren't radical enough, the band was joined by an R&B rhythm section for one tune. The evening also included a string quartet performing "Dedication to Poets and Writers," Coleman's first "classical" composition, inspired by his studies with Gunther Schuller. Coleman broke even with the receipts from this show, and New York had certainly taken further notice. A recording of the concert was released in 1964 by ESP (*Town Hall Concert 1962*), not long after label founder Bernard Stollman began documenting New York's free-jazz sounds.

About this time, Coleman decided to up his asking price, perturbed by the high wages of musicians of equal or lesser talent who played more commercial music. This noble effort put him out of work for much of the next year, disillusioning him greatly. He took a two-year sabbatical from performance, during which time he opened his own club and kept developing his musical ideas in private. He also chose an unusual way to inject freshness into his art: he took up the trumpet and violin, without any professional lessons. Needless to say, that did little to quell other musicians' questions about his sanity, particularly since he used his new toys more as turbulent noisemakers than melodic devices.

In 1965, Coleman relented and lowered his fees, reunited the trio, and landed a gig at the prestigious Village Vanguard in New York's Greenwich Village. His trumpet and violin led him down fresh paths as he explored new textures and sounds. Shortly thereafter, a prime financial opportunity arose when Coleman was commissioned to write the score for the film *Chappaqua*. The score (which featured tenorman Pharoah Sanders, soon to join John Coltrane's last group) was more powerful than the film itself and was not used, but Coleman was paid handsomely for his efforts. Those funds enabled him to finance a European tour with Izenzon and Moffett. This junket, partially documented on a pair of Blue Note releases (1965, *At the Golden Circle, Stockholm, Vols. 1 and 2*) and *The Great London Concert* (1965, Freedom), spread Coleman's new jazz gospel across the continent, helping to ignite the free movement in Europe. The Stockholm albums are especially exciting, illustrating the sympathetic bonds between the performers. Izenzon, a distinctive asset, unfailingly holds onto the leader's coattails through the maze of "Faces and Places" on the first volume.

It was in this period that Coleman began to formulate his *harmolodic* theory of performance. This concept, which takes its name from *har*mony, *mo*tion, and me*lody*, is a nearly impenetrable method of musical creation using motivic variations and different clefs to determine the key in which each instrument plays. All of the players operate both democratically and empathically, reacting and interacting without the usual hierarchy of melody versus rhythm instruments. Borrowing a page from George Russell's Lydian Concept, harmolodics permits the performers to shift the music's tonal center up and down the scale at will, using a sliding-clef principle.

Coleman spent several years honing the concepts of harmolodics before presenting it to the world. It was first mentioned in the liner notes to *Skies of America* (1972, Columbia), a symphonic work recorded by the London Symphony Orchestra and recently revived in New York. Harmolodics remains the basis of his musical conceptions today; Coleman consistently refers to his music as "harmolodic" instead of free jazz, avant-garde, or anything else. He seems to understand how specialized these ideas are; in the liner notes of *Sound Museum—Hidden Man* (1996, Harmolodic/Verve), Coleman asserted, with postmodern flair, that "Harmolodics is not a style. Those who judge the concept of harmolodic playing are using outdated terms to describe their knowledge. All listeners are equal in their opinions." The exact value of a musical philosophy that cannot be accurately described with any known terminology is debatable, but nonetheless it has remained the center of Coleman's focus since the 1970s.

As suggested earlier, starting in the mid-1960s, Coleman began to write monumental symphonic works, string quartets, and other pieces for ensembles that lie outside of standard jazz instrumentation. "Dedication to Poets and Writers" was intriguing but left no room for improvisation. *Saints and Soldiers* (1967, RCA) marked a step forward in his writing for strings, and by *Skies of America* his orchestral concepts were close to full realization. Legend has it that when some of the string players on that date complained that a section was unplayable, the perturbed Coleman took out his alto and played the entire piece note for note, effectively shutting up the highbrows who had doubted his capabilities. While his string projects were seriously complex, Coleman headed in a different direction within his jazz groups. The final curtain for Izenzon and Moffett was the soundtrack for a Belgian film, *Who's Crazy* (1966, Affinity). Though the music is not as oppressive as the *Chappaqua* score, it is power- ful stuff that rises above mood music or innocuous padding.

That project and the first trio finished, Coleman reversed gears. His search for rhythmic simplicity, almost a naiveté, led him in September 1966 to include his ten- year-old son, Denardo, as the drummer on *The Empty Foxhole* (Blue Note). Haden returned for this trio session and responded well to the new setting. While the six tracks are not among Coleman's best works, the ideas he attempted to transmit about returning to the basics are distinct. Between young Denardo's simplistic drumming and the leader's primitive trumpet and violin, Haden comes off as downright sophis- ticated. Once again, most of New York's critics and musicians had a field day verbally assaulting the altoist for hiring his kid to beat on the drums . . . for a Blue Note date, yet!

Haden did not stay for long after this set, and Garrison came back after John Coltrane's death in July 1967 left him unemployed. Coltrane drummer Elvin Jones also joined the band early in 1968, along with one of Coleman's old high school friends, the energetic Texas tenorman Dewey Redman. The brilliant Garrison stuck with Coleman for a while but eventually became uncomfortable with the demands of the altoist's music. He had also remained with Coltrane until the end, driving the frantically free sounds of the tenorman's final bands, but the avant-garde began to weigh heavily upon the bassist. In 1967, in the midst of these shifting paradigms, Coleman produced and guested on altoist Jackie McLean's *New and Old Gospel* (Blue Note). The session, one of the few times that Coleman ever appeared as a sideman, is surely one of the most unusual things in McLean's discography. Coleman plays trum- pet exclusively, investing it with church and blues elements that support McLean's scattershot vision.

Garrison, Jones, and Redman recorded two dates with Coleman in April and May 1968, which were issued on the Blue Note albums *Love Call* and *New York Is Now!* Blue Note's art department tried an interesting marketing strategy for *Love Call*, along the lines of Miles Davis's albums of this period: the record's sleeve depicts two young, attractive black women in contemporary attire. The music, however, was well removed from the pop scene. "Love Call" illustrates precisely Coleman's objective in taking up the trumpet. He uses it as a paintbrush, flitting through keys like pages in a book. The rhythm section is inarguably strong, but on both discs, Jones and Garrison seem to not quite grasp Coleman's aim. *New York Is Now!* opens with another landmark track, "Garden of Souls," wherein the altoist quickly quotes several pop songs in his solo as he previously had in Stockholm. The low point is the closing track, "We Now Interrupt for a Commercial," on which the screeching violin is a bit too much to bear.

In 1969, both Cherry and Haden rejoined Coleman in time to record *Crisis* (1969, Impulse) live at New York University on March 22. Dewey Redman had been a band member for about a year and had firmly established his reputation as an unorthodox mastermind. Denardo, now a more experienced drummer at age twelve, rounded out the group. *Crisis* is one of the altoist's most musically successful efforts, though it never attained the status of his earlier releases. "Broken Shadows" continues his tradition of "dirges," his slow, painfully majestic compositions. This was one of the first instances of a later recurrent theme in Coleman's harmolodic music, continual restating of a principal melodic line throughout a piece while solo improvisations take place around it.

On June 16, 1969, Ornette, Denardo, Redman, and Haden recorded another controversial disc, *Ornette at 12* (Impulse). The title refers to the age of Denardo (which is his middle name; his first name is Ornette) at that time. The young drummer's technique, or lack thereof, helped fan the fire set by critics who had insisted all along that his father's "music" required no musical knowledge to perform. Yet hindsight reveals that Denardo's inexperience was vital in keeping him from sagging into cliché or trying to do too much, the curse of many drummers. The interaction between the two saxophones is also marvelous on this underestimated date.

By this time, Coleman had opened up his loft space on Prince Street in New York, a performance mecca for just about anyone in town who was interested in experimenting or just dropping by. Artists House became one of the principal cauldrons for free blowing, along with Ali's Alley, owned by ex-Coltrane drummer Rashied Ali, and Sam Rivers' Studio RivBea. On February 14, 1970, Coleman called in Redman, Haden, and Ed Blackwell for a fun set issued on *Friends and Neighbors: Ornette Live at Prince Street* (Flying Dutchman). This disc, all but forgotten until BMG reissued it on CD in 1997, interestingly documents the dynamics that the lofts' open-doored forums generated. Gil Evans and Pharoah Sanders were among the audience that night as the show kicked off with a group sing-along. "Forgotten Songs" has an Aylerish folk-march vibe to it. In hindsight, it seems almost an homage to Ayler instead of to the American folk idiom, but the tenorman's death would not come until November. The disassociated sax lines give a sense of collage.

Coleman enlisted Izenzon, Haden, and Blackwell for a rather strange project in 1970, backing Yoko Ono on the seven-minute auditory adventure "AOS" (*Plastic Ono Band*, Apple). Apart from her unfair notoriety as John Lennon's second wife and the alleged reason for the Beatles' breakup, Ono was an honored member of the Fluxus performance-art movement fronted by George Maciunas. Her screeching vocal performances, abstract poetry, and unusual musical reasoning had been fertilized through the Fluxus experience, and she was open to almost any kind of artistic encounter that pushed the envelope. "AOS" is unusual even for a Coleman performance, but it is more or less successful in retrospect. It is apparent that Ono and Coleman listened attentively to each other instead of vying for dominance, and that mutual respect paid off.

In 1971, Coleman signed a three-year contract with Columbia, resulting in more controversially excellent music but only three albums, including his symphonic work *Skies of America* (1972). David Measham conducted the London Symphony Orchestra on the twenty-one unified themes, which Coleman had to radically cut and paste after the British musicians' union refused to let his quartet play along with the orchestra. The altoist turns in some of his most inspired improvisations, and this marks the earliest realization of his harmolodic modulation principles. The album remains daunting to both "classical" and jazz aficionados, only proving the point that it should be accepted on its own merits and listened to openly.

The pinnacle of the Columbia period came early with *Science Fiction* (1971), which only recently received the praise it deserves after languishing for nearly thirty years. Coleman again raised the bar by including poet David Henderson, Indian vocalist Asha Puthli, and two studio trumpet players, Gerard Schwarg and Carmon Fornarotto, on various tracks. Trumpeter Bobby Bradford, who had briefly been part of Coleman's group a decade before, returned for these sessions. Bradford's personal ideas were quite different from Cherry's, adding bold new seasoning. "Street Woman" and "Civilization Day" feature the classic quartet of Coleman, Cherry, Haden, and Higgins in exceptional form. The musicians' individual abilities and the leader's musical concepts had advanced so far since the mid-1950s, there is no mistaking these tracks for outtakes from the Contemporary or Atlantic years. Coleman was beginning to show a deeper interest in rock music and technology, and he took the unusual step of running Haden's bass through a wah-wah pedal, *á la* Jimi Hendrix, for the delectably oddball "Rock the Clock." A Columbia/Legacy reissue, *The Complete Science Fiction Sessions* (2000), adds outtakes that are interesting if not essential.

Eight tracks from 1971 to 1972 were collected on *Broken Shadows* (1993, Columbia), a collector's item with a few good points to recommend it. Cherry, Redman, Haden, Blackwell, Higgins, and Bradford are present in various combinations, and unusual guest spots by mainstream jazz pianist Cedar Walton and guitarist Jim Hall pull the alto player in different directions. Much of the album has a Third Stream air about it. It's unfortunate that Bradford again parted company with the altoist too soon, as the collaborations here showed real promise. For Coleman, however, it was time to switch gears once more.

In the mid-1970s, Ornette traveled to Africa in search of new sonic adventures. He discovered ways to blend the native melodic and rhythmic notions of Nigeria and Morocco into his own harmolodic conceptions. His amazing collaboration with the Master Musicians of Joujouka from Morocco, documented on *Dancing in Your Head* (A&M, 1976), is an early masterpiece of "world music" synergy. As the Joujoukas had been performing their native version of harmolodics for centuries, Coleman was able to relate to their vital music on many levels. The crushing energy of the short "Midnight Sunrise," with jazz critic Robert Palmer accompanying on clarinet, is absolutely exhilarating.

Dancing in Your Head also marked the debut of Prime Time, Coleman's hot electric band. In 1975, Dewey Redman had departed, giving Coleman the impetus to fully alter course again. First, he chose to renounce his policy against working with chordal instruments in his ensembles. His musical vision had developed to the point where he felt those instruments could now interact better within his structures instead of hindering them. Secondly, he chose to expand the ensemble's size and include electric voicings. On *Dancing*, the Prime Time lineup was electric bassist Jamaaladeen Tacuma (né Rudy McDaniel), electric guitarists Bern Nix and Charlie Ellerbee, and drummer Ronald Shannon Jackson. Jackson had just spent some time in the Cecil Taylor Unit, preparing him to deal better with the complexities of harmolodics. Prime Time blended free jazz, rock, and funk on the two variations of "Theme from a Symphony" on *Dancing*. The sound was wild, fresh, and, above all, danceable. Who ever expected Ornette Coleman to play dance music for any generation? As usual, the critics and jazz purists all but burned Coleman in effigy, but a new revolution was declared and the public took notice.

Ornette experimented with the Prime Time sound for a few years, adding a second drummer and bassist to the mix in an update of the doubled instrumentation on *Free Jazz*. The next recording, *Body Meta* (1976, Verve), was not as cohesive and remains a marginal work. In that same year Haden, Cherry, Redman, and Blackwell formed Old and New Dreams in homage to Coleman's legacy. (See the entry for Old and New Dreams.)

In 1977, Coleman taped a set of duets with Charlie Haden. *Soapsuds, Soapsuds* (1977, Artists House) was an underappreciated disc on which Coleman played fine tenor sax and, well, improving trumpet. Who knows what they were thinking when they chose to play the theme from the TV soap, *Mary Hartman, Mary Hartman*, but it's fairly successful. *Soapsuds* documents the duo's warm interaction without other players to get in the way. The following year, Coleman produced the debut disc of guitarist James "Blood" Ulmer, with whom he had worked in Prime Time. Ulmer had worked in hard funk with George Clinton and in jazz with organist Big John Patton, but he detected his muse in Coleman's harmolodic notions.

In 1979 came the next Prime Time disc, *Of Human Feelings* (Antilles). Denardo and Calvin Weston were dual drummers, Tacuma the sole bassist, and Ellerbee and Nix rounded out the band. The set was more successful by far than *Body Meta*, although Coleman's basic, repetitive compositions took getting used to. Coleman and Prime Time spent the next few years alternately resting and touring to promote the harmolodic agenda.

Coleman also got involved in the development of a remarkable project in his hometown, Fort Worth. The Caravan of Dreams, a performing arts center housed in an immense geodesic dome, offered a quality concert venue and recording studio in an area that desperately needed help in encouraging the arts. The facility was state-of-the-art, including a nightclub and rooftop grotto, and Coleman was a principal supporter. As part of his promotional efforts, he taped three albums there, beginning with *Opening the Caravan of Dreams* and the lesser *Prime Design/Time Design* (both 1985, issued on the Caravan of Dreams label). The third, *In All Languages* (1987, Caravan of Dreams), was a double album featuring Prime Time on one record and the quartet of Coleman, Cherry, Haden, and Higgins on the other. The groups interpreted several of the same songs in their own fashions, offering an intriguing insight into the flexibility of Coleman's conceptions.

In 1985, Coleman achieved wider exposure and acceptance in another surprising way, collaborating with the tremendously popular jazz guitarist Pat Metheny on *Song X* (1985, Geffen). Metheny, one of the brightest stars in the ECM Records stable, had been influenced by Coleman for years, had covered some of the altoist's tunes on his own albums, and had recorded repeatedly with Redman and Haden. It seemed to be high time, then, that Metheny's significant influence was introduced to a public that was unknowingly preconditioned to accept his music. Haden, Denardo, and drummer Jack DeJohnette are present on this appealing disc, one that grows on the listener gradually. It is tailored more toward the average Coleman fan than those who melt at Metheny's melodicism, but the guitarist excels in the position of coleader here.

In the 1980s, Denardo became his father's record producer and business manager. The company Harmolodic, Inc. was established to manage the altoist's business affairs, from concert bookings to a record label and website. Coleman composed his first ballet, *Architecture in Motion*, and created the soundtrack for the film *Naked Lunch*. He appeared in concert on a few occasions with the Grateful Dead, another unlikely group of musicians that held him and Coltrane in the highest regard. The appearance of Dead guitarist Jerry Garcia on the Prime Time album *Virgin Beauty* (1988, Portrait) brought further attention and comparatively huge record sales, though Garcia's contribution to three tracks was minimal. Of greater interest is the band's long-awaited return, *Tone Dialing* (1995, on Coleman's Harmolodic imprint in partnership with Verve). With the exception of the annoying "Search for Life" (Coleman did as badly with rap as Miles Davis), the album is an invigorating return to form. Percussionist Badal Roy is excellent on the track bearing his name, their Bach prelude is hilariously hip, and "Kathelin Gray" is expanded nicely for this larger format. The album is notable for the presence of keyboardist Dave Bryant, the first time in years that Coleman had recorded with a keyboard of any kind.

The year 1996 saw more changes of direction. Having given the keyboards a trial run, Coleman made a striking duet album with German pianist Joachim Kühn. *Colors* (1997, Verve) was produced by Denardo, and the resultant beauty of interplay is dazzling. The disc contains some of Coleman's best writing in years, and Kühn responds marvelously to the altoist's unpredictable spins. Reviewers did not know what to make of *Colors* because it was such a radical departure for Coleman, but its appetizing vitality and its uniqueness in both men's discographies make it a definite point of interest.

Around the same time, Coleman hired the impressive pianist Geri Allen for a new quartet with Denardo and bassist Charnett Moffett, son of his old friend Charles. Coleman had performed two duets with Allen on her album *Eyes in the Back of Your Head* (1995, Blue Note) and opted to involve her in his next project. Typical of the altoist, this was no small task. The quartet recorded two discs under the heading "Sound Museum": *Hidden Man* and *Three Women* (both 1996, Harmolodic/Verve). Both albums include markedly different interpretations of the same thirteen songs, with one tune different on each album. The discs are similar in concept to the halves of *In All Languages*, and the contrasting interpretations of shared songs make it well worth picking up both "Sound Museum" releases.

Coleman has received honorary degrees from the New School for Social Research, Boston Conservatory of Music, CalArts, and the University of Pennsylvania. He was awarded a MacArthur Fellowship "genius grant" in 1994, the Rex Foundation's Ralph J. Gleason Award in 1996, and the Japanese Praemium Imperiale in 2001. Coleman has continued to be one of the supreme innovators in jazz. He has instructed and influenced a small but steady stream of performers who carry the harmolodic banner in their own work, including Ulmer, Jackson, and Tacuma. With Prime Time, his new quartet, and various other projects, Ornette Coleman continues to expand the envelope of jazz.

Coleman, Steve (b. Chicago, IL, 20 September 1956): alto saxophonist, composer, producer, and bandleader. Coleman comes from a background in soul, funk, and R&B,

which colored his development in 1985 of the universal musical concept, M-BASE ("macro-basic array of spontaneous extemporization"). Like Lester Bowie, Coleman has a strong appreciation for the full spectrum of black musical experiences and has fused them into a new artistic philosophy that crosses accepted boundaries. From his first group, Five Elements (*Motherland Pulse*, 1985, JMT), Coleman gathered the M-Base Collective, which included Geri Allen, Cassandra Wilson, altoist Greg Osby, and trombonist Robin Eubanks. Strata Institute is a like-minded collective, which Coleman also heads up. Besides his early gigs with the Thad Jones–Mel Lewis Orchestra, Coleman has ventured further out with the Dave Holland Quartet, Sam Rivers All-Star Orchestra, and Cecil Taylor's large ensemble.

Collective Black Artists (CBA): musicopolitical collective founded by bassist Reggie Workman, pianist Stanley Cowell, and trumpeter Jimmy Owens. The CBA, like the AACM, was intended to encourage musicians to be self-reliant and to produce albums and concerts by themselves instead of relying upon the white-dominated music industry that was choking the very life out of jazz. Rahsaan Roland Kirk and Lee Morgan were among the group's other members.

Colombo, Eugenio (b. Rome, Italy, 10 December 1953): reedman. As a composer and performer, Colombo briskly ties jazz, modern classical, and Mediterranean musics together with the expected Italian thread of humor. A member of the Italian Instabile Orchestra, Colombo is equally revered in his homeland as a soloist and sax-quartet member. His most evident influences are Eric Dolphy and Roland Kirk. His collaborators include Giorgio Gaslini, Alvin Curran, Misha Mengelberg, Mario Schiano, and vocalist Giovanna Marini. Colombo has recorded a handful of albums as a leader; perhaps the best is the ambitious *Tales of Love and Death* (2000, Leo).

Colson Unity Troupe: ensemble led by tenorman/pianist Adegoke Steve Colson and his wife, singer Iqua Colson. The Colsons were among the lesser-known fringe of free players in the 1970s, and they are principally known for the uneven recording *No Reservation* (1980, Black Saint), with reedman Wallace McMillan, bassist Reggie Willis, and drummer Dushun Mosley. Steve Colson has appeared on recordings by David Murray, Andrew Cyrille, and Baikida Carroll, and is a member of Bright Moments.

Coltrane, Alice (Turiya Aparna Satchidananda, née Alice McLeod; b. Detroit, MI, 27 August 1937): pianist, organist, and harpist. Trained in classical piano, Coltrane played in church and gained early jazz experience with Bud Powell, Yusef Lateef (whose group also featured Alice's brother, bop pianist Ernie Farrow), Kenny Burrell, and other major figures. She studied in Paris with Bud Powell in 1959. In 1962, she toured with vibist Terry Gibbs, at which time she met John Coltrane. They married in 1965, and Alice joined his group in 1966 after McCoy Tyner's departure. Coltrane was into his own deep spiritual searching at the time, and Alice encouraged him to dissolve his acclaimed quartet and explore his emotions freely through his music. She, along with Jimmy Garrison and Rashied Ali, provided the foundation for the free explorations of Coltrane and Pharoah Sanders.

After John's death, Alice continued as a leader, making recordings of Eastern spiritual influence beginning with *A Monastic Trio* (1968, Impulse). Her most famous album was *Journey in Satchidananda* (1970, Impulse). Her sidemen during this period included Sanders, Ali, Garrison, Archie Shepp, Frank Lowe, drummer Ben Riley, and tenorist Joe Henderson. She moved to California in 1972 and founded a retreat called the Vedantic Center. She has rarely performed since, releasing two albums in the late 1970s and appearing with her sons at a 1987 tribute to her husband. She has written inspirational books and hosted a television show focusing on spirituality and music.

Coltrane, John (b. Hamlet, NC, 23 September 1926; d. New York, NY, 17 July 1967): saxophonist, composer, and bandleader. Through his high-profile work with Miles Davis and his own successful albums, Coltrane (often known simply as "Trane") was one of jazz's most recognized figures when he embraced free music in the mid-1960s. He soon gained equal eminence in that genre, second perhaps only to his erstwhile mentor, Ornette Coleman. Quickly enough, Trane became a superior innovator in his own right. By the time of his death, he had become arguably the most influential jazzman since Louis Armstrong, impacting not only jazz players but rock musicians as well.

A deeply spiritual performer, Coltrane continually searched for ultimate truth; this was a key factor in his music up to the end. It led him to both extreme intensity and meditative lulls, and often he seemed anxious to search beyond the limitations of his horn. He could play with head-spinning rapidity, ripping through and around the chord changes as fast as fingers and breath would allow; this technique was aptly dubbed "sheets of sound." His strong personal style was easily identifiable from the space of his service with Miles Davis, but toward the end of his life, Trane's phrases were punctuated by multiphonics and shrieking harmonics well beyond the horn's normal range, part of his search for new horizons and musical truth.

Coltrane's father was a tailor who dabbled in music, his grandfather an A.M.E. church elder. John was a quiet boy, and when both his father and grandfather passed away when he was twelve, young John became even more introverted. His family then consisted of his mother Alice, cousin Mary, and Mary's mother. He studied alto sax during and after high school and entered the navy in 1945.

In May 1946, Coltrane made his first recording, a take of Tadd Dameron's "Hot House," with other navy musicians. (The track is available on the anthology *The Last Giant*, 1993, Rhino.) Following his service, Trane came to Philadelphia and began a career as an R&B player with King Kolax, Joe Webb, and singer Big Maybelle. Altoist and vocalist Eddie "Cleanhead" Vinson convinced John to switch from alto to tenor in 1947, whereupon he hired the promising young man. John then spent a year touring with Jimmy Heath and Howard McGhee before heading back to Philadelphia.

In 1949, Coltrane joined Dizzy Gillespie's big band and became immersed in New York's bop scene. After the band dissolved, Gillespie retained the tenorist for his septet. "We Love To Boogie" (1951) was Coltrane's first recorded solo. This was an important tenure, helping John build a quick mind and formidable chops. It was also,

unfortunately, the time in which he became addicted to heroin. After leaving
Gillespie, Coltrane played with saxman Earl Bostic, then spent 1953 to 1954 working with one of his idols: former Ellington altoist Johnny Hodges. Between Gillespie's
fiery bebop, Bostic's R&B, and Hodges's refined swing, Coltrane gained a wealth of
knowledge. He also derived inspiration from tenorman Dexter Gordon, whose wit and
vibrancy made him one of the era's shining stars.

In 1955, Trane began his first stint with Davis. The quintet, which included pianist
Red Garland, bassist Paul Chambers, and drummer Philly Joe Jones, was among the
most popular groups in jazz. The next year was especially fruitful for Davis's band, as
they recorded several albums' worth of material for the Prestige label (*Miles, Relaxin'*,
Workin', *Steamin'*, *Cookin'*). Coltrane was instrumental in the quintet's success but
suffered from drug and alcohol addictions. Davis fired him more than once but usually took him back soon thereafter. Despite his personal problems and rather formulaic soloing, Coltrane's capabilities loomed large on these sessions.

In 1956, he recorded *Tenor Madness* (Prestige) with Sonny Rollins, another controversial tenorman whose influence was widespread. Rollins was noted for his thematic improvisations, building solos from segments of the melody in a way similar to
Cecil Taylor's later motivic elaborations. Davis again gave Coltrane his walking papers
in 1957, encouraging him to clean up his act and quit wasting his great promise. Trane
was briefly replaced in Davis's ensemble by Rollins, who, like Davis, had recently
overcome his own drug battles.

The saxophonist returned home to Philadelphia, secluded himself at his mother's
house, and after a week of partaking of nothing but water, quit his habits cold turkey. He also devoted time to spiritual pursuits, which he said helped him overcome
his urges far better than medicine or social pressures could. Rejuvenated, Coltrane
joined the Thelonious Monk quartet in 1957. Though their association only lasted
six months or so and resulted in but a single recording (*Thelonious Monk with John
Coltrane*, Jazzland) due to contractual problems, Monk helped redirect the
saxophonist's focus toward breaking the inhibiting rules of jazz tradition.

That year Coltrane formed his own group and landed an important recording contract with Prestige. He cut a long string of ever-improving albums for the label, usually featuring the phenomenal bassist Paul Chambers, who also worked with Davis.
Traneing In, *Soultrane*, *Black Pearls*, *Bahia*, and *Stardust* (most issued several years after being recorded) contain glowing gems that express Coltrane's equal comfort with
ballads, standards, and original bop tunes. He also taped a one-off session for Blue
Note, which became an instant classic: *Blue Train* (1957), with Chambers, trumpeter
Lee Morgan, trombonist Curtis Fuller, pianist Kenny Drew, and Philly Joe Jones.
Hearing his attempts to seemingly squeeze as much mileage out of the chord structures as possible, it was evident that Coltrane was frustrated with the restraints of
traditional musical forms, his imagination running far ahead of what jazz had to offer
at the time.

When Trane returned to Davis's group early in 1958, he became part of a significant chapter in jazz history. The band performed at the Newport Jazz Festival that
year, and some critics who generally applauded the concert complained that Coltrane's
angry tone hindered the group. These assaults led writer Ira Gitler to vehemently
defend Coltrane's approach to improvisation, famously describing his use of rapidly

cascading notes as "sheets of sound." Vindicated, Coltrane continued to pursue the technique with varying success.

In the mid-1950s, feeling that bebop had gotten boring and stale, Davis began to investigate more complicated harmonies and chord substitutions. Soon, inspired by George Russell's work with the Lydian mode, Davis looked into basing improvisations on modal scales rather than chord progressions. *Kind of Blue* (1959, Columbia) became the definitive document of Davis's modal adventures. Coltrane, pianist Bill Evans, and altoist Julian "Cannonball" Adderley were integral parts of this great innovation, and the album's unparalleled popularity opened new doors of opportunity for all involved.

Modality gave Coltrane some of the structural release he had been desperately seeking. His next album was a shock to jazz's system and a mixed blessing for him. *Giant Steps* (1959, Atlantic) featured Paul Chambers, pianist Tommy Flanagan, and drummer Art Taylor on a set of originals, with the title track as crowning glory. Trane's solo on "Giant Steps" is an exuberant lava flow of arpeggiated chords and wide intervallic leaps, an almost endless river of sixteenth notes that bespeaks his long endurance and vivid imagination. His powerful tone is balanced nicely by Taylor's restrained high-hat ride and Flanagan's judicious use of space. The tune is amazingly dense, a new chord falling on almost every beat. This is an ironic 360-degree turn from the modal avoidance of chords that Coltrane had practiced with Davis. While "Giant Steps" was an impressive showcase for Coltrane's chops, it inspired countless imitative performances by musicians of lesser merit. It also did not hold up well under the critics' microscopes, as they pointed out the repetitive, simplistic structure beneath the flood. The more mercenary jazz writers implied that it was merely a case of sound and fury signifying nothing. "Countdown" is similarly hell-bent for leather, the tenor barely supported as Taylor struggles to keep pace. The beautifully long-toned "Naima," which features Jimmy Cobb and Wynton Kelly in place of Taylor and Flanagan, is dedicated to the saxophonist's first wife and serves as a calm after the storm.

In 1960, Coltrane caught a performance on soprano sax by ex-Cecil Taylor sideman Steve Lacy and became enraptured with the horn's sound. Though Lacy had played soprano exclusively for the previous decade, to modest acclaim, Coltrane brought the slim horn into a new vogue. Having decided to reconfigure his quartet, he auditioned several musicians, among them pianist Steve Kuhn and Ornette Coleman's drummer, Billy Higgins. In May, Trane settled on the superior team of pianist McCoy Tyner and drummer Elvin Jones, both of whom remained with him for five years. This quartet, with a succession of bass players beginning with Steve Davis, became even more influential than Miles's group, sealing Coltrane's position as the most popular man in jazz.

In 1960, the quartet recorded the breathtaking *My Favorite Things* (Atlantic), a *tour de force* of substitute harmonies that consistently ranks among the most favored jazz albums of all time. Coltrane's reconstruction of the Rodgers and Hart title tune (from *The Sound of Music*) is perennially beloved. Harmonies are substituted throughout the piece, replacing standard chords with alternates that still support the melody but provide an altogether different mood. During the solo spots, Tyner concentrates on certain chords for long periods, extending the tense emotionality of Coltrane's flights. The principle is related to Davis's modal trials but is taken to new levels, resulting in catharsis.

Over the next few years, as Coltrane's profile built steadily, his personal finances expanded well beyond the expected level for a jazzman. This monetary freedom permitted Coltrane to experiment more widely with new sounds and to offer support to struggling younger musicians like tenorman Albert Ayler. He seemed to be on top of the world. However, Coltrane's combined search for new frontiers and spiritual contentment pulled him away from the financially equitable styles he had been performing. Coleman's *Free Jazz* made a deep impression upon Trane, and he sought to explore similar ground. As his success grew in the meantime, the quartet recorded several more dates for Atlantic.

The Avant-Garde (1960, Atlantic) teamed Coltrane with several of Coleman's associates: trumpeter Don Cherry, this session's coleader; bassists Charlie Haden and Percy Heath; and drummer Ed Blackwell. The album title is rather misleading as the music is not too overboard here, more modal than free. Three Coleman compositions ("Focus on Sanity," "The Blessing," and "The Invisible") are revisited, along with the trumpeter's "Cherryco" and Monk's "Bemsha Swing." Cherry is about as complementary to Coltrane's tone as Davis had been, and Blackwell is the edgiest of all with his enterprising rhythmic embellishments. Though not as inventive as one might expect, the session has many rewarding moments, and no doubt it inspired Coltrane to look further outward. His later hiring of Eric Dolphy and Freddie Hubbard, and use of two bassists, all features of Coleman's *Free Jazz*, are telling enough. Coltrane told critic Ralph J. Gleason, "I feel a need to learn more about production of music and expression and how to do things musically, so I feel a need for another horn for that reason" (from Gleason's liner notes for *Olé* [1961, Atlantic]). In Dolphy and Hubbard, the leader found highly complementary foils.

Dolphy initially joined Coltrane in 1961 for the large-ensemble endeavor *Africa/Brass*, the leader's first recording for Impulse. Dolphy arranged three tracks, an unusual take on "Greensleeves," and Coltrane's "Africa" and "Blues Minor." *Africa/Brass* is unique in Trane's discography for its extended lineup: Tyner, Jones, bassists Art Davis and Reggie Workman, trumpeter Booker Little, trombonist Britt Woodman, reedman Garvin Bushell, tubaist Bill Barber, four French horns, and three euphoniums. It was an auspicious debut for Dolphy in Coltrane's realm.

Two days later, Trane recorded *Olé* (Atlantic) with Tyner, Jones, Art Davis, Workman, Dolphy, and Hubbard. The title track is a Spanish-tinged opus reminiscent of *Sketches of Spain* (1960, Columbia), Davis's Iberian endeavor with arranger Gil Evans. Coltrane's soprano sax motifs are exciting, although like Tyner he seems unable to escape the aura of "My Favorite Things" for long; his final solo is especially redolent of that earlier record. *Olé* is an often overlooked signpost on the leader's path to freedom, with a strong bass duo and Dolphy's excursions (now pretty, now furious) pointing the way.

Coltrane's search for the right bassist ended in 1961 with the selection of Jimmy Garrison, who had worked with a variety of boppers from Curtis Fuller to Lennie Tristano. The bassist provided another Coleman link, having recently performed on *Ornette on Tenor*. Garrison's infallible ear and imagination made him an ideal accompanist for the saxophonist and his sidemen. Garrison was paired with Workman on *Live at the Village Vanguard* (Impulse), taped on two November dates at the New York club. Dolphy, Jones, and Tyner were on hand. "Chasin' the Trane" is one of the leader's definitive performances, his barreling marathon solo topping out the nearly sixteen-minute track. "Spiritual," which points to Coltrane's developing interest in meditative music, is a magnificent feature for soprano and bass clarinet. The 1997 reissue (subtitled *The Master Takes*) adds "India" and "Impressions," taped the same day as "Spiritual" but issued in 1962 on *Impressions*.

It was in this period that *Down Beat* coeditor John Tynan infamously labeled Coltrane's music "anti-jazz." Tynan's attack polarized the jazz journalists, with few writers taking the middle ground. Coltrane was aggrieved but undaunted. His next release, *Ballads* (1961, Impulse), seemed designed to give the naysayers what they desired from him. Beloved for the prettiness of its themes, the album contains some of Coltrane's least daring solos in years.

The following spring, with Dolphy moved on to new pastures, the quartet cut the simply titled *Coltrane* for Impulse. If *Ballads* was a peace offering, *Coltrane* was a firm declaration of where the leader was really at. Not quite as out-looking as *Olé* or the Vanguard set, the recording represents a slight return to form. The next album, *Bye Bye Blackbird* (1962, Impulse) was a further step forward. This live disc, not much over a half-hour in length, contains extended performances of the title track and "Traneing In." All four players are in grand form, and the tunes build to phenomenal climaxes, overstepping themselves time and again.

Trane set his musical advances aside for a day to share space with an elder giant of jazz in September 1962. *Duke Ellington and John Coltrane* (Impulse) put the legendary composer/pianist in Tyner's chair for an enjoyable set of six Ellington compositions and Coltrane's "Big Nick." The results are quite entertaining, and it's interesting to speculate about how Coltrane might have fared with the full Ellington orchestra.

March 1963 brought another unexpected turn. The quartet went into the Van Gelder studios to record with vocalist Johnny Hartman, with whom Coltrane had worked in Gillespie's band fifteen years prior. *John Coltrane and Johnny Hartman* (Impulse) marks the saxophonist's only major work with a singer and remains a classic despite its unseemly timing in Coltrane's career. Amiable renditions of ballads like "Lush Life" and "My One and Only Love" showcased a side of the tenorman that he had been pulling away from, but few clues indicate discomfort.

The 1963 Newport Jazz Festival was the setting for another triumph by the quartet. *Newport '63* (Impulse) documents a phenomenal concert with Roy Haynes in the drum chair. It includes what some consider the definitive performance of "My Favorite Things," boiling over with passion but never sailing off into atonality; the wondrous opus "Impressions"; and (because the Newport set was so short) "Chasin' the Trane" from the Village Vanguard show. Newport sold what remained of a skeptical public on Coltrane's contemporary vision for jazz, confirming the validity of his new path.

Live at Birdland was recorded in October 1963. "Alabama," a hallmark of Coltrane's compositional skills, interprets a speech by Martin Luther King Jr. and was inspired by the deaths of four young girls in a Birmingham church bombing. Its depth of passion testified as to Coltrane's heartsickness with the condition of black America and his passionate spiritual searching. "Alabama" is one of his most important moments on record.

The year 1964 was slower for the quartet, as they only made two studio albums. The first, *Crescent* (Impulse), contains five memorable Coltrane themes, including the compelling title track and "Lonnie's Lament." Not long after these sessions were completed, Dolphy died in Europe from diabetic complications. His passing may have been a principal catalyst for the quartet's next disc, their most universally inspirational project.

In December, Coltrane and company recorded a four-part suite that the saxophonist considered his gift to God, a love offering in return for his escape from addiction and the many blessings that followed. *A Love Supreme* (Impulse) is a continuous exaltation of God's love and glory, an earnest topic that would run throughout Trane's future efforts. The "Acknowledgement" theme is mostly variations on a four-note sequence that modulates through the chromatic scale, taken up at times by voices chanting "A Love Supreme" in the pattern. It is followed in turn by his "Resolution" to seek out God, "Pursuance" of spiritual enlightenment, and finally a closing "Psalm" of worship and praise. Though the music can tend toward the static, the power of Coltrane's conviction as translated into music is inarguable. It expresses his desire for positive change in people's lives and his understanding that a greater power guides us all. Later, as Coltrane sought to clarify that power's true nature, he effectively abandoned tonal music to open new artistic pathways on that endless search.

In February 1965, the band recorded *The John Coltrane Quartet Plays* (Impulse), his first official step into more atonal environments. Casual shoppers who flipped through the stacks would have noticed that the album bore two original song titles, "Brazilia" and "Song of Praise," and two fairly strange choices for a performer of Coltrane's stature: "Nature Boy," previously rendered as aural cheese by Nat "King" Cole, and the Disney melody "Chim Chim Cheree." As it was, the quartet didn't hold onto the melodies for very long before Coltrane was off on abstruse improvisations that barely, if at all, related to the themes. Fans who wondered what the tenorman was up to with "A Love Supreme" now had more questions.

Coltrane's next projects confirmed that he was entirely serious about breaking new ground in jazz form and function. The relentless *Transition* was the next step out. The quiet ballad "Welcome" is the only calm amid the unrelenting atonal storm. Tyner sounds especially ill at ease on the session, and Jones can barely hold down the fort on the long tenor-drums duet, "Vigil," which closes the disc. *Transition* was an early sign that all was not well with the quartet.

Coltrane's next move was even more unexpected. On June 28, 1965, at Van Gelder's studio, he recorded two takes of an ambitious free-jazz work entitled *Ascension* (Impulse). The project, Coltrane's initial leap into the avant-garde, is on a par with Coleman's *Free Jazz* as a milestone of improvised music. As with the Coleman piece, *Ascension* seemed to wallow in chaos but was actually grounded in a different kind of musical logic. The group and its musical conception were similar to the Coleman session: democracy in the group interaction, a few set reference points to inspire alternating collective and solo improvisations. Instead of short written lines, however, *Ascension* was rooted in Phrygian and Aeolian modal scales with various centers. The young band included trumpeters Dewey Johnson and Freddie Hubbard, altoists Marion Brown and John Tchicai, tenormen Pharoah Sanders and Archie Shepp, and bassist Art Davis, in addition to Tyner, Garrison, and Jones.

Ascension was perhaps a more accomplished exercise in total group communication than *Free Jazz*, as the interactions are more inspired and exciting. The density of sound was far beyond what Coleman or anyone else had explored at the time. Some of the musicians were distinctly uncomfortable with such freedom and soon strayed from free jazz altogether, while others used the date to kick-start lifelong careers in free improvisation. Hubbard had taken part in *Free Jazz* five years prior and would sporadically play free for the next decade. Tyner, disenchanted with his employer's immoderate change of direction, parted company with Coltrane within a year after this session. Sanders remained in the group until Trane's death. His powerful, avant-garde approach to the horn peaked Coltrane's interest and led to an eventually permanent position.

Ascension begins with the full ensemble playing chantlike structured passages, supported by Elvin Jones's splashing torrents and tumbling punctuations. Several seconds in, the form begins to wear down as the saxophonists interject honks and high runs. Quietness soon gives way to seeming chaos from all hands. Such ensemble passages come and go between solos, foggy visions of form and unity appearing and fading back into the mist. The bassists are usually lost in the mix during the ensemble ventures, emerging more clearly under the solo spotlights and their own brief duet.

It is interesting to study the individual solo turns to note the musicians' stages of development and comfort with such freedom. Coltrane's solo bears his distinctive tone and phrasing. He enters with a quick repeated phrase, then moves into shimmying, howling lines that sometimes use high-pitched notes as reference points. He rarely uses multiphonics in his solo, sticking mostly to melodic phrase repetitions and punctuating blats. Dewey Johnson's solo is characterized by rapid, unmelodic note flurries with short pauses for breath. Johnson was a young, little-known player whose performance shows that he was deeply into the spirit of the session, even if his inexperience restricted his ideas somewhat. The next turn is by Sanders, who begins with short repetitive phrases that span the full range of the horn. He frequently climbs into the upper reaches with wild honks and overblowing, held screams, multiphonics, and crushing miasmas that sound like white noise or feedback. He briefly returns to the short repetitions and ends his solo with a series of low honks.

Freddie Hubbard's turn is distinctively different from Johnson's, as evidenced by the use of fast tremolos, well-structured descending and ascending lines, and nearly stock bebop phrases. His solo structure is infinitely more melodic than Johnson's rapid flourishes. Toward the wrap-up, he blows several sweeping bleats that seem to be momentarily echoed by Johnson, then the solo decays into low-pitched groans. Next up is Shepp, beginning with astonishing, short, sharp phrases like cries of pain, building into ripping voicelike lines, squeals, multiphonics and pitch extremes. Shepp's soloing has been likened to someone "screaming through blood" and gives John Tchicai a hard act to follow. The now legendary Danish saxophonist is restrained and seems rather unsure of himself in this particular spotlight. His turn is notably quieter and more relaxed than any of the prior solos. Tchicai mostly blows wavering lines with a Dolphyesque flavor. His different usage of repetitive phrases sounds almost as if he is carrying on a tribal call-and-response with himself. Marion Brown's foray is more energetic than Tchicai's, rather like Shepp in his intensity and exploration. His blowing has a multiphonic edge spread across cries, flurries, and interesting phrase variations. He maintains a commanding presence despite being a little-known player at the time.

Coltrane is especially prominent in the next ensemble passage. His repeated tenor phrases build quickly as a lead-in to the piano solo. Tyner's turn is melodic and logical as if played over a written chord structure, much like his performances in the quartet setting. He pounds a few chords but there is little freedom here, even in a Monkish style. Tchicai may have seemed rather ill at ease in his solo, but Tyner seems unwilling to even attempt a truly free improvisation. Instead, he creates more of a spontaneous composition, at sharp odds with the other occurrences.

Davis and Garrison begin their bass duet with bowed phrases, which sound like rusty, creaking doors and scratching dogs. The duet reveals intriguing interplay and trade-offs on rhythmic and melodic playing. One bassist resorts to *col legno* tapping of a flamenco-like rhythm on the strings while the other bass scurries and trips about. Elvin Jones's short drum solo is pure thunderation, with heavy pounding and wide rolls across the whole kit. Had he remained with Coltrane during the last portion of his career, Jones might well have remained a suitable foil for the tenorman. Then the ensemble returns, building to tremendous intensity. The horns settle into rough structure and die off in phases. "Ascension" ends with a piano tremolo and cymbal shimmers, a blessed release.

Coltrane immediately followed *Ascension* with another appearance at Newport on July 2. As captured on *New Thing at Newport* (Impulse), along with Shepp's smashing performance, the quartet session is disquieting for the palpable tension between the players. The unusually structured "One Down, One Up" has trouble getting off the ground, and "My Favorite Things" almost seems a battle between Coltrane and Tyner. Many of the festivalgoers embraced Coltrane's new sound, while others who likely had not yet heard the tide of change on *Plays* or *Transition* were nonplussed. Shepp played with the quartet at the Down Beat Festival in Chicago a couple of weeks later.

Sun Ship (Impulse), recorded in August 1965, exacerbated the painful unease within the quartet. Coltrane's compositions had almost ceased to be such, basically becoming small sketches that bookended improvisations. The title track's theme is merely a hiccupping phrase repeated over and over with slight alterations, echoed by Jones in spots. "Dearly Beloved" is a mournful, wavering ballad, while both "Amen" and "Attaining" extend the prayerful thematics of *A Love Supreme*. Jones is highly responsive in contrast to Tyner's undeviating normalcy. It is unfair to label Tyner as insufficient, given his immense talents as a mainstream jazzman and the harrowing difficulties of Coltrane's late music. His seeming inflexibility is no greater than most any other pianist would have demonstrated in the period. The complexity of this sort of music is perhaps exactly why Ornette Coleman ceased to use pianists. The piano's chordal, tempered nature is simply not as compatible with certain free forms as other instruments. Garrison dominates more than half the length of "Ascent," unaccompanied and dotting melodies with strums.

Coltrane's spiritual hunting took another turn in October with *Om* (Impulse). In Hindu mythology, "Om" is said to be the first sound uttered in the universe, the summation of God's name and nature. His interest in exploring Hindu spirituality was no doubt instigated by his second wife. Alice McLeod had studied piano and harp as a child, performing in church groups while learning jazz from Bud Powell, Kenny Burrell, and Yusef Lateef. She had met Coltrane in 1963 while touring with vibraphonist Terry Gibbs, and they married in 1965. Alice had a profound interest in Eastern religions, which colored her music and her personal life, and she helped guide John in his all-consuming spiritual pursuits. From the overtly Christian leanings of A Love Supreme, Coltrane looked into Hinduism, African religions, and a bit of cosmology in his last couple of years. For Om, Coltrane retained Pharoah Sanders and added Joe Brazil and Donald Rafael Garrett to the band. Garrett, a double threat on bass and bass clarinet, had worked with Muhal Richard Abrams's Experimental Band in Chicago before coming to New York. Brazil played percussion and flute on Om, but little is known of him beyond this date. Om is probably the most difficult item in Coltrane's catalog to endure in one sitting, though it is rewarding once the listener grows accustomed to it.

Coltrane kept Sanders and Garrett on along with his original rhythm section, then hired two other musicians for Kulu Se Mama and Selflessness (both on Impulse) in October 1965. Frank Butler had been a popular hard-bop drummer, employed by Dave Brubeck and Duke Ellington among others. Less is known about percussionist/vocalist Juno Lewis, who was almost never heard from again after these recordings. The tracks on which these men joined the group once again upped the ante of Coltrane's musical bravery, though they were a comparatively comforting denouement in the wake of Om.

In November came Tyner and Jones's swan song with Coltrane's group. Meditations (Impulse) was the next logical protraction from A Love Supreme, more prayerful themes serving as solo springboards. The leader continued his mission of building intensity through dynamics, tone color, and rhythmic diversity on the date, part of which was originally issued as First Meditations. As Coltrane told jazz writer Nat Hentoff (taken from Hentoff's liner notes for Meditations, 1965, Impulse):

> Once you become aware of this force for unity in life, you can't ever forget it. It becomes a part of everything you do. In that respect, this is an extension of A Love Supreme since my conception of that force keeps changing shape. My goal in meditating on this through music, however, remains the same. And that is to uplift people, as much as I can. To inspire them to realize more and more of their capacities for living meaningful lives. Because there certainly is meaning to life.

For Meditations, drummer Rashied Ali was added to the lineup of Trane, Sanders, and the principal rhythm section. Ali, a Philadelphian, moved into free music after working with Sonny Rollins. He became a key associate of Sanders, Albert Ayler, Paul Bley, Bill Dixon, and other outward-looking musicians around New York. Coltrane was duly impressed and hired him to replace the hand percussionists with whom he had been experimenting. Elvin Jones apparently thought little of the idea, since he and Tyner left the fold shortly after this session.

The melody of "The Father And The Son And The Holy Ghost," built around its title's rhythms, emerges after a long period of drum swells and saxophone staccatos. From this precise sound, Albert Ayler would construct his tune "Love Cry" in 1967, as an homage to the late Coltrane. At intervals Sanders picks up a tambourine or string of bells for percussive emphasis. The track flows seamlessly into "Compassion," which showcases the reedmen's empathy. Sanders's solo is rough as sandpaper and almost unbearably intense. Clearly, he is begging for compassion, not extending it. When Coltrane enters in the background, his high-range rips resemble a screeding violin more than a tenor. The leader returns to the modulating theme of "The Father . . ." briefly before the keening staccatos resume and Jones takes the piece out. Unlike previous sessions with Sanders, the fierce overblowing by both saxophonists finds a clearer context within *Meditations*, resulting in room for the most exciting elements to develop organically. The remaining pieces ebb and flow together in a continuation of the contemplative mood.

Now that his two longtime companions were out of the picture, Coltrane took Alice on as pianist for his quintet with Sanders, Garrison, and Ali. Some controversial live shows followed, culminating in May 1966 with the recording of *Live at the Village Vanguard Again!* (Impulse). The leader's return to the club where he had triumphed five years earlier was not easy. The band delivered only two extended takes of "Naima" and "My Favorite Things." While Sanders had excelled at interpreting the original material Coltrane had used him on for the past year, he did not suit the audience's expectations for older selections. In effect, Sanders sort of kills the mood uniformly, sticking to his trademark screeches and howls on one of Coltrane's most attractive compositions and his show-tune theme. The date is not a complete loss. Alice is a welcome replacement for the grounded Tyner, building upon his penchant for arpeggios with a more atonal approach better suited to her husband's current aesthetic, and Ali is as vital to the new sound as Sunny Murray had proved to Cecil Taylor's advances.

In February and March 1967, despite the onset of a yet-undiagnosed illness, Coltrane held sessions at the Van Gelder studios that were released on *Expression* (1967, Impulse) shortly after his death. These were principally quartet dates with Alice, Ali, and Garrison, with Sanders joining in only on "To Be." That track is profound, surreal, in its questioning of life as channeled through Coltrane's flute and Sanders's piccolo. Trane had not played the flute much at all until his last days, yet on this track it seems as much an extension of his mortal soul as the saxophone. The piano arpeggiations play a prominent role in the mood of the album, supporting and responding to Coltrane on the Afro-Brazilian meditation "Ogunde" and strongly spiritual "Offering." Ali's rhythms and the leader's melodic reason keep the tracks from sounding too much alike. The CD reissue adds "Number One," a less focused effort that finds Ali full of energy but Coltrane with less to say.

Another collection of sides from February 15, 1967, was finally issued by Impulse in 1995 under the title *Stellar Regions*. Again, it features the quartet lacking Sanders. "Offering," which also appears on *Expression*, was the only previously released track from this session. This disc is more uniformly interesting than *Expression* in some ways, particularly the performers' levels of energy. Alice Coltrane performs more interesting bop-modal lines here instead of sticking to raining arpeggios; her solo on "Seraphic Light" is outstanding in its conception. The lessons that Coltrane drew from Albert Ayler and Ornette Coleman, all the ripping lines, honks, and overblows, are brought to full fruition in his own improvisations here.

February 22, 1967, was one of Coltrane's last studio dates, the recording of *Interstellar Space* (Impulse). This time around, it was just him and Ali in an enigmatic duo setting, interpreting themes inspired by the cosmos. Trane's spiritual quest had taken him from the many faiths of men out to the heavens themselves. This set, which was not released until 1974, shows the real promise of their intuitiveness, a bonding that had often been held back by Sanders's powerful saxophone or Jones's and Tyner's bebop restraint. Coltrane vacillates between nearly pastoral calm and raging fury, with Ali responding psychically to each mood shift. It is the true culmination of the cosmically personal abstraction that Coltrane had been seeking and a highlight of Ali's own respectable discography.

By that spring, Coltrane's health problems were getting the better of him, and he had to cut back drastically on his performance schedule. His final public appearance was on April 23, 1967, at the Olatunji Center of African Culture, founded by his old friend, percussionist Babatunde Olatunji, as a venue for black cultural events. Issued in 2001, *The Olatunji Concert* (Impulse) documents the first of two sets played that evening; apparently, the second set was not recorded. The group included Coltrane, Alice, Sanders, Garrison, Ali, bata drummer Algie DeWitt, and a second percussionist, probably Jumma Santos. Typical of Coltrane's late live sets, there were only two compositions on tap: "Ogunde" and the final rendition of "My Favorite Things." Health aside, Coltrane was able to give Sanders a taste of his own strong medicine for a few moments on this daunting final blowout.

Coltrane died of liver disease on July 17, 1967, survived by Alice and their three sons, John Jr., Oran, and Ravi, who was named after Ravi Shankar and who has become an acclaimed saxophonist in his own right. Trane's legacy lives on in his family, frequently reissued recordings, and the performers and fans he continues to inspire.

Company: an improvisational ensemble concept created by guitarist Derek Bailey in 1976 as an extension of his experiences with the Music Improvisation Company. The personnel of the "group" have shifted constantly over the years, from duo to medium-sized combo, with Bailey the only real constant. Participants have included Evan Parker, Steve Lacy, Fred Frith, Lee Konitz, Dave Holland, Lol Coxhill, Anthony Braxton, Han Bennink, John Zorn, and at least sixty others. The Company principle is to unite a group of improvisers, let them gather their own individual thoughts, bounce them off one another, and see what comes of it. One recent lineup featured Bailey, Rhodri Davies, Simon H. Fell, cellist Mark Wastell, and tap-dancer Will Gaines (*Company in Marseilles*, 1999, Incus). Perhaps the best recording is *Company 5* (1977, Incus), with electrifying performances by Braxton, Lacy, Honsinger, Maarten Altena, Evan Parker, Leo Smith, and Bailey himself. From 1977 until 1994, Bailey held annual "Company Week" celebrations, five-day festivals of no-holds-barred improvised music. The inceptive events were held in London, but subsequent weeks were conducted in New York, Japan, and elsewhere. Bailey suspended the celebrations in 1994 due to budgetary concerns but still convenes Company ensembles on occasion.

Connors, Loren MazzaCane (b. New Haven, CT, 1949): guitarist and vocalist. The enigmatic Connors's musical background includes violin, trombone, electric bass, blues, and classical, but he has built his career upon freely improvising with electric and acoustic guitars. Now and then, he has billed himself as "Guitar Roberts." In the

1970s, he studied art at Southern Connecticut State University and the University of Cincinnati, but music remained his principal calling. Connors labored for years as a sort of cult figure, releasing a large number of indie albums with poor distribution that made it into the hands of a few interested players. After marrying singer Suzanne Langille, he took a sabbatical to write award-winning poetry and haiku. Connors returned to music in 1990, and *Come Night* (1991, What Next) was his first solid post-hiatus release. In 1992, he was diagnosed with Parkinson's disease, but that hardly curtailed his output. Instead, he moved away from quieter acoustic works and into distorted electric guitar mayhem that better reflected his inner turmoil. The distance between his early works on *Unaccompanied Acoustic Guitar Improvisations* (4 CDs, 1999, Ecstatic Yod) and *The Murder of Joan of Arc* (2003, Table of the Elements) is remarkable. Connors has recorded with Alan Licht, Langille (*Enchanted Forest*, 1999, Secretly Canadian), Keiji Haino, koto artist Brett Larner, and Derek Bailey.

Contemporary: record label established in Los Angeles in 1951 by Lester Koenig. Contemporary quickly became the label of choice for musicians out of the West Coast cool school, largely alumni of Stan Kenton's bands: Shelly Manne, Art Pepper, Howard Rumsey and the Lighthouse All-Stars, and others. Contemporary also recorded notable black artists like Sonny Rollins, Harold Land, and Hampton Hawes. The earliest recordings by Ornette Coleman's quartet and Cecil Taylor's *Looking Ahead!* (1958) marked the label's only serious ventures toward free jazz. The company also handled subsidiary labels that concentrated upon Dixieland jazz and classical music. After Koenig's death, Contemporary and its subsidiaries were eventually sold to Fantasy, which has since led a vigorous reissue program.

Cooper, Jerome (b. Chicago, IL, 14 December 1946): drummer and percussionist. Cooper studied drums with Captain Walter Dyett in Chicago, continuing his studies in college in 1967–1968. He played with Oscar Brown Jr. and tenorist Kalaparusha Maurice McIntyre, then relocated to Europe, where he performed with Steve Lacy, Alan Silva, Noah Howard, Roland Kirk, and the Art Ensemble of Chicago. In 1971, Cooper formed the Revolutionary Ensemble with Sirone and Leroy Jenkins, remaining a member until its demise six years later. Within that trio, his most prominent group, Cooper played piano, flute, and bugle in addition to drums. Later Cooper performed with Cecil Taylor, Sam Rivers, and Anthony Braxton. He maintains a good semblance of form in his playing while allowing freedom for the other musicians to explore and tends to be underestimated as a free drummer.

Cooper, Lindsay (b. Hornsey, England, 3 March 1951): reeds player, composer, and bandleader. Well instructed in piano and bassoon, Cooper graduated from the Royal Academy of Music and spent a year in New York, where she became interested in new jazz and rock developments. The experience led her to dump her classical ambitions, and in 1971, she became involved in the Canterbury scene, which united jazz and progressive rock, spawning ensembles like Soft Machine, Matching Mole, and Henry Cow. She played on Mike Oldfield's landmark *Tubular Bells* session, a precursor of the New Age movement, then joined Henry Cow in 1974. She made two records (*Unrest*, 1974, and *Western Culture*, 1979) with the band, and others with the side project Slapp Happy, Egg, Hatfield and the North, the Art Bears, and her first group, Comus.

In 1975, Cooper began working with some of England's more hard-core improvisers, including Lol Coxhill and Derek Bailey. She assembled the Feminist Improvising Group with vocalist Maggie Nicols, Swiss pianist Irène Schweizer, and other performers, took up the soprano sax, and became renowned for her work as a composer and player of film scores. Among her better projects in the 1980s were the quartet News From Babel and her avant-jazz vocal project, *Oh Moscow* (1989, Victo), with Phil Minton. In 1991, Cooper was diagnosed with multiple sclerosis, which has now curtailed most of her activities. She has, however, composed music for dance performances and an exceptional theatrical work, *Sahara Dust* (1992, Intakt), about the 1991 Gulf War.

Cooper-Moore (Eugene Ashton; b. Virginia, 1946): pianist, composer, and instrument inventor. The reasons for his change of name are not very clear; he established a solid reputation as Gene Ashton several years beforehand. He began studying piano at the age of eight and became enamored with jazz at twelve through the recordings of Ahmad Jamal and Charles Mingus. Ornette Coleman's *This Is Our Music* was the catalyst that eventually led Ashton to look into free jazz. He attended Catholic University of America but dropped out in dissatisfaction. Club hopping exposed him to the ESP crowd—Sun Ra, Bill Dixon, Albert Ayler.

Ashton had a slightly better experience at Berklee, after which he joined an R&B group. As of that time, the late 1960s, he still hadn't begun to play free jazz himself. But at Berklee he met David S. Ware, who shared his interest in the music. Both men played in The Rosewater Foundation, led by percussionist Jim Riley (now Jumma Santos). A couple of years later, Ashton and Ware formed Apogee, with drummer Marc Edwards and bassist Chris Amberger. The group opened for Sonny Rollins at the Village Vanguard, a most auspicious opportunity for a young band. Apogee did not last long, but Ware and Ashton became fixtures of New York's new wave of free jazz.

Cooper-Moore has worked regularly with William Parker, both in the Little Huey Creative Music Orchestra (*Sunrise in the Tone World*, 1997, Aum Fidelity) and In Order To Survive (self-titled, 1995, Black Saint), as well as with Bill Cole's Untempered Ensemble (*Seasoning the Greens*, 2002, Hopscotch) and poet Martha Cinader. His records include *Triptych Myth*, with bassist Tom Abbs and drummer Chad Taylor, and *America*, with Assif Tsahar (both 2003, Hopscotch). Cooper-Moore is a musical consultant for the Harlem Interfaith Counseling Service and resident storyteller at New York's Prospect Park. He builds unusual instruments as a sideline, including traditional one-string diddly-bos.

Cora, Tom (b. Yancey Mills, VA, 1953; d. Draguignan, France, 9 April 1998): cellist. Raised on a diet of gospel and country music as a youth, Cora worked as a drummer on a local children's TV show, then played jazz guitar at a club in Washington, D.C. Soon Cora gave up the guitar in favor of the cello, studying with Luis Garcia-Renart and learning elements of Eastern European and Turkish musics. In the late 1970s, he toured Europe with Karl Berger and Don Cherry, then moved to New York in 1979. Cora developed a friendship with Eugene Chadbourne, playing in his oddball Shockabilly ensemble, plus occasional improvisational gigs alongside John Zorn, David Moss, and other key Downtown figures. Cora was a founding member of Curlew, then joined Fred Frith in Skeleton Crew from 1982 to 1987. Cora expanded his arsenal to include drums, bass, and various foot-operated musical contrivances of his own design. In 1986, he began to perform as a solo cellist, played in a duo with Hans Reichel, and toured the Soviet Union with Frame. Cora formed an enthralling partnership in the "trio" Third Person, with electronic percussionist Samm Bennett and a third member that varied with each performance or recording. In the 1990s, Cora frequently collaborated with Dutch rock band The Ex and composed on commission for films and orchestras until he died of melanoma.

Corea, Chick (Armando; b. Chelsea, MA, 12 June 1941): pianist, electric keyboardist, composer, and bandleader. Corea, of Spanish heritage, studied piano from age four and gained an interest in jazz through recordings by Charlie Parker, Dizzy Gillespie, and other bebop figures. Bud Powell and Horace Silver were among his greatest influences. He began his career as a sideman with the Latin groups of Willie Bobo and Mongo Santamaria, and in this time, he began incorporating Spanish colorations into his playing and writing. His compositions were first recorded in the mid-1960s by trumpeter Blue Mitchell. Corea's debut as a leader was *Tones for Joan's Bones* (1966) on Vortex, an Atlantic subsidary; the album clearly shows the influence of the post-bop movement prevalent in jazz at the time.

From 1968 to 1970, Corea was a member of Miles Davis's electric band, often performing alongside fellow keyboardist Keith Jarrett on albums like *Miles Davis at Fillmore* (1970, Columbia). While with Davis, he gained an interest in free improvisation but wished to explore outside the electric context. This led to Corea's trio with Barry Altschul and Dave Holland, documented on *The Song of Singing* (1970, Blue Note). With Anthony Braxton added, the group became known as Circle. A very influential ensemble, Circle only lasted until 1971. (See entry.)

Corea's involvement in Scientology led him to abandon free music in favor of a style that better appealed to mass audiences. In the early 1970s, after a productive stint with tenorist Stan Getz and the start of a collaboration with vibist Gary Burton, Corea founded the jazz-rock group Return to Forever. Initially a Latin-flavored acoustic group, it went electric in about 1973 and lasted until 1980. The following year he formed a trio with bassist Miroslav Vitous and drummer Roy Haynes, which has returned periodically to free jazz, and in 1985 Corea assembled his internationally popular Elektric Band. He has also led the Akoustic Band, with similar personnel, and more recently recorded a poignant tribute to his main inspiration, Bud Powell.

Cortez, Jayne: poet, ex-wife of Ornette Coleman and mother of Denardo Coleman. Cortez is a respected poet who has collaborated with free musicians on several occasions. On *Celebrations and Solitudes* (1974, Strata-East), she was backed by bassist Richard Davis. *Everywhere Drums* (1990, Bola Press) presents her excellent work with the Firespitters, son Denardo's group, as her gripping verse is backed by firm, harmolodic-funk rhythms.

Cosmosamatics: improvising quartet, founded in 2000 by saxophonists Sonny Simmons and Michael Marcus. Bassist William Parker and drummer Jay Rosen rounded out the original lineup. That group recorded their self-titled debut (2001, Boxholder), which featured guests including reedman James Carter, tabla player Samir Chatterjee, and bassoonist Karen Borca. For *Cosmosamatics II* (2002, Boxholder), Parker was replaced by Curtis Lundy. Their music is reminiscent of Simmons's early Coleman-inspired recordings, and their repertoire has included tributes to Eric Dolphy and Charles Mingus.

Coursil, Jacques (b. Paris, France, 1939): trumpeter and bandleader. Coursil was one of the first French nationals to be heard playing free jazz outside of his homeland. His intellectual conception and deep concern with the sound of his horn placed him in the same circles as Anthony Braxton, with whom he collaborated during the saxophonist's residence in Paris. His West Indian heritage gave Coursil an appreciation for Caribbean musical styles along with classical and jazz forms, all of which he used as elements in his personal bag of tricks.

After high school, Coursil came to America, where he studied jazz under pianist Jaki Byard and drummer Sunny Murray. Both men were involved in free jazz to different degrees, but it was Murray who convinced Coursil to pursue the path of freedom. The drummer also featured Coursil on his self-titled ESP record in 1966. Gigs with Rashied Ali, Marion Brown, tenorman Frank Wright (*Your Prayer*, 1967, ESP), pianist Burton Greene (*Aquariana*, 1966, ESP), and the Sun Ra Arkestra opened his eyes to new possibilities in jazz, although he was eventually put off by Ra's nearly fascistic ideology and cosmic weirdness. Coursil then recorded with Bill Dixon's big band and with his own quintet featuring Brown. That group cut what would have been his debut recording for ESP. Unfortunately, neither that disc nor the Dixon session ever saw the light of day, save a single track issued on a sampler.

Coursil is principally recognized for two albums issued by BYG in 1969. *The Way Ahead* is a quartet date with altoist Arthur Jones, bassist Beb Guerin, and drummer Jacques Delcloo, who was the A&R man for BYG. The music is more organized and tuneful than many of the albums resulting from the label's recording spate, although there are definite passages of freedom within. Coursil is the finest soloist, since Jones's ideas are sometimes fraught with uncertainty. Anthony Braxton and Burton Greene supplemented the quartet on *Black Suite* (1969, BYG), the better of the two releases. Braxton's presence seems to be inspirational to everyone, since Jones rises to the occasion admirably and Greene holds onto the reedman's coattails to great effect. Coursil reaches his pinnacle as a trumpeter, crafting original melodic phrases out of thin air that few others could have imagined. As with *The Way Ahead*, the rhythm section is mostly along for the ride. The horns and piano work the real magic.

Following his brief heyday at the close of the 1960s, Coursil descended into obscurity and rarely recorded again. He continued to gig around New York City, spreading his influence quietly but effectively around the young set. Coursil made perhaps the biggest impression on one of his high-school French students, John Zorn, who openly acknowledges his teacher's inspiration. Eventually Coursil left the jazz world altogether to become an educator. He is a professor of linguistics at the French West Indies University in Martinique and has been a visiting professor of Francophone studies at Cornell University.

Cowell, Stanley (b. Toledo, OH, 5 May 1941): pianist. Classically trained from age four, Cowell was inspired by Art Tatum and Bud Powell. He studied at Oberlin College Conservatory, playing with Roland Kirk at the time, and at the University of Michigan. In the late 1960s, he alternated between free jazz and post-bop, performing with Marion Brown, Max Roach, and the quintet of Harold Land and Bobby Hutcherson. In 1969, Cowell joined Music Inc., with trumpeter Charles Tolliver, and recorded two of his most powerful albums as a leader, *Blues for the Viet Cong* and *Brilliant Circles*, both on Polydor. He formed Collective Black Artists with Reggie Workman in 1970, and in 1971 cofounded the label Strata-East with Tolliver. Cowell worked with the Heath Brothers from 1974 to 1984, received a National Endowment for the Arts grant in 1981, and that same year began teaching at City University of New York.

COWWS Quintet: ensemble that includes multi-instrumentalist Rüdiger Carl, bassist Jay Oliver, violinist Phillip Wachsmann, guitarist Stephen Wittwer, and pianist Irène Schweizer. The moniker is composed of their surname initials. On occasion, Oliver has been replaced by Arjen Gorter, as on Carl's *Book/Virtual COWWS* (FMP).

Coxhill, Lol (Lowen; b. Portsmouth, England, 19 September 1932): tenor, soprano, and sopranino saxophonist. Always an advocate of jazz in Britain, has was initially inspired by Charlie Parker and worked as a club promoter as a teenager. After a brief service in the Royal Air Force, Coxhill became a vital session player backing up the cream of British post-bop musicians. In the 1960s and early 1970s, he accompanied visiting American soul, jazz, and blues artists while performing avant-jazz in duo and ensemble settings. His 1971 album *Ear of the Beholder* (Daffodil) gained him his first national attention. From 1973 onward, Coxhill became well known as an improviser and solo performer, playing at festivals and collaborating with jazz and rock musicians and experimental theater troupes. His recordings include projects with Trevor Watts Moiré Music, Spontaneous Music Ensemble, Company, Dedication Orchestra, and AMM. Coxhill was a founding member of the Recedents, an electroacoustic improv group, and the trio Melody Four with Steve Beresford and reedman Tony Coe. He has often worked as an actor and master of ceremonies.

Create(!): Long Beach, California–based improvising ensemble. The core trio consists of bassist Orlando Greenhill (a member of the contemporary Christian folk-jazz-rock band Havalina Rail Company), guitarist Chris Schlarb, and drummer Steve Richardson. They have released two albums on the Sounds Are Active label, augmented by various horns, voices, MCs, and electronics. The members have characterized their music as "Improvdrumn'jazzworshiphopnoise."

Crispell, Marilyn (b. Philadelphia, PA, 20 March 1947): pianist. Crispell began studying piano at the age of seven and graduated from the New England Conservatory in 1969 but left music for several years to work in the medical field. She returned in 1975 with a new interest in the more outward jazz of Thelonious Monk, Cecil Taylor, and Paul Bley, influences that forever determined her artistic direction. While studying at the Creative Music Studio, she met Anthony Braxton. Her long, fruitful partnership with the saxophonist began with the 1978 tour by the Creative Music Orchestra and culminated in a spectacular mid-1980s stint in Braxton's quartet with Mark Dresser and Gerry Hemingway (see Braxton's entry).

Besides working with Braxton, Crispell has led outstanding sessions on Music & Arts, Black Saint, Leo, Okkadisk, and other labels. The live *Labyrinths* (1987, Victo) is an excellent solo date; *Overlapping Hands: Eight Segments* (1990, FMP) pairs Crispell and Irène Schweizer with scintillating results. Another fine partnership has been with Hemingway, resulting in recordings like *Crispell and Hemingway Duo* (1992, Knitting Factory Works). Other mates include Henry Kaiser, Urs Leimgruber, François Houle, Steve Lacy, and the Parker/Guy/Lytton Trio (*After Appleby*, 2000, Leo, as well as *Odyssey*, 2001, Intakt, with just Guy and Lytton).

Cryptogramophone: label founded in 1998 by violinist Jeff Gauthier. The death of a good friend, the sadly underappreciated bassist Eric Von Essen, led Gauthier to recognize that too much excellent music was not being properly documented on the West Coast, despite the best efforts of the Nine Winds label. Cryptogramophone was created to take up the slack, and to specifically document Von Essen's compositions. Among the featured artists are Gauthier, Nels and Alex Cline, bassists Steuart Liebig and Mark Dresser, "hyperpianist" Denman Maroney, and drummers Jeanette Wrate, Peter Erskine, and Scott Amendola. So far, three discs of Von Essen's compositions, as performed by various musicians, have been issued, as have several unrelated recordings.

Cunningham, Bob (b. Cleveland, OH, 28 December 1934): bassist. Cunningham moved to New York in 1960 and signed on with Dizzy Gillespie's band, with which he toured the Middle East and recorded at the Monterey Jazz Festival. Throughout the 1960s, he worked with a number of bebop and free musicians, among them Eric Dolphy, Walt Dickerson, Freddie Hubbard, Frank Foster, Art Blakey, Sun Ra, Pharoah Sanders, and Rashied Ali. Cunningham recorded with the Jazz Composers Orchestra in 1968 and Leon Thomas in 1970, then joined Yusef Lateef on tours and records from 1970 to 1976. He has worked as a leader and sideman, with occasional commissions as a composer.

Curlew: avant-jazz-rock ensemble, led by saxophonist George Cartwright. The band has crafted some consistently intriguing fusions of hard rock, free jazz, and the classical avant-garde since its inception in the mid-1980s. Among its members have been guitarist Davey Williams (a key component of Curlew's sound), cellist Tom Cora, drummer Pippin Barnett, and an unsteady string of bass players including Fred Frith, Bill Laswell, and Ann Rupel. *Live in Berlin* (1986, Cuneiform) documents the band at their finest.

Curson, Ted (b. Philadelphia, PA, 3 July 1935): trumpeter. Curson studied music in high school with his neighbors, Jimmy, Percy, and Albert "Tootie" Heath. He played with Charlie Ventura in 1953 and moved to New York in 1956 at Miles Davis's suggestion. He played with pianist Red Garland and Austrian vibist Vera Auer, performed briefly with Cecil Taylor in 1959, then joined Eric Dolphy in Charles Mingus's band. Influenced by Clifford Brown and the obscure ex-Coltrane sideman Johnnie Splawn, Curson's empathy with Dolphy and Mingus is documented on the albums *Mingus at Antibes, Pre-Bird,* and *Presents Charles Mingus.* In 1962, he formed a group with tenorman Bill Barron, which moved *en masse* to Europe to find work. He settled in Denmark from 1964 to 1976, then returned to New York. Curson paid tender homage to his old cohort on *Tears for Dolphy* (1964, Fontana).

Cusack, Peter: guitarist, bouzouki player, and composer. Cusack was a founding member of Alterations in 1977 but tends to be neglected when cataloguing the annals of British improvisation. He got his start in free music in the early 1970s, appearing alongside Fred Frith, Henry Kaiser, Eugene Chadbourne, and Keith Rowe on the collection *Guitar Solos 3* (1974, Red). In the 1980s, Cusack helped found Bead Records and the London Musicians Collective, two important ventures in furthering British improvised music. He developed a keen interest in field recording, fruits of which can be heard in the radio pieces on *Where Is the Green Parrot?* (1999, Recommended). Cusack has played the bouzouki in several settings including Alterations, explored electronic music at the STEIM studio in Amsterdam, and collaborated with Mario Schiano, Chris Burn, Luc Houtkamp, John Butcher, sound sculptor Max Eastley, and dance and theater companies.

Cuypers, Leo (b. Maastricht, Netherlands, 1 December 1947): pianist. Cuypers played the drums as a child, then taught himself to play piano and later supplemented his knowledge with conservatory lessons. In 1969, he appeared with the Baden-Baden Free Jazz Orchestra and Lester Bowie (*Gettin' to Know Y'all*, MPS). He is best known for his work in the Willem Breuker Kollektief from 1974 through 1983, at which point he left over a disagreement with Breuker. Among the better WBK albums in which he is featured are *De Onderste Steen* (1974), *European Scene* (1975), and *Driebergen-Zeist* (1983). He and Breuker cofounded the BVHaast label. Cuypers played with Misha Mengelberg and Theo Loevendie in the 1970s and led his own groups. *Theatre Music* (1978, BVHaast) was his debut as a session leader; *Johnny Rep Suite/Zeeland Suite* (rec. 1974/1977, issued on CD 1995, BVHaast) are some of his best works. In 2000, Atavistic's Unheard Music imprint reissued his classic 1981 session, *Happy Days Are Here Again,* with Breuker, Han Bennink, and Arjen Gorter. *Songbook* (1995, BVHaast) is an excellent solo session.

Cyrille, Andrew (b. New York, NY, 10 November 1939): drummer, noted for his restraint and subtlety of touch. In his youth, Cyrille played in a drum and bugle corps and in a trio with guitarist Eric Gale. He studied at Juilliard from 1958 and worked with Mary Lou Williams, Roland Kirk, Coleman Hawkins, Howard McGhee, and other prominent jazz figures. He made the move into free jazz in 1964, when he replaced Sunny Murray as Cecil Taylor's drummer. He carved a formidable niche in Taylor's unit until his departure in 1975, as well as playing with Grachan Moncur III, Marion Brown, and Jimmy Giuffre. Cyrille partnered with Milford Graves and Rashied Ali for the mid-1970s concert series "Dialogue of the Drums" (1974, Institute of Percussive Arts), and in 1975 he gathered the group Maono with David S. Ware and trumpeter Ted Daniel (*Metamusicians Stomp*, 1978, Black Saint). Cyrille has worked with Carla Bley, John Carter, Muhal Richard Abrams, and Charlie Haden's Liberation Music Orchestra. In the 1980s, he led his own quartet, performed in the drum quartet Pieces of Time with Graves, Famoudou Don Moye, and bebop titan Kenny Clarke, and was a member of The Group with Billy Bang and Marion Brown.

D

Dafeldecker, Werner (b. 1964, Vienna, Austria): bassist, composer, and bandleader. Dafeldecker began to come into international prominence in the 1990s with Polwechsel, which he founded with cellist Michael Moser and the groups Ton Art, Shobotinski, and SSSD. He started the Durian label in 1995 to document his music and that of other Austrian improvisers. Among his best records are his debut, *Bogengange* (1995, Durian) and *Eis 9* (2000, Grob).

Daisy, Tim (b. Waukegan, IL, 1976): drummer. Daisy is a young percussionist on the rise, having come to jazz at age seventeen. Influenced by Milford Graves, Paul Lovens, and Eddie Prévost, Daisy performs in Triage with Vandermark 5 saxman Dave Rempis and bassist Jason Ajemian (*Premium Plastics*, 2001, Solitaire; *Twenty Minute Cliff*, 2003, Okkadisk). When Vandermark needed a drummer for an Ornette Coleman tribute concert in 1999, Rempis suggested his bandmate Daisy, who replaced Tim Mulvenna as the Vandermark 5's drummer in 2003.

Daley, Joe (d. 1994): tenor saxophonist. A highly influential performer in the early days of free jazz, Daley has been all but forgotten with the passage of time. His one readily available album is *Trio at Newport '63* (1963, RCA), with bassist Russell Thorne and drummer Hal Russell, who later applied Daley's influence to his own NRG Ensemble. Among the other musicians Daley impacted were tenormen Ellery Eskelin and Assif Tsahar.

Damiani, Paolo (b. Rome, Italy, 6 March 1952): bassist, cellist, conductor, and composer. A member of the Italian Instabile Orchestra and leader of France's Orchestre National de Jazz (*Charmediterranéan*, 2000, ECM), Damiani taught at the Milan and L'Aquila Conservatories and founded the Testaccio Music School and a youth jazz orchestra, the IS Ensemble. He has performed and recorded with Norma Winstone, Kenny Wheeler, Eugenio Colombo, Tony Oxley, Gianluigi Trovesi, Albert Mangelsdorff, and his own ensembles, among others. *Eso* (1993, Splasc(h)) with Trovesi and trumpeter Paolo Fresu on hand, is one of his best.

Dara, Olu (Charles Jones; b. Natchez, MS, 1941): trumpeter, cornetist, vocalist, and guitarist. Dara's professional name was drawn from the Yoruba language, reflecting his interest in African American history. From the mid-1970s on, Dara was one of the principal free trumpeters in New York, where he had relocated in 1963. He soon amassed an impressive resumé of sideman gigs and recordings under Art Blakey, David Murray, Henry Threadgill, Don Pullen, Hamiet Bluiett, Charles Brackeen, and other prominent figures who benefitted from his bold and brassy presence. Dara occasionally led groups (Natchezsippi Dance Band, Okra Orchestra) but did not record as a leader until 1998. Surprisingly, when he reached that milestone, it was as a reputable singer and guitarist drawing from blues and folk idioms. While they are entertaining in their own right, his pair of Atlantic discs (*In the World: From Natchez to New York*, 1998, and *Neighborhoods*, 2001) bear little or no relation to the free jazz work that first made his name known to the music industry. Dara has continued to play cornet and trumpet in jazz settings with Tim Berne and the Dirty Dozen Brass Band.

Darriau, Matt: saxophonist, composer, leader of Pachora and Paradox Trio. Darriau first came to public attention as a member of George Schuller's big band, Orange Then Blue. Darriau began blending jazz and Eastern European folk elements in the early 1990s with the Paradox Trio, a quartet that included electric cellist Rufus Cappadocia, Macedonian percussionist Seido Salifoski, and Brad Shepik. Darriau expanded his concepts with Pachora, bringing them to fuller realization on their three recordings. Unlike similar-minded performers, such as John Zorn, Darriau brings a more genuine ethnic flavor to his groups by using traditional flutes, bagpipes, and percussion instruments. He has worked with trumpeter Frank London's Klezmatics, Les Miserables Brass Band, and the swing-era repertory group Ballin' the Jack.

Dato, Carlo Actis (b. 21 March 1952): reedman, bandleader, and composer; one of Italy's most prominent and prolific performers, who had made over fifty recordings by the new millennium. Dato is a wise, witty professional and educator who has played free music since founding the Art Studio in the 1970s. Like many of his compatriots, he plays in the Italian Instabile Orchestra.

Dato's first three records as a leader were *Noblesse Oblige* (1986), *Oltremare* (1987), and *Zig Zag* (1989, all on Splasc(h)), now reissued in a two-disc package (conveniently entitled *Noblesse Oblige/Oltremare/Zig Zag*, 1999, Splasc(h)). The small-group dates unveil his interest in humor and European folk musics à la Willem Breuker. Bizarre vocals, klezmer motifs, and damaged tangos lie among the tarnished treasures. The multiethnic references continue on *Ankara Twist* (1989, Splasc(h)). The leader is in his best form on baritone sax and bass clarinet, setting the stage for reedman Piero Ponzo to cavort in off-kilter counterpoint. Dato's next several records (*Bagdad Boogie*,

1992, Splasc(h); *Urartu*, 1994, Leo; *Blue Cairo*, 1995, Splasc(h)) tend to be of a piece, following the same ethnic-free-humor motif.

On *Son Para El Ché* (1997, Splasc(h)) Dato broke the mold by electrifying his band and sharpening up the tunes. The ethnic elements remain key to the conception, but the plugged-in instrumentation breathes more life into the format. Tracks like "Dead Chicken for Breakfast," "Nefertari," "Lazymambo," and the title track balance world-music complexity with avant atonality, an authentic jazz feel . . . and you can dance to it!

Japanese saxophonist Kazutoki Umezu teamed with Dato for the delicious *Wake up with the Birds* (1999, Leo). The pairing successfully updated the Italian's ethno-avant mode by cutting away rhythmic support to leave the bare interaction of reeds. Dato also met with Oriental ingenuity in TAO, with Japanese bassist Yasuhiko Tachibana and violinist Keisuke Ohta. As *Tomorrow Night Gig* (2002, Leo) attests, this team is not as up to snuff as many of Dato's other unions. Tachibana seems to have trouble keeping up with the beat, even on comparatively simple things like the calypso "Red," and Ohta's fusiony effects and esoteric singing do not help.

Dato's solo masterpiece is *The Moonwalker* (2001, Leo), a busker's tour through the back streets of exotic lands. Intermingled with the eighteen improvisations are sound-snippets from the real world, be it children in song or an active Moroccan bazaar.

Dauner, Wolfgang (b. Stuttgart, Germany, 30 December 1935): pianist, leader, and composer. Dauner studied music at the Musikhochschule in his hometown. He played in saxophonist Joki Freund's sextet and at festivals in the early 1960s, and in 1964 made the album *Dream Talk* on CBS Records, one of the earliest European free recordings. He led groups including the Radio Jazz Group Stuttgart (1969), the jazz-rock band Et Cetera (1970) and the ponderously named Free Sound and Super Brass Big Band (1975). Also in 1975, he founded the United Jazz + Rock Ensemble with Charlie Mariano, Kenny Wheeler, Ian Carr, and other top European jazzers. He has written and performed works with *musique concrète* inclusions, synthesizers, and tape loops, as well as orchestral works and media scores.

Davies, Hugh (b. London, England): instrument inventor and composer. Since 1971, Davies has performed entirely on found objects and electroacoustic instruments of his own invention, such as shozyg (amplified objects mounted inside the covers of volume SHO-ZYG of an encyclopedia), porcupine, and springboards. Formerly an assistant to Karlheinz Stockhausen, Davies comes by his interest in electroacoustics honestly. In 1968, he was a founder of the Music Improvisation Company with Derek Bailey, Evan Parker, and percussionist Jamie Muir (*Music Improvisation Company 1968–1971*, 1971, Incus).

Davies graduated from Oxford's music program in 1964, about the time that a serious interest in the avant-garde began to take hold in England. After working with Stockhausen for two years, he engaged in electronic music research at French Radio's Groupe de Recherches Musicales. In 1967, he began working on his new instruments, of which the shozyg was the first real success. In that same year, Davies founded the Goldsmith's College Studio of Electronic Music at the University of London. He has also consulted and researched at Middlesex University and the Gemeentemuseum at The Hague. In 1982, Davies helped found the International Confederation for Electroacoustic Music in London.

Davies has written commissioned works for dance and music theater groups, and pieces specially designed to be performed underground. He performs in a trio with percussionist Roger Turner and guitarist John Russell, and has collaborated with Bailey, Parker, Fred Frith, London Improvisers Orchestra, and even the pop-rock group Talk Talk (*Spirit of Eden*, 1988, Nettwerk). Principal recordings under Davies' name include *Shozyg: Music for Invented Instruments* (1982, FMP) and *Warming up with the Iceman* (2001, Grob).

Davies, Rhodri (b. Aberystwyth, Wales, 1971): harp player. Davies graduated with honors from the University of Sheffield's music program, then studied contemporary harp at University of Huddersfield. He was first exposed to free improvisation there, which led him to move to London in 1995. Davies has been the premier improvising harpist in Europe since then, performing with John Butcher (*Vortices and Angels*, 2000, Emanem), Derek Bailey and Company (*In Marseille*, 1999, Incus), Chris Burn (*Navigations*, 1997, Acta), Simon H. Fell, Phil Durrant, Axel Dörner, London Improvisers Orchestra, John Zorn, Evan Parker, and various Japanese improvisers. He has long had a bond with cellist Mark Wastell, working with him in duos and ensembles like IST and The Sealed Knot. His first appearance on record was IST's *Anagrams to Avoid* (1995, Siwa); he debuted as a session leader on *Pure Water Construction* (1997, Discus). In the mainstream, he is the harpist of choice for classical diva Charlotte Church.

Davis, Anthony (b. Paterson, NJ, 20 February 1951): pianist and composer. He received his BA in music in 1975 from Yale, where he became involved in free jazz inspired by the AACM's activities. In 1975, he and trombonist George Lewis had a free group, Advent, and from 1974 to 1977, he was a member of Leo Smith's New Dalta Akhri. He moved to New York in 1977, where he met and played with Leroy Jenkins; the following year he began a long working relationship with flautist James Newton. In 1981, he formed the fine Third Stream ensemble Episteme, with Newton and cellist Abdul Wadud. Davis has composed an opera, X, based on the life of Malcolm X. Davis does not include much room for free jazz in his compositions, though he does write atonally. His works tend to be complex and heavily notated, and he has dabbled in minimalism inspired by Javanese gamelan. He is presently a member of Smith's Golden Quartet.

Debris: Boston-based improvising quintet, established in 1986. Most recently comprising guitarist and mandolinist Arthor Weinstein, saxophonists Steve Norton and Andrew D'Angelo, bassist Bob Ross, and drummer Curt Newton, Debris blends modern compositional techniques with elements of jazz, rock, and free improv. *Terre Haute* (1998, Rastascan) is a typically bracing album.

DeJohnette, Jack (b. Chicago, IL, 9 August 1942): drummer and bandleader, a versatile performer who can blend seamlessly into most any performance situation. In his skillful unification of bop and free styles, DeJohnette seems a bridge between Max Roach's power and Sunny Murray's fluidity. His musical conception is colored by his studies of the piano, which he took up at age four. Impressed in his teen years by Ahmad Jamal's melodicism, DeJohnette worked along similar lines before he moved to the drums instead. A short apprenticeship with John Coltrane led him to pursue a new interest in outward-looking jazz, culminating in a spot on the AACM roster upon its founding.

In 1966, DeJohnette moved to New York to resume his working relationship with Coltrane and altoist Jackie McLean, another inspiration. Charles Lloyd's popular quintet offered him an opportunity for further exposure, as did DeJohnette's debut disc, *The DeJohnette Complex* (1968, Milestone). In 1969, he replaced Tony Williams in Miles Davis's band, just in time to record the seminal electric experiment *Bitches Brew* (Columbia). After three years, he quit the Davis group to lead his own bands. DeJohnette explored fusion with Compost (*Compost*, 1972, Columbia) and Directions; the latter group took a free turn, as New Directions, with the addition of Lester Bowie and bassist Eddie Gomez. In the mid-1970s, he began partnering with guitarist John Abercrombie, who remains a collaborator.

A contract with ECM brought DeJohnette a steady stream of work, both as a sideman and a leader. Arthur Blythe and David Murray figured prominently in the drummer's next unit, Special Edition (*Album Album*, 1984, ECM), skating easily between free and mainstream jazz forms. After a fashion, however, DeJohnette became more interested in jazz-rock fusion and pulled Special Edition away from free jazz. In recent years, he has held down a regular gig in Keith Jarrett's critically beloved trio with Gary Peacock.

Delmark: label founded by Bob Koester in 1953 in St. Louis, MO. (Delmark was named after Delmar Street in St. Louis, plus a "K" for Koester.) Frustrated that only a few labels were issuing blues LPs, he decided to help fill the gap, a sound choice in the hometown of the electrified blues. In 1958, after releasing Delmark's first modern jazz album (a now-obscure session by Bob Graf) and recording bebop and "jump" artists like tenorman Jimmy Forrest, Koester moved his operation to Chicago.

In 1966, some local jazz writers made Koester aware of the new music and social programs created by the AACM. After he and producer Chuck Nessa attended concerts by Roscoe Mitchell and Muhal Richard Abrams, they became enthused about these changes to the very substance of jazz. Koester chose to record the AACM's artists and expected that the albums would eventually sell enough to recoup their costs. While that *still* has yet to happen for some releases, Delmark provided a vital function in bringing Chicago's new jazz to the public ear.

The first album, Roscoe Mitchell's *Sound*, sold better than Koester had expected, but the AACM's sales figures were a rollercoaster ride. Anthony Braxton's two-LP set of sax solos, *For Alto*, surprised them by becoming one of their best sellers. Their subsequent reissue program proved even more successful, validating Prestige label head Bob Weinstock's famous assertion that "jazz isn't for releasing, it's for re-issuing!"

Koester was satisfied with providing the artists an outlet and promotional funds but mostly stayed out of the way, leaving the production tasks up to Nessa, who eventually formed his own label. Promoting the new music was difficult at best until Nessa and Koester got a grip on who their audience really was: a small but loyal target audience of open-eared jazz listeners, as opposed to the avant-garde classical critics and musicians they originally targeted.

Koester feels that the AACM lived up to its initial promise and continues to do so today. Delmark is now maintained by continued album sales, occasional licensing opportunities, and income from the Jazz Record Mart. Like most labels and performers, Delmark receives no monetary support from foundations or the government. The label's most recent catalog includes releases by Roscoe Mitchell, the Ethnic Heritage Ensemble, and NRG Ensemble, as well as contemporary blues and mainstream jazz sessions.

Denley, Jim (b. Bulli, New South Wales, Australia): flautist and saxophonist. Along with Jon Rose, Denley is one of Australia's best free improvisers but remains unfairly obscure. He studied violin as a child and flute at the New South Wales Conservatorium. His professional career began in 1977, and Denley first gained public attention with the touring sound-sculpture show New Musical Constructions, which he coordinated with Peter Ready. In 1981, he cofounded the Relative Band with Rose, then moved to projects like The Machine for Making Sense (*On Second Thoughts*, 1994, O.O. Discs). Denley began visiting London in the 1980s to get a sense of the improv scene there, establishing associations with John Butcher, Chris Burn, Derek Bailey, and other key figures. With Butcher, Burn, and Marcio Mattos, he formed the quartet Embers; Mattos and Denley also collaborate in the pan-European group Lines (self-titled, 1997, Random Acoustics) with Axel Dörner, Martin Blume, and Philipp Wachsmann. In 1987, Denley married violinist Stevie Wishart, with whom he has worked professionally (*Tibooburra*, 1997, Split). He has been a regular member of the Chris Burn Ensemble for several years (*Navigations*, 1997, Acta) and issued his solo album, *Dark Matter* (Tall Poppies), in 1995.

Detail: European free group, founded in 1981 through the partnership of Norwegian saxophonist Frode Gjerstad and English drummer John Stevens. Detail was originally a trio with Gjerstad, Stevens, and Norwegian keyboardist Eivin One Pedersen. South African expatriate bassist Johnny Mbizo Dyani joined in 1982, shortly before Pedersen left due to artistic conflicts. Detail performed as a trio, augmented by occasional guests (including Bobby Bradford), until Dyani's death in 1986. Bassists Paul Rogers and Kent Carter followed in turn. In 1989, Detail toured Norway with Billy Bang. The trio continued to perform, with Carter in the bass position, until Stevens's death in 1994. *Last Detail: Live at Café Sting* (1995, Cadence) documents the group's wall-melting final performance in Gjerstad's hometown of Stavanger, Norway.

Diaz-Infante, Ernesto (b. Salinas, CA, 10 June 1968): guitarist and pianist. A graduate of CalArts, Diaz-Infante is one of the Bay Area's principal improvising musicians today. He has held residencies all around the world and has a hand in several West

Coast festivals, including curating Creative Music Thursdays at the Luggage Store Gallery in San Francisco. Besides his principal instruments, Diaz-Infante has performed on flute, percussion, and vocals. He has collaborated with Rotcod Zzaj (a.k.a. multi-instrumentalist Dick Metcalf; *Sirius Intrigues*, 1999, Zzaj), recorded for nearly a dozen labels, and performed with W.O.O. Revelator, nmperign, pianist Dan DeChellis, guitarist Donald Miller, and saxophonist Blaise Siwula. His recordings include *Solus* (2000) and *Crashing the Russian Renaissance* (2000, both on Pax). Diaz-Infante coleads The Abstractions with Rent Romus.

Dick, Robert (b. New York, NY, 4 January 1950): flautist and composer. One of the true geniuses of the flute, Dick has pulled the instrument well beyond the technical peaks attained by Eric Dolphy. A graduate of Yale School of Music, Dick gleans as much from the inspirations of Dolphy and Jimi Hendrix (*Third Stone From the Sun*, 1993, New World) as he does the classical canon. He blows the full gamut of flutes, from the piccolo to the gigantic vertical contrabass, using a number of specialized techniques.

In Europe, where he is usually based, Dick performs in the ADD Trio with guitarist Christy Doran and drummer Steve Argüelles. While in New York, he frequently works in the ambient band King Chubby, in duo with pianist Anthony deMare, or in the ensemble New Winds. Dick debuted on disc in 1982 with *Whispers and Landings* (Lumina) and has built a good rapport with the Soldier String Quartet (*Jazz Standards on Mars*, 1995, Enja). He has also performed with the groups Flute Force and First Avenue, bandleader Klaus König, Steve Lacy, John Zorn, and minimalist composer Steve Reich. Dick has received commissions from the NEA and New York Music Ensemble, and has twice been awarded the Composers Fellowship.

Dickerson, Walt (b. Philadelphia, PA, 1931): vibraphonist. Although he was about as adventurous and technically adept at Bobby Hutcherson in the 1960s, Dickerson has become something of a footnote as a jazz vibist. He entered the army after graduating from Morgan State College in 1953. After his discharge, he resided in California for several years, working with Andrew Hill and Andrew Cyrille before they made a serious impact on free jazz. He moved to New York in about 1960 and debuted on record with the promising *This Is Walt Dickerson!* (1961, Prestige). As he was already demonstrating some comfort with free-jazz tenets, Dickerson was switched to the associated New Jazz label for his next albums (*A Sense of Direction*, 1961; *Relativity*, 1962). He spent some time in Sun Ra's Arkestra in the mid-1960s and continued to make occasional albums. A substantial career boost came when Dickerson signed with Steeplechase Records in 1975. That contract resulted in over a dozen recordings, including duos with Sun Ra (*Visions*, 1978) and Pierre Dørge (*Landscape with Open Door*, 1979). Since the early 1980s, Dickerson has been rather scarce, preferring to keep close to home in the Philadelphia area.

Dickey, Whit: drummer. Dickey is best known as a member of David S. Ware's circle of influence in New York. In 1992, Dickey replaced Marc Edwards as drummer in Ware's spectacular quartet, contributing to four albums including the bracing *Third*

Ear Recitation (1992, DIW). Dickey has also recorded with Matthew Shipp's trios and quartets, and guitarist Joe Morris's band. In 1998, Dickey made his first album as a leader (*Transonic*, Aum Fidelity), followed by *Big Top* in 2000 (Wobbly Rail). He is dependable as a drummer, faithful to the pulse but flexible enough to grant the ensemble elbowroom.

Die Like A Dog Quartet: ensemble including reedman Peter Brötzmann, bassist William Parker, drummer Hamid Drake, and trumpeter Toshinori Kondo. The group's first album was *Die Like A Dog: Fragments of Music, Life and Death of Albert Ayler* (1994, FMP), an apt tribute to the free-jazz great who died like a dog in the East River. In the midst of the four long group improvisations, snippets of Ayler themes, like the perennial "Ghosts," appear briefly in the mist and then flicker out. Short interpretations of the old standard "St. James Infirmary" are perfect addenda to the bittersweet tribute, which acknowledges Ayler's music directly and in spirit. Kondo's electronically enhanced horn completes the haunting portrait.

In November 1997, the Die Like A Dog Quartet performed at the Total Music Meeting in Berlin, turning in three long sets that are documented on *Little Birds Have Fast Hearts, No. 1* and *No. 2* (1997, FMP). This time there is no canon like the Ayler material to refer to, even briefly; all is spontaneously improvised and absolutely frenetic. Parker and Drake pave the way with brisk turns and spills, trying to trip up the dextrous hornmen with little success. On the second volume, Brötzmann stretches out on both clarinet and tarogato, complementing the cloudless pitch of Kondo's trumpet.

From Valley to Valley (1998, Eremite) was recorded at the Fire in the Valley Festival in Massachusetts. On this date, bright young trumpeter Roy Campbell, whose novel approach brings a rejuvenating change of pace to the group, replaced Kondo. Just as capable a technician as Kondo, Campbell plays his horn unadorned and uses its clarion sound as a foil for Brötzmann's burriness. The session illustrates the cellular level of intuition and listening among the performers, including a "finishing of sentences" comparable to that between Ornette Coleman and Don Cherry. The disc begins with the tenorman blasting out hard blues patterns of long notes while Campbell scampers and wails beside him. The trumpeter settles down into similar long figures, then thirty-odd seconds in they achieve a letter-perfect harmony; the exact same thing happens one minute later. Campbell's soloing is deftly humorous, with horse whinnies and screeches interspersed. In the background, Parker walks steadfastly through nonexistent chords while Drake crashes and tumbles like roaring rapids. Brötzmann begins snaky lines in a battle for dominance. The horns move in parallel, responding to each other like street kids playing the dozens. When Campbell proverbially takes his ball and goes home, Brötzmann rejoices in his victory with an ecstatic sax scream. His celebration is short-lived, as Campbell soon returns to resume the fight. Over ten minutes along, Parker's spotlight finally arrives, and he dances furiously with Drake in a rapturously psychic duet. As the cowbells chide the bassist, Parker retaliates time and again with brisk retorts. By the time the semimelody returns, we are practically exhausted by the brutal energy.

Kondo came back into the fold for *Aoyama Crows* (2002, FMP), the quartet's fifth release. The trumpeter takes an earthier path through the music this time around, better grounded in the blues while still peering outward. Brötzmann's performance is more accessible as well, not to say that either has grown complacent. The heightened unity that comes from a long period of working together has simply paid off in a new comfort level, permitting the players to let down their guard and follow as friends instead of strangers.

DIW: Japanese jazz and improv label, founded in the early 1970s as a spinoff of Disk Union. Among the label's first releases were live sessions by Kaoru Abe. The label eventually branched out to cover worldwide improv artists including Peter Brötzmann, David Murray, Music Revelation Ensemble, Milford Graves, Art Ensemble of Chicago, Marion Brown, Ronald Shannon Jackson, and Misha Mengelberg. The early 1980s series "Live from Soundscape" presented performances at the New York jazz club by Sun Ra, Frank Lowe, Material, and various groupings.

Dixon, Bill (b. Nantucket, MA, 5 October 1925): trumpeter, composer, and bandleader. Dixon has been rather underrecognized since the early 1960s despite his efforts to support independent artists, a good number of daring albums, and many years as a respected music educator. While not quite the sonic alchemist that Lester Bowie was, Dixon's ability to produce a dazzling array of sounds from his horn made him invaluable as a colorist. His trumpet technique is emotionally evocative, sometimes in the vein of Lester Bowie; his improvisations recall Ornette Coleman and Eric Dolphy, particularly his use of wide intervals. His solo recordings (gathered on both *Solo Works (Odyssey)*, 2001, and the smaller *Collection*, Cadence Jazz, 1999) offer some special insight into his phenomenal chops and fertile imagination. Like many free players, he has a particular fondness for pairing up bass players, which usually works like a charm.

Dixon started down a career path as a painter, now a sideline he still nurtures whenever possible (check out the abstract beauty of some of his album covers), but got into music after serving in the Navy. In 1961, he began his association with Cecil Taylor and formed his own group with Archie Shepp not long afterward. (See the Taylor and Shepp entries.)

Dixon gathered forty artists and groups in 1964 for the "October Revolution in Jazz" at Manhattan's Cellar Café, which helped bring the city's free movement into the public eye. He followed with the Jazz Composers Guild, a good-intentioned but poorly organized attempt at a new music support group. The failure of the Guild in 1965 did not dissuade Dixon from his noble goals; two years later he founded the Free Conservatory of the University of the Streets, an AACM-like organization dedicated to teaching inner-city youth about the arts.

After the demise of his quartet with Shepp, Dixon's next album was *Intents and Purposes: The Jazz Artistry of Bill Dixon* (1967, RCA), one of the mighty label's few excursions into free territory. That album has long been unavailable but contained some highly intriguing material for its day. The personnel was an unusual mix of freemen and mainstream jazzers, including bass trombonist Jimmy Cheatham, English horn player George Marge, saxmen Robin Kenyatta and Byard Lancaster, and bassists

Jimmy Garrison and Reggie Johnson. The music is as variegated as the lineup, wedging jazz sentiments into the open spaces of avant-garde art music.

In 1968, Dixon began his long tenure at Vermont's Bennington College, where he remained until 1996; only a brief residence at the University of Wisconsin in the early 1970s interrupted his stay. During that time, he made few recordings, most of which were the solo efforts mentioned earlier. Dixon's major interest in the period was teaching music to excited young performers like Marco Eneidi and drummer Jackson Krall, West Coast freemen who rose to subsequent fame in Glenn Spearman's ensembles. Dixon traveled the globe conducting his popular workshops and continued to compose and paint during his "down time" from regular recording.

Dixon was contracted in 1980 to record for Soul Note, an Italian label associated with the famed free-jazz imprint Black Saint. Giovanni Bonandrini's dual babes were specifically intended to document American players for the European audience, since few other Continental labels bothered to do so and U.S. labels had feeble distribution abroad. Dixon did not disappoint Bonandrini. In *Italy, Vols. 1 and 2* (1980, Soul Note), recorded in the summer of that year, were outstanding samples of his avant-jazz eclecticism. The ensembles here include two more trumpeters, Arthur Brooks and Stephen Haynes, whose rather classical tonalities clash deliciously with the leader's rough-edged variability. Saxophonist Stephen Horenstein is brusquely effective, and the strapping Alan Silva leaves most of the rhythm-keeping duties to drummer Freddie Waits. "For Cecil Taylor" pays fitting due to Dixon's mentor, mirroring the pianist's complexity. Taylor's handprints are often evident in Dixon's performances, though the cerebral nature of his music might be a little closer to Anthony Braxton's contemporary classical bent.

Dixon, Silva, second bassist Mario Pavone, and drummer Laurence Cook dealt more uneven cards on the weighty *November 1981* (Soul Note). At least half the tunes contain the brooding darkness that tends to characterize Dixon's compositions, which in this case is hard to deal with on initial exposure. The details and sound reasoning behind the duskiness emerge with further listens, and the flawlessness of the basses' interaction becomes quite clear. Pavone and Cook were again on hand for the bass-heavy *Thoughts* (1985, Soul Note), which included three more behemoth low-enders: Peter Kowald, William Parker, and tubaist John Buckingham. Eneidi's alto is hard-pressed to drag its way out of the consequent quicksand, but Dixon's trumpet and piano are ready to assist.

"Schema VI-88" on *Sons of Sisyphus* (1988, Soul Note) typifies the intellectualism behind Dixon's work at times. Like some of Roscoe Mitchell's most minimally constructed pieces, the track is centered on a single tone, which is manipulated and danced around. The well-chosen quartet has the taste and creativity to make the process anything but monotonous, and the bass and tuba cavort among each other with ease in this smaller configuration. The two Dixon/Pavone duets derive ecstasy from tranquility in ways that few other teamings have achieved.

American and British free concepts are successfully combined on *Vade Mecum, Vol. 1* (1994) and *Vol. 2* (1997, both Soul Note). Dixon and William Parker unite with English veterans Barry Guy and Tony Oxley on these busy, satisfying dates. Because the trumpeter is right at home with nonjazz-based forms of music that have inspired European improvisers, the sometimes divergent styles are easily reconciled within his compositions. Likewise, the popularity of Cecil Taylor among Europeans gave Oxley and Guy a familiar basis for relating to the two Americans. The bassists' vast differences in approach are hardly irreconcilable; in fact, their distinctiveness from one another is a valuable asset in filling up the spaces. The matrix they achieve with the bendable Oxley's drumming gives Dixon free rein to take off into the great beyond with flutters, screeches, and hot blasts of air.

Dixon and Oxley duet graciously on *Papyrus, Vols. 1 and 2* (2000, Soul Note). If there is any sort of formal composition here, it is kept to a minimum. The openness and sensitivity with which the two giants interact is nothing short of wonderful. Dixon's piano playing on a few tracks is reminiscent of Taylor's only in its angularity; no insult to the man, who needs not be tied to his old friend's apron strings to be intensely original. Oxley, who has worked with Taylor himself, shows ultimate respect for his partner. The inherent sparseness is not for everyone.

Berlin Abbozzi (2000, FMP) brings bassists Klaus Koch and Matthias Bauer to play with the Dixon/Oxley team. The three long tracks are even darker than usual for Dixon's work, the cloudiness being abetted by vast gaps in the sound, the distancing effects used to modify the trumpeter's tone, and the almost autistic conversation carried on between the bassists with little regard for the other men. Oxley's drums are all dings and whispers, a coffeehouse beatnik snapping his fingers and whispering "Yeah, man," as Dixon lays down the contents of his soul. Apropos, as Dixon's nonchalant, comfortable manner has often given the impression of a Beat poet. His music is comparable in some ways, too: radically different, painfully human, alternately confrontational and apologetic, and accessible once we tuck away our preconceptions.

Dolphy, Eric (b. Los Angeles, CA, 20 June 1928; d. Berlin, Germany, 29 June 1964): multi-instrumentalist and composer. Dolphy was one of the most influential musicians to emerge from primordial free jazz, single-handedly changing the public perception of jazz and his instruments in particular. On alto sax, flute, and bass clarinet, which he pioneered as a viable solo horn, Dolphy developed his own unique vocabularies, which have since become part of the basic accepted techniques: vocalizations, sound effects, widespread intervals, and general expansions of the bop tradition. Like Ornette Coleman, Dolphy expressed a human vocal quality through his horns, touching his listeners in ways to which they were unaccustomed. Though he had a nodding interest in the music of white avant-gardists like Edgard Varése (he even performed Varése's solo flute piece "Density 21.5"), his experiments usually remained true to the African American roots of jazz. He achieved an impressive solidity in his playing, greatly influencing performers like John Coltrane and Arthur Blythe, while keeping up a consistent level of soulfulness. Dolphy drew inspiration from Charlie Parker (especially his rhythmic sense), Monk, Mingus, Coltrane, and Coleman even as he became inspirational in his own right. Almost everyone who worked with Dolphy showered him with platitudes: transcendent, powerful, saintly. Although his recording career barely spanned six years, Dolphy contributed more to the evolution of jazz than many musicians have in a lifetime.

Dolphy worked in Los Angeles with Roy Porter's big band, cutting his first records before entering the army in 1950. He returned to town two years later, gigging around quietly wherever he could find work. In 1958, he was discovered by drummer Chico Hamilton, who sought a replacement for Buddy Collette in his famed quintet. On *Gongs East* (1958, Warner Bros.), his first major recording, Dolphy immediately presented himself as an innovative voice. Within a year, thanks to his association with Hamilton, Dolphy's name was recognizable enough that he moved to New York and immediately found work with Charles Mingus. The bassist latched onto the young reedman shortly after his arrival, featuring Dolphy prominently in some of his best recordings and concerts of the era.

Dolphy was an essential sideman, always shaping the outcome of the sessions with the subtlety of a potter. In 1960, he dabbled briefly in the Third Stream with John Lewis and Gunther Schuller (*Jazz Abstractions*, Atlantic), nudged Ken McIntyre toward free improv (*Looking Ahead*, New Jazz), and cut the seminal *Free Jazz* (Atlantic) with Coleman's double quartet. Oliver Nelson's *Blues and the Abstract Truth* (1961, Impulse) is an impressive showcase for his skills, particularly on the classic "Stolen Moments." His work with Mingus and Coltrane during his last years is captured on several brilliant recordings. Coltrane's *Impressions* (1961, Impulse) contains the perennially popular "India," one of Dolphy's greatest achievements on bass clarinet. He is also inspirational on Coltrane's lush, ambitious *Africa/Brass* project, arranged by Dolphy, and *Live at the Village Vanguard* (both 1961, Impulse). (See Coltrane's entry.)

Dolphy's own albums are excellent almost to the whole, with many textural shifts and bright new ideas to recommend them. The three tracks on *Eric Dolphy at the Five Spot* (1961, New Jazz) document his collaboration with Mal Waldron, himself a Mingus alumnus. *Outward Bound* (1960, New Jazz), recorded on the same day as *Free Jazz*, marks his new personal trek toward parts unknown, though it is more restrained than the Coleman session.

Conversations (1963, FM) is a true gem. Dolphy tackles "My Love" on solo alto, his experiments perhaps inspiring Anthony Braxton's own solo efforts a few years along, and duets admirably with bassist Richard Davis on the extended "Alone Together." His scintillating flute is featured on a revamping of Fats Waller's "Jitterbug Waltz" alongside trumpeter Woody Shaw. "Music Matador" is the centerpiece, featuring no less than four winds: Clifford Jordan on soprano sax, Prince Lasha on flute, Sonny Simmons on alto, and Dolphy on humorously growling bass clarinet. Davis and Charles Moffett complete the ensemble on this free-tempered romp through Latin clichés. Later reedmen like David Murray, Hamiet Bluiett, and John Surman drew from Dolphy's bass clarinet investigations.

Out to Lunch (1964, Blue Note) is Dolphy's masterpiece, recorded just four months before his death. The ensemble includes Davis, trumpeter Freddie Hubbard (from the *Free Jazz* session), vibraphonist Bobby Hutcherson, and young drummer Tony Williams. The album contains loving homages to two players who inspired Dolphy. "Hat and Beard," dedicated to Thelonious Monk, bears a jostling rhythm that typifies the pianist's approach. "Gazzelloni" gives the nod to Severino Gazzelloni, an avant-garde and classical flautist who developed a distinctive approach to creating untraditional sounds, methods that Dolphy had extrapolated upon for the past few years. The charming "Something Sweet, Something Tender" is one of Dolphy's most-covered compositions. "Straight Up And Down" mimics a drunk's walking movements, and the title track is a twelve-minute free festival that pits Dolphy against Hutcherson in brilliant interplay. *Out to Lunch* is one of the inarguable classics of jazz, a must-own.

In 1964, Dolphy embarked on a successful tour of Europe with Mingus's quintet. One of those gigs, held in Paris on April 18, is documented on *Revenge!* (1996, Revenge!) The two-disc set includes six Mingus compositions. All the instrumental performances are exemplary and, as he had at Antibes four years prior, Dolphy stole the show with his nearly flawless exhibition.

Dolphy played a few concerts on his own after Mingus's tour ended. *Last Date* (1964, Fontana) documents one of his final concerts, on June 2, with the European rhythm section of drummer Han Bennink, pianist Misha Mengelberg, and bassist Jacques Schols. The first sound heard after the applause is a savage bass clarinet rip that leads into Monk's "Epistrophy," Dolphy swinging mightily over Mengelberg's cloddy triplets and a stable rhythm. The reedman's technique was often characterized as speaking through the horn, and that is most evident here; it's as if he's reciting a manically humorous Beat poem. "You Don't Know What Love Is" begins with blissfully fluttering flute, then Schols emerges to bow somber long tones. Dolphy also plays flute on "South Street Exit," this time with a bop sensibility that fragments into unexpected note choices. The other two Dolphy originals, "Miss Ann" and "The Madrig Speaks, The Panther Walks," feature the leader on alto sax. The remaining tune, "Hypochristmutreefuzz" by Mengelberg, is a near-shuffle with a rapid bass clarinet melody followed by a Monkish piano solo. The pianist, who with Bennink would later become a star of European free improv, wears his influences on his sleeve on this session. Some have argued that this rhythm section was not well suited to Dolphy, while others strongly disagree. The date definitely points toward different directions the reedman might have pursued.

Dolphy had been eagerly anticipating his return home to America, as he was to be married soon. But his diabetes flared up a couple of weeks after the *Last Date* session, and he entered a coma. On June 29, 1964, just nine days after his thirty-sixth birthday, Eric Dolphy died of heart failure related to diabetes. One can only speculate whether he would have stuck to the avant-garde, delved into a jazz-rock fusion like Miles Davis would, or retreated into more traditional jazz forms. Conjecture is moot; all that remains is his profound legacy.

Doneda, Michel (b. 1954): soprano saxophonist. In the early 1970s, Doneda played in jazz and dance bands around France but was intrigued by the outside explorations of artists like Steve Lacy and Alan Silva. The soprano antics of Lacy led Doneda to adopt the straight horn as his principal instrument, and he has built his own personal style since that time. In the 1980s, he founded the free trio Hic et Nunc ("here and now") and the Institut de Recherches et d'Échanges Artistiques, a street-theater troupe. Louis Sclavis befriended the young man and took him on tour; from there Doneda made more connections in the French improvisational scene. He began working with vocalist Beñat Achiary and recording for Nato, which led Doneda to further work opportunities around Europe. In 1986, he formed a trio with Daunik Lazro and Lê Quan Ninh, which toured the continent and recorded (*26 Janvier 1988*

Vandoeuvre-les-Nancy, 1999, Vand'oeuvre). Doneda waxed the albums *L'Élémentaire Sonore* and *Soc* (both In Situ) in 1992, in which he moved away from jazz toward less idiomatic music. His collaborators include Barre Phillips (*No Pieces*, 1996, Émouvance), Urs Leimgruber, and poet Serge Pey. Among his best records are *Open Paper Tree* (1994, FMP), *Temps Couché* (1998, Victo), and the solo *L'Anatomie des Clefs* (1998, Potlatch).

Doran, Christy (b. Dublin, Ireland): guitarist. Doran's father was an Irish ballad singer who instructed his son in the art of music from his childhood. Doran grew up in Lucerne, Switzerland, where he formed early relationships with free-leaning musicians like reedman Urs Leimgruber and drummer Fredy Studer. The three men collaborated in the band Om with bassist Bobby Burri, then Studer and Doran explored Jimi Hendrix's music in an ensemble that included trumpeter and vocalist Phil Minton. Other collaborators include Joe McPhee, Carla Bley, Herb Robertson, Robert Dick, Ray Anderson, and Han Bennink (the latter two in a trio). Doran's group New Bag (*Black Box*, 2001, Cue) hybridizes avant-jazz with Indian and other ethnic musics. Doran's other recordings include *Red Twist and Tuned Arrow* (1986, ECM) and *What a Band* (1991, HatArt).

Dørge, Pierre (b. Copenhagen, Denmark, 28 February 1946): guitarist and leader of the New Jungle Orchestra. He has had an impressive presence on the European jazz scene since the early 1960s and has worked with countryman John Tchicai in many situations over the past three decades, from duos to the group Thermaenius. Founded in 1980, the New Jungle Orchestra updates the Ellington school of big-band jazz with heavy doses of Monk and the avant-garde (self-titled album, 1982, Steeplechase). Dørge also had a fruitful association with Johnny Dyani, recording the amazing *Three* (1984, Steeplechase) as a trio with Dyani and vibraphonist Khan Jamal.

Dörner, Axel (b. Köln, Germany, 1964): trumpeter. Dörner is a phenomenal technician, perhaps as advanced as Bill Dixon or Lester Bowie, focusing upon the slightest possible tones and noises as sound sources in performance with amplification as an aid. He originally studied piano in high school and the Arnhem Conservatory, then moved to the trumpet in his twenties. A number of free groups, including Lines and The Remedy, benefited from his analytical approach to the horn. In 1994, he moved to Berlin and began working with saxophonist Rudi Mahall, interpreting the works of Thelonious Monk and teaming with drummer Sven-Åke Johansson. Since the mid-1990s, Dörner has worked on occasion with American improvisers, including Fred Lonberg-Holm, Michael Zerang, and Butch Morris, while fostering continental associations with Alex von Schlippenbach, John Butcher, and Chris Burn. He is also a member of King Übü Örchestrü.

Douglas, Dave (b. Montclair, NJ, 24 March 1963): trumpeter, composer, and bandleader. Douglas, like Lester Bowie, draws from a large pool of inspirations to craft his particular brand of cutting-edge jazz. Coltrane's freedom, Stravinsky's boldness, and

Burmese folk songs all have a place in Douglas's striking aesthetic, expressed through a variety of means.

Douglas studied piano and trombone in his youth before settling on the trumpet. As an exchange student in Spain, he learned much about improvisation to augment his high-school jazz studies. Tenures at Berklee College of Music and the New England Conservatory followed, then a period at New York University. A significant position in Horace Silver's touring band first brought Douglas to the public ear, and work began to flow steadily.

Douglas's debut as a leader, 1993's *Parallel Worlds* (Soul Note), announced the arrival of a prominent new voice on trumpet, as he used a variety of sound production techniques to color his performances. He has led his own quartets, quintets, and sextets, blended jazz and Balkan styles in Tiny Bell Trio, and fronted his String Group with violinist Mark Feldman and cellist Erik Friedlander. He is a vital member of both John Zorn's Masada and Myra Melford's The Same River, Twice, two of the more significant recent ensembles to ride the frontiers of jazz. Among his surprising side jobs have been work with The Band, Sheryl Crow, jazz diva Patricia Barber, Anthony Braxton, Japanese techno-pop band Cibo Matto, and duets with Han Bennink. In 2000, Douglas paid tribute to pianist Mary Lou Williams on *Soul on Soul* (RCA Victor), performing her compositions and originals inspired by her vision. One of his more recent groups is Alloy, a three-trumpet unit with Roy Campbell, Baikida Carroll, vibist Bryan Carrott, Mark Dresser, and Susie Ibarra.

Doyle, Arthur (b. Birmingham, AL, 26 June 1944): reeds player. Doyle is one of the most extreme reeds players since Albert Ayler, in conception if not technique, which has alienated him from an already tenuous audience. While at Tennessee State University, Doyle began his career in Nashville bop, blues, and soul bands. He played big-band swing in Detroit and R&B in Birmingham before coming to New York in 1967. Doyle fell into the nascent loft-jazz circle there and met Milford Graves (*Babi Music*, 1976, IPS) and Pharoah Sanders. Sun Ra offered Doyle a spot in the Arkestra after a sit-in gig, but the saxophonist opted to join Noah Howard's band instead (*The Black Ark*, 1969, Polydor). He became frustrated with the business and laid off music for several years but returned fully in 1976.

Guitarist Rudolph Grey was impressed by Doyle's fiery playing and developed The Blue Humans around Doyle and Beaver Harris (*Live N.Y. 1980*, 1995, Audible Hiss). The reedman stayed for two years before moving to Paris for better work options. A bad move, as it turned out, because trumped-up charges landed Doyle in jail for five years. While imprisoned, he could not perform but took the time to compose a large body of work. Upon being freed in 1987, he returned to New York and began interpreting the 300-odd tunes he had written behind bars. *Arthur Doyle Plays and Sings from the Songbook* (1992, Audible Hiss) presents a sampling of the pieces, which are extremely difficult with their stream-of-consciousness lyrics and strange rhythms. Doyle gradually worked himself back into the scene through gigs with Grey, Sunny Murray (*Dawn of a New Vibration*, 2000, Fractal), Wilber Morris, Sonic Youth guitarist Thurston Moore, Rashid Bakr, and his own ensembles (*A Prayer for Peace*, 2000, Zugswang). *Live at the Glenn Miller Café* (2001, Ayler) presents the saxophonist in his good form, although he doesn't even play on three tracks.

Drake, Hamid (b. Monroe, LA, 1955): drummer and percussionist, one of the hardest working musicians on the contemporary free scene. The young Drake served a valuable apprenticeship with Fred Anderson in the late 1970s, playing in his quartet and making the acquaintance of other AACM members. As his profile increased, Drake was drawn into much work around Chicago, gigging with the ensemble Liof Munimula, duetting on an annual basis with Michael Zerang, and forming the DKV Trio with Ken Vandermark and Kent Kessler (*Baraka*, 1998, Okkadisk). He interprets Sun Ra's compositions with Vandermark in Spaceways Incorporated, and has played Latin jazz, reggae, and original African-inspired music as well. Drake's strongest associations so far have been with Peter Brötzmann—Die Like A Dog, duos, and larger ensembles—and William Parker. He has performed with Pharoah Sanders, Georg Graewe, Marilyn Crispell, and Joe Morris while remaining in Anderson's band (*Birdhouse*, 1995, Okkadisk).

Dresser, Mark (b. Los Angeles, CA, 1952): bassist and composer. One of his earliest regular gigs was Black Music Infinity, an early West Coast free unit with Arthur Blythe, David Murray, James Newton, Bobby Bradford, and drummer Stanley Crouch. A graduate of UC San Diego and alumnus of the city's symphony, Dresser studied in Italy on a Fulbright Scholarship. In the mid-1980s, he relocated to New York City, and shortly thereafter he became part of Anthony Braxton's heralded quartet with Marilyn Crispell and Gerry Hemingway. His head-turning technical skills were a perfect match for the level of virtuosity in that ensemble. (See Braxton's entry.) Dresser has composed on commission and worked in several settings, including Gregg Bendian's Interzone, Tim Berne's Caos Totale, Arcado String Trio, and Dave Douglas's String Group. Dresser has written chamber works and silent film scores, recorded several compelling solo discs (*Invocation*, rec. 1980, issued 1995, Knitting Factory Works), lectured worldwide, and performed with Ray Anderson, vocalist Greetje Bijma, and Maarten Altena.

Drumm, Kevin (b. South Holland, IL): experimental guitarist. Though he came up in Chicago, Drumm has not been very active in the city's large free-jazz circles, concentrating instead on less idiomatic improvisations in the style of AMM. He performs on tabletop and prepared guitars, creating unusually captivating mechanical soundscapes with few hints of melody. Drumm has recorded solo, in duets with Bhob Rainey, Axel Dörner, and Taku Sugimoto, and as a member of MIMEO and Jim O'Rourke's avant-rock group Gastr del Sol.

Dudek, Gerd (Gerhard Rochus Dudek; b. Opole, Poland, 23 September 1928): reeds player, brother of bandleader Ossi Dudek, in whose ensemble Gerd performed during his late twenties. Trained on clarinet in his youth, Dudek played mainstream jazz around Berlin before discovering free jazz in the mid-1960s. He joined Manfred Schoof's daring quintet in 1965 and took part in the debut of Globe Unity Orchestra the following year. Since that time, he has been a semiregular member of the Orchestra and has performed with Alex von Schlippenbach outside that milieu as well. Other collaborators include Albert Mangelsdorff, Peter Brötzmann, Don Cherry, Joachim Kühn, Tony Oxley, and Mal Waldron. Dudek recorded his debut as a leader in 1977 (*Open*, FMP) but did little else under his own name until he contracted with the Konnex label in the early 1990s.

Dunmall, Paul (b. Welling, Kent, England, 1953): saxophonist. As a teenager, Dunmall studied instrument repair while honing his playing skills. He toured the continent with the prog-rock band Marsupilami in the mid-1970s. His decision to follow the Indian sect Divine Light Mission and play with its orchestra led him to America. He found a kindred spirit in Alice Coltrane, who rehearsed with the young Briton. Dunmall played rock and blues with Johnny "Guitar" Watson, then returned home to England where he played free music with John Stevens and folk-rock with Danny Thompson. In 1979, Dunmall cofounded the jazz quartet Spirit Level, which endured for a decade. Since that time, Dunmall has worked extensively with Keith Tippett's Mujician, the London Jazz Composers Orchestra and its members, and in duo with drummer Tony Levin. His debut recording was *Soliloquy* (1986, Matchless).

Durian: Austrian record label, founded by Werner Dafeldecker in 1995. Artists include Franz Hautzinger, electronic musician Peter Brandlmayr, Fennesz, and Burkhard Stangl.

Durrant, Phil (b. England, 1957): violinist and electronic musician. Durrant studied piano and violin at the London College of Music and began his career in 1977. He founded the X-OPF label in 1985 and debuted there with *Planet Oeuf*. He has performed with John Russell and John Butcher (*Conceits*, 1987, Acta), Chris Burn Ensemble, Thomas Lehn, Radu Malfatti (both on *Beinhaltung*, 1997, Fringes), Derek Bailey, Tom Cora, Phil Minton, Evan Parker, John Zorn, MIMEO, Pat Thomas, the Quatuor Accorde string quartet, Assumed Possibilities (with Burn, Mark Wastell, and Rhodri Davies), Lunge, and a number of choreographers.

Duval, Dominic (b. New York, NY, 27 April 1944): bassist. Duval started on saxophone in the fifth grade, which no doubt had a serious effect on his melodic bass playing later in life. As a teenager, he saw Miles Davis, Cecil Taylor, and other jazz figures at the local clubs in Brooklyn. After a few jobs in the garment industry, Duval joined the army and played in the service band. Following his discharge, he kicked some bad habits but laid off of performing for a few years. Eventually, through some jam-session connections, Duval met trombonist George Zorco and formed a loft-based band; that gig was followed by resort and hotel work. From 1980 to 1993, Duval again dropped out of the music business, concentrating instead on his family and a window-cleaning business. After a work-related injury, he began to concentrate on the bass again and landed a job with pianist Michael Jefry Stevens. Connections with Dave Douglas, Mark Whitecage, and drummer David Bromberg led to a new but short-lived band (Artists Colony), a recording, and runner-up status in the Hennessy Jazz Search. Duval sent a tape to Robert Rusch at Cadence, just as Rusch was formulating the CIMP label. Duval, Whitecage, and drummer Jay Rosen got together as a trio and first recorded for CIMP in January 1996. The Duval/Rosen relationship has persisted to the point that they are practically the label's house rhythm section. A recent project of promise is Trio X, with trumpeter and saxophonist Joe McPhee. *Anniversary* (1999, CIMP) is an invigorating solo bass disc.

Dyani, Johnny ("Mbizo") (b. East London, South Africa, 30 November 1945; d. Berlin, Germany, 11 July 1986): bass player. Dyani was one of the South African expatriates who added vitality to England's embryonic free-jazz scene in the early 1970s. He came from a musical background, studying piano and voice in his youth and taking up the bass at age thirteen. In his late teens, Dyani was hired by Chris McGregor as bassist for the Blue Notes, which departed from South Africa in 1964 to tour Europe. Two years later, Dyani happened to be in Argentina when the chance arose to record with Steve Lacy and Enrico Rava (*The Forest and the Zoo*, 1966, ESP). That encounter helped to spread his name further around Europe's jazz community.

Dyani played cross-cultural music in the early 1970s with Don Cherry and Turkish percussionist Okay Temiz, who later performed in the band Xaba with Dyani and Mongezi Feza. Gigs with McCoy Tyner, Dollar Brand (aka Abdullah Ibrahim), and Alan Shorter led to more opportunities with expatriate Americans and central European free players like Han Bennink and Irène Schweizer. With Detail, Pierre Dørge's New Jungle Orchestra, and various side projects including his own bands (*Witchdoctor's Son* and *Song for Biko*, both 1978, Steeplechase), Dyani was one of the most beloved figures in European jazz until his unfortunate death at age forty.

E

Earth People: ensemble based in New York City, uniting hot funk, poetry, free jazz and other stylings. Originally assembled for the 2001 TV production "Waking the Living," the group centers around saxophonist Jason Candler, drummer André Martinez, and guitarist/synth player Doug Principato. Auxiliary members include bassoonist Karen Borca, reedmen Daniel Carter and Sabir Mateen (both from Test), violinist/vocalist Rosi Hertlein, bassist François Grillot, keyboardist Mark Hennen, and the vocalist known only as M. On occasion, their performances have featured guests, including Roy Campbell, Kali Fasteau, Gunter Hampel, Rashid Bakr, and Raphé Malik. Their debut album is *Simple . . . Isn't It?* (2001, Undivided Vision).

Ehrlich, Marty (b. St. Louis, MO, 1955): reedman. Ehrlich was a founding member of the Black Artists Group and made his recorded debut with Human Arts Ensemble in 1972. He attended the New England Conservatory, moving to New York after graduation. Ehrlich's facility on the full range of clarinets, saxophones, and flutes opened doors regularly, permitting him to work with great freemen like Anthony Braxton, hometown hero Julius Hemphill, Myra Melford, Muhal Richard Abrams, John Lindberg, and Bobby Bradford. Ehrlich has been a member of the New York Jazz Collective, New York Composers Orchestra, and Bobby Previte's Weather Clear Track Fast, and leads his own reeds-and-strings group, the Dark Woods Ensemble. He has recorded solid sessions for Enja (*Pliant Plaint*, 1987), New World (*Emergency Peace*, 1990), Tzadik (*Sojourn*, 1999), and other labels.

Ellis, Lisle (b. Campbell River, B.C., Canada, 17 November 1951): bassist. Ellis has been a perpetual partner of his countrymen Paul Plimley and François Houle and a member of the NOW Orchestra while maintaining a residence and much activity in America. From 1975 to 1979, Ellis studied at the Creative Music Studio in New York. He has resided in the San Francisco area since the early 1990s and is part of the Bay

Area's vital improvising community. His employers have included pianist Matthew Goodheart and Glenn Spearman. With Rova saxophonist Larry Ochs and drummer Donald Robinson, Ellis is a member of the trio What We Live and the Trummerflora Collective. He has performed with Joe McPhee, Dave Douglas, Scott Fields, Wadada Leo Smith, Jon Raskin, and Jeb Bishop. His own recordings include *Elevations* (1995, Victo) and *The Children in Peril Suite* (1998, Music & Arts).

El'Zabar, Kahil (b. Chicago, IL, 11 November 1953): percussionist and bandleader. Associated with the AACM, El'Zabar is one of Chicago's premier percussionists and instigators of musical exploration. His most visible project thus far has been the exciting Ethnic Heritage Ensemble, first recorded in 1982 (*Three Gentlemen from Chikago*, Moers Music). His EHE associates, in trio and quartet formats, have included trombonist Joseph Bowie, reedmen Ed Wilkerson and Ernest Dawkins, and percussionist Atu Harold Murray.

El'Zabar also heads the Ritual Trio, with Malachi Favors and Ari Brown (*Conversations*, 1999, Delmark, teams them with Archie Shepp) and the Juba Collective, and is a member of the all-star group Bright Moments (see separate entry). His side gigs have included work with David Murray, Ari Brown, Ed Wilkerson's Eight Bold Souls, singer Kurt Elling, and the alternative-rock group Sonia Dada. El'Zabar's forte is his mastery of African musics, including a large array of percussion instruments and methods, which he weaves into dense matrices to support his bandmates. El'Zabar's music reflects upon the full histories of African and Afro-American culture.

Emanem: British record label, founded by former record salesman Martin Davidson and his wife, Madelaine, in 1974. (Their first names are the "M and M" from which the label's name derives.) At the time, Davidson felt that the European free scene, particularly that in London, was not being documented extensively enough. The first artists he contacted were Steve Lacy, John Stevens, and Derek Bailey, who willingly contributed to the catalog. The roster eventually included heavyweights like Paul Rutherford, the Spontaneous Music Ensemble, and the duo of Bailey and Anthony Braxton. For much of the label's history, Davidson kept it funded through his day job as a computer programmer. After a few years' absence, Emanem returned to the market in 1995 with a catalog of classic reissues, new and previously unreleased material.

Emery, James (b. Youngstown, OH, 1951): guitarist, composer, and bandleader. Proficient on acoustic and electric guitars, Emery is one of the few improvisers (along with Derek Bailey and Spencer Barefield) to concentrate more upon the acoustic instrument. One of his earliest recordings was Leroy Jenkins's *For Players Only* (1975), a JCOA project. Two years later, Emery joined the String Trio of New York with bassist John Lindberg and violinist Billy Bang. Their debut album, *First String* (1979, Black Saint), presented a new, bracing, free-edged form of chamber jazz to the market.

Emery is capable of playing as straight and lyrically as any mainstream jazz guitarist but is never afraid to venture outward with extended techniques and harmonies.

Besides leading his own record dates (*Luminous Cycles*, 2000, between the lines, is excellent), Emery has performed with Henry Threadgill, Charles Bobo Shaw, guitarist Brandon Ross, Anthony Braxton, Franz Koglmann, and Gerry Hemingway.

Empty Bottle: jazz, rock, and improvisation venue, located in Chicago's Ukrainian Village. One of the city's most important contemporary music outlets, the 400-seat club has presented outward music since 1992, featuring acts as diverse as the Vandermark Quartet, bachelor-pad-music icons Combustible Edison, and alternative rock bands like Veruca Salt and Morphine. The club conducts an annual improvised music festival along with other popular events.

Eneidi, Marco (b. Portland, OR, 1 November 1956): alto saxophonist. Eneidi grew up in the San Francisco area, where he began studying the clarinet at age nine. In high school, he experimented with Dixieland, American folk music, and blues guitar but did not begin seriously concentrating on music as a career until after graduation. He fell under the spell of Jimmy Lyons after seeing a performance by Cecil Taylor's band at the Keystone Korner. Eneidi was hired as a touring musician around local schools, nursing homes, and hospitals, which lasted only about one year until he was fired for being too experimental and not wearing socks!

In 1981, Eneidi moved to New York and quickly fell into the free scene there. He began to associate musically with, besides Lyons, William Parker, Jemeel Moondoc, Don Cherry, Roy Campbell, Dewey Redman, Denis Charles, Bill Dixon, and many other principal figures. Their tutelage proved invigorating for the young altoist, but he did not find many recording opportunities. In 1987, he formed his own label, Botticelli, and issued his first album as a leader, *Vermont Spring* (since reissued as *Vermont 1986*), with Parker and Charles. Subsequent recordings on the label featured Wadada Leo Smith, bassoonist Karen Borca, Wilber Morris, and the undersung tenor saxophonist Glenn Spearman.

Eneidi and Spearman formed the Creative Music Orchestra in 1995 after returning to northern California. The CD *Creative Music Orchestra* (1995, Botticelli) featured a twenty-piece band with strings, African drums, and dual bassists performing the "American Jungle Suite." The following year, the ensemble expanded its scope. *Marco Eneidi and the American Jungle Orchestra* (1997, Botticelli) presents the band's new face, with Smith in a lead role and a lineup that included Spearman, Oluyemi Thomas, pianist Matthew Goodheart, Rova members Jon Raskin and Bruce Ackley, and avant-classical bassist Bertram Turetzky. The two-disc package includes Eneidi's musings on the Nez Perce and Lakota cultures, along with the monumental "Landscapes" suites.

Since Spearman's passing in 1998, Eneidi has carried on his memory with an annual Bay Area festival. Besides his Botticelli releases, Eneidi has recorded the sharp trio album *Cherry Box* (2001, Eremite) with Parker and Donald Robinson.

Eremite: record label, founded by Michael Ehlers in 1996. Based in Amherst, Massachusetts, Eremite documents some of the most exciting free music in the current scene. Its inaugural release was Jemeel Moondoc's *Tri-P-Let* (1996), which helped to finally break the undersung altoist out onto the market. The catalog also includes excellent material from William Parker's Little Huey Creative Music Orchestra, Ellery Eskelin with Andrea Parkins, Glenn Spearman, Denis Charles, Raphé Malik, Noah Howard, and the members of Test, together and separately. The label has a hand in conducting the annual Fire in the Valley Festival and, in concordance with the Conway New Music Society, a concert series at the Amherst Unitarian Meetinghouse.

Erstwhile: electroacoustic improvisation label. Founded in 1999 by Jon Abbey, Erstwhile's main focus is on teams of improvisers who might not normally work together. The label debuted with *Extracts* by VHF: Simon Vincent on drums and tone generator, Simon H. Fell on bass, and Graham Halliwell on alto sax and percussion. Erstwhile's growing catalog features Keith Rowe, Greg Kelley, Axel Dörner, Kevin Drumm, Phil Durrant, Thomas Lehn, Gerry Hemingway, Günter Müller, John Butcher, Polwechsel with Christian Fennesz, Otomo Yoshihide with Voice Crack, and MIMEO with John Tilbury.

Eskelin, Ellery (b. Wichita, KS, 16 August 1959): saxophonist, composer, and bandleader. Eskelin was raised in Baltimore. His mother, Bobbie Lee, was a professional organ player; his father, Rodd Keith, a singer-songwriter and purveyor of tunes set to clients' mailed-in lyrics. Eskelin took up the tenor sax, still his primary instrument, at the age of ten. His abundant talents, coupled with some of his mother's connections, resulted in pro gigs from the time he was in high school. At Towson State University, he studied jazz under Hank Levy, along with classical woodwind repertoire. After graduation, he toured the Americas with trombonist Buddy Morrow, then relocated to the brighter prospects of New York City. Eskelin studied with two Miles Davis alumni, George Coleman and David Liebman, and gigged around town with whomever he could find to take him under a wing.

In the mid-1980s, Eskelin became interested in free jazz, and he soon found himself working with Paul Smoker, an underappreciated trumpeter who recognized the usefulness of Eskelin's experiments with timbre and technique. He joined bassist Drew Gress and drummer Phil Haynes in Smoker's Joint Venture, which cut their self-titled debut record for Enja in 1987. Haynes also enlisted the young tenorman for his group 4 Horns and What?

In the following year, with Gress and Haynes, Eskelin formed his first trio, an ensemble format that has proved especially rewarding for him. *Setting the Standard* (1988, Cadence Jazz) presented Eskelin's first attempts to exercise his personal sax vocabulary as the sole horn in an ensemble. The balance of structure and improvisation in the trio was striking and inspired him to seek further development of his ideas. Four years later, after a lean period, Eskelin joined drummer Joey Baron's quartet, Barondown, which expanded upon what Baron had learned from his service in John Zorn's less jazzy Naked City.

Eskelin's next trio, with tubaist Joe Daley and percussionist Arto Tuncboyaciyan, was perhaps too exotic for its time and did not survive for long. *Figure of Speech* (1993, Soul Note) captures the group in a rather unstable situation. One year later, the saxophonist hit paydirt with the ultimate trio, featuring Jim Black on drums and Andrea Parkins on accordion and sampler. Despite the bizarre instrumentation, the trio made a positive impression upon the new-music community with their bold approach and democratic creative processes. Since their debut recording, *Jazz Trash* (1995, Songlines), the trio has continued to push the boundaries of contemporary music. Their most recent disc, *12(+1) Imaginary Views* (2001, HatOlogy), contains a dozen of their finest reactive improvisations and a wild reading of Thelonious Monk's "Oska T."

Outside the trio, Eskelin has recorded over a soundscape of Parkins's samples on *Green Bermudas* (1997, Eremite), collected some of his father's rare recordings for issue on Zorn's Tzadik label, and participated in a tribute to soul-jazz tenorman Gene Ammons. He occasionally performs solo tenor concerts and works regularly with Mark Helias and Gerry Hemingway in their own ensembles. Eskelin's mighty tenor has graced records and performances by George Gruntz's Concert Jazz Band, the New York Composers Orchestra, Jaki Byard's Apollo Stompers, Dennis Chambers, Joe Lovano, Ray Anderson, Carlos Ward, Mike Stern, Han Bennink, and dozens of other musicians.

ESP (or ESP-Disk): label founded by Bernard Stollman in 1963. Its first release was actually an instructional guide to Esperanto, the failed "international language" of which Stollman was an aficionado. After becoming attracted to the powerful free jazz pouring out of New York City, Stollman decided to begin recording as much of the scene as possible. He hired Albert Ayler's trio to record for the label, and *Spiritual Unity* (1964) became an instant landmark of the movement. Recordings by Sun Ra, Burton Greene, Ornette Coleman, Noah Howard, Paul Bley, the New York Art Quartet, Bob James (later a major pop-jazz star), and Pharoah Sanders's debut followed.

Despite good intentions, Stollman's ambitions often outstripped his capabilities. Allegations of fraud came when he failed to pay royalties on a regular basis; the totally blank second side of Ayler's *Bells* angered consumers and critics alike; and the reissues of bebop-era material by Charlie Parker, Bud Powell, and Billie Holiday hit fatal roadblocks. By the mid-1970s, ESP was washed up, its last few releases barely worth their vinyl. Reissues have been sporadic; a once-fruitful deal with the German ZYX imprint fizzled in the late 1990s, and ESP's catalog has since been handled by Charly and Get Back.

Ethnic Heritage Ensemble: see **El'Zabar, Kahil**.

Ewart, Douglas (b. 1946): reedman. Ewart is a seriously talented performer, particularly on bass clarinet and his own handcrafted bamboo flutes. Nonetheless, he remains one of the lesser-known Chicagoans. He can be heard to good advantage with the bands of Muhal Richard Abrams (*Lifea Blinec*, 1978, Novus) and Henry Threadgill (*X-75*, 1979, Arista/Novus), and on George Lewis's masterful *Homage to Charles Parker* (1979, Black Saint). He has also performed and recorded with his Inventions Clarinet Choir (*Angels of Entrance*, 1998, Aarawak), including Anthony Braxton and Roscoe Mitchell, and a promising quintet.

Experimental Band: ensemble led by Muhal Richard Abrams from 1961 to 1965. Unrecorded, it was the catalyst that led to the formation of the AACM in 1965. (See entries for AACM and Abrams.)

Eyges, David: cellist. Eyges is an outstanding technician, mining the old blues spirit with classical tools. He is one of the principal players of the electric cello in jazz, using it to great advantage with Arthur Blythe (*Synergy*, 1997, In & Out; *Today's Blues*, 1997, CIMP), Paul Bley (*Emerald Blue*, 1994, Venus), and Jaki Byard (*Night Leaves*, 1997, Brownstone). He emerged in the jazz scene in the mid-1970s with his record *The Captain* (1977, Chiaroscuro; reissued 2002, Midlantic). Eyges often partnered with such compatible musicians as drummer Bob Moses (*Bittersuite in the Ozone*, 1974, Amulet) and Byard Lancaster, who supported Eyges and Sunny Murray on the cellist's breakout disc, *Crossroads* (1981, Music Unlimited). A respected soloist, Eyges released two fine albums in 2002 (*Wood*; *Sky*, both Midlantic).

F

Fasteau, (Zusaan) Kali: multi-instrumentalist, vocalist, and bandleader. Fasteau, the former wife of Donald Rafael Garrett, specializes in an impressively brocaded style of improvised music, colored by her use of exotic instruments from around the world: soprano sax, piano, cello, sanza, sheng, ney, shakuhachi, and percussion devices, to name a few. She studied voice and several instruments during her childhood in Paris and New York, obtained degrees in anthropology and world music, and joined in New York's free community prior to the loft-jazz movement. Fasteau toured the world for over a decade, absorbing as much cultural richness as she could manage while performing with the likes of Archie Shepp, Noah Howard, and Sun Ra. In the mid-1970s, she and Garrett formed the Sea Ensemble, the first major platform for her free-world-jazz fusions. Since the 1980s, Fasteau has released several albums on her own label, Flying Note (*Worlds Beyond Words*, 1989, is a gem), and performed with William Parker, Dewey Redman, Daniel Carter, Rashied Ali, and Jeanne Lee. She reunited with Noah Howard and Bobby Few on the marvelous trio date *Expatriate Kin* (1997, CIMP).

Favors (Maghostut or **Maghostus** or **Magoustous), Malachi** (b. Chicago, IL, 22 August 1937; d. 2 February 2004): bassist. One of the most respectably talented bassists in free music, Favors is remembered almost exclusively for his membership in the Art Ensemble of Chicago. A powerful swinger and excellent soloist, Favors tended to subsume himself beneath his bandmates, occasionally writing or stepping to the fore.

Favors took up the bass at age fifteen and studied with Wilbur Ware as a young man. His first recording was made with tenorman Paul Bascomb in 1953. As a member of Andrew Hill's trio with drummer James Slaughter, Favors recorded his first full album *So In Love* (1956, Warwick). Favors further explored bebop with Dizzy Gillespie and Freddie Hubbard before joining Muhal Richard Abrams's Experimental Band. There he met Roscoe Mitchell, and the two men began investigating the free jazz and hard bop that was coming out of New York City. From that point, Mitchell developed his Art Ensemble, which became their principal gig for most of the next three decades. (See entry for Art Ensemble of Chicago.)

Favors recorded with most of the Art Ensemble's members in contexts outside of that band. His own solo bass recording, *The Natural and the Spiritual* (1977), was issued on the group's AECO imprint. Favors recorded in duo with Muhal Richard Abrams (*Sightsong*, 1975, Black Saint) and Tatsu Aoki (*2x4*, 1998, Southport), and worked with Charles Brackeen, Sunny Murray, Dewey Redman, Archie Shepp, Dennis Gonzalez, Yosuke Yamashita, and Alan Silva, among others. He was a member of Bright Moments, Kahil El'Zabar's Ritual Trio, and Wadada Leo Smith's Golden Quartet. Favors died of stomach cancer, which he had kept concealed from his musical friends.

Favre, Pierre (b. Le Locle, Switzerland, 2 June 1937): drummer. Favre was a self-taught Dixieland revivalist who regularly worked with visiting American jazzmen from his late teens. In the mid-1960s, like many Europeans, Favre found a keen interest in free jazz, which has continued to hold most of his attention. His quartet with Evan Parker, Irène Schweizer, and Peter Kowald was one of middle Europe's finest groups (*Pierre Favre Quartet*, 1968, Wergo). Peter Brötzmann, Joe McPhee, John Stevens, Albert Mangelsdorff, and Andrea Centazzo have also hired the Swiss drummer, whose horizons have expanded as he has investigated contemporary classical music and other facets of the avant-garde. Since 1984's *Singing Drums*, Favre has enjoyed a fertile relationship with the ECM label, appearing on his own sessions and those led by bandoneonist Dino Saluzzi and saxophonist John Surman. His most recent disc as a leader is the fine *Punctus* (2001, Splasc(h)).

Fefer, Avram: reedman and bandleader. Fefer began playing clarinet at age eight in Seattle and switched to saxophone six years later. He sidestepped from music long enough to obtain a BA in psychology from Harvard, then resumed his musical studies at Berklee and the New England Conservatory. In 1989, he worked in a trio with drummer Mike Sarin and pianist John Medeski, then settled in Paris for several years. He performed alongside expatriate musicians and visitors including Archie Shepp, Bobby Few, and Sunny Murray, all the while absorbing the many ethnic forms of music that Paris's homogeneous culture offered. Drummer Igal Foni became a tight, long-lasting partner. In 1995, he moved to New York and began working in the free-funk ensemble Tone Poets with guitarist David Fiuczynski. Fefer has experimented with electronic and ambient musics, and has performed in the ensembles of David Murray, Joseph Bowie, Butch Morris, and the Mingus Big Band. He leads his own trio (*Calling All Spirits*, 1999, Cadence Jazz) and has issued several recordings with other lineups.

Feldman, Mark (b. Chicago, IL): violinist. Classically trained, Feldman has made an indelible mark on free jazz by performing with many of the finest avant-gardists: John Zorn, Dave Douglas's String Group, Muhal Richard Abrams, Ray Anderson, Maarten Altena, John Abercrombie, and Pharoah Sanders, to name but a few. From 1980 to

1986, he lived in Nashville and worked extensively around country-music circles. Feldman then relocated to New York and worked as a studio musician behind such disparate performers as They Might Be Giants, Diana Ross, Sheryl Crow, and the Manhattan Transfer. He has been a member of the Arcado String Trio and Chromatic Persuaders, and has worked in big bands around Europe and the United States, making over two hundred recordings across almost all genres of contemporary music. His solo debut was *Music for Violin Alone* (1995, Tzadik).

Fell, Simon H. (b. Dewsbury, England, 13 January 1959): bassist, composer, and label administrator. One of the second generation of British improvisers, following the Parker/Bailey/Watts revolution, Fell is a strong composer whose interests lean toward the contemporary avant-garde more than jazz. After his graduation from Cambridge in 1984, Fell established his Bruce's Fingers label and began issuing records of his new compositions. The first, *Compilation I* (1985), is a very interesting collection of nonet works, which slides freely between true jazz feel and serious improvisation. It also highlights his impressive skills as a bassist, which have garnered much praise in settings like his trio with saxophonist Alan Wilkinson and drummer Paul Hession (*Registered Firm*, 1998, Incus). Some album titles indicate the humor with which Fell approaches life and music: *Two Steps to Easier Breathing* (1988) and *Eight Classic Jazz Originals You Can Play* (1991, both Bruce's Fingers), the title of which is deceptive. At London's Termite Club, Fell played dates with George Haslam and Lol Coxhill that resulted in a pair of discs (*Termite 1* and *Termite 2*, both 1989). Fell has also performed with Company, Butch Morris's London Skyscraper Project (and its offsprings, the London Improvisers Orchestra), Peter Brötzmann, John Butcher, and the trios VHF, Badland, and IST. Butcher, Hession, Wilkinson, Rhodri Davies, vibist Orphy Robinson, and longtime sax associate Charles Wharf appear on Fell's magnum opus, *Composition No. 30: Compilation III* (1998), admirably uniting the spirits of Cage and Mingus.

Fennesz (Christian; b. Vienna, Austria): guitarist and electronic musician. Fennesz was an underground artist who emerged into higher visibility with his dense improv EP *Instrument* (1996, Mego). A profoundly deep thinker who spreads thick layers of texture on his recordings, Fennesz has worked with rock-improv band Maische, Orchester 33 1/3, Jim O'Rourke, Werner Dafeldecker, and Polwechsel. He is respected as a producer and multimedia artist.

Festival International de Musique Actuelle Victoriaville: Annual improvised music festival, held in Victoriaville, Québec, Canada, since 1983. Directed by Michel Levasseur, the festival spans forms from mainstream jazz to the extreme avant-garde. The Victo record label is associated with the festival and has documented many of the finest performances there.

Few, Bobby (b. Cleveland, OH, 21 October 1935): pianist. Few was raised in the same neighborhood as Albert Ayler, and one of his earliest recorded appearances was on

Ayler's *Music Is the Healing Force of the Universe.* In the early 1970s, after Ayler's death, Few joined the jazz migration to Europe and settled in Paris. He performed with Archie Shepp, Alan Silva, Noah Howard, Sunny Murray, and Zusaan Kali Fasteau over the years. However, his major gig for the past couple of decades has been with Steve Lacy (see Lacy's entry) as the pianist in Lacy's popular sextet. He made a staggering number of concert appearances and recordings with Lacy until the saxophonist returned to America in 2002. Few has recorded a handful of albums under his name, including three live discs for Boxholder.

Feza, Mongezi (b. Queenstown, South Africa, 1945; d. London, England, 1975): trumpeter. Feza was one of the South African expatriates who revitalized British jazz in the mid-1960s and contributed to the resultant ethnic strain of free jazz. Influenced by the forceful bop of Clifford Brown as much as by the glistening melodies of his homeland, Feza became a professional musician and was invited by Chris McGregor to join The Blue Notes while still in his teens. In 1964, he joined them on the European tour that became their escape from apartheid.

Besides McGregor's Blue Notes and the later Brotherhood of Breath, Feza collaborated with altoist Dudu Pukwana and bassist Johnny Dyani in Afrocentric groups like Assegai, Spear, and Xaba (the latter was Dyani's trio with Turkish percussionist Okay Temiz). He also associated with white British jazzmen and Canterbury crossover rockers: Robert Wyatt, Henry Cow, Gary Windo, Tony Oxley's Dedication Orchestra, and Keith Tippett's massive ensemble Centipede (on *Septober Energy,* 1971, RCA). In 1975, not long after completing *Diamond Express* (1977, Freedom) with Pukwana, Feza died from pneumonia, which compounded a mysterious nervous illness. Though Feza never recorded as a leader, his legacy lives on in the many albums he made with his longtime friends; *Spirits Rejoice* (1978, Ogun), under Louis Moholo's name, is a treasure.

Fields, Scott (b. Chicago, IL): guitarist and composer. Fields is one of the few improvisers of recent vintage to try out a fusion of free jazz and Schoenberg's serial techniques. His system, developed by Professor Stephen Dembski of the University of Wisconsin at Madison, can be heard on *Disaster at Sea* (1996, Music & Arts). The resulting music is dense and complex, yet without the stodgy academicism that characterized early serialism.

In his younger days, Fields became enamored with the AACM's innovations, and he built a friendship with Joseph Jarman that endured through the subsequent hills and valleys of his career. After some unsteady experiments with a free-rock organ trio, Fields returned to academia to learn more about musical theory and practicum. However, he switched majors to concentrate on journalism, a tangential move that lasted about ten years. After his father's death, Fields returned to music as a creative outlet. Around 1992, he met Dembski and began to explore the professor's modified serial principles. Those concepts remain at the core of his ensemble but are not Fields's only stock-in-trade. *Five Frozen Eggs* (1997, Music & Arts) is an admirable project with Hamid Drake, Marilyn Crispell, and bassist Hans Sturm.

Fine, Milo: multi-instrumentalist and bandleader. At times, the Milo Fine Free Jazz Ensemble has barely qualified as an "ensemble," being the duo of Fine and guitarist Steve Gnitka (*Hah*, 1976, HatHut). Usually Fine concentrates on drums, piano, and clarinet, a fairly odd combination of instruments played by a highly unusual performer. He began playing drums at age nine and took up the piano at age fourteen. In 1969, Fine formed the group Blue Freedom, which eventually mutated into his conceptual Free Jazz Ensemble. He has collaborated with Borbetomagus (*Borbeto Jam*, 1985, Agaric), with Gnitka and Joe McPhee in a trio (*MFG in Minnesota*, 1978, HatHut), and with dance troupes in the Minneapolis area. Fine runs his own label, Shih Shih Wu Ai, its name drawn from the Buddhist philosophy of nonobstruction (*Get Down! Shove It! It's Tango Time!*, 1986), and is a former music critic for *Cadence*.

Fire in the Valley Festival: annual festival in Amherst, Massachusetts. Begun in 1996, the festival is produced by Michael Ehlers, who also heads the Eremite record label. Fire in the Valley is centered more steadily upon the free-jazz tradition than the wider avant-garde spectrum covered by other festivals. Among the featured artists in the past have been Test, Die Like A Dog, Joe Morris, and Alan Silva. Several excellent performances have been released on CD by Eremite.

Firespitters, The: ensemble of former Prime Time members who perform with poet Jayne Cortez. The core group includes guitarist Bern Nix, electric bassist Al MacDowell, and drummer Denardo Coleman, the son of Cortez and Ornette Coleman. *Taking the Blues Back Home* (1996, Polygram) adds Frank Lowe, altoist Talib Kibwe, harmonica player Billy Branch, guitarist Carl Weathersby, and two African kora players.

Flaherty, Paul (b. Hartford, CT, 6 November 1948): saxophonist. He started saxophone studies at age ten but gave up on formal education in high school. After jamming along with jazz records to learn the ropes, Flaherty began his career in 1971 but struggled for several years as a bandleader and member of the group Orange. For most of the 1980s, Flaherty painted houses and played sax on street corners. He began a partnership with drummer Randall Colbourne in 1988 that drew positive attention and resulted in ten recordings (*Endangered Species*, 1989, Cadence Jazz). His powerful, Aylerish tone can be best heard on albums like *Anahad* (1999, Cadence Jazz), co-led with Colbourne, and *Sannyasi* (2002, Wet Paint), with trumpeter Greg Kelley. In the mid-1990s, Flaherty administered the Zaabway record label and runs Wet Paint today.

Flying Luttenbachers: free jazz/rock ensemble, convened in 1990 by ex-punker Weasel Walter after he discovered the free improvisation of Hal Russell. Inspired, Walter originally assembled a disastrous free-punk ensemble called the Sound Improvisation Collective, which quickly fell apart due to an understandable lack of direction. Walter met Russell himself and began taking saxophone lessons to further familiarize himself with jazz concepts. Along with second saxophonist Chad Organ and bassist Bill

Pisarri, they formed the Flying Luttenbachers. (The name is derived from Russell's true surname, with "Flying" added to suggest a daring troupe, like the wire-walking Wallendas.)

The band recorded their first album in February 1992 for Walter's ugEXPLODE label (reissued by Coat Tail in 1996 as *Destructo Noise Explosion: Live at WNUR 2-6-92*). Shortly thereafter, Russell became involved in his NRG Ensemble and was replaced by saxophonist Ken Vandermark. Jeb Bishop joined as the band's bassist but switched to trombone later on. Since then, the Luttenbachers have issued eight albums of varying content, constantly wobbling between punk rock and jazz influences; the most recent is *Infection and Decline* (2002, Troubleman).

FMP: Free Music Production, a record label created by engineer/producer Jost Gebers and bassist Peter Kowald in 1969 following a number of antiestablishment music festivals in Berlin, including the Total Music Meeting and the Free Music Workshop. FMP has taken pride in presenting top-quality free music in defiance of popular tastes. Once boasting one of the largest catalogs of free albums by European and American artists, FMP has now deleted many of these instead of reissuing them in CD form. The label's crowning glories include its first release, Manfred Schoof's *European Echoes*, and eleven CDs documenting the 1988 Cecil Taylor Festival in Berlin, once available as a boxed set but now limited to the individual albums. The label hosts summer and winter music festivals in Berlin.

Fonda, Joe (b. Amsterdam, NY, 16 December 1954): bassist and coleader, with pianist Michael Jefry Stevens, of the Fonda-Stevens Quintet. Fonda is a powerful player and deft technician who first came to prominence with Anthony Braxton's mid-1990s ensembles, the period in which Braxton concentrated on piano. *Octet (New York) 1995*, on the reedman's Braxton House label, is an excellent document. Since 1996, the Fonda-Stevens group has recorded half a dozen albums for Music & Arts and Leo; 1997's *Parallel Lines* (Music & Arts) is one of the best, demonstrating the leaders' supple interaction. Fonda has also supported saxophonist David Bindman, Herb Robertson, Wadada Leo Smith, Chris Jonas, and Mark Whitecage.

For 4 Ears: Swiss improv label, founded by drummer Günter Müller in 1990 to showcase his own music and that of his associates. Featured artists include trombonist Hans Anliker, altoist Dimitri Visotzky, Jim O'Rourke, Christian Marclay, the European Chaos String Quartet, Voice Crack, Lê Quan Ninh, violinist Hans Burgener, Butch Morris, Urs Leimgruber, Sachiko M, and drummer Fredy Studer, often with Müller as a supporting performer.

Freedom of the City Festival: annual festival inaugurated in London, England, in 2001. Held at Conway Hall in the Holborn area, the first festival of "radical improvised music" included over a hundred improvisers working in jazz, electronic, and nonidiomatic forms.

Freeman, Chico (Earl Lavon Freeman Jr.; b. Chicago, IL, 17 July 1949): reedman and bandleader, the son of saxophonist Von Freeman. He first played trumpet in high school but switched to tenor sax while at Northwestern University. After graduation, he joined the AACM, dividing his time between edgy jazz and R&B gigs for the next five years. Freeman's first recording was a long-gone album for the small Dharma label; his second, *Morning Prayer* (1976, India Navigation), featured AACM members like Henry Threadgill, Muhal Richard Abrams, and Douglas Ewart, with the leader on saxes, flute, and panpipes. It set the standard for his unusual yet accessible style.

In 1977, Freeman moved to New York and began working with some of the city's finest fringe artists: Sun Ra, Don Pullen, Jack DeJohnette, Sam Rivers, Kip Hanrahan, Ahmed Abdullah, and others. He has also continued to lead his own groups. Among his finest records are *The Outside Within* (1978, India Navigation), *Peaceful Heart, Gentle Spirit* (1980, Contemporary), and the Latin-jazz triumph *The Emissary* (1995, Clarity). Freeman joined The Leaders in 1984 and has co-led occasional dates with his father.

Freeman, Von (Earl Lavon Freeman Sr.; b. Chicago, IL, 3 October 1922): tenor saxophonist. Though Freeman is not specifically a free saxophonist, his bop-heavy resumé includes work with Sun Ra, Malachi Favors, Fred Anderson, Andrew Hill, and Muhal Richard Abrams. He is the father of saxman Chico Freeman, the brother of guitarist George and drummer Bruz, and was a sort of father figure to the young Chicagoans who constituted the AACM in the 1960s. Despite a long and impressive career working with the likes of Horace Henderson, Charlie Parker, Lester Young, Otis Rush, and Roy Eldridge, Freeman did not record as a leader until 1972 (the decidedly unfree *Doin' It Right Now*, Atlantic). His Nessa recording *Serenade and Blues* (1975) gives a better impression of his free leanings.

Friedlander, Erik (b. New York, NY, 1960): cellist. Friedlander began playing cello in his youth and studied music at Columbia University. An encounter with bassist Harvie Swartz led him to become seriously interested in music as a profession, and the young cellist debuted on Swartz's *Underneath It All* (1980, Gramavision). Friedlander had spent his life listening to jazz, as his father was a photographer who contributed album covers to Atlantic Records, but he took a left turn into the free end of things in the mid-1980s when he began working with Dave Douglas's String Group (*Parallel Worlds*, 1993, Soul Note) and John Zorn. In 1994, Friedlander assembled his group Chimera, with reedmen Andrew D'Angelo and Chris Speed and bassist Drew Gress (*Chimera*, 1995, Avant). Since then, Friedlander has led other ensembles, continued to work in classical settings, and recorded with Marty Ehrlich's Dark Woods Ensemble, Myra Melford's The Same River, Twice, Laurie Anderson, Brazilian vocalist Ana Caram, Anthony Coleman, Bob Belden, and Broadway singer Betty Buckley, among others.

Fringe, The: Boston-based free jazz collective, founded in 1972. The members are saxophonist George Garzone, bassist John Lockwood, and drummer Bob Gullotti. The band holds down a regular Monday night gig at the Lizard Lounge downtown. Among their recordings are *It's Time for The Fringe* (1993, Soul Note) and *The Fringe in New York* (2000, NYC Records, issued under Garzone's name) with guest vibraphonist Mike Mainieri.

Frisque Concordance: free quartet of pianist Georg Graewe, reedman John Butcher, drummer Martin Blume, and bassist Hans Schneider. *Spellings* (1992, Random Acoustics) is the premier document of their densely microtonal improvisations.

Frith, Fred (b. Heathfield, U.K., 17 February 1949): postmodern guitarist, bassist, and violinist. A choirboy and violin student in his youth, Frith took up the guitar in his teens and joined the burgeoning British folk scene. In 1968, he cofounded the avant-rock group Henry Cow, a band comparatively more adventurous in its songwriting and improvisations than Pink Floyd or most of the other early British progressive rock bands.

In 1978, after Henry Cow's dissolution, Frith relocated to New York and became part of the nascent avant- music crowd. Among his associates in the Downtown community have been John Zorn (who included Frith on bass in his Naked City project), cellist Tom Cora, and electric harpist Zeena Parkins (Frith's cohorts in Skeleton Crew). Frith has also performed with Brian Eno; in duo with guitarist/saxophonist Hans Reichel; with Company, Material, and the "mystery band" The Residents; and in a stunning quartet with ex-Captain Beefheart drummer John French and guitarists Richard Thompson and Henry Kaiser. His group Maybe Monday features Lawrence Ochs (of Rova), koto player Miya Masaoka, and Kronos Quartet cellist Joan Jeanrenaud (*Digital Wildlife*, 2001, Winter & Winter).

Frith has composed for dance, film, and theatrical projects, as well as impressive works for groups such as Rova (*Freedom in Fragments*, 2002, Tzadik), the Ensemble Moderne, and the Lelekovice String Quartet. He draws much inspiration from writers and painters. Nicolas Humbert and Werner Penzels' award-winning documentary film *Step across the Border* chronicles Frith's life and career.

Fuchs, Wolfgang (b. Landau, Germany, 1949): reeds player. Fuchs studied guitar and mandolin in his childhood, then moved on to the reeds and jazz while attending the Music Academy of Karlsruhe. In 1974, he came to Berlin and met the circle of free improvisers there. In 1978, he recorded *Momente*, the first of several albums for FMP. Fuchs assembled his acclaimed tentet, the King Übü Orchestrü, in 1983 with some of Europe's finest improvisers, among them Philipp Wachsmann, Günter Christmann, Paul Lytton, Radu Malfatti, Luc Houtkamp, and saxophonist Peter Van Bergen. His interest in pan-European collaborations has led to some interesting projects, such as *Duets, Dithyrambisch* (1990, FMP) with Evan Parker, Louis Sclavis, and Hans Koch, and the trio "Holz für Europa" with Koch and Van Bergen (*Comité Imaginaire*, 1997, FMP). Fuchs has participated in Total Music Meetings, Cecil Taylor's Workshop Orchestra (*Melancholy*, 1990, FMP), Butch Morris's conduction event London Skyscraper, and has duetted with King Übü members, including electronic musician Georg Katzer, guitarist Jean-Marc Montera, and bassist Fernando Grillo.

Fuhler, Cor (Cornelis; b. Barger-Oosterveld, Netherlands, 1964): pianist, electronic musician, and composer. He is an experimenter of good repute, having developed ways to sustain and modify the piano's tone through E-bows, tone wheels, and pickups. He is the inventor of the keyolin, a keyed violin, and mbirinthesizer, an electronically modified African thumb piano, among other instruments. Fuhler came out of Amsterdam's Sweelinck Conservatory in 1989 and studied jazz and improvisation under Misha Mengelberg. In 1994, he began working with the ensemble Palinckx (*Border—Live in Zurich*, 1996, Intakt), and in 1995 formed a trio with Han Bennink and bassist Wilbert de Joode (*Bellagram*, 1998, GeestGronden; *Zilch*, 1998, Conundrum). He has performed in duo with Gert-Jan Prins (*The Flirts*, 2001, Erstwhile), participated in multimedia and theater events, investigated live sampling as "DJ Cor Blimey and His Pigeon," and worked with Jim O'Rourke, Keith Rowe, MIMEO, Michael Moore, Paul Lovens, Tristan Honsinger, Evan Parker, Luc Houtkamp, and a host of others.

Fujii, Satoko (b. Tokyo, Japan, 9 October 1958): pianist. Fujii draws from Cecil Taylor's sphere of influence, whipping up torrents of sound, which she tends to color with tinges of Oriental beauty. She studied classical music for literally her entire childhood but became frustrated when she seemingly lost her ability to improvise because of that strict regimen. She studied jazz with local professionals and obtained a scholarship to Berklee in 1985. Within two years, Fujii graduated and was gigging around Japan's better jazz spots while teaching on the side. In 1993, she returned to America to study with George Russell and Paul Bley at New England Conservatory. *Something About Water* (1995, Libra) includes her duets with Bley, which pointed her toward the avant-garde. Three years later, she recorded an experimental big-band album, *South Wind* (1998, Leo), as critically acclaimed as her prior records had been. Fujii has led her own trios, sextets, and large ensembles; recorded duets with her husband, trumpeter Natsuki Tamura, and Mark Feldman; and performed in rock-flavored units as well. Fujii has worked with several American improvisers, including trombonists Joey Sellers and Curtis Hasselbring, and reedmen Andy Laster, Briggan Krauss, Chris Speed, and Tony Malaby.

Fully Celebrated Orchestra: Boston-based free jazz quartet. Led by altoist Jim Hobbs, the band's members include trumpeter Taylor Ho Bynum (replacing Keici Hashimoto), bassist Timo Shanko, and drummer Django Carranza. Their best recording to date is *Marriage of Heaven and Earth* (2002, Innova). The band blends traditional jazz forms with freedom, folk styles, and ethnic musics.

Futterman, Joel (b. Chicago, IL, 30 April 1946): pianist. At first glance, an acolyte of Cecil Taylor, Futterman has taken the master's approach and personalized it into his own fluid commodity. He was a semipro by fourteen and was well known to the early AACM members, though he did not take an active part in the organization. In 1973, he relocated to Virginia Beach, where the relative absence of high-profile jazz players enabled Futterman to work out his own personal philosophy of performance. A long period of relative obscurity, with a handful of albums issued on his JDF label, was broken by an exciting partnership with altoist Jimmy Lyons. Unfortunately, the good times only lasted until Lyons's death in 1986, at which time Futterman went into a depressed seclusion for three years.

Finally, coaxed out of retirement, Futterman joined Raphé Malik for some enjoyable sessions (*To The Edge*, 1992, Konnex). Collaborations with Hal Russell, Kidd Jordan, and William Parker helped further fuel the pianist's climb to greater attention. *Southern Extreme* (1998, Drimala), with Jordan and drummer Alvin Fielder, is brisk and invigorating, indicating a sense of healing. In the past few years, Futterman has also taken up soprano sax and flute, with pleasant results. Recent releases on IML Music, *InterView* (2000) and *The Present Gift* (2001), show him to be one of the more thoughtful piano improvisers of the present scene.

G

G-T-Ch Trio: Russian improvising ensemble, sometimes called the Ganelin Trio. One of the ensembles graciously permitted to record for the state-run Melodiya label, its preferred name was the G-T-Ch Trio after its members' initials. Vyacheslav "Slava" Ganelin was born in Moscow in 1944, but his parents moved to Lithuania when he was four. He studied piano in his youth and became interested in jazz through the more open policies of the Lithuanian arts community. In 1961, when an official jazz conference was convened at the National Conservatory in Vilnius, young Ganelin was a featured player. He developed a steady following among the city's jazz-minded musicians and met drummer Vladimir Tarasov and saxophonist Vladimir Rezitsky. Tarasov, born in 1947, had come to Vilnius in 1968 after studying music in Arkhangelsk and Leningrad. Their trio had the honor of performing at the legendary Tallinn Jazz Festival in 1968, where Keith Jarrett and Charles Lloyd made a triumphant appearance in the interest of global brotherhood.

Rezitsky left the trio in 1971 and was replaced by Vladimir Chekasin, also born in 1947 in Sverdlovsk. This trio, dubbed G-T-Ch at some point, created its own personal style of free-form jazz, which drew inspiration from Eastern European folk musics and the modern avant-garde. While its energy level was similar to that of the Cecil Taylor Quartet, the trio was distinguished by its leaderless democracy (hence its chafing at the "Ganelin Trio" title) and its vast, AACM-like array of instruments: Ganelin played piano, trombone, trumpet, guitar, and basset keyboard; Tarasov, a wide assortment of drums, percussion, and bells; Chekasin, a mind-boggling variety of horns and small devices, including the rare basset horn, an alto clarinet in F.

In 1976, after performing at the Warsaw Jazz Jamboree in Poland, the trio was signed to Melodiya. Its first album was *Con Anima* (1976), its second *Concerto Grosso* (rec. 1978, issued 1980, both Melodiya). The two performances, both of long single selections, are now available on a single disc (2001, Golden Years of New Jazz). "Con Anima," over forty-one minutes in total length, demonstrates the gist of G-T-Ch's style. It is almost overwhelmingly energetic from start to finish, with tidal waves of percussion and scorching saxophone crashing over Ganelin's brisk piano flourishes. Influences and thematic hints are strung together in the manner of Ives, overlapping or clashing in terrifying ways and broken by vehement solo passages by each member. Tarasov makes it a habit to not vary the dynamics of his playing, maintaining a flat level of energy for his friends to leap over or duck under as they choose. Even for those familiar with Ayler and Taylor, these sessions are a little much to take the first time, but they make for an exhilarating ride. The music is a heartfelt gesture of disdain toward their nation's totalitarian regime.

Strictly for Our Friends (1985, Leo) was recorded live in Moscow in 1978 and was one of the earliest pirated records released by Leo Records. The trio is at its creative peak on the eight tracks, which range from four to almost ten minutes in length. Ganelin wrings passages of beauty out of the piano, which are embellished and extrapolated upon by Chekasin on his bevy of reeds. The exceptionally flexible Tarasov picks up on his cohorts' leads and most logically frames them in open-ended rhythms. The sound quality is not as good as on *Poco A Poco* (1988, Leo), also recorded in 1978. However, the latter disc has some off-putting rough edits, which suggest that the eleven-part suite was pieced together from longer, flowing improvisations. Smatterings of Coltrane and Russian folk dances peep out as through the "Laugh-In" wall of windows. Ganelin's sparsely composed sections are yielding enough to permit the men wide-ranging freedom. *Catalogue: Live in East Germany* (1979, Leo) is the best conceived of the Leo albums, compositionally superior with a serial structure through which the players cycle with steady variations. The men's improvisations are somewhat restrained, but Chekasin gets in plenty of furious outbursts.

Ancora da Capo (1980, Leo), originally issued in two parts, is an intellectually rigorous suite driven along more by Ganelin's rigid, formal basset keyboard lines than by Tarasov's resolutely irregular drums. The composed themes are actually used as end goals instead of initial inspirations, a highly unusual structure with few parallels in jazz (perhaps "Them Dirty Blues" by Cannonball Adderley would be a reasonable parallel, as it mostly consists of long improvisations before a swinging melody closes things out). Tarasov's multiple rhythmic streams frequently recall Sunny Murray. The drummer positively swings on the second half, which in CD format is a different product than the *Ancora da Capo, Vol. 2* LP originally issued in 1980.

The full contents of *Con Fuoco* (1979, Leo) are now available on *Encores* (2000, Leo), which also includes several other live tracks recorded between 1978 and 1981. The most surprising thing about this fabulous release is the trio's takes on two moldy standards, Weill's "Mack the Knife" and Gershwin's "Summertime." These renditions are as teasingly subversive as you might imagine. Other witty delights include "Who's Afraid of Anthony Braxton" and the sarcastic "It's Too Good To Be Jazz." Ganelin even throws some itchy electric guitar into the works.

"Too Close for Comfort" and Béla Bartók's "Mikrokosmos" studies for piano are both obliterated in good faith on . . . *Old Bottles* (1985, Leo). Both sources inform the maniacal improvs on "Non Troppo," recorded in 1983. From the subdued introduction through the Warholian transformation of recognizable materials, G-T-Ch personalizes this music in ways that would do John Zorn proud. "Too Close" also figures into 1982's "New Wine," the second half-hour track on this compilation. Meters and tempos again shift gears on a whim thanks to Tarasov's liquidity; his drum solo is a special highlight. There is little here that resembles conventional use of harmony, just innumerable gut reactions to minute changes and hints.

The drummer swings like mad on sections of *Con Affetto* (1983, Leo), on which the very long introductory track gives a full view of the jazz-history continuum. Ganelin's tubby basset keyboard does little to hold Tarasov back this time, instead plugging along practically ignored by the rest. Chekasin emulates Dixie, swing, bop, Trane, and everything in between on this opus for his reed chops. On the series of encores, G-T-Ch manages to assassinate "Mack" with his own "Knife."

In the summer of 1986, the trio traveled to the United States for the first time. There they met up with the Rova Saxophone Quartet and recorded *San Francisco Holidays* (1992, Leo), a pleasurable event for all involved. Musical *glasnost* prevails from the second the trio launches into "Ritardando," building from tiny drums and piano flutters to Chekasin's hellfire amid Tarasov's breakneck pulses. Yet another stab at "Mack the Knife" precedes a stimulating but short group improv between G-T-Ch and Rova. If this date was their payback for Rova's *Saxophone Diplomacy*, it gave ample evidence that Communist separatism was doomed.

In the mid-1980s, Ganelin began to assert himself as a more dominant force in the trio's conception. He is the strongest link on *Ttaango . . . in Nickelsdorf* (1986, Leo), a limited-edition LP that presaged the group's collapse. No more is there the sense of freewheeling democracy that had characterized G-T-Ch from its inception. Ganelin has a heavy hand on piano and almost cheesy synthesizer, practically obscuring Chekasin's best efforts.

In 1987, the trio formally dissolved amid a whirl of ill feelings. Chekasin and Tarasov continued to play and record together (*1 + 1 = 3*, 1988, Leo), while the pianist assembled another unit that still performed under the now misleading name of Ganelin Trio. *Opuses* (1989, Leo) features Ganelin, Victor Fonarev on bass and cello, and Mika Markovich on drums, with vocalist Uri Abramovich guesting. These capable new sidemen are sadly undermined by Ganelin's hard domination of the session. Only on "Opus 3" do they manage to fight their way through his morass of keyboards and have their say. *The Trio Alliance* (1995, Leo) is much better, perhaps due to the refusal of saxman Petras Vysniauskas and percussionist Arkadi Gotesman to be subjugated. It is possible that Ganelin himself had seen the error of his ways; he performs with a taste and restraint absent from his music for too long. The first part of the program is the familiar stylistic collage: jazz, folk motifs, carnival tunes, and freedom. Part two features each player in a solo turn before the stentorian energy explodes.

Ganelin has never been afraid to try out the latest technology, though it does not always serve him well. A case in point is *On Stage Backstage* (2000, Leo), a solo performance in which he uses synthesizers to emulate a tuba, strings, flügelhorn, even a full big band. Ganelin also plays on a drum kit at intervals. His piano playing is as pristine as ever, but the dated synthesizers are a poor choice. In attempting to give solo performances of works for orchestra, string quartet, and other ensembles, Ganelin only succeeds in demonstrating his need for resolute accompanists like his trio-mates. In 2001, the original three men reunited for an acclaimed tour, and hopes are high for more of the same.

Ganelin Trio: see **G-T-Ch Trio**.

Ganelin, Vyacheslav (born Moscow, USSR, 1944): pianist, composer, and bandleader. See **G-T-Ch Trio**.

Garbarek, Jan (b. Mysen, Norway, 4 March 1947): tenor saxophonist. Besides playing with various Norwegian musicians, Garbarek studied and performed with George Russell in the early 1960s. He was featured prominently on Russell's landmark *Electronic Sonata for Souls Loved by Nature* (1969, Flying Dutchman), the same year that he recorded his own *The Esoteric Circle* (Freedom). Garbarek's interesting blend of folk, free, and rock forms got him noticed by producer Manfred Eicher, who in the late 1960s was just conceiving ECM Records. Garbarek's deal with ECM made him an international jazz star, and his association with the label continues to this day. His signature style has become one of ECM's hallmarks, even as he has evolved from the freer leanings of *Afric Pepperbird* (1970) and *Sart* (1971) toward folkier forms. He has recorded with Keith Jarrett's Scandinavian Quartet and other prominent labelmates, as well as key figures in European improv and folk musics. Two projects with the Hilliard Ensemble, a vocal ensemble dedicated to Renaissance music, have revealed other facets of Garbarek's estimable talents.

Garrett, Donald Rafael (b. El Dorado, AR, 28 February 1932; d. 17 August 1989): multi-instrumentalist. Brought up in musically fertile Chicago, Garrett studied the acoustic bass and clarinet as a youth. He worked with Muhal Richard Abrams in the 1950s and was a founding member of Abrams's Experimental Band and, later, the AACM. Garrett split his duties between the growing avant-garde scene and hard bop, recording with Rahsaan Roland Kirk, Ira Sullivan, and Eddie Harris, as well as Dewey Redman's debut, *Look for the Black Star* (1966, Freedom).

Garrett played a prime role in many of John Coltrane's experiments between 1963 and 1965, including *Om*, *Selflessness*, and *Kulu Se Mama* (all collected on *The Major Works of John Coltrane*, Impulse). His bass clarinet and upright bass add important textures to these exotic, often underappreciated settings. Later Garrett moved to San Francisco, where he first worked with reedman Gerald Oshita and drummer Oliver Johnson, then landed gigs with Archie Shepp and Pharoah Sanders. In the mid-1970s, he married multi-instrumentalist Zusaan Kali Fasteau and worked with her in the duo Sea Ensemble (*We Move Together*, 1976, ESP) for several years.

Garrison, Jimmy (b. Miami, FL, 3 March 1934; d. New York, NY, 7 April 1976): bassist. Garrison grew up in Philadelphia's rich jazz scene after learning to play the bass in his youth. After gigging with bop trumpeter Kenny Dorham, saxophonists Jackie McLean and Lee Konitz, and other key jazzmen, Garrison met Ornette Coleman in 1959 and took part in *The Art of the Improvisers* (Atlantic). Despite some further excellent work with Coleman's groups, Garrison became most renowned for his vital role in John Coltrane's bands from 1960 to the saxophonist's death in 1967. His hard-edged, blues-heavy style and distinctive bowing on solo spots set him apart from the more cerebral bassists of the day. Until his own death from cancer, Garrison continued to work frequently with artists like Pharoah Sanders, Alice Coltrane, and Sonny Rollins. His son Matthew is a respected bassist today, and William Parker is one of Garrison's best-known students.

Gaslini, Giorgio (b. Milan, Italy, 22 October 1929): pianist, composer, and bandleader. Gaslini is fourteen years Enrico Rava's senior but did not bring his brand of Italian jazz to the global market until after the trumpeter's breakout with Steve Lacy. He has an academic background in serialism and aleatory composition, which colors his music. In fact, Gaslini's *oeuvre* is so multidirectional that he simply refers to his creations as "total music." His glistening piano approach has been a central sound in the Italian Instabile Orchestra.

By the age of sixteen, Gaslini was already active with a jazz trio, and at nineteen he performed at a Florence jazz festival. Film and symphony work in early adulthood did not detract from his love for jazz. Like many of his compatriots, Gaslini bears a bottomless appreciation for Monk and Ayler, and he has worked with the cream of improvisers: Lacy, Don Cherry, Tony Oxley, Roswell Rudd, Anthony Braxton, and violinist Jean-Luc Ponty.

Lacy, Oxley, and Ponty all figure in the surprising *Giorgio Gaslini Meets . . .* (1976, Pausa). Gaslini pours on the Monk and even hints at Carla Bley's sound on "Fabbrica Occupata," which fabric is practically rent to shreds by the soprano saxophone and Oxley's behemoth drums. *Multipli* (1987, Soul Note) features a commanding all-Italian lineup. Jelly Roll Morton's "Chicago Breakdown" (compare this more "traditional" version with the one on Air's *80 Below '82*, 1982, Antilles) shares time with seven Gaslini originals like "Ornette Or Not."

Gaslini's solo interpretations of Monk and Ayler works are among the most interesting of the large crop. On *Gaslini Plays Monk* (1981, Soul Note) he is original enough to not simply ape the essential Monk style, choosing to analyze and reshape the tunes as Lacy and Misha Mengelberg have in their own investigations. Gaslini injects a freshness into his interpretations that the overdone Monk canon sorely needs. *Ayler's Wings* (1990, Soul Note) is a more daunting prospect, given the transient flexibility of the late saxophonist's writings and his constant revisions of them. If Ayler had been composing in the classical era, he may have devised something like Gaslini's unassuming translations of "Truth Is Marching In" and "Ghosts." Monk had a knack for making the piano sound as if it were producing microtones, and Gaslini puts that effect to good use in substituting for Ayler's scraping tonal variations.

Gauthier, Jeff (b. Santa Monica, CA, 4 March 1954): violinist and administrator of the Cryptogramophone label. Gauthier is a prominent improviser on the Southern California scene, working regularly with the Cline brothers and Vinny Golia. Inspired by twentieth-century classical developments, progressive rock, and jazz from the bebop revolution onward, he melds a large number of influences into his personal approach.

Around 1978, following his graduation from CalArts, Gauthier formed the forward-looking Quartet Music with Nels Cline, Alex Cline, and bassist Eric Von Essen. Since 1991, he has led his quintet, the Goatette (a play on his childhood nickname, "The

Goat") with the Cline brothers, bassist Joel Hamilton, and pianist David Witham. *Mask* (2002, Cryptogramophone), the group's third CD, features compositions by Gauthier, Von Essen, the Clines, and Ornette Coleman. Aside from an abundance of classical work across the nation, Gauthier has played jazz with Gregg Bendian, Yusef Lateef, Adam Rudolph, and Mark Dresser, and has produced mainstream jazz albums. He coordinated the Inner Ear new music concert series in Los Angeles and performed on the Grammy-winning *Credo* (2000) by Kristof Penderecki and the Oregon Bach Festival Orchestra and Chorus.

Gayle, Charles (b. Buffalo, NY, 28 February 1939): saxophonist and composer. Gayle began his studies on piano but switched to tenor sax in his early twenties; he has also played trumpet, bass, and soprano sax. For the most part, he has been self-taught. He was a marginal figure in New York's free scene in the 1960s and 1970s, teaching at State University of New York at Buffalo and gigging with Rashied Ali, Ronnie Boykins, and Eddie Gale. During the same period, he regularly performed for change in the city's subways. A recording deal with ESP during the label's boom never materialized, and Gayle did not record until 1988. His first significantly popular album was *Touchin' on Trane* (1991, FMP), recorded by Rashied Ali in a German hotel room. Gayle was a featured performer in the 1984 Sound Unity Festival and *Rising Tones Cross*, Ebba Jahn's documentary about the festival. Work with Cecil Taylor and a contract with Silkheart Records increased his profile. By the mid-1990s, Gayle had become a force to be reckoned with; he is one of the most visceral, impassioned saxophonists on the contemporary scene. He has also played piano and bass clarinet regularly since the early 1990s. He has performed in duo with Sunny Murray (*Illuminators*, 1996, Audible Hiss) and backed punker poet Henry Rollins in the company of Rashied Ali.

A devout Christian, Gayle's work is deeply inspired by Jesus Christ's teachings. Once homeless on the Big Apple's streets, Gayle credits his faith with his increase in public acceptance, though it has also cost him work when he refused to remain silent during concerts and just play his horn. His more traditionally structured works, like those on *Ancient of Days* (1999, Knitting Factory Works), stick close to post-bop forms while permitting Gayle to venture outside. He is clearly inspired by Albert Ayler, though his tunes are more complex than Ayler's folksy melodies.

Gelb, Philip (b. Brooklyn, NY, 12 April 1965): shakuhachi player and composer. The traditional Japanese flute is not frequently heard, even in the wide-open spaces of free improvisation, making Gelb a rare commodity. He began studying the instrument in 1988 while studying anthropology at the University of Florida. Gelb's fascination with experimental music led him to bring the shakuhachi into that environment while directing Florida State University's New World Ensemble. In that position, Gelb hosted some of the world's finest improvisers, including Wadada Leo Smith, Derek Bailey, Butch Morris, Richard Teitelbaum, and George Lewis. Following a grant to attend the Atlantic Center for the Arts, Gelb began working with Japanese composer Yuji Takahashi and dancer Eri Majima. A resident of the San Francisco area, Gelb is an associate of Deep Listening guru Pauline Oliveros. Their trio with pianist Dana

Reason has been captured on several recordings (*Between/Waves*, 1999, Sparkling Beatnik, with Rova member Jon Raskin; *The Space Between*, 2003, 482 Music, with bassist Matthew Sperry). Gelb has also recorded as a solo artist with violinist Carla Kihlstedt and with koto players Brett Larner, Shoko Hikage (both on *Indistancing*, 1999, Leo), and Miya Masaoka.

Giuffre, Jimmy (James Peter; b. Dallas, TX, 26 April 1921): progressive saxophonist and clarinetist. He graduated from North Texas State in 1942, entered the service shortly thereafter, and worked his way up through the ranks of the big bands of Jimmy Dorsey, Buddy Rich, and Boyd Raeburn. Woody Herman's orchestra was especially fertile ground; Giuffre's tune "Four Brothers" made a name for both himself and the bandleader.

In the early 1950s, Giuffre began playing clarinet and baritone sax along with his tenor. After a brief period in the cool vein, circulating around Shorty Rogers's cadre of Stan Kenton sidemen, he went full-force into avant-jazz, creating fascinating, if often inaccessible, music over the next two decades. His drumless trios, variously including guitarist Jim Hall, trombonist Bob Brookmeyer, and bassists Ralph Peña and Jim Atlas, gained acclaim for their rare sound. The year 1957 saw an underground hit, "The Train and the River," which was featured on the TV special "The Sound of Jazz." The 1960s trios with Paul Bley and Steve Swallow resulted in some of his finest moments, none more than the legendary *Free Fall* (1962, Columbia), a tremendous breakthrough in collective improvisation.

For most of the 1960s and 1970s, Giuffre worked as an educator, only rarely heading out to the concert stage and even less frequently to the studio. Sporadic records came out on Choice and Paul Bley's IAI label, and Giuffre continued to stretch boundaries with the inclusion of electronic instrumentation in his groups. *Dragonfly* (1983) and 1985's *Quasar* (both on Soul Note) marked an unexpected return to the forefront of contemporary jazz, if only briefly. A ballyhooed reunion of the Bley/Swallow trio in 1992 was fun but short-lived.

Gjerstad, Frode (b. Stavanger, Norway, 24 March 1948): alto saxophonist. One of the few of his countrymen to avoid the more ethereal "ECM" style of tenorist Jan Garbarek, Gjerstad has most frequently performed with foreign musicians because of Norway's lack of a dynamic free-jazz movement. He began his musical education on trumpet but switched to saxophone when one was needed in a local R&B band. The free music of Eric Dolphy and Albert Ayler impacted him dramatically, and from the early 1970s, Gjerstad committed himself to outside jazz. He founded the Circulasione Totale label at that time, but it was several years before the imprint was seriously active. In 1981, he began a close performing relationship with English drummer John Stevens, which resulted in the formation of the band Detail (see separate entry) and which flourished until Stevens's death in 1994.

Gjerstad leads the Circulasione Totale Orchestra, a workshop ensemble of young Norwegian players, which includes electric instrumentation and rock rhythms. He has toured with Evan Parker, Peter Brötzmann, and Borah Bergman, played in trios with bassist William Parker and either Rashid Bakr (*Seeing New York From the Ear*, 1996,

Cadence Jazz) or Hamid Drake on drums, and in a fine quartet with Louis Moholo. Gjerstad has received several performance and composition grants, and in 1997, he was named Norwegian Jazz Musician of the Year.

Globe Unity Orchestra: European ensemble organized by pianist Alexander von Schlippenbach. Assembled in the autumn of 1966 through a commission from the Berlin Jazz Festival, the core of Globe Unity consisted of the leader's quintet with Manfred Schoof and the trio of saxist Peter Brötzmann, bassist Peter Kowald, and drummer Sven-Åke Johansson. The group's debut performance was of Schlippenbach's extended composition "Globe Unity" at the Philharmonie in Berlin, under commission by the Berlin Jazztage Festival. *Globe Unity* (1966, Saba), issued under Schlippenbach's name, is rich in the atonal cacophony resulting from his concepts of group interaction in a minimal framework. The pianist was so pleased with the project's outcome that he decided to maintain the orchestra as a regularly function-ing unit. *Globe Unity Orchestra 1967/70* (2001, Atavistic) demonstrates the further expansion of Schlippenbach's ensemble formulae with crushing intensity.

Initially, the most prominent voices in the Orchestra were Brötzmann and Kowald. However, as time went on, Schlippenbach became the principal composer and titu-lar leader of Globe Unity. Other members have included the ceaselessly creative Han Bennink, Kenny Wheeler, Paul Rutherford, Albert Mangelsdorff, Evan Parker, and a trio of expatriate Americans: Alan Silva, Steve Lacy, and tubaist Bob Stewart. The eventual international composition of the Orchestra suited its moniker perfectly. A nine-piece edition recorded *Rumbling* (FMP) at the 1975 Berlin Free Music Festival. Misha Mengelberg's "Alexanders Marschbefehl" has little room for collective impro-visation within its twisted dance-march framework. On the more open title track, composer Lacy engages in brutal soprano sax fisticuffs with Parker, no clear winner decided. The players' radically different approaches are distinct here: Lacy's concep-tion is liquid but always melodic, while Parker's is almost alien in its toothy abrasiveness. Lacy might have felt at home on Monk's prickly "Evidence," a trouble-some tune he has interpreted innumerable times.

Jahrmarkt/Local Fair (1977, Po Torch) includes a pair of compositions by Peter Kowald, who heads up this affair. The style of composition is in a way Ives by way of AEC, complex collages of jazz themes, folk musics, marches, and whatnot. Parker, Wheeler, Schoof, trombonist Gunter Christmann, tenormen Gerd Dudek and Rüdiger Carl, British drummer Paul Lovens, Italian trumpeter Enrico Rava, and even Anthony Braxton are on hand. The disc was literally recorded in the Wuppertal town square, and several local performers took part in the colorful process: a Greek quartet with bouzouki (a long-necked lute) and clarinet; a horde of thirty accordionists; and a tra-ditional brass band. The resultant morass is completely insane and jaw-numbingly humorous, the very epitome of global unity.

In the 1970s, Globe Unity had begun to shift from formally structured works with plenty of elbow room for free soloing to flat-out group-improv chaos. The move was a wise one, actually earning them a wider audience with little compromising of prin-ciples. In 1986, the group recorded *20th Anniversary* (FMP), a shattering performance of over an hour's length. Schlippenbach, Lovens, Parker, Wheeler, Mangelsdorff,

Christmann, and Dudek are present, along with trombonist George Lewis, tubaist Bob Stewart, reedman Ernst-Ludwig Petrowsky, trumpeter Toshinori Kondo, and bassist Alan Silva. The music is a landmark in collective improvisation, sounding more organized than *Free Jazz* or *Ascension*, despite the absence of composed material. This release was Globe Unity's swan song; their final performance was at the 1987 Chicago Jazz Festival, after which Schlippenbach suspended activities due to time and financial constraints.

Globokar, Vinko (b. Anderny, France, 7 July 1934): trombonist and composer. Globokar grew up in Slovenia and began his jazz career there. He returned to France to study trombone and conducting, which he has practiced around the world. In 1967, he accepted a professorship in Köln, where he founded the group New Phonic Art with reedman Michel Portal, keyboardist Carlos Roque, and percussionist Jean-Pierre Drouet. Globokar has performed with Evan Parker and Derek Bailey, and has had a number of compositions written for him. He is admired as a composer in his own right, with nearly a hundred modernistic instrumental and vocal works on file (*Les Emigrés [The Emigrants] [1982–1986]*, 1991, Harmonia Mundi).

Gold Sparkle Band: ensemble founded in Atlanta, Georgia, and based in New York City since 1998. The core unit has included drummer Andrew Barker, saxophonists Charles Waters and Rob Mallard, brass player Roger Ruzow, and previously Chris Riggenbach, Andrew Burnes, or Adam Roberts on bass. Their four albums to date (*Earthmover* [1995, Third Eye], *Downsizing* [1997, Nu] *Nu Soul Zodiac* [1998, Squealer], and *Fugues and Flowers* [2002, Squealer]) draw inspiration from Albert Ayler with a good measure of the AACM's tactics mixed in. The nature of this "Band" is flexible, ranging from the duo of Barker and Waters to the full-sized Nuzion Big Band (*Hallelujah!*, 1997, Third Eye).

Golia, Vinny (Vincent) (b. The Bronx, NY, 1 January 1956): reeds player, composer, and bandleader. One of the consummate multi-instrumentalists in jazz, Golia performs on well over two dozen instruments, from the full series of saxophones (his bass sax technique is especially enviable), clarinets, and flutes to exotica like the Chinese sheng, ancestor of the harmonica, and double-reeded suona. He began his career as a painter but became a professional musician in 1971. Two years later, he moved to Los Angeles and joined Horace Tapscott's milieu, a fertile ground for developing Golia's keen ears as a performer and composer. His circle of longtime comrades includes Nels and Alex Cline, keyboardists Tad Weed and Wayne Peet, Gregg Bendian, Steve Adams, and Tim Berne. Many of these and more have been documented on Golia's award-winning label, Nine Winds, since 1977.

Golia is as acclaimed a solo performer as a bandleader. Beginning with 1980's *Solo* (Nine Winds), Golia has developed his reed vocabulary along lines somewhat similar to Anthony Braxton, exploring different methods of sound production and timbre. His large-group records, spreading from *Compositions for Large Ensemble* (1982) to the monumental *The Other Bridge* (1999, both Nine Winds), also tend to recall

Braxton in their uniqueness, scope, and dynamic range. Yet Golia is an utterly individual voice, not earnestly indebted to Braxton or any other particular performer. World musics and contemporary classical innovations play some part in his works, with jazz usually the primary component. He has also composed for film, dance companies, and multimedia situations.

Graewe (or Gräwe), Georg (b. Bochum, Germany, 1956): pianist and composer. A marvelously subtle technician, it is hard to tell by listening to his records that Graewe began his musical journey as a teenage rock guitarist. Jazz soon became equally important as an entertainment preference, and Graewe formed his first quintet in 1974. He has since worked with the cream of European and American improvisers, most significantly in trio with drummer Gerry Hemingway and cellist Ernst Reijseger (*The View from Points West*, 1991, Music & Arts), and the tentet known as GrubenKlang-Orchester. Graewe's more recent quartet crosses national boundaries, featuring German reedman Frank Gratkowski and two Chicagoans, Kent Kessler and Hamid Drake. He is also a member of Frisque Concordance (see entry) and a composer of chamber and modern classical works. In 1993, Graewe founded his record label, Random Acoustics. Among Graewe's past collaborators are Anthony Braxton, Ken Vandermark, Evan Parker, John Tchicai, Dave Douglas, Jöelle Léandre, Scott Fields, Marilyn Crispell, Mats Gustafsson, and John Butcher.

Grassi, Lou: drummer, percussionist, and bandleader. Grassi is one of several performers whose stars have shone brighter thanks to the Cadence Jazz and CIMP labels. A drummer since the age of fifteen, Grassi spent time in the U.S. Navy School of Music and U.S. Army Band, where he began to look into free jazz. After his discharge in 1968, Grassi studied percussion at Jersey City State College. He received an NEA Fellowship in 1974, which permitted him to study drums with Beaver Harris and arranging with Marshall Brown. He also worked with Sheila Jordan and Jimmy Garrison in that period but specialized in older forms of jazz: ragtime with Max Morath, traditional jazz with the Dixie Peppers.

A fortuitous meeting with German pianist Andreas Boettcher led Grassi back into free jazz, which became the mainstay of his career, though he continues to play Dixieland on occasion. He joined the Improvisers Collective in 1994 and assembled the first incarnation of his Po Band with Herb Robertson, Perry Robinson, trombonist Steve Swell, Burton Greene (temporarily), and Wilber Morris. The ensemble debuted at the collective's 1995 festival, a performance captured on *Pogressions* (1995, Cadence Jazz). The hourlong, three-part suite is held together mostly by Grassi's drumming, as grounded in bebop as he is flexibly free. The Po Band has recorded with several guests: Marshall Allen (*PoZest*, 2000), Joseph Jarman (*Joy of Being*, 2001), and John Tchicai (*ComPOsed*, 2002, all on CIMP). Grassi is a frequent performer on CIMP and Cadence projects, supporting Rob Brown, Roswell Rudd, Paul Smoker, guitarist Bruce Eisenbeil, sax player Bob Magnuson, and others.

Gratkowski, Frank (b. Hamburg, Germany, 1963): reeds player. Since the mid-1990s, Gratkowski has emerged as one of Europe's more creative reedmen. He is a regular

quartet partner of Georg Graewe, Kent Kessler, and Hamid Drake, and has collabo-
rated with Tony Oxley (*Enchanted Messenger*, 1994, Soul Note), Michael Moore (*Tunes
for Horn Guys*, 1995, Ramboy), Ernst Reijseger, Klaus König Orchestra, Wolter
Wierbos, Tom Rainey, Phil Minton, and others. Gratkowski's albums as leader include
Gestalten (1995, JazzHausMusik), *Quicksand* (2000, Meniscus), and *Arrears* (2002,
Cactus).

Graves, Milford (b. New York, NY, 20 August 1941): drummer and percussionist. As
well versed in African and Asian musical traditions as in jazz, Graves is one of the
most exciting and unpredictable drummers to come out of America's third wave (post-
Coleman, post-Shepp) of free jazz.

By the time he graduated from high school, Graves was trained on the trap set, Latin
percussion, and tablas. In his twenties, after backing South African expatriates Miriam
Makeba and Huge Masekela, he became involved in free jazz. His first recordings were
made in 1964 with Giuseppi Logan (*Quartet*) and the New York Art Quartet (self-titled,
both on ESP). Graves's own *Percussion Ensemble*, an early manifestation of his love for
all-percussion groups, was issued the following year by ESP. He participated in Bill
Dixon's 1964 "October Revolution in Jazz," and two years later recorded duets with
pianist Don Pullen for the pair's own label, SRP (short for Self-Reliance Project, in the
spirit of creative independence from the music industry).

Graves briefly joined Albert Ayler's band in 1964 as a second drummer alongside
Sunny Murray. The hard intensity of that group's music inspired John Coltrane to
hire Rashied Ali as a second drummer for his own band. In 1967, Graves officially
replaced Beaver Harris as Ayler's drummer, performed at Newport and Coltrane's funeral, and then recorded *Love Cry* (1967, Impulse). He left the Ayler band when
Impulse began pulling the saxophonist toward less pleasurable and creative music. In
the 1970s, Graves worked regularly with Andrew Cyrille, duetting and playing in trio
concerts with Rashied Ali (Cyrille's *Dialogue of the Drums*, 1974, IPS). He began
teaching at Bennington College in 1973, alongside Bill Dixon.

World tours and drum quartets with Cyrille, Don Moye, and bebop giant Kenny
Clarke kept Graves busy for much of the 1980s, along with his practice as an herbal-
ist. In the 1990s, Graves experienced a career resurgence as new opportunities opened
up. Recordings with David Murray (*Real Deal*, 1994, DIW) and solo projects for John
Zorn's label, Tzadik (*Grand Unification*, 1998, and *Stories*, 2000), preceded the New
York Art Quartet's long-awaited reunion (*35th Anniversary*, 2000, DIW).

Greene, (Narada) Burton (b. Chicago, IL, 14 June 1937): pianist. In his youth,
Greene trained in classical music for eight years at the Chicago Fine Arts Academy
and got into jazz during college. After five years in the Army reserve, Greene lived
in California temporarily. In 1962, he moved to New York where he met bassist Alan
Silva and pianist Billy Green. He performed with Silva in the *Free Form Improvisation Ensemble* (rec. 1964, issued 1995, Cadence Jazz), experimented with the then-
new Moog synthesizer (his "Slurp" was one of the first pieces for jazz synth), and was
a founding member of the short-lived Jazz Composers' Guild in 1964. Greene recorded
two albums for ESP and did a few other projects before he tired of the racism and

unpredictability of the American music business. Greene moved to Paris in 1969 with other American jazzmen. Since 1970, he has lectured at the Utrecht Conservatorium in the Netherlands. Greene has recorded many good albums for a number of European labels, including HatHut, BYG, Horo, and BVHaast. At times, he has gotten away from jazz to explore ragas or klezmer, most recently with Klezmokum. His autobiography is *Memoirs of a Pesty Mystic; or, From the Ashcan to the Ashram and Back Again* (Redwood, NY: Cadence Jazz Books, 2001).

Gress, Drew (b. Trenton, NJ, 1959): bassist. Gress was one of avant-jazz's fastest rising stars in the 1980s, beginning with his quartet, Joint Venture. Gress holds down the low end of Dave Douglas's String Band along with cellist Erik Friedlander, in whose group, Chimera, Gress also participates. The bassist is one-third of Paraphrase, working with altoist Tim Berne and drummer Tom Rainey. Other employers have included Don Byron, Ray Anderson, Uri Caine, and Ellery Eskelin. Gress has taught at the University of Colorado at Boulder and has been the recipient of grants from NEA and Meet the Composer. In 1998, his own quartet, Jagged Sky, debuted with *Heyday* (Soul Note).

Grimes, Henry (Alonzon; b. Philadelphia, PA, 3 November 1935): bassist. Trained at Juilliard, Henry Grimes's too-brief career spanned early R&B, cool jazz, and freedom before he mysteriously called it quits. Grimes first made a name for himself touring with honking Philly tenormen like Willis "Gator" Jackson and Arnett Cobb, then performed with Gerry Mulligan, Lee Morgan, Sonny Rollins, Jimmy Giuffre, Thelonious Monk, Chet Baker, Lennie Tristano, Mose Allison, and even Benny Goodman in the 1950s and early 1960s. Giuffre and Tristano helped open the bassist's ears to more outside music, and in 1961, he found himself playing radically free in Cecil Taylor's group (*Into the Hot*, issued under Gil Evans's name on Impulse). His complete openness of technique, parting from rhythmic accompaniment in favor of loose pizzicatos and bowing, inspired a generation of younger bassists. Grimes partnered up with clarinetist Perry Robinson for a time, then worked in Albert Ayler's band for three years. In 1965, Grimes cut *The Call*, a rather unsuccessful trio date for ESP, then played briefly with Don Cherry.

In 1967, for reasons known only to himself, Grimes packed his bass away for the last time and left music permanently. Communications with his former associates were very rare, and in 1979 and 1984, he was rumored to have died. In 2002, rumors began to circulate that Grimes was alive and had contacted Perry Robinson for the first time in over two decades. Social worker and avant-jazz fan Marshall Marrotte tracked Grimes down in Los Angeles and interviewed him in October 2002. In that interview, published in the Winter 2003 issue of *Signal To Noise*, the former bassist revealed that he had gone to L.A. in 1967 to seek work as an actor, endured bouts of manic-depression and homelessness, and had removed himself so far from the scene that he was completely unaware of the deaths of Ayler, Cherry, Ed Blackwell, and a number of other past associates. Having been provided with a bass, courtesy of William Parker, Grimes has resumed his career to exceptional reviews.

Grob: Köln, Germany label founded by Hans Grob in 1998. Its recorded artists include Thomas Lehn/Paul Lovens, Keith Rowe, Gert-Jan Prins, MIMEO, Eugene Chadbourne, John Butcher/Phil Minton, Elliott Sharp/Bobby Previte, and the trio of Fred Lonberg-Holm, Jim O'Rourke, and Flying Luttenbachers drummer Weasel Walter.

Grossman, Richard (b. Philadelphia, PA, 1937; d. October 1992): pianist. Philly was good to Grossman when he was coming up, offering the chance to jam with jazzmen like bassists Henry Grimes and Jimmy Garrison before free jazz really took off. But it was the sounds of the Ornette Coleman Quartet in the late 1950s that led Grossman to California, where he merged into the Los Angeles scene that bore John Carter, Bobby Bradford, Horace Tapscott, and Vinny Golia. Grossman's approach to piano tempered freedom with truly palpable beauty. He recorded a mere handful of albums for Golia's label, Nine Winds, and for HatHut before his untimely death in 1992. Among the best are *Where the Sky Ended* (2000, HatHut) and *Trio in Real Time* (1991, Nine Winds), both with bassist Ken Filiano and drummer Alex Cline.

Ground Zero: Japanese noise-improv group, led by Otomo Yoshihide from 1990 to 1998. The other core members were usually bassist Hideki Kato and drummer Masahiro Uemura; additional personnel came in and out as situations dictated. Around ten albums were released, the last being *Last Concert* (1999, Amoebic).

Gruppo di Improvvisazione Nuovo Consonanza (GINC): Italian electronic music ensemble. Founded in 1964, the defiant group, like Musica Elettronica Viva and AMM, attempted to unite the electronic concepts of Stockhausen and Luigi Nono with other improvised musical forms. It counted among its members Giancarlo Schiaffini (who later went on to establish both Gruppo Romano Free Jazz and the Italian Instabile Orchestra), Franco Evangelisti, Antonello Neri, Mario Bertoncini, Giovanni Piazza, Egisto Macchi, and Ennio Morricone, who was later celebrated as a soundtrack composer. Frederic Rzewski, a founder of Musica Elettronica Viva, also participated in the group's activities for a while. Profoundly noisy and amelodic, GINC was devoted to redefining the very definition of music. Their nonidiomatic approach and ensemble democracy was inspirational to a number of European improvisers. The self-titled 1995 CD collection on the Editions RZ label is the best source for hearing their experiments.

Gruppo Romano Free Jazz: Italian improvisational group, founded in 1967. Not very well documented, Gruppo Romano was assembled by Giancarlo Schiaffini three years after Gruppo di Improvvisazione Nuovo Consonanza (see above entry) was founded. Its members included reedman Mario Schiano, Marcello Melis, and Franco Pecori. *Ecstatic* (1967, Splasc(h)) is the vital document of their whimsically creative brand of free jazz.

Guelph Jazz Festival: annual event held in Guelph, Ontario, Canada, since 1993. Unlike the major jazz festivals in the United States, Guelph and Victoriaville are dedicated to cutting-edge, avant-garde jazz by the likes of the Sun Ra Arkestra, Joe McPhee, Andrew Hill, and Don Byron. Guelph also includes photography exhibits, lectures, panel discussions, and performance workshops as well as concerts at large and small venues over a four-day span.

Gustafsson, Mats (b. Umeå, Sweden, 29 October 1964): reedman. Over the past two decades, Gustafsson has risen from relative obscurity to become one of the contemporary scene's top improvisers. He studied flute and saxophone in his youth and created the "fluteophone" (still part of his arsenal) by attaching a sax mouthpiece to the flute's body. He began experimenting with drummer Kjell Nordeson in the early 1980s before relocating to Stockholm. In 1988, he formed Gush with pianist Sten Sandell and drummer Raymond Strid (*Saw*, 1988, Radium), then fell in with the German cadre of free improvisers through his friendship with Sven-Åke Johansson. An invitation to participate in a Company event followed two years later, breaking him out to the British scene.

Chicago proved an inspirational locale in the 1990s, as Gustafsson then began a fruitful partnership with Ken Vandermark and Hamid Drake. After Gustafsson, Nordeson, and bassist Peter Jansson formed the Aaly Trio in 1995, Vandermark became a frequent colleague (*Stumble*, 1998, Okkadisk, is one of four albums so far). Gustafsson has performed with the members of Sonic Youth and Peter Brötzmann's Chicago Octet and Tentet, taken part in Gunter Christmann's Vario projects, and recorded several discs under his own name. Among the best are *For Don Cherry* (1995, Okkadisk), *Impropositions* (1996, Phono Suecia), and his solo tribute to Steve Lacy, *Windows* (2000, Blue Chopsticks). Besides free improv, Gustafsson has collaborated with visual artists, dancers, theater troupes, and poets in multimedia events.

Guy, Barry (b. London, England, 22 April 1947): Bassist, composer and bandleader. Guy is a founding father of the British free movement and has extended the vocabulary of the double bass as an improvisational instrument. Guy's initial background was in baroque music. In 1970, he founded the London Jazz Composers' Orchestra, remaining its leader to the present day, alongside his New Orchestra (*Inscape–Tableaux*, 2000, Intakt). He also administrates the Maya record label. Besides his own activities and those of the LJCO, Guy has worked with the cream of British and American freemen, including Tony Oxley, Evan Parker (in a famed trio with Paul Lytton), Howard Riley, Marilyn Crispell, Bill Dixon, John Stevens, and Rova. *Study-Witch Gong Game 11/10* (1994, Maya), recorded with the New Orchestra Workshop (NOW) of Canada, is an excellent study of his compositional development methods.

H

Haden, Charlie (Charles Edward; b. Shenandoah, IA, 6 August 1937): bassist, composer, and bandleader. Perhaps most famous as Ornette Coleman's bass player during the birth of free jazz, Haden came from undeniably different roots. His family performed country-and-western music around the Midwest and had their own radio show around the time that little Charlie was born. He sang with the family band before his second birthday and took up the bass after the show and family moved to Springfield, Missouri. Haden contracted polio at fifteen and was no longer able to sing, but the bass proved helpful as physical therapy. He developed a special touch that gave his playing a keen, bright resonance unlike almost anyone else's at the time.

In 1957, having gained an interest in jazz, Haden moved to Los Angeles and got involved with the bebop and cool scene there. After gigging with Art Pepper, Elmo Hope, and Hampton Hawes, Haden was hired by pianist Paul Bley for his trio. The two met Coleman one night when he was kicked off the bandstand after trying to sit in with Gerry Mulligan. Though the ill-tempered baritonist had not been impressed by Coleman, Haden and Bley surely were. They soon began working with Coleman and Don Cherry on Bley's regular gigs at the Hillcrest Club. In 1959, Coleman and Haden headed for New York, where they nearly single-handedly instigated the free jazz revolution by performing at the Five Spot and recording bold albums for Atlantic. (See Coleman's entry.)

After leaving Coleman's band, Haden recorded beautiful duets with pianist Denny Zeitlin yet stayed close to free jazz with Cherry, Gato Barbieri, Archie Shepp, and Roswell Rudd. In 1969, Haden assembled his Liberation Music Orchestra, an ambitious big band that interpreted politically charged music from Spain, Latin America, and other locales, as well as originals. Their self-titled debut (1969, Impulse) is a landmark of large-band writing and arranging, thanks largely to Carla Bley's hand. For this project, Haden revamped "Song for Ché," a tribute to Latin American revolutionary Ché Guevara, which he had previously recorded with Coleman, and the altoist's tune "War Orphans." Haden actively expressed his socialist interests for several years, and his political stances led to his arrest in 1971. At the Festival de Cascais in Portugal, Haden dedicated "Song for Ché" to the black liberation movements in the Portuguese colonies of Africa, causing a positive commotion in the crowd. Arrested as an instigator, Haden was released with a stern warning to never return to the country. Three years later, the Portuguese revolution ignited and Marcello Caetano's fascist government was overthrown.

In 1976, Haden recorded *The Golden Number* (A&M), a collection of duets with Coleman, Cherry, Shepp, and his old bebop-era employer, Hampton Hawes. The disc illustrated how well Haden could still straddle the many forms of jazz. That same year he formed Old and New Dreams with ex-Coleman alumni Cherry, Ed Blackwell, and Dewey Redman. (See separate entry for Old and New Dreams.) In 1979, he began performing in a trio with saxophonist Jan Garbarek and Egberto Gismonti, which opened doors for him with the ECM label (*Magico*, 1979). Haden has worked with Keith Jarrett, Geri Allen, and drummer Ginger Baker, and duetted with guitarist Pat Metheny (*Beyond the Missouri Sky*, 1996, Verve) and pianist Hank Jones, among others.

In the 1980s, after reforming the Liberation Music Orchestra, Haden joined the faculty of CalArts and helped to strengthen the school's jazz program. The year 1986 saw the advent of Quartet West, his popular mainstream collaboration with saxophonist Ernie Watts, pianist Alan Broadbent, and drummer Larance Marable. Quartet West remains his top priority, with sideline gigs as he chooses. In 2001, Haden won a Grammy for *Nocturne* (Verve), his duet album with Latin pianist Gonzalo Rubalcaba. His daughters Petra and Rachel are musicians, as is son Josh; another daughter, Tanya, works in animation.

Haino, Keiji (b. 1952): guitarist and vocalist. The Japanese equivalent of Sonny Sharrock, Haino is an energetic improviser who emerged at age nineteen with the ensemble Lost Aaraaff. He often vocalizes along with his guitar playing and has contributed vocals to sessions by Fred Frith (*Speechless*, 1981, Ralph/East Side Digital) and Derek Bailey (*Songs*, 2000, Incus). His first recording as a leader was *Watashi-Dake?* (1980, PSF). Haino has made several albums with the progressive rock group Fushitsusha (*The Caution Appears*, 1995, DSA) and recorded with kindred spirits Loren MazzaCane Connors (*Volume 1* and *Volume 2*, 1996, Menlo Park) and Peter Brötzmann (*Shadows: Live in Wels*, 2000, DIW). John Zorn has produced some of his work, including *Tenshi No Gijinka* (1995, Tzadik).

Hampel, Gunter (b. Göttingen, Germany, 31 August 1937): multi-instrumentalist, composer, and bandleader. Hampel is one of the most prolific and beloved musicians in modern creative music. He is a capable performer on several instruments but is principally recognized for the peculiar pairing of vibraphone and bass clarinet. Like many of Europe's improvisers, he got into jazz after World War II, when American soldiers who listened to Willis Conover and the latest jazz hits on Armed Forces Radio occupied Göttingen. During his architectural studies, Hampel kept active as a bandleader and composer. His quintet with Alex von Schlippenbach and Manfred

Schoof, assembled in 1964, was one of the continent's earliest, most popular free jazz ensembles (*Heartplants*, 1965, MPS).

Hampel came to Americans' attention early on by recording for the small but influential ESP label. *Music from Europe* (1966) was a manifesto of sorts to demonstrate his brotherhood with the U.S. improvisers. Hampel, on bass clarinet, flute, and vibes, romps through three intricate originals with Willem Breuker on various reeds, bassist Piet Veening, and drummer Pierre Courbois. The subsections of the suite "Assemblage" bear titles that suggest a rather cold, cerebral music: "Dissociation," "Consolation," and so on. But these titles have no bearing on the actual music, which is warmly executed and charming in its abstractness. As for "Heroicredolphysiognomystery," sort that one out for yourself. Dolphy is in there somewhere, and suitably so!

Since the late 1960s, Hampel has issued several dozen releases on his own record label, Birth, starting with the classic *8th of July, 1969* with Anthony Braxton, Willem Breuker, drummer Steve McCall, bassist Arjen Gorter, and Hampel's then-wife, vocalist Jeanne Lee. Lee alternates magnificently between the roles of frontwoman and extra "horn." She declares the mysterious lyrics of "We Move" over McCall's mockery of a horse trot and Hampel's loping piano stride, while Braxton and Breuker fight over new territories, and Gorter holds down a clunky ostinato. On "Morning Song," Breuker's gruff bass clarinet improv is a highlight. The title track is quite short, a thank-you from Hampel on vibes with McCall offering the sparest acknowledgments in return. Free jazz had begun to make some impact in Europe a few years prior, but it took the exodus of American freemen in the late 1960s and early 1970s to kickstart the movement and set it aflame. *The 8th of July 1969* holds a special place in the history of European free improv as an immaculate document of the genre's potential. From that point on, Hampel, Breuker, and Gorter would become standard-bearers in the vanguard of European improvisation.

Most of Hampel's recordings on Birth tend to be similar in spirit and body, small group operations on his quirky but appealing originals. Most are quite enjoyable, and a few truly stand out from the pack. One of those is *All the Things You Could Be if Charles Mingus Was Your Daddy* (1980, Birth), a live set by his Galaxie Dream Band. The forty-four-minute title track is a bone-crusher in the Mingusian spirit, with Lee and Mark Whitecage in excellent form. Like most free vocalists worth their salt, Lee again functions as a fourth horn as much as a singer.

Time Is Now (1992, Birth) is a different band altogether, but the blueprint of the compositions remains the same: free intro, structured thematic material with wide openings for individual direction. This live show was played in support of a dancer, Shaun Vargas. Hampel and his bandmates devise musical frameworks that are both free and danceable, a comparatively rare combination.

In May 1997, Hampel reunited his original "Heartplants" quintet of Schlippenbach, Schoof, bassist Arjen Gorter, and drummer Pierre Courbois for a Freie Musik Workshop performance. *Legendary, The 27th of May 1997* (1998, Birth) shows just why these free pioneers made such an impression on European audiences more than thirty years prior. Though Schoof's technique was vastly different from Lester Bowie's, the two shared the innate ability to drive an ensemble. The irrepressibly jazzy Schlippenbach is still a vital foil for the vibist, building up chords upon chords as the band's flame burns higher. Like *Free Jazz* and *Ascension*, the dense, preset ensemble passages build up excitement to signal the impending improvs on "All the Things . . ." and "Spielplatz."

Hano, Shoji (b. Kokura, Japan, 1 March 1955): drummer. He debuted at the Kokura Festival at age four and took up the full trap set in his teens after becoming interested in the hard bop of Art Blakey and Max Roach. Hano moved to Tokyo in 1974 and began exploring the avant-garde at that time. Two years later, he formed a trio with Toshinori Kondo and pianist Yoshito Osawa, touring the nation in 1977. Hano gave solo concerts at Kyoto University and nightclubs, along with playing in Odowara and the Easy Music Band and gigging with Kaoru Abe and trombonist Masahiko Kono. In the 1980s, Hano began performing with visiting American and European improvisers—Peter Brötzmann, Hans Reichel, Henry Kaiser, Eugene Chadbourne. He took a sabbatical to experiment with uniting his musical interests with the Shintaido martial art, then debuted the new concept in 1985 to reasonable acclaim. He continued to perform solo and in group formats, and in 1990 he joined Reichel and Brötzmann on separate tours and concert dates. Since that time, he has collaborated with Chadbourne, Johannes Bauer, Keshavan Maslak, Billy Bang, Vladimir Chekasin, and in a trio with altoist Werner Lüdi and bassist William Parker.

Happy Apple: Minneapolis trio of saxophonist Michael Lewis, bassist Erik Fratzke, and drummer David King. As irreverent as John Zorn's early work, the trio is documented on *Please Refrain from Fronting* (2001, Happy Apple).

Harada, Masashi (b. Hiroshima, Japan): pianist, percussionist, and vocalist. Harada studied traditional vocal and percussion techniques as a child, then attended the New England Conservatory. His studies continued in Japan and Finland during his downtime from the Conservatory, from which he received two degrees by 1993. He later studied piano with Avram David.

Harada is notable for the visual aspects of his art, which add greatly to the live experience but reduce the impact of his recordings. Renowned for his photographs of paintings on ice, he brings the same kind of transience to his music by responding to contextual changes with new directions. As an extension of his concepts of generative improvisation, which involves the full human body as an instrument, he developed the discipline of "condanction," conducting an ensemble through dance movements. These experiments can be heard on *Enter the Continent* (2000, Emanem), although again it might help to see how Harada's movements affect the ensemble. Harada has performed with Barre Phillips (*Voluminous Venture* [2001, Cadence Jazz]), John Cage, Joe Maneri, and Cecil Taylor.

Harmolodics: A complex theory of performance and improvisation formulated by Ornette Coleman beginning in the late 1950s. Assembled from the words *har*mony, *mo*tion, and me*lody*, the term refers to Coleman's idea of using all three concepts equally in creating music to achieve a sense of unity among the players. Improvisations are based not on chordal structures but on variations of the melodic, harmonic, and rhythmic structures, guided by individual and group intuition and the logic of the composition itself. Besides Coleman's own groups, harmolodics has been explored by Ronald Shannon Jackson's Decoding Society, James Blood Ulmer, bassist Jamaaladeen Tacuma, and other Coleman disciples.

Harriott, Joe (Arthurlin; b. Kingston, Jamaica, 15 July 1928; d. London, UK, 2 January 1973): free and world-fusion altoist, and one of the first free-leaning Europeans to capture his ideas on record. A transplant to Britain, Harriott was initially a Parker-inspired bopper who gained notoriety in the bands of Ronnie Scott, Tony Kinsey, and other Brits. Following Parker's death, Harriott decided to move away from such fast-paced but chordally restricted music. He developed new notions about ensemble democracy and texture that were similar to Ornette Coleman's, although the men were most likely unaware of each other at the time.

Harriott's first recording was *Southern Horizons* (1959, Jazzland), now difficult to come by. His second, *Free Form* (1960, Jazzland), was released around the same time that Coleman's records began to reach European ears, which led to Harriott being unfairly denounced as a poseur. "Formation" seems pretty straightforward at first, with Harriott and trumpeter Shake Keane playing unison bebop lines over the steadfast pianist Pat Smythe, bassist Coleridge Goode, and legendary drummer Phil Seaman (the only band member not of West Indian extraction). A quick, choppy second stanza, followed by a suspended-rhythm passage, indicates a different logic behind the tune. Harriott's solo is rhythmically free, his tone closer to Parker than Coleman. Keane's ideas are tentative, like Don Cherry's had been with Coleman. The title track and "Tempo" are breakneck bebop runs that shatter into fragments of openness as the two horns call and respond, while the pace of "Impression" rises and falls with the energy level. "Straight Lines" is about the closest thing here to Coleman's work, with clearly defined bebop roots. Throughout the disc, Seaman riffs and tumbles like an aural football team.

Abstract (1962, Columbia) provided evidence that Harriott's ensemble notions were further removed from Coleman's individual concepts than was thought before, but still he found little appreciation for his breakthroughs. Harriott eventually moved away from free music into a fusion of jazz with Indian forms, garnering overdue plaudits of critics. *Indo-Jazz Fusions* (1967, Columbia), a collaboration with Indian violinist John Mayer, is a building block of "world music," with a few free ideas still audible. His untimely death in 1973 halted a remarkably colorful career.

Harris, Beaver (William Godvin Harris; b. Pittsburgh, PA, 20 April 1936; d. New York, NY, 22 December 1991): drummer. Originally a Negro League baseball player, Harris decided to concentrate on music as a career upon taking up the drums at age twenty. After his discharge from the Army, he performed with Sonny Rollins, Horace Silver, Benny Golson, and Joe Henderson in the early 1960s, then changed directions toward free jazz after falling in with Archie Shepp, Marion Brown, Albert Ayler, and Grachan Moncur III. In 1968, he formed the 360 Degree Music Experience, with

Moncur and pianist Dave Burrell. Harris kept the cooperative fresh with a rotating cast of players (among them Hamiet Bluiett, Don Pullen, bassist Cameron Brown, steel drummer Francis Brown, and others) for the remainder of his life. Harris also worked with mainstream luminaries like Cecil Taylor, Al Cohn, Thelonious Monk, and Chet Baker. Unlike many free drummers, Harris always kept the pulse close to the front. He was continually underappreciated despite his familiarity with many musical styles.

Harth, Alfred "23" (b. Kronberg, Germany, 28 September 1949): multi-instrumentalist and composer. Harth's unusual nickname represents the number of instruments he plays. Harth was one of the first performers signed to the ECM label (*Just Music*, 1969). He was an art and sociology teacher in the mid-1970s but has mostly concentrated on his music career, to international acclaim. Some of his sessions, like *This Earth!* (1983, ECM), are marked by starkness of emotion. Harth has conducted several projects with pianist/guitarist Heiner Goebbels, including the Sogenanntes Linksradikales Blasorchester (self-titled compilation, 2002, Trikont). Since 2001, Harth has made his home in South Korea, where he works with many national improvisers like trumpeter Choi Sun-bae. Harth is presently a member of Otomo Yoshihide's New Jazz Quintet. His past collaborators include John Zorn, David Murray, Peter Brötzmann, Wilber Morris, Lindsay Cooper, and drummer Chris Cutler's band Cassiber. Harth's bands have included Hale Peat, the electronic group Imperial Hoot, and Die Flyby No Net.

Haslam, George (b. Preston, Lancashire, England, 22 February 1939): baritone saxophonist. Haslam, mostly self-taught, was influenced by Gerry Mulligan and Lester Young. He worked with jazz and dance bands through the 1950s and 1960s. In the 1970s, he began to venture into free jazz to expound upon his love for different world musical styles. He has performed in Mexico, Hungary (where he learned to play the tarogato, the national instrument), Argentina, Cuba (becoming the first British jazzman to perform in either of those two nations), and elsewhere. In 1989, he formed the Slam Productions label. He works as a music educator and conducts jazz workshops worldwide. Haslam has played with Elton Dean, Lol Coxhill, Paul Rutherford, Mal Waldron, and a host of other Europeans and Americans. *Pendle Hawk Carapace* (2002, Slam) is a sharp duo with drummer Paul Hession.

HatHut: Werner X. Uehlinger's first label, founded in Switzerland in 1975. The imprint was originally founded to document the music of Joe McPhee but quickly expanded to include other American and European artists as well. In the 1990s, the HatHut name generally ceased to exist except as an umbrella, as Uehlinger's interests were dispersed among several subsidiary labels: HatArt, Hat[Now]Art, HatNoir, and HatOlogy. Among the artists represented on the imprints are McPhee, Steve Lacy, Ellery Eskelin, Anthony Braxton, Morton Feldman, Myra Melford, Matthew Shipp, Cecil Taylor, pianist Marc Copland, the Vienna Art Orchestra, Franz Koglmann, and Polwechsel.

Hautzinger, Franz: Austrian trumpeter. His particular specialty is the quarter-tone trumpet, which permits him to play in microtones. Hautzinger studied at the Graz Academy and Vienna Conservatory, then began to teach at the Vienna University of Music in 1989. With saxophonist Helge Hinteregger, he performed in the duo ZOSB and, along with bassist Werner Dafeldecker, the group Striped Roses. Burkhard Stangl has been a reliable partner in projects like the amelodic *Dachte Musik* (2001, Grob). Hautzinger's other band affiliations include Trio F, Nouvelle Cuisine, Mühlbacher usw., London Improvisers Orchestra, and Zeitkratzer. He has collaborated with Derek Bailey (2002, Grob) and has led several sessions including his debut, *Bent* (1996, Extraplatte), and *Gomberg* (2000, Grob); the latter mostly involves valve clicks and lip buzzes.

Haynes, Phil (b. Hillsboro, OR, 15 June 1961): drummer, composer, and producer. At age twenty-three, Haynes moved to New York City and quickly assimilated into the avant-jazz scene there. He ran a rehearsal space called the Brooklyn Corner Store, which drew a good number of prime improvisers including Mark Dresser, Dave Douglas, Tim Berne, Ellery Eskelin, and Don Byron. He joined Paul Smoker's quartet Joint Venture in 1988 and has led his own ensembles, among them *4 Horns and What?* (1991, Open Minds), Free Country, the organ combo Hammond Insurgency, and a quintet with Herb Robertson. Haynes has also recorded in a trio with German guitarist Andreas Willers and reedman Gebhard Ullmann (*Trad Corrosion*, 1995, Nabel).

Helias, Mark (b. Brunswick, NJ, 1 October 1950): bassist and composer. Helias did not start playing the bass until he was twenty, but he was proficient enough to graduate from Yale with a music degree in 1976. There he met Ray Anderson, and in 1977, they formed the trio BassDrumBone with drummer Gerry Hemingway. His connection with Anderson led to some formidable free-jazz gigs with Anthony Braxton, Anthony Davis, Dewey Redman, and other major improvisers.

In 1981, Anderson and Helias founded Slickaphonics, an electric band that melded free jazz and funk in a rather twisted fashion. Three years later, the bassist began his long association with the Enja label by taping *Split Image* (1984), the first of seven albums for Enja thus far. Inspired by Don Cherry's fusion of world musics and jazz, Helias enlisted the cornetist into his ensemble Nu along with Carlos Ward, Ed Blackwell, and Brazilian percussion master Nana Vasconcelos. As a sideman, Helias has performed with Muhal Richard Abrams, Cecil Taylor, Ellery Eskelin, Marty Ehrlich, Christy Doran, Marilyn Crispell, and Michael Moore, and has taken part in Butch Morris's conduction ensembles. He has also appeared on and produced more than half a dozen of Anderson's albums.

Hemingway, Gerry (b. New Haven, CT, 1955): drummer. After performing in relative obscurity for several years, with only a couple of small-label sessions and one Ray Anderson date (*Harrisburg Half-Life*, 1980, Moers) under his belt, Hemingway was hired by Anthony Braxton in 1983 and immediately made a powerful impression. The young drummer found himself in fertile, inspiring territory among Braxton, Mark

Dresser, and Marilyn Crispell, and he remained in the quartet for over a decade. (See Braxton's entry.) In 1990, Hemingway resumed recording as a leader, fronting his quintet with Dresser, Ernst Reijseger, Michael Moore, and Wolter Wierbos (*Down to the Wire*, 1991, HatArt). He has worked with Crispell on bracing sessions (including *Circles*, 1990, Victo) and joined Reijseger in a trio with pianist Georg Graewe. Hemingway's other credits include recordings with John Cale, Mark Helias, Don Byron, Franz Koglmann, and Jeanne Lee.

Hemphill, Julius (b. Fort Worth, TX, 1940; d. 2 April 1995): saxophonist. He began on clarinet, then switched to baritone sax in high school after hearing Gerry Mulligan play the beast with such facility. He played around town with John Carter and various blues or R&B bands, though he apparently did not encounter Ornette Coleman at that time. Hemphill spent two years in the Army, then played with Ike Turner's soul-blues band before moving to St. Louis in 1968. He soon became part of the Black Artists Group, bonding with the Bowie brothers, Baikida Carroll, and two fellow saxophonists who would play prominent roles in his career: Hamiet Bluiett and Oliver Lake. Besides participating in BAG activities, Hemphill formed the Mbari label and began to issue his own powerful recordings like *Dogon A.D.* (1972, reissued by Freedom) and *Blue Boyé* (1977, reissued by Screwgun, a label administered by Hemphill follower Tim Berne). His hard, fleet, relentless alto sax approach had a tremendous influence on younger players of the day.

In 1974, Hemphill relocated again, this time to New York, where he made a life-changing recording with Anthony Braxton. On one track of *New York, Fall 1974* (Arista/Freedom), Hemphill and Braxton performed in a sax quartet with Bluiett and Lake. The experience was inspirational enough that, two years on, the three friends from St. Louis were invited to play in a similar quartet with David Murray. From that meeting came the World Saxophone Quartet, one of the most inspirational ensembles in post-bop jazz. (See the WSQ's entry.)

Outside the WSQ, Hemphill had occasional opportunities to record as a leader. *Roi Boyé and the Gotham Minstrels* (1977, Sackville) and *Flat-Out Jump Suite* (1980, Black Saint) are two excellent documents of this period in Hemphill's career. The latter features an acutely sympathetic group: Olu Dara, Abdul Wadud, and percussionist Warren Smith. In 1988, Hemphill recorded some of his large-band arrangements (*Julius Hemphill Big Band*, Elektra/Musician) with good results. He also composed a "saxophone opera," *Long Tongues*.

The following year, with his health failing, Hemphill departed the WSQ. The absence of his commanding presence and composing skills threw the quartet for a loop, yet the group motored on. In 1991, Hemphill assembled an excellent all-saxophone sextet to expand upon his ideas for performing *sans* the rhythm section. *Fat Man and the Hard Blues* (1991, Black Saint) is a reasonably successful document of what such a unit could achieve. But by the next recording, 1993's *Five Chord Stud* (Black Saint), Hemphill's health problems had left him unable to play. From that point on, his role in his sextet was purely as its composer and guiding light. Since Hemphill's death, the sextet has continued to carry his name and extend the legacy he built.

Higgins, Billy (b. Los Angeles, CA, 11 October 1936; d. Inglewood, CA, 3 May 2001): drummer. Higgins was beloved not only for his kind and encouraging disposition, but also for his astounding flexibility as a percussionist. Equally adept at free improvisation and firm bebop rhythms, Higgins was an asset on dozens of sessions on both sides of the free fence. More boppish than Ed Blackwell, less elastic than Sunny Murray, Higgins occupied a comfortable spot on the drum continuum that guaranteed him steady work.

Higgins came up as a rock and R&B drummer, but sidestepped into jazz in the group Jazz Messiahs with Don Cherry and tenor saxophonist James Clay. The Cherry association earned Higgins a job with Ornette Coleman's first recording band after the altoist came to Los Angeles in the mid-1960s. His time with Coleman resulted in some of the most innovative and enduring recordings of the decade. (See Coleman's entry.)

Higgins's first recording as a leader was *Soweto* (1979, Red), a nod to his interest in African cultures and music. His post-Coleman resumé read like a who's-who of jazz giants: Sonny Rollins, Dexter Gordon, Thelonious Monk, Art Pepper, Milt Jackson, Jackie McLean, Steve Lacy, Pat Metheny, David Murray, Mal Waldron, Charles Lloyd, Cedar Walton. Higgins opened the World Stage venue in Los Angeles in the mid-1980s, envisioning a place for young jazz explorers to try out their ideas and record. His final record session was Charles Lloyd's *Hyperion with Higgins* (2001, ECM); the drummer passed away from liver and kidney failure shortly before the album's release.

Hill, Andrew (b. Chicago, IL, 30 June 1937): pianist and composer. Hill's music was an advancement of bebop, riding on the edge of the avant-garde without becoming completely free. He is widely respected by musicians and especially pianists, but his music has never received its due. Hill began playing piano at age thirteen, studying with modern composer Paul Hindemith. He was a freelance jazz/R&B pianist through the 1950s, then relocated to New York in 1961 to work with Dinah Washington. Hill's experiences with Rahsaan Roland Kirk opened his ears to new sounds, and since 1962, he has led his own ensembles playing an adventurous brand of post-bop. His sidemen have included John Gilmore, Sam Rivers, Joe Henderson, Eric Dolphy, Freddie Hubbard, and Kenny Dorham. From 1963 to 1966, he recorded several explorative albums for Blue Note; 1964's *Point of Departure* is a particularly fine document of his innovative style. He became a public school teacher in the early 1970s. Since then, Hill has mostly concentrated on his education career, recording occasionally for various labels. The late 1990s saw a significant resurgence in his career, with new recording and touring opportunities.

Holland, Dave (b. Wolverhampton, W. Midlands, England, 1 October 1946): bassist, composer, and bandleader. One of the principal bassists in free jazz, Holland has expanded his horizons to become a poll-winning mainstream artist. He played ukulele, guitar, and electric bass in his youth, with some piano lessons on the side. Holland took up the upright bass in his teens when he became interested in the bebop styles of Ray Brown and Leroy Vinnegar. Soon he was gigging around town as a professional bassist. He studied a wide range of musical disciplines at the Guildhall School of Music and Drama. After graduation, impressed by what Jimmy Garrison and Gary Peacock were doing in free contexts with Coltrane and Ayler, Holland began working with pianist John Taylor, Kenny Wheeler, and John Surman in exploring the free jazz that was stretching across Europe. At the same time, he backed visiting American jazzmen like Ben Webster and Coleman Hawkins on their visits to London.

In 1968, Miles Davis hired Holland to play in his new electric ensemble, once again broadening the young bassist's horizons. *In a Silent Way* and *Bitches Brew* (both 1969, Columbia) brought Holland into the American marketplace for the first time. After leaving Davis, the bassist worked with Chick Corea and Barry Altschul in a trio that sprouted into Circle with the addition of Anthony Braxton. This was the freest music Holland had explored yet, and it is sad that infighting brought Circle to a close within two years. Holland's 1972 album *Conference of the Birds* (ECM), with Sam Rivers, Braxton, and Barry Altschul, is one of the most acclaimed free jazz recordings. (See Braxton's entry for details.) Holland dabbled in further freedom under Rivers, got into new fusion sounds with Stan Getz, and performed on some of Thelonious Monk's last dates. In 1975, Holland, Jack DeJohnette, and guitarist John Abercrombie formed the formidable Gateway Trio, a favorite among audiences and critics ever since. Several years later, following two astonishing solo excursions (bass: *Emerald Tears*, 1977, and cello: *Life Cycle*, 1982, both on ECM) came Holland's first quintet, an exciting unit with Kenny Wheeler, altoist Steve Coleman, trombonist Julian Priester, and drummer Steve Ellington. The group inspired Holland to continue exploring small-group settings as a player and composer.

Holland also got involved in education in the 1980s, assuming a position at the New England Conservatory and conducting summer workshops at the Banff School in Alberta, Canada. He has remained active as a sideman (Jim Hall, Joe Lovano, Herbie Hancock, Gary Burton) and leader of quartets, quintets, and most recently a big band. Holland's new-century recordings, *Not for Nothin'* (2001) and *What Goes Around* (2002, both ECM), cemented his reputation as one of jazz's premier bassists and bandleaders.

Honsinger, Tristan: cellist. Usually assumed to be European due to his name, Honsinger was born in New England and studied music at Baltimore's Peabody Conservatory before relocating to Amsterdam in the 1970s. Once there, he joined the Instant Composers Pool (ICP), which opened new doors for Dutch improvisation. He often worked with visiting Americans and Britons, among them Evan Parker, Cecil Taylor (both of those on *The Hearth*, 1998, FMP), Steve Lacy, and Louis Moholo. In 1978, he relocated to Florence and remained there for several years, recording *Earmeals* (1978, Moers Music) and performing with members of Gruppo di Improvvisazione Nuovo Consonanza. Honsinger has taken part in Company events and cut albums with Borbetomagus (*Industrial Strength*, 1983; *Borbeto Jam*, 1985, both Agaric), and Toshinori Kondo (*What Are You Talking About?*, 1983, DIW). He is a key member of Tobias Delius's quartet. His best recordings as a leader are *Map of Moods* (1996, FMP) and *A Camel's Kiss* (1999, ICP), both powerful solo outings.

Hooker, William (b. New Britain, CT, 18 June 1946): drummer and poet. He took up his instrument as a child and was already performing in public by the age of twelve.

As a member of the Flames, he backed doo-wop, rock, and R&B performers. In college, he studied both jazz, specifically the bop of Blue Note Records, and the twentieth-century classical avant-garde while continuing his practical drum training. Hooker first explored free music on a trip to California, then in 1974 he became involved in New York City's loft-jazz movement.

Like many free musicians of the period, Hooker had to create his own record label in order to document his music. Reality Unit Concepts issued two albums, *Is Eternal Life* (1978) and *Brighter Lights* (1986). The debut disc featured Hooker in duo and trio settings with David S. Ware, Jemeel Moondoc, and David Murray. On subsequent projects, Hooker hired whichever local musicians were willing and available. A 1988 contract with Silkheart Records brought more exposure for the titanically powerful drummer and his remarkably original conceptions. Guitarists Lee Ranaldo and Thurston Moore, of the avant-rock band Sonic Youth, were among the young rockers who embraced the drummer. Moore produced *Subconscious* (1994, Ecstatic Peace), and both he and Ranaldo have recorded with Hooker (*Shamballa* [1993, Knitting Factory Works] with Moore and Elliott Sharp; *The Gift of Tongues* [1995, Knitting Factory Works] with Ranaldo and Zeena Parkins). Hooker has also performed in a trio with keyboardist Doug Walker and Borbetomagus guitarist Donald Miller. He recites his original poetry on some sessions, and he has collaborated with turntable artists (like DJ Olive on *Armageddon*, 1995, Homestead) and electronic musicians with varying degrees of success.

Hopkins, Fred (b. Chicago, IL, 11 October 1947; d. Chicago, 7 January 1999): bassist. When the third wave of free jazz seriously took off in the early 1970s, AACM member Hopkins found himself as one of the first-call bassists on the scene. He is perhaps most famous as the bassist for Air, but his resumé also includes work with Muhal Richard Abrams's large bands, David Murray, Anthony Braxton, Marion Brown, John Carter, Bobby Bradford, Ari Brown, Arthur Blythe, Hamiet Bluiett, Oliver Lake, and Kalaparusha Maurice McIntyre. Never a leader, Hopkins was ever reliable as a sideman until health problems overtook him a few years before his death.

Horo: Italian label, founded in 1976. The catalog includes releases by Sam Rivers, Sun Ra, the Gil Evans Orchestra, Archie Shepp, Max Roach, Burton Greene, Roswell Rudd, Steve Lacy, Ran Blake, MEV, Don Pullen, Lee Konitz, and a large number of Italian performers.

Horvitz, Wayne (b. New York, NY, 1955): keyboardist, composer, and bandleader. He studied piano and guitar in his youth but dumped the guitar once he heard blues pianists like Otis Spann. In his twenties, Horvitz became part of John Zorn's cadre in the New York underground improv scene. He played with Zorn in the Sonny Clark Memorial Quartet and Naked City for several years, and more recently he cut *Downtown Lullaby* (1998, Depth of Field) with Zorn, Elliott Sharp, and Bobby Previte. Other associates include accordionist Guy Klucevsek, Anthony Coleman, Fred Frith, Butch Morris, and Curlew. Horvitz has led a number of different ensembles since the 1980s, among them The President, Ponga, Pigpen, and the Four Plus One Ensemble.

His most widely acclaimed group has been the funk-jazz-groove organ quartet Zony Mash. Formed around 1994 when Horvitz moved to Seattle, the band's music is engaging but bears few marks of freedom. Horvitz is also a respected producer, having worked on recordings by Peter Apfelbaum's Hieroglyphics Ensemble and singers Fontella Bass and Jay Clayton.

Houle, François (b. Québec, Canada, 1961): clarinetist. Houle is one of the few free musicians to focus exclusively on the clarinet. His impressive technique, similar to Anthony Braxton's extended vocabulary for alto sax, has made him an appreciated fixture of Canadian improv. He is a member of the Vancouver New Music Ensemble and has worked with Peggy Lee, Dylan van der Schyff, Paul Plimley, Lisle Ellis, and a number of other fellow countrymen. His resumé includes recordings with Scott Fields Ensemble, Joëlle Léandre, Evan Parker, Wayne Horvitz, violinist Eyvind Kang, the group Standing Wave, and various dramatic and modern classical projects. Houle's debut under his own name was *Hacienda* (1992, Songlines). He presently leads a trio with guitarist Scott Fields and bassist Jason Roebke (*Hornet's Collage*, 1999, and *Cryptology*, 2001, both on Nuscope).

Houtkamp, Luc (b. The Hague, Netherlands, 1953): saxophonist and composer. Houtkamp studied briefly at the Vrije Academie, concentrating on electronic composition, but gained most of his knowledge on his own time. From his mid-twenties, he began working his way into Europe's free-improv scene, teaming with John Russell, Sven-Åke Johansson, Han Bennink, Ernst Reijseger, Konrad Bauer, George Lewis, Derek Bailey, and Jon Rose (*Violin Music for Restaurants*, 1994, Megaphone). He has been a member of Klimaat, the Hommage Saxophone Quartet, Four In One, the Relative Band, and the King Übü Orchestrü (*Binaurality*, 1992, FMP). Most of his recordings have been on the Dutch Ooyevaer and X-OR labels, but one solid recommendation is *Luc Houtkamp in Chicago* (1997, Entropy).

Howard, Noah (b. New Orleans, LA, 6 April 1943): alto saxophonist. A perennial underdog, Howard was brutally neglected as a performer until the 1990s, when a new wave of interest in his bop-inflected free style caught the ears of independent record labels. Around 1963, Howard moved to the San Francisco area, where he played with Dewey Redman, Sonny Simmons, and a number of other freemen who would soon head out for the brighter lights of New York. Howard did so in 1965, just in time to meet Archie Shepp, Sonny Sharrock, and the artists affiliated with ESP Records. He cut two albums for the label (*Noah Howard Quartet* and *At Judson Hall*, both 1966) with his group, neither of which made much of a dent in the tiny market. *The Black Ark* (1969, Polydor) was a more significant offering, done around the time he joined Frank Wright's quartet for a tour of Europe (*One For John*, 1969, BYG). Howard settled in Belgium in the late 1970s and has remained there, recording off and on for European labels with figures like Han Bennink, Thomas Borgmann, Denis Charles, and Misha Mengelberg. Howard has released sessions on his own label, Altsax, as well as CIMP (*Expatriate Kin* with Zusaan Kali Fasteau and Bobby Few, 1997), Cadence Jazz

(*In Concert* with Few and drummer Calyer Duncan, 1997; *Between Two Eternities* with drummer Bobby Kapp, 1999), Eremite (*Patterns/Message to South Africa*, rec. 1971/ 1979, issued 1999), Ayler, and Boxholder.

Hubbard, Freddie (Frederick Dewayne Hubbard; b. Indianapolis, IN, 7 April 1938): trumpeter and composer. One of the finest trumpeters in his heyday, Hubbard came up in the hard bop era, blew free with Coleman and Coltrane, went almost fatally commercial in the 1970s, and returned to serious jazz not long before his chops fell apart. Among Hubbard's earliest employers were the Montgomery brothers, guitarist Wes and bassist Monk, who latched onto the young trumpeter for his stylewise resemblance to Clifford Brown. In 1958, Hubbard went to New York and began playing with Eric Dolphy, whose outside-leaning explorations perked up his Midwestern ears. He played regulation bop with several top names—Sonny Rollins, Quincy Jones, J.J. Johnson, Philly Joe Jones—then met John Coltrane and Ornette Coleman through Dolphy.

Coleman's *Free Jazz* was Hubbard's first serious exposure to free playing, and he sounded a bit out of sorts on the session despite giving it a good shot. He continued to explore outside techniques with Coltrane (*Olé*, 1961, Atlantic), tenorman Oliver Nelson (the classic *Blues and the Abstract Truth*, 1961, Impulse) and his own recordings beginning with *Open Sesame* (1960, Blue Note). Two other prime settings were Eric Dolphy's *Out to Lunch* (1964, Blue Note), which pitted the horns against vibist Bobby Hutcherson, and Coltrane's landmark disc *Ascension* (1965, Impulse), by which time Hubbard sounded infinitely more confident. His contract with Blue Note ended that year, however, and he moved back into hard bop with Herbie Hancock and Max Roach.

Since the late 1960s, Hubbard has remained far from free jazz. His 1970s recordings for CTI and Columbia were increasingly commercial and have not held up with the passage of time. In 1977, he returned to form somewhat with Hancock's V.S.O.P. ensemble, a touring unit that looked back at the history of bop. Hubbard re-signed with Blue Note in 1985, but not long afterward, he became seriously hindered by lip trouble and other personal problems that have mostly kept him out of the limelight.

Human Arts Ensemble (HAE): group formed by drummer Charles "Bobo" Shaw under the umbrella of the Black Artists Group in St. Louis, Missouri. After the BAG folded, Shaw opened membership in the pivotal Human Arts Ensemble to performers of all races. The racial admixture guaranteed better financial support for the Ensemble while its art and politics were left mostly unscathed. White performers such as John Lindberg and John Zorn came and went through the Ensemble's open doors until it folded in New York in about 1978.

The HAE's classic *Under the Sun* (1973) was originally issued on their own label, Committee for Universal Justice, and reissued by Arista/Freedom in 1975. Its two long tracks represented an exquisite meld of jazz, funk, blues, freedom, and ethnic sounds, a mixture that helped the album sell surprisingly well in its day. "A Lover's Desire" and "Hazrat, the Sufi" both draw from Middle Eastern musics, modified by Butch Smith's funky bass on the former track and AACM-ish group improv on the latter.

J. D. Parran and Marty Ehrlich are the stars, their seething reeds propelling the unit into the clouds. Oliver Lake and Lester Bowie also contribute to the music's appealing character.

Hutcherson, Bobby (b. Los Angeles, CA, 12 January 1941): vibraphonist, composer, and bandleader. The vibes are comparatively rare in free jazz, or straight jazz for that matter, and no vibist bears a higher profile in the New Jazz than Bobby Hutcherson. His landmark sessions with Jackie McLean and Eric Dolphy, not to mention his own Blue Note records, place him at the upper echelons of free jazz. His harmonic sense and pinpoint technical accuracy still amaze audiences.

Hutcherson grew up playing piano and surrounded by jazz; his siblings were friends with Dexter Gordon and Dolphy. He switched to the vibes in high school after hearing a Milt Jackson record. Lessons with West Coast jazz great Dave Pike built up his technical skills, and Hutcherson played dance gigs on the side as he worked with tenormen Curtis Amy and Charles Lloyd. He began to experiment with four-mallet playing, a talent that landed him a quintet job with trombonist Al Grey and saxman Billy Mitchell. Hutcherson drew the most attention when the quintet played Birdland in 1961, and he soon found himself hanging with the Blue Note crowd. As much as he enjoyed mainstream gigs, it was outsiders like Andrew Hill, Jackie McLean, and Eric Dolphy who really piqued his interest. McLean's *One Step Beyond* (1963, Blue Note) was Hutcherson's baptism of fire, proving the young man had what it took to change the face of jazz vibes.

Dolphy's legendary *Out to Lunch* (1964, Blue Note) was a triumph for both performers. Their interaction bordered on the magical, and Hutcherson received *Down Beat*'s TDWR award for vibes that year. In 1965, he led his first Blue Note session, *Dialogue*, with Hill, Freddie Hubbard, Sam Rivers, Richard Davis, and Joe Chambers. Also in that year, he appeared at Newport with Archie Shepp (*New Thing at Newport*, Impulse). Subsequent Blue Note albums like *Components* (1965), *Stick-Up!* (1966), *Oblique* (1967), and *San Francisco* (1970, with tenorman Harold Land) remain some of his best recordings ever. Hutcherson stayed with the label through its decline in popularity, but finally moved to Columbia in 1978. He gradually backed away from free playing while sustaining a high level of musicianship that kept his career afloat (despite occasional disappointments like *Linger Lane*, 1974, Blue Note). He played Montreux with bop trumpeter Woody Shaw in 1973, worked further with Land, and started making respectable hard bop albums for Landmark in 1984 (*Good Bait*). He remains active as a touring and recording performer.

I

Ibarra, Susie: drummer and percussionist. Ibarra's technique is one of the most refreshing in modern free music, at times reminiscent of Milford Graves in her use of small percussion devices and dynamic control. Ibarra, of Filipino descent, grew up in Texas and came to New York after graduating from high school. She studied at Mannes and Goddard Colleges, with an emphasis on musics of the South Pacific, and took private lessons with Graves, Denis Charles, Danny Kalanduyan, and Vernel Fournier.

Ibarra married saxophonist Assif Tsahar in the mid-1990s; their duo set *Home Cookin'* (1999, Hopscotch) was the inaugural release on their own label. Ibarra seems to be quite comfortable in duo settings. *Drum Talk* (1998, Wobbly Rail) presents one of her weekly duo dates with Denis Charles, and on *Daedal* (1999, Incus) she teams with Derek Bailey with interesting results. In 1997, she joined the David S. Ware Quartet, replacing Whit Dickey, in time to record *Wisdom of Uncertainty* for the new Aum Fidelity label. (See Ware's entry.) The following year, based upon her performances with Ware and Matthew Shipp's trio, Ibarra was named "Best New Talent of the Year" by *Jazziz* magazine.

Ibarra leads an unusual trio with pianist Cooper-Moore and violinist Charles Burnham (*Radiance*, 1999, Hopscotch), and has performed and/or recorded with William Parker's groups In Order To Survive and Little Huey Creative Music Orchestra, Dave Douglas's Trilogy, Ori Kaplan's Percussion Ensemble, John Zorn, Pauline Oliveros, Eugene Chadbourne, Arto Lindsay, Thurston Moore, Yo La Tengo, Cibo Matto, John Lindberg, Zeena Parkins, Evan Parker, Butch Morris, and her own trio, quartet, and the Electric Kulintang ensemble. Ibarra has served several residencies and taught at Juilliard, The New School, Sarah Lawrence College, and Manhattan School of Music. A skilled solo artist and composer, Ibarra has collaborated on the opera *Shangri-La* with poet Yusef Komunyakaa and written for the Kronos Quartet.

ICP Orchestra: see **Instant Composers Pool**.

Ictus: label founded in 1976 by percussionist Andrea Centazzo and his wife, Carla Lugli. It was inaugurated with *Clangs* by the duo of Centazzo and Steve Lacy. The label issued a reasonable number of albums over the next eight years by artists like Centazzo, Andrew Cyrille, and Lol Coxhill, but eventually folded due to financial woes. It was revived in 1995, originally as a means of gathering funds for Bosnian refugees.

Imagine the Sound: 1981 documentary film by Ron Mann, director of *Grass* and *Comicbook Confidential*. One of the first documentaries about free jazz, Mann's film focuses specifically upon four major pioneers: Paul Bley, Bill Dixon, Archie Shepp, and Cecil Taylor. Concert clips alternate with enlightening interview footage. The film, a Canadian production, is issued and distributed by Janus Films and Public Media, Inc.

Impetus: label founded in 1979, originally to promote the music of Amalgam. The label's catalog includes albums by Evan Parker, John Stevens, Frøde Gjerstad, Maggie Nicols, Howard Riley, and other European players.

Impulse: record label originally administered by ABC/Paramount, now part of the Verve Music Group under the Universal umbrella. Impulse was one of the most important labels of the free jazz movement, documenting the paths of John Coltrane, Pharoah Sanders, Marion Brown, Archie Shepp, and others, as well as releasing more standard jazz fare. Producer Bob Thiele's discerning ears and musical taste played a major role in Impulse's successful marketing of free jazz in the late 1960s and early 1970s. Beyond the mid-decade point, Impulse began concentrating more heavily upon mainstream jazz—presently their biggest star is pianist/vocalist Diana Krall—but the label has consistently reissued excellent free sessions from its heyday.

Incus: the first independent, musician-owned label in the U.K., founded in 1970 by Tony Oxley, Michael Walters, Derek Bailey, and Evan Parker. The directors (minus financial backer Walters) recorded the first two Incus sessions, one of which was never released and is now lost; the master tapes for the second session, *The Topography of the Lungs*, have apparently been damaged or lost as well. The label released a huge amount of music for an independent label, including many sessions featuring Bailey. Now administered by Bailey and designer Karen Brookman, Incus (Latin for anvil, one of the small bones of the middle ear) has expanded into video production, limited-edition CD-Rs, and a festival of improvised music.

Instant Composers Pool (ICP): loose collective led by pianist Misha Mengelberg and including, at times, such performers as Han Bennink, Willem Breuker, Peter Bennink, John Tchicai, Arjen Gorter, and Maarten Altena.
    In 1966, following Mengelberg's triumphant appearance at the Newport Jazz Festival, the pianist judged a music competition where he was impressed by young Breuker's spirit. He and Bennink began to collaborate with the reedman regularly, and

within a couple of years, the three had developed the ICP concept. The name stems from Mengelberg's somewhat accurate term for spontaneous improvisation, "instant composing." The "pool" meant that performers would be drawn from a loose group of musicians interested in the ICP's ideas, with personnel varying according to availability or the session's requirements.

The ICP label was established to promote albums by the Pool and its constituents. Its first release was *New Acoustic Swing Duo* (1968) by Breuker and Bennink. Breuker plays soprano, alto, and tenor saxes, Eb and bass clarinets, while Bennink vocalizes and hammers on a trap set, tabla, a large parade bass drum, rattles, sticks, bells, cymbals, blocks, and what-have-you. Highlights include a dedication to Tchicai and the twenty-one-minute closer "Gamut." A penchant for the strange and wonderful soon exhibited itself among the ICP flock, as exemplified by the label's third release: Breuker's *Lunch Concert for Three Barrel Organs* (1969, ICP).

Confusingly, three different albums were issued on ICP with the generic title *Instant Composers Pool* on the sleeve. A 1968 session with a complex intestinal knot illustrated on the cover (catalog #ICP002) features the trio of Mengelberg, Bennink, and Tchicai. A 1971 date, packaged in a round, plush-edged box, combines Mengelberg and Bennink in various groupings with Tchicai, Breuker, Gunter Hampel, Anthony Braxton, saxophonist/bagpiper Peter Bennink (Han's brother), bassists Altena and Gorter, Steve McCall, and a mandolin ensemble. Yet another release from 1971 is a simple, entertaining Mengelberg/Bennink duo.

In 1969, the ICP core met up with Evan Parker and Derek Bailey, a fortuitous teaming that resulted in some excellent cross-cultural exchanges. *Groupcomposing* (1970, ICP) includes two long spontaneous improvisations by Mengelberg, the Bennink brothers, Parker, Bailey, Paul Rutherford, and Peter Brötzmann. *Fragments* (1970) places Bailey in a more solid quartet context with Mengelberg, Han Bennink, and Tchicai, and *Han Bennink/Derek Bailey* (1969) is a duo set for guitar and drums. Solo discs by Bennink, Altena, Mengelberg, and cellist Tristan Honsinger have also been issued on the label.

Despite the cooperation of Breuker and Mengelberg on mutually beneficial projects like the BIMHuis, they came to disagree vehemently about the ICP's direction. Matters of time, repertoire, personnel, and finance became insurmountable sticking points. In 1973, Breuker broke away to establish his Kollektief band, leaving Mengelberg in charge. By the time of *Tetterettet* (1977, ICP), Mengelberg had taken to hand-signal conducting. That particular group was a tentet, large enough that Mengelberg felt the need for some semblance of order within the spontaneity. Thus the ever-flexible ICP Orchestra concept was born.

The fascinating *Japan Japon* (1982, ICP) draws not only from Japanese influences but cultures of the whole world. The group includes tubaist Larry Fishkind (a regular contributor), Mengelberg, Bennink, Brötzmann, Michael Moore, Keshavan Maslak, Toshinori Kondo, and trombonists Wolter Wierbos and Joep Maassen. Most of those players also figure in Mengelberg's dream project, *Two Programs* (1986, ICP), an outstanding evaluation of compositions by Thelonious Monk and Herbie Nichols. Mengelberg wears his heart on his sleeve, lovingly recasting tunes that had influenced him since his teen years. Like Gil Evans and Steve Lacy, Mengelberg has a propensity for rehashing the same compositions with different ensembles, exploring as many harmonic and textural variations as possible. He is as obsessive about the Nichols and Monk repertoires as Evans was about Mingus and Jimi Hendrix, and many surprises result from his tenacity.

In 1992, the ICP Orchestra recorded two volumes entitled *Bospaadje Konijnehol* (ICP), which means "Forest Path Rabbithole." The tracks are full of the whimsy and accessible abstraction that had come to characterize their performances. The first disc's recastings of old Ellington themes are the biggest draws; they get postmodern, crazy facelifts, with Michael Moore's clarinet as an outstanding decoration.

After a layoff of several years, the ICP returned with *Jubilee Varia* (1999, Hatology), an unusual exercise in textural variations. Though the music is quite appealing, this is an atypical addition to the ICP catalog. A bit steadier in conception is *Oh, My Dog!* (2001, ICP), wherein the band sticks it to Ives on "A Close Encounter with Charles' Country Band," pokes fun at the rigors of travel on other tracks, and has much fun throughout. Honsinger plays a plum role, contributing five compositions, which feature himself and violinist Mary Oliver.

Intakt: Swiss label cofounded by pianist Irène Schweizer, with a catalog of dozens of releases including Schweizer and the London Jazz Composers' Orchestra.

Iskra 1903: British improvising trio, originally consisting of Paul Rutherford, Barry Guy, and Derek Bailey. Named after a Communist newspaper published by Lenin at the turn of the twentieth century, the trio generated a phenomenal level of energy despite the absence of drums (*Chapter One*, 1972, Incus). Eventually Bailey was replaced by Philipp Wachsmann on violin and electronics (*Buzz Soundtrack*, 2002, Emanem). For a few years in the 1970s, Rutherford led an expanded edition he dubbed Iskra 1912 (*Sequences 72 & 73*, 1974, Emanem), including Kenny Wheeler, Evan Parker, Tony Oxley, Maggie Nicols, Trevor Watts, Howard Riley, and several other improvisers.

I.S.O.: Japanese trio founded in June 1997 by percussionist and electronic musician Ichiraku Yoshimitsu. The other members are Sachiko M on samplers and sine-wave generators, and Otomo Yoshihide on turntables and electric guitar. *I.S.O. Live* (1998, Zero Gravity) gives a solid impression of their heavy, complex sonic constructions.

Italian Instabile Orchestra (IIO): large ensemble, a gathering place for the esteemed improvisers of Italy. The IIO's past lineup reads like a roll call of avant nobility: Giorgio Gaslini, Sebi Tramontana, Giancarlo Schiaffini, Carlo Actis Dato, Mario Schiano, Gianluigi Trovesi, Pino Minafra, Tiziano Tononi, Paolo Damiani, Bruno Tommaso. All these men and the other IIO members have had distinguished careers in jazz, classical, and other circles, and their union results in a sum greater than its parts.

The group utilizes theatricality and humor in the Breuker/AEC fashion, as when Minafra sings or speaks through a megaphone. The IIO was originally slapped together by Minafra for a feature spot in the 1990 Festival di Noci, but the audience response was so positive that he decided to maintain it as a semi-regular entity. To give some indication of their flexibility, the IIO's past featured guests have included Lester Bowie, Cecil Taylor, and Breuker, whose bold sense of humor was right at home among the Italians.

The group debuted with *Live in Noci and Rive-de-Gier* (1991, Leo), compiled from two early concerts. The layering of themes in compositions like Damiani's "Detriti" (roughly, "castoffs") is akin to that of the Art Ensemble of Chicago, jewels strung into minisuites through which the listener weaves like museum dioramas. Schiaffini's "La Czarda Dell'Aborigeno" is a bent folk-dance, Minafra's "Noci . . . Strani Frutti No. 1" a free-spirited skirmish. Eugenio Colombo's crotchety "Ippopotami" conjures apropos images of hippos sparring playfully in the river.

Skies of Europe (1995, ECM) is composed of two suites. Tommaso's six-part "Il Maestro Muratore," or "The Master Mason," is dedicated to sculptor Constantino Nivola; Dato's bass clarinet is most prominent. Gaslini's "Skies of Europe" is in seven parts: two inspired by avant artist Marcel Duchamp, the others by Wassily Kandinsky, Marlene Dietrich, Erik Satie, and Italian film giants Michelangelo Antonioni and Federico Fellini. Understandably, the requisite tidbits of Nino Rota are discernible in the last section. Spots of brilliance abound, but the frequent lack of structure causes problems. The iffy recording quality also does not help. Still, *Skies* is a very interesting exercise in cross-cultural creativity. More successful is *Litania Sibilante* (1999, ECM). Its title, roughly meaning "Whispered Litany," is also an anagram of the orchestra's name. A guest spot by Italian superstar Enrico Rava adds to the appeal of this fine set, of which the most surprising feature is a take on the Billie Holiday theme "Lover Man." Schiaffini's arcane title track and Minafra's wild-eyed "Herr Fantozzi" are also something special.

Iyer, Vijay (b. New York, 1971): pianist and composer. The son of Indian immigrants, Iyer studied violin at age three and piano at age six. He earned his PhD in music and cognitive science from U.C. Berkeley in 1998, three years after making his debut recording, *Memorophilia* (1995, Asian Improv). Besides his trio with drummer Brad Hargreaves and bassist Jeff Brock, the album features two other Iyer-led groups: Poisonous Prophets (with guitarist Liberty Ellman, bassist Jeff Bilmes, and drummer Elliot Humberto Kavee) and Spirit Complex (with Kavee, George Lewis, tenorman Francis Wong, and cellist Kash Killion). Like many labelmates, Iyer is interested in the fusion of jazz and improvisation with Eastern musics. He performed with Steve Coleman in M-BASE-associated groups like Five Elements and Mystic Rhythm Society (*Myths, Modes & Means: Live at Hot Brass*, 1995, RCA). Altoist Rudresh Mahanthappa (*Black Water*, 2002, Red Giant) has been another frequent duo and ensemble partner. *Panoptic Modes* (2001, Red Giant) remains one of Iyer's best sessions. Since the early 1990s, he has been working on software to enhance live musical performance. Iyer is a member of Fieldwork (*Your Life Flashes*, 2002, Pi), Midnight Voices, Amiri Baraka's Blue Ark, and Burnt Sugar. Recently he issued the quartet date *Blood Sutra* (2003, Artists House) and the antiracism project *In What Language?* (2003, Pi) with poet/rapper Mike Ladd. Other collaborators include Gerry Hemingway, Miya Masaoka, Rova, Butch Morris, and Cecil Taylor. A former resident of the San Francisco Bay Area, Iyer has lived in New York since 1998.

Izenzon, David (b. Pittsburgh, PA, 17 May 1932; d. New York, NY, 8 October 1979): bassist. Izenzon took up the bass fairly late in life, at age twenty-four. Five years later he joined the emerging free jazz movement in New York City, working with Archie Shepp (in a great band including drummer J. C. Moses), Bill Dixon, Paul Bley, Sonny Rollins, and other artists on both sides of the free fence. Izenzon broke out to higher visibility when Ornette Coleman hired him for his groundbreaking trio with drummer Charles Moffett. His amazing technique, particularly with the bow, placed him on an equal footing with the formidable altoist. The trio's first run lasted less than a year before Coleman put it on hiatus, at which time Izenzon took whatever gigs came up. After participating in Dixon's "October Revolution in Jazz," the bassist returned to the trio in 1965 and remained for the next few years. He also took part in Coleman's 1970 collaboration with Yoko Ono. (See Coleman's entry.)

In 1968, Izenzon moved into academia, teaching at Bronx Community College while continuing to gig with Jaki Byard and then lesser-known artists like Paul Motian, Charles Brackeen, and Perry Robinson. Izenzon obtained his doctorate in psychotherapy in 1973 and switched careers, but still occasionally performed before his death in 1979. John Lindberg paid tribute to his fellow bassist on 1997's *Luminosity: Homage to David Izenzon* (Music & Arts).

J

Jackson, D.D. (b. Ottawa, Ontario, Canada, 25 January 1967): pianist. Jackson graduated from the Manhattan School of Music and Indiana University, studying with Don Pullen and Jaki Byard along the way. Pullen became his mentor, encouraging the young Canadian to explore as much of the musical world as he could. Jackson debuted as a leader with *Peace-Song* (1994), one of many releases on Justin Time. As Pullen's final days approached, Jackson assisted his guru in completing his final composition, "Earth Eagle First Circle." In 1998, he contributed piano and liner notes to David Murray's *The Long Goodbye: A Tribute to Don Pullen* (DIW). Since 1998, Jackson has played piano, organ, and synthesizer in a trio with Hamiet Bluiett and African hand drummer Mor Thiam (*Same Space*, 1998; *Join Us*, 1999, both Justin Time). He has performed and recorded with Henry Threadgill, Billy Bang (*Bang On!*, 1997, Justin Time), Canadian soprano saxophonist Jane Bunnett, Dewey Redman, poet Paul Haines, Kip Hanrahan, and Vincent Chancey (*Next Mode*, 1998, DIW). One of his best albums is . . . *So Far* (1999, RCA).

Jackson, Ronald Shannon (b. Fort Worth, TX, 12 January 1940): drummer and bandleader. Jackson has brought the funk to free music like no other drummer before him, adapting Ornette Coleman's harmolodic ideas to his uniquely flexible Decoding Society band along with blues, funk, rock, and influences that are more eclectic.

He began his pro career at age fifteen, working in Fort Worth jazz and R&B bands alongside tenorman James Clay. In his mid-twenties, Jackson went to New York and found plenty of opportunities, playing mainstream jazz behind Kenny Dorham, Betty Carter, and Stanley Turrentine, fringe forms with Charles Mingus and Jackie McLean, and free with Byard Lancaster. At a Charles Tyler session, Jackson met Albert Ayler and became impressed with the saxophonist's vision. He joined Ayler for sporadic gigs, even turning down a long-term job offer from Mingus. The two men never did record together (except for a poorly bootlegged live disc: *In Memory of Albert Ayler*, 1965,

Jazz Door), but Ayler's tutelage made an earnest stamp on Jackson, which prepared him for future tenures with Coleman and Cecil Taylor.

After a hiatus of several years, Jackson joined Coleman's electric outfit, Prime Time, fitting perfectly into the band's embryonic hybrid free-funk. In 1978, he played with Cecil Taylor, another eye-opening experience that resulted in three excellent albums: *The Cecil Taylor Unit* (1978), *Three Phasis* (1979, both on New World), and *One Too Many Salty Swift and Not Goodbye* (1991, HatArt, 2 CDs). (See Taylor's entry.)

In 1979, after pushing harmolodics to a new level within James Blood Ulmer's group, Jackson founded his Decoding Society. The new unit deftly whirled together rock, funk, and ethnic elements. Its personnel over the years included Byard Lancaster, guitarist Vernon Reid (later of the smash black rock band Living Colour), Billy Bang, and tenorman Zane Massey. Given its intriguing instrumentation and cutting arrangements, the Decoding Society's version of harmolodics ended up more widely popular than Prime Time's often static grooves. The group has made over a dozen albums, but the best are likely those recorded between 1982 (*Mandance*, Antilles) and 1984 (*Decode Yourself*, Island).

In 1986, Jackson joined Last Exit, a titanic supergroup that included free guitar maniac Sonny Sharrock, Peter Brötzmann, and electric bassist Bill Laswell. (See Last Exit's entry.) He also performed in the early 1990s with Power Tools and Ulmer's Music Revelation Ensemble, and has returned to the Decoding Society whenever possible.

Jamal, Khan (b. Jacksonville, FL, 23 June 1946): vibraphonist. Though born in Florida, Jamal is indelibly linked to Philadelphia's jazz circles. He learned to play the vibes at age eighteen, influenced by Lem Winchester and the more outward-looking Walt Dickerson. Jamal soon landed a job with the Cosmic Forces, a group that leaned toward free jazz. Byard Lancaster was another early employer and influence who taught Jamal to open up to new directions. In the 1970s, he performed with Sunny Murray's Untouchable Factor, appearing on the *Wildflowers* compilation (1977, Douglas). Later posts with Jemeel Moondoc, Billy Bang, and Joe Bonner led to a spot in Ronald Shannon Jackson's Decoding Society. His debut as a leader was *Don't Take No* (1982, Vintage Jazz), and arguably his best work was recorded for Steeplechase between 1984 and 1985 (*Dark Warrior*, *Three*, *The Traveller*). Recently Jamal collaborated with Omar Hill, Roy Campbell, and the African Rhythm Tongues project, and released *Cool* (2002, Jambrio).

Jang, Jon (b. Los Angeles, CA, 11 March 1954): pianist, composer, bandleader, and label head. Jang grew up in the Bay Area community of Palo Alto and took up the piano at the relatively late age of nineteen. He graduated from the Oberlin Conservatory in 1978 and released his first recording, *Jang* (RPM), the next year. He and tenorman Francis Wong founded the Asian Improv label in 1987 to specifically document the music of Asian immigrants in America (*Never Give Up!*, 1989). His ensembles have included the large Pan-Asian Arkestra (*Tiananmen!*, 1993, Soul Note), an octet, a sextet, and a trio, as well as Asian-tinged groups led by baritone saxophonist Fred Ho (or Houn; Afro-Asian Music Ensemble: *We Refuse to Be Used and Abused*,

1987, Soul Note) and Anthony Brown (*Far East Suite*, 1999). *Big Bands Behind Barbed Wire* (1998), recorded by the Asian American Jazz Orchestra, was a memorial to the Japanese-American musicians who performed in American internment camps during World War II. Jang has collaborated with the Kronos Quartet, the L.A. Philharmonic's New Music Ensemble, Max Roach, James Newton, David Murray, theater groups, dancers, and performance artists. Kronos, the Rockefeller Foundation, the NEA, and other organizations have commissioned compositions, and he has received awards from ASCAP several times. Jang has also lectured at U.C. Berkeley and U.C. Irvine.

Janssen, Guus (b. 1951): pianist, harpsichordist, and administrator of the Geest-Gronden record label. Like Cor Fuhler, Janssen came out of the Sweelinck Conservatory in Amsterdam with a firm background in classical and jazz theory. He has performed with John Zorn, George Lewis, Han Bennink, Theo Loevendie, the Schoenberg Ensemble, Nieuw Sinfonia Amsterdam, and other artists. In 1981, Janssen received the Boy Edgar Award, Holland's premier prize for jazz achievement. His compositions have been commissioned and performed by many of Europe's finest ensembles. *Harpsichord* (1991) sums up his odd but appealing way with the archaic keyboard, and *Noach: An Opera Off Genesis* (1994, both GeestGronden) is an epic radio opera speculating on Noah's post-deluge decline.

Jarman, Joseph (b. Pine Bluff, AR, 14 September 1937): saxophonist, composer, and founding member of the AACM and Art Ensemble of Chicago. Jarman originally played drums in high school under the famed Captain Walter Dyett, who taught music to urban teenagers in the 1950s. He took up the reeds while in the Army and had a solid background in theater by the time he met fellow saxophonist Roscoe Mitchell in 1958.

By his admission, Jarman was without direction until Mitchell encouraged him to check out Muhal Richard Abrams's Experimental Band, which Jarman joined in 1961. Afterward, with clearer focus, he developed new modes of musical expression with the tools provided by Abrams and friends. Although Anthony Braxton's *For Alto* (1968) was the first collection of solo sax performances to come out of the AACM's recording deal with Delmark, Braxton and other Association members had been inspired by Jarman's solo explorations a year prior.

Jarman joined Mitchell's sextet in 1962; both he and Mitchell helped form the AACM three years later. In 1966, Jarman formed his own ensemble with Fred Anderson, pianist Christopher Gaddy, trumpeter Bill Brimfield, bassist Charles Clark, and drummers Steve McCall and Thurman Barker. *Song For* (1966) was the second AACM album on Delmark, recorded four months after Roscoe Mitchell's *Sound*. Jarman's playing on this and other discs of the period reflects the energy and showmanship that were borne from his theatrical training. On "Little Fox Run," drummers Barker and McCall stir a boiling groundswell of improvised rhythms beneath the off-key horn harmonies. Anderson and Brimfield contribute edgy, buzzsaw-quick solos but are left in the dust as Jarman veers and screeches through his frighteningly intense improvisation. "Non-Cognitive Aspects of the City" is an open structure for poetic recitations, bookended by abrasive solos and Barker's rollicking drums.

In 1967, Jarman took part in a recording session with Mitchell, trumpeter Lester Bowie, and bassist Malachi Favors, who had also been in Mitchell's sextet. *Numbers 1 and 2* was issued under Bowie's name by the Nessa label that year. This marked the first meeting of the Art Ensemble of Chicago's original members, but the group was not official for a while. Jarman and the others plugged along with their own projects, with the saxophonist issuing *As If It Were the Seasons* (Delmark) in 1968. But within a year, both Christopher Gaddy and Charles Clark were dead and Jarman was devastated. He accepted the offer to join Mitchell's Art Ensemble in 1969, the year that the group went to Europe for an extended stay. (See Art Ensemble of Chicago.)

Within the Art Ensemble context, both Jarman and Mitchell played on the full range of saxophones, flutes, and clarinets as whim and situation called for. Their stylistic differences were fairly clear, which helped listeners to determine who played what at any given time on records: Mitchell was the better technician, chasing odd harmonic avenues, while Jarman was more gruff, bluesy, and focused upon tone color. His appreciation of theater and poetry, combined with Favors and drummer Don Moye's studies of African culture and musics, helped strike a vital balance with Bowie's R&B/blues leanings and Mitchell's interests in the classical avant-garde.

During the 1970s, Jarman performed in various settings, including duos with Don Moye (*Egwu-Anwu*, 1978, India Navigation, and *Black Paladins*, 1979, Black Saint). In the late 1980s, Jarman's study of Buddhism intensified, and he was eventually compelled to take time off from performing in order to give his fullest attention to spiritual pursuits. He left the Art Ensemble in 1992 and did little playing or recording for the next several years. He finally returned to music as a featured guest with performers like Reggie Workman, the Scott Fields Ensemble, and Marilyn Crispell. He has recorded with drummer Lou Grassi's Po Band (*Joy of Being*, 2001, CIMP) and, in 1999, recorded *Pachinko Dream Track 10* (Music & Arts) with San Francisco–based pianist Glenn Horiuchi. More recently, he has worked in a trio with Leroy Jenkins and Myra Melford (*Equal Interest*, 2000, Omnitone) and come back into the Art Ensemble of Chicago following Lester Bowie's death.

Jarrett, Keith (b. Allentown, PA, 8 May 1945): pianist, composer, and bandleader. Jarrett was an unlikely figure to score a smash worldwide hit in 1975, an era when disco and country-rock swept the globe. But *The Köln Concert* (ECM), a double-disc live date recorded in Germany, became one of the biggest-selling instrumental albums of all time, thanks to the rapturous beauty of Jarrett's spontaneous piano performance. He has shown many faces before and since that time, but *Köln* typifies the eternal mystery that is Keith Jarrett.

Jarrett began playing the piano at age three, and his status as a bona fide prodigy was quickly evident. Within a few short years, he was regularly giving recitals, then performing professionally. At Berklee School of Music in 1962, Jarrett formed his first trio, influenced by the music of pianist Bill Evans. Three years later, he was hired by drummer Art Blakey as pianist for the Jazz Messengers. Jarrett only held that position for a few months before being hired by the adventurous saxophonist Charles Lloyd, who brought the pianist on a landmark tour of the Soviet Union. Jarrett took up the soprano sax, which he has continued to use on occasion, during his three years with Lloyd. The pianist landed his own contract in 1967 with Vortex, a subsidiary of

Atlantic, for which he cut two albums (*Life Between the Exit Signs*, 1967, and *Restoration Ruin*, 1968). He then moved to the parent label, which released *Somewhere Before* (1968), a well-intentioned but less than successful pop-jazz crossover, and a date with vibist Gary Burton.

In 1969, Jarrett joined Miles Davis's new electric jazz-rock group, playing alongside second keyboardist Chick Corea (*Live at the Fillmore*, 1970, Columbia). That job gave Jarrett even greater exposure but permanently burned him out on the concept of electric keyboards. He left Davis in 1971, not long before he signed to a highly rewarding contract with ECM. *Facing You*, issued that year, announced Jarrett's estimable presence to the world in a better fashion than his previous labels. His alternately brisk and delicate piano technique benefitted from ECM's pristine recording methods, and the association has endured into the new century (aside from a few side projects for Atlantic, Columbia, and Impulse).

Jarrett's early 1970s projects generally centered around two separate ensembles: the "American Quartet" of Dewey Redman, Charlie Haden, and Paul Motian, augmented by percussion at times (*Fort Yawuh*, 1973, Impulse); and the "European Quartet" with Jan Garbarek, bassist Palle Danielsson, and drummer Jon Christensen (*Belonging*, 1974, ECM). *Ruta and Daitya* (1972, ECM) is an uncharacteristic but strong duo session with Jack DeJohnette.

In 1972, Jarrett began giving his spontaneous solo concerts, which quickly set the standard for pianists across the world. The performances were almost universally popular, despite Jarrett's disconcerting habit of singing along with himself in high-pitched, scat-like utterances (a tendency that rubbed off on guitarist/labelmate Pat Metheny). This was about as far as Jarrett ever ventured into the territory of free jazz. While he undoubtedly spun his fanciful creations off the top of his head in completely free spirit, he was never as incendiary or loose as Cecil Taylor or the other major freemen. Jarrett investigated the music of Bach and other classical giants in the 1980s, then formed his extremely popular trio with DeJohnette and bassist Gary Peacock, which remains his priority today. Jarrett battled chronic fatigue syndrome during the 1990s but came back with a vengeance. *Always Let Me Go: Live in Tokyo* (2002, ECM) is a good document of the trio's freewheeling exploration of standards and infrequent originals.

Jarvis, Clifford (b. 1941; d. 26 November 1999): drummer. Jarvis was an adaptable, thoughtful, but woefully undersung percussionist who came to New York in 1959 after studying at Berklee. Along with mainstream jobs under Barry Harris, Elmo Hope, and Chet Baker, Jarvis leaned toward free jazz on dates with Yusef Lateef, Freddie Hubbard, and Jackie McLean. A fifteen-year stint with Sun Ra began in 1962 and included work on many of the Arkestra's best recordings (*When Angels Speak of Love*, 1966, Saturn). The following decade brought opportunities for free work with Alice Coltrane (*Reflections on Creation and Space*, 1968) and Pharoah Sanders (*Thembi*, 1971, both on Impulse). From the mid-1970s onward, Jarvis stuck more to straight-ahead jazz dates, with Archie Shepp and Harry Beckett among his more ambitious employers.

Jaume, André (b. Marseille, France, 7 October 1940): reedman, composer, and bandleader. In his youth, Jaume was a devoted fan of Dixieland jazz, thanks to increasingly available recordings and concerts by soprano sax icon Sidney Bechet. But as his youthful studies on tenor sax progressed, Jaume became more attracted to the bebop movement. He landed a spot in Guy Longnon's fledgling jazz school when it opened in 1966, remaining there for three years and absorbing the jazz legacy.

In the early 1970s, after working with bassist Barre Phillips, Jaume formed a trio with Raymond Boni and percussionist Gérard Siracusa. The group gigged occasionally around town, landing jobs at cafés and clubs that were willing to give their brand of jazz an outlet. In 1976, the influential bandleader Jef Gilson, whose big band was a major incubator of young talent, hired Jaume. While performing with Gilson at the Nancy Festival, Jaume made the acquaintance of Joe McPhee. Since that meeting, the two have become friends and frequent collaborators. (See McPhee's entry.) With McPhee's assistance, Jaume toured America in 1985, during which time he furthered his sax and clarinet studies under Jimmy Giuffre. Jaume had set his clarinet aside until Giuffre encouraged him to take it up again. A good thing, since he has emerged as one of the most consistently entertaining clarinetists of the modern era.

In 1999, Jaume devoted a full album to the soprano, alto, and bass varieties of the horn (*Clarinet Sessions*, on his own CELP label). In 1980, he convened an octet to work on some new notions of ensemble composition and performance. He was especially interested in writing for strings and low brass, both of which play principal roles in *Musique Pour 8: L'Oc* (1981, HatArt). Jaume's impressionistic compositions are rich in timbre and flow, sometimes reminiscent of Giuffre. Trombonist Yves Robert is a revelation.

Jazz Composers Guild: short-lived collective based in New York City and founded by Bill Dixon in 1964. The Guild was a cooperative designed to promote free music without dealing with biased nightclubs and agents. Among the members were saxophonists John Tchicai and Archie Shepp, pianists Cecil Taylor and Paul Bley, trumpeter Michael Mantler, and organist/composers Sun Ra and Carla Bley. Despite the Guild's noble aspirations, it fell apart in 1965 due to weak management and in-fighting, which allegedly began over Shepp's decision to promote his music outside of the Guild's supervision. After its dissolution, Mantler and Bley reorganized as the JCOA (see next entry).

Jazz Composers Orchestra Association (JCOA): nonprofit foundation created in 1966 by organist and composer Carla Bley and her husband, trumpeter Michael Mantler, from the ashes of the Jazz Composers Guild. The JCOA was designed initially as a fund-raising entity to support the Jazz Composers Orchestra, maintained by the Guild as a showcase for the work of promising new writers. It was roughly contemporary to the AACM but did not gain much notice until after the Chicago organization had come into the public conscience.

The JCOA provided a much-needed outlet for creative musicians, composers, and arrangers whose works were not accessible to the mainstream jazz audience due to financial concerns and label intolerance. The Mantlers developed their own record label and established the Grog Kill recording studio at their home in Willow, New York. They also created the New Music Distribution Service (NMDS) to distribute independent and collective projects by modern creative musicians who could not get distribution through the major American companies.

For the most part, JCOA music tended to be more accessible to the white public than that of the AACM and similar groups, due in part to its members' academic backgrounds. Mantler, an Austrian immigrant, was well versed in European musical traditions, as was his American wife; therefore, much of their own work was centered on classical or contemporary styles and elements as opposed to jazz themes. Pianist Cecil Taylor, featured prominently on the JCOA's eponymous debut album, had also received conservatory training in his youth. Because of their more structured, Eurocentric focus, the group was almost the antithesis of the Afrocentric Chicago clan, though their final ambitions were the same. The collective included a wide cross-section of freemen, among them Don Cherry, Leroy Jenkins, Grachan Moncur III, Clifford Thornton, Argentine tenorman Gato Barbieri, and guitarist Larry Coryell.

The JCOA recordings were often sprawling, some might say overambitious efforts, epitomized by the double-LP set *Jazz Composers Orchestra* (1968) featuring Cecil Taylor, and the more ostentatious *Escalator Over the Hill* (1971, both JCOA). The latter was a bizarre modern opera (or "chronotransduction," meaning it spanned across the lines of time), written by Bley and writer Paul Haines over the course of four years. The opera, which featured ex-Cream bassist/vocalist Jack Bruce, typified the blending of tradition and abstract performance that was a trademark of the Association's productions. Other outstanding JCOA projects included Don Cherry's *Relativity Suite* (1971) and works by Thornton (*The Gardens of Harlem*, 1971) and Mantler.

The JCOA and NMDS are now defunct, though Bley and company still carry on the lofty aspirations of the collective through various projects. Her present record label, Watt, has continued the association's commitment to quality new music with releases by Bley's own orchestra and smaller bands, Mantler's projects of varied scopes and sizes, and albums by their daughter, singer/organist Karen Mantler, and bassist Steve Swallow.

Jazz Group Arkhangelsk: Russian improvising ensemble. Led by reeds/keys player Vladimir "Volodya" Rezitsky, the band was formed in the early 1970s in the farthest reaches of Siberia. Their first album with Western distribution was *Portrait* (1991, Leo), which featured percussionist brothers Nikolai and Oleg Yudanov, synth player Vladimir Turov, and bassist Nikolai Klishin. In 1995, Rezitsky issued his excellent album *Hot Sounds from the Arctic* (Leo), including saxman Tim Hodgkinson, drummer Tim Ryder, and Tuvan vocalist Sainkho Namtchylak.

Jenkins, Leroy (b. Chicago, IL, 11 March 1932): violinist and composer. Jenkins was the first violinist to make a serious impact on the development of free jazz. Jenkins severed his instrument's classical and traditional bonds and carried it to a new level in his work with the AACM, the Cecil Taylor Unit, the Creative Construction Company, and the Revolutionary Ensemble. Jenkins is capable of leaping from phrases of intricate orchestral beauty and technical detail to pure volcanic hell within the course of a piece, while always fitting glovelike into the context of the music. Classicism, the blues, and early jazz forms are significant elements of his style.

Jenkins began his violin studies at age eight. Like Joseph Jarman, Ronnie Boykins, and his future partner, Jerome Cooper, Jenkins studied at Du Sable High School under Captain Walter Dyett, performing on both violin and alto sax. After completing his studies at Florida A&M University, Jenkins taught music in Mobile, Alabama, for a few years, then moved his career venue back to Chicago. He was an early member of the AACM and made his first records under the Association's auspices with Anthony Braxton and Leo Smith (Braxton's *3 Compositions of New Jazz*, 1968, Delmark). In 1969, the trio moved to Paris, where drummer Steve McCall joined the group, then known as the Creative Construction Company. (See Braxton's entry.) Jenkins spent two years in Paris performing with the CCC, Ornette Coleman, and local musicians who were interested in the free sound. He returned to America in 1970 and soon found his way to New York, where he resided briefly with Coleman and worked with Braxton, Archie Shepp, Cecil Taylor, and other important freemen.

The Revolutionary Ensemble, Jenkins's trio with bassist Sirone and percussionist Jerome Cooper, was born in 1971. Jenkins carried the AACM's philosophy of ensemble democracy, as well as the preponderance of doubling on various instruments, over to the trio with resounding success. While some of the Ensemble's records were truly excellent, hardly anything has made it to the CD format thus far. (See separate entry for Revolutionary Ensemble.) During that interval, Jenkins also performed with Rashied Ali and Don Cherry, joined the Jazz Composers Orchestra Association, and made his first album under his own name, *For Players Only* (1975, JCOA).

The Revolutionary Ensemble broke up in 1977, at which time Jenkins toured Europe as a solo violinist (*Solo Concert*, 1977, India Navigation) and led his own groups. Created via a commission from the National Endowment of the Arts, *The Legend of Ai Glatson* (1978, Black Saint) features Jenkins, Anthony Davis, and Andrew Cyrille. The title refers not to a mythical folk hero, but is "nostalgia" backward. It is difficult, however, to find the nostalgia in the abstract track "Ai Glatson." "Brax Stone" is a nod to Jenkins's past partner, and "Albert Ayler (his life was too short)" is a cutting, folksy lament similar to Ayler's own compositions.

Throughout the 1980s, Jenkins kept busy, recording with Muhal Richard Abrams (*Mama and Daddy*, 1980, Black Saint), Cecil Taylor (*It Is in the Brewing Luminous*, 1990, HatArt), and his own groups. A former board member of the Composers' Forum, Jenkins has written several works on commission for various ensembles. In the 1990s, his career experienced a serious resurgence, beginning with the triumphant *Leroy Jenkins Live!* (1992, Black Saint). Jenkins is presently a member of Equal Interest with Joseph Jarman and Myra Melford. His biography is Carl P. Baugher's *Turning Corners: The Life and Times of Leroy Jenkins* (Redwood, NY: Cadence Jazz Books, 2001).

Johansson, Sven-Åke (b. Mariestad, Sweden, 1943): drummer, percussionist, and accordionist. He was one of the first major drummers in European free jazz, playing with Peter Brötzmann and Peter Kowald as early as 1965. With those men, Johansson made two of the primary documents of Euro-freedom, *For Adolphe Sax* (1967) and *Machine Gun* (1968, both FMP). That label's subimprint, SAJ, was derived from the drummer's initials. Johansson made Berlin his home in 1968 and has remained there since. His favor of sound control over sheer energy is explicit in his solo drum recording *Schlingerland* (1972, FMP/SAJ; reissued 2000, Atavistic Unheard Music), one of the few discs available under his name.

Johansson had a longtime partnership with Alex von Schlippenbach, working as a duo (*Live 1976/1977*, 2000, FMP) and in ensembles like Manfred Schoof's quintet and Globe Unity Orchestra. *Smack Up Again* (1997, Two Nineteen), with Schlippenbach, Axel Dörner, and others, looks at the "cool school" and beyond in a funhouse mirror with wacky takes on compositions by Thelonious Monk, Art Pepper, Ornette Coleman, and Harold Land. Dörner is a principal player on Johansson's minimalist *Six Little Pieces for Quintet* (1999) and *Barcelona Series* (2001, both HatOlogy). The drummer has also worked with reedman Dietmar Diesner, pianist Per Henrik Wallin, Rüdiger Carl, Hans Reichel (*Bergisch-Brandenburgisches Quartett*, 1982, Amiga), Derek Bailey, and John Corbett. Johansson is also an appreciable artist who has designed various album covers, and a composer with several radio-based and chamber pieces under his belt.

Jonas, Chris: saxophonist and bandleader. Jonas began his career as a painter and designer, activities that have positively impacted his development as a live musician. Since 1991, he has been a popular figure among New York's free community, working with Cecil Taylor, Anthony Braxton (*Anthony Braxton Trio [Wesleyan]*, 2001, Leo), the Brooklyn and Great Circle Saxophone Quartets, and William Parker's Little Huey Creative Music Orchestra (*Mayor of Punkville*, 2000, Aum Fidelity). Jonas leads the sextet The Sun Spits Cherries (*The Vermilion*, 2001, Hopscotch), his own quintet, and the Brooklyn Creative Orchestra. He occasionally composes for multimedia presentations.

Jordan, Edward "Kidd" (b. Crowley, LA): tenor saxophonist. Jordan's resumé tells a journeyman's tale, detailing his work with Stevie Wonder, Ray Charles, Aretha Franklin, Cecil Taylor, Ornette Coleman, Alan Silva, Dennis Gonzalez, and Hamiet Bluiett's Clarinet Family. He has always been underappreciated, given his large measure of talent, and has labored quietly as an educator (at New Orleans' Southern University) and arts advocate. Jordan has established educational programs in Africa and was knighted by the government of France for his contributions to the arts, yet he has never received his full due in America. He recorded in the 1980s with his Improvisational Arts Quintet (*The New Orleans Music*, 1988, Rounder), has worked extensively with pianist Joel Futterman (*Southern Extreme*, 1998, Drimala), and more recently led his Elektra Band. He is one of comparatively few free jazzmen working in New Orleans and is the father of two musical sons, trumpeter Marlon and flautist Kent.

Joseph Holbrooke: an early, short-lived British free improvising group, consisting of Derek Bailey, Tony Oxley, and bassist Gavin Bryars. The ensemble was named for an early twentieth-century composer who had set Welsh folktales and the works of Poe to music. It is not clear if the group ever performed their namesake's works. It began as a fairly mainstream unit, performing head-solos-head tunes drawn from bebop and early Ornette Coleman. By the group's demise in 1966, however, Joseph Holbrooke was a serious free ensemble working through completely spontaneous means. Unfortunately, except for one ten-minute *Rehearsal Extract* (1965, issued 1999, Incus) of the group playing "Miles' Mode," there are no other recordings of Joseph Holbrooke in action. In 2000, the group reunited for a series of successful performances in Europe and America.